Indian Rural Economy

Indian Rural Economy

A Mustafa

Director,
Sathak Institute of Management Studies,
Mohamed Sathak Engineering College
Kilakarai-623806, Ramnad District
Tamil Nadu State

SERIALS PUBLICATIONS
NEW DELHI (INDIA)

First Published – 2010

ISBN: 978-81-8387-272-0

Published by

SERIALS PUBLICATIONS
4800/24, 1st Floor, Ansari Road
Darya Ganj, New Delhi-110002 (India)
Phone : 23245225. Fax : 91-11-23272135
E-mail: serials@satyam.net.in

CONTENTS

FOREWORD

Dr. A. Mustafa, Director, Sathak Institute of Management Studies, Mohamed Sathak Engineering College, is an eminent and efficient Professor in Management Studies. His four decades of teaching experience is reflected in his writings. He is a scholarly personality, well-known in the academic circle as prolific author who has written about 25 books relating economics and business administration. There is dearth of books on Indian Rural Marketing, Indian Agriculture, and Microfinance. The author has presented a very good account of all the three aspects of our economy.

I hope that the students will be much benefited by this book. I congratulate the author and the SERIALS Publishers for having broughtout this book with latest facts and figures in a fitting manner.

With my best wishes

03-01-2009

Dr. N. Namasivayam
M.Com.,Ph.D., L.F.I.I. D.C.P.
D.M.I.M., P.G.Dip. in Tax Laws
Prof. & Head, Dept. of Commerce
M.K. University, Madurai-625021

PREFACE

India is a country of villages. There are about 6,50,000 villages. India's 700 million villagers now account for the majority of consumer spending in the country, more than $100 billion a year. Agriculture is the main source of livelihood in India. This book by 2028, India is expected to have the fifth-largest consumer economy in the world due to sustained growth among all sectors of Indian economy. Most of our Indian universities offer "Rural Development as one of the papers in their curricula. "Indian Rural Economy" is written keeping in view with the syllabi of both U.G. and P.G. courses offered by the Universities in India. It is brought out specifically to provide a comprehensive knowledge of Rural Market and Rural Agricultural Marketing in India. This book will enable the students to follow and master rural economy and answer questions vividly.

In the preparation of this book, I collected materials from various books, journals, magazines, newspapers and downloaded information from various websites. I thank the Serials Publications for publishing my book. I hope that this book will find favour, as in the past, with the students of B.A., and M.A., having rural economics both as a major and as an ancillary paper in the Credit Based Choice System introduced by the Universities and Autonomous colleges in India. This book will also be highly useful to Foreign Universities offering a study on Indian Economy.

02-01-2009 **A. Mustafa**

1

INDIA'S ECONOMY

INTRODUCTION

The economy of *India*, measured in *USD exchange-rate* terms, is the *twelfth largest* in the world, with a GDP of around $1 trillion (2008). It recorded a GDP growth rate of 9.1% for the fiscal year 2007–2008 which makes it the second fastest big emerging economy, after China, in the world. At this rate of sustained growth many economists forecast that India would, over the coming decades, have a more pronounced economic effect on the world stage. Despite this phenomenal rate of growth, India's large *population* has an estimated *per capita* income of $2,563, measured by PPP, and $941, measured in nominal terms, *as of 2007*.

India's economy is diverse and consist of various activities including manufacturing, agriculture and services. Although most of the Indian workforce still earns its livelihood directly or indirectly through agriculture and manufacturing, high tech services are a growing sector and play an increasingly important role in India's economy. The advent of the digital age, and the large number of young and educated populace fluent in English, is gradually transforming India as an important 'back office' destination for global *outsourcing* of *customer services* and technical support. India is a major exporter of highly-skilled workers in software and financial services, and *software engineering*. Other sectors like *manufacturing*, *pharmaceuticals, biotechnology, nanotechnology, telecommunication, shipbuilding, aviation, tourism* and *retailing* are showing strong potentials with higher growth rates.

India followed a *socialist*-inspired approach for most of its independent history, with strict government control over *private sector* participation, *foreign trade*, and *foreign direct investment*. However, since the early 1990s, India has gradually opened up its markets through *economic reforms* by reducing government controls on foreign trade and investment. The *privatisation* of publicly owned industries and the opening up of certain sectors to private and foreign interests has proceeded slowly amid political debate.

India faces a fast-growing population and the challenge of reducing economic and social *inequality*. *Poverty* remains a serious problem, although it has declined significantly since independence.

India has the *world's fourth largest wind power* industry, with an annual power production of 8,896 MW.

India's total cultivable area is 1,269,219 km² (56.78% of total land area), which is decreasing due to constant pressure from an ever growing population and increased urbanisation.

India has a total water surface area of 314,400 km² and receives an average annual rainfall of 1,100 mm. *Irrigation* accounts for 92% of the water utilisation, and comprised 380 km² in 1974, and is expected to rise to 1,050 km² by 2025, with the balance accounted for by industrial and domestic consumers.

By 2028, India is expected to have the fifth-largest consumer economy in the world due to sustained growth among all sectors of Indian economy.

India *is fourteenth* in the world in factory output. They together account for 27.6% of the GDP and employ 17% of the total workforce. However, about one-third of the industrial labour force is engaged in simple *household manufacturing* only.

Economic reforms brought foreign competition, led to privatisation of certain public sector industries, opened up sectors hitherto reserved for the public sector and led to an expansion in the production of fast-moving *consumer goods*.

Table 1

Indian Companies have been Listed in the Forbes Global 2000 Ranking for 2008. The 10 Leading Companies are

World Rank	*Company*	*Industry*	*Revenue (billion $)*	*Profits (billion $)*	*Assets (billion $)*	*Market Value (billion $)*
193	Reliance Industries	Oil & Gas Operations	26.07	2.79	30.67	89.29
198	Oil and Natural Gas Corporation	Oil & Gas Operations	18.90	4.11	33.79	54.11
219	State Bank of India	Banking	15.77	1.47	188.56	33.29
303	Indian Oil Corporation	Oil & Gas Operations	42.68	1.82	25.39	16.36
374	ICICI Bank	Banking	9.84	0.64	91.07	29.85
411	NTPC	Utilities	7.84	1.60	20.34	41.57
647	Steel Authority of India Limited	Materials	7.88	1.45	8.05	26.37
738	Tata Steel	Materials	5.83	0.97	11.48	14.63
826	Bharti Airtel	Telecommunications Services	4.26	0.94	6.61	39.16
846	Reliance Communications	Telecommunications Services	3.13	0.65	13.08	29.63

Post-liberalisation, the Indian private sector, which was usually run by oligopolies of old family firms and required political connections to prosper was faced with foreign competition, including the threat of cheaper Chinese imports. It has since handled the change by squeezing costs, revamping management, focusing on designing new products and relying on low labour costs and technology.

The *Indian economy* has been passing through the trajectory of high growth for several years. The overall Gross Domestic Product (GDP) is estimated to grow at 8.4 per cent, with the agriculture and allied sector projected to bounce back with 3.9 per cent growth during 2005-06. The Government has also been consolidating its fiscal position, creating a conducive climate for investment activities. Investment demand in the *economy* is picking up, reflecting the growing dynamism in the industrial sector. The exports have also assumed vibrancy. Thus, the *Indian economy* as a whole is poised for still higher growth in the coming years.

Spread across 650,000 villages, with an average population of 1,100, *rural* villagers were long imagined by city dwellers as primitive, impoverished and irrelevant, something to drive past on the way to something else.

That is no longer the case.

A new prosperity is sprouting in *rural* India, with tens of millions entering the pressure-cooker-and-television-owning class and tens of thousands becoming sippers of Scotch, owners of premium tractors and drivers of multiple sedans.

The opening of this new frontier of consumer demand from 700 million people could tip India's role in the global *economy* from seller to buyer, from a vendor of outsourced skills to a source of consumers for the world's wares. Multinational corporations, from Coca-Cola to Nokia, appear increasingly keen to understand *Indian* villagers.

At the extreme of the trend are the "crorepatis,"Hindi for those making the equivalent of $220,000 or more a year. Here in the northern state of Haryana, *rural* dwellers are now nearly twice as likely to be crorepatis as city dwellers in Bangalore, the high-technology hub, according to the National Council for Applied Economic Research, the leading collector of data on *rural* India.

It may be a trickle, but India's urban prosperity is flowing to the countryside.And well-to-do villages like Hasangarh are early testing grounds of whether the benefits of India's economic makeover and opening to the world will flow to its villagers, many of them living in its very poorest *rural* nooks.

The transformation of such villages will also add fuel to the debate over democracy's influence on economic development.India has been faulted for growing more lethargically than China, in part because of its democracy.

But the new *rural* prosperity suggests that the high cost of democracy also has a hidden benefit. By compelling each politician to deliver results to his own narrow constituency, democracy spreads economic change more thinly. But that in turn broadens the consensus in favor of change, perhaps making liberalization more sustainable in India than in China, said Yasheng Huang, a Chinese-born scholar at the Massachusetts Institute of Technology and an expert on the two countries.

"In China in the 1990s, you have a combination of a leadership who had an urban bias and of an authoritarian system that suppressed the voices of the poor, and the end result was the rising *rural*-urban disparity and the high level of social tensions," Huang said in an e-mail interview.

"If you have an urban bias, then it is better to have a democracy because then the voters can rise up to correct that bias, especially, as in India, where poor people actively vote."

In China, a widening income gap between town and country is worrying officials. But in India, the gap is narrowing. In 1990, for every $100 earned by an *Indian* villager, an urbanite made $82 more. Today, the difference has dropped to $56.

Yet the new *rural* riches are far from ending poverty. In India, 390 million people still live on $1 a day or less.

What is changing is the nature of the rich-poor divide. That divide was once synonymous with the urban-*rural* split. The only way to get rich was to live in town, and to reside in the country was to be bound to interminable poverty.

But increasingly, the *rural economy* is a microcosm of the national *economy*, with its own rich and poor. The *rural* rich are 1,000 times as likely as the *rural* poor to own a motorcycle, 100 times as likely to own a color television and 25 times as likely to own a pressure cooker, according to a survey of 96,000 *rural* households by the research council.

That distribution of wealth may or may not be equitable. But in creating the possibility of making it in *rural* India itself, the new *rural* prosperity is transforming *rural* India's image from economic nonentity to emerging market within the emerging market.

India's 700 million villagers now account for the majority of consumer spending in the country, more than $100 billion a year. Millions step into consumerism each year, graduating from the economics of necessity to the economics of gratification, buying themselves motorcycles, televisions, transistor radios and pressure cookers.

Diverse forces are fueling the trend. The government has invested billions of dollars in development, including road building and *rural* electrification, and has forced banks to lend to farmers. Hearty monsoons have fattened farmers' profits. Widening educational access has helped farmers' children to get city jobs and send money home.

India Vs China There are greater similarities rather than differences in the policies followed and their outcomes in the the periods of economic repression and reform in India and China.

China carried its repression further as it has its reforms than India. But in both countries the liberalization of foreign trade and the ending of planning gave a boost to growth. The major difference has been in their respective investment rates, with China's at over 40 per cent of gross domestic product (GDP) being roughly twice that of India's. But, given the continuing deadweight of the State Owned Enterprises on the Chinese growth path, this has not led to a commensurate difference in their growth rates during their reform periods, with Chinese growth between 1978-98 being 9.7 per cent per annum on official and over 7 per cent per annum on the best independent estimates, whilst India grew by 6.1 per cent per annum from 1991-2000.

But the growth in China has been more labor intensive than India's. This was the unintended consequence of the end of collectivization in agriculture which led to an explosion of labor intensive small-scale rural industry for export.

This export led industrialization was facilitated by the much better and more extensive infrastructure created in China, and by the freedom to hire and fire as well as the absence of any 'social' burdens carried by firms in this fast growing non-state sector.

India by contrast continues to hobble the development of small-scale and labor intensive industry with its policy of reservations, and refusal to repeal the archaic labor laws it inherited from the Raj. In both China and India the dynamics of their growth have been provided by areas which the State had overlooked as being of little importance: the small-scale rural industries in China, and the information based service sector in India.

These were the areas where capitalism was allowed to take its natural course and once foreign markets were opened with the liberalization of foreign trade, the native wit and entrepreneurship of the economic agents not subject to the dead hand of the State, generated a dynamism which no planner could have created.

Unlike the Indian, the Chinese policy elite has fully embraced capitalism. The new (often Western trained) mandarins who run the Chinese state recognize, as many in India still do not, that this is the only route to both prosperity and power for their nation — and like mandarins of yore, it is the Chinese State and not any ideology that they serve.

India by contrast seems stuck with its 'Left' still unwilling to abandon its past dirigisme, who continue to block the necessary privatization of its public enterprises.

These differences in the embrace of global capitalism are reflected in both the much greater trade liberalization undertaken by China and its more relaxed attitudes to foreign investment.

Thus, whereas exports were 19 per cent of Chinese GDP in 1998, they were about 8 per cent in India. Whilst the stock of foreign direct investment (FDI) was $261 billion in China in 1998, it was a mere $13 billion in India.

Moreover, the foreign investment in China which has flowed to the non-state sector from the Chinese diaspora to finance industrial exports has loosened the constraint on its growth from its weak domestic capital markets.

The multinationals, by contrast, have been lured into joint ventures with state enterprises to service the large domestic market and have usually lost their shirts.

In both countries wherever growth has occurred, there have been dramatic reductions in poverty. However, whilst labor intensive industrial growth seems to be spreading faster to the hinterland in China through fierce locational competition for joint ventures with foreign investors, the Hindu heartland in the eastern Gangetic plain still remains mired in its ancient equilibrium.

While inequality had increased in China since the planned period, there is no clamor in an ostensibly Communist country for egalitarianism. This is because like India, China for millennia has been a hierarchical society. It was the foreign Enlightenment virus of socialism which for half a century infected their intelligentsia, but whereas the Chinese seem to have overcome it, India's intellectuals unfortunately still remain deeply infected. From this it would seem that there is no contest in the growth race between the hare and the tortoise. But there are some signs that appearances may be deceptive. The fragility of the Chinese financial system is a case in point. Though India's financial system is healthier, it shares with China the problem of unsustainable fiscal deficits fuelled by economically unjustifiable subsidies. China might be able to tackle this problem more easily if it used its foreign exchange reserves creatively. By contrast, the political roadblocks to ending the subsidies debauching the Indian budget remain significant. Nevertheless, India currently has a head start in both the instruments it can provide for savings as well as in the mechanisms through the financial system for their efficient deployment.

There are two other advantages which India has over China as part of the legacy of the Raj: the rule of law, and the English language. Even though China has, in the most recent revision of its Constitution, put private firms on an equal footing as state owned firms, entrepreneurs are still suspicious of the State. Forbes recently published a list of the top 50 Chinese millionaires.

It explains why most of these new entrepreneurs rely on self or foreign financing of their firms and are reluctant to put their head above the parapet by listing their companies on the stock exchange. This cannot bode well for the future of Chinese growth. India's advantage in having a large pool of English speaking people is likely to be eroded in a generation. Apart from the much higher literacy rate in China, it has now decreed that everyone from the age of five will have to learn English—the commercial and scientific lingua franca of the world.

Given its fiercely meritocratic education system, without any quotas or firmative action, it is on the way to producing one of the most highly skilled populations in the world. This is a danger India needs to guard against, by helping the spread of private schools in the rural areas and abandoning the Mandalism which has already done great harm to its system of university education. If affirmative action is extended to the private sector, it would further handicap India in its ongoing race with China.

(25 million people of *Indian* origin live outside India. On the other hand 45 million people of Chinese origin live outside China-but they remitt just $ 25 billion into China).

Last, but not least, whilst China with the ageing of its population is likely to see an end to the savings bonanza promoted by the demographic transition accompanying its one child policy, when the dependency ratio declines as the birth rate and population growth rate fall, India is first entering its own demographic transition. These life cycle effects will raise Indian savings for the next few decades. This should allow a substantial rise in India's investment rate, just as after 2010 demographic effects lead to falling Chinese savings rates. If by then India has completed the second generation of reforms, built up its infrastructure and fully integrated itself into the world economy, we might find that the tortoise overtakes the hare. This race between the two Asian giants is set to be the cost of dramatic event of this century.

- China's GDP is somewhere around 2 trillion dollars while our's is at around 700 billion dollars.They are said to be growing at around 9.5% of their GDP while we at 7.5% of ours.China is a huge communist country while we are a relatively smaller democracy.

  Leaving aside the economy and coming to the military side, we have around a 1000 nuclear warheads while China has around 5000.

If they had been hardcore communists like the Soviets, their economy would have collapsed like that of the USSR. But they are smart people who have learnt from the past. The only thing red about the Chinese today is their blood and their flag. They are more capitalistic than India what with the Govt. having to keep it's communist coalition partner in good humour. As if this is not enough, the Chinese have made learning English compulsory for their kids. There are no Asian giants; only one giant and that is China which wants to compete with the sole super power, the US. Still everybody wants to compare India.

INDIAN FARMERS VITAL STATISTICS : FATAL FIGURES

- Hardly 10 per cent of Indian farmers are covered by crop insurance.
- Debt drove nearly 1 lakh members of farming community to commit suicide between 1998 and 2003, says a government report.
- 17,000 farmers and their kin killed themselves each year for six years.
- 12% of all suicides in the country was in the farming community.
- 2002 worst year. 16% of suicides among farmers.
- Agriculture provides nearly 600 million direct and another 200 million indirect jobs.

- The total annual rural debt of Punjab was Rs 24,000 crore in 2003-04—is more than its gross annual earnings from agriculture. (Source: The Telegraph, April 24, 2006).
- There is a total of about 455 million acres of land that is cultivated in India and only about a third of it is covered by irrigation.
- The four states of Andhra Pradesh, Karnataka, Maharashtra and Kerala have recorded over 8,900 suicides between 2001-2002 and 2005-2006.
- 70% of the Andhra's 78 million people are dependent on agriculture.
- Due to the acute distress, more than 1500 farmers committed suicide, mainly in Wayanad district, which is unprecedented in the history of Kerala.
- Rural development expenditure as percentage of GDP between 1985-1990 was 14.5%, which came down to 5.9% in 2000-01.
- The expenditure on agriculture research is only around 0.3 per cent of GDP.

Our farmers are committing suicide, not only in Andhra but also in Maharashtra *Rural* India is being left behind as GDP surges in Urban areas.

Vidarbha remains a grim statistic. One suicide in every eight hours. More than half of those who committed suicide were between 20 and 45, their most productive years. The Maharashtra government says as many as 1920 farmers committed suicide between January 1, 2001 and August 19, 2006. Nearly 2.8 million of the 3.2 million cotton farmers are defaulters, reports Jaideep Hardikar(Daily News & Analysis).

SUICIDE COUNT

There are no authentic figures on the exact number of farm suicides in Vidarbha, but the Maharashtra government accepts a figure of 1920 from January 1, 2001 to August 19, 2006. The Vidarbha Jan Andolan Samiti (VJAS), a farmers' movement, puts the toll at 782 from June 1, 2005 to August 26, 2006. And, in the last three months, there has been a suicide every eight hours.

INDIAN VILLAGES

Villagers in India manifest a deep loyalty to their village, identifying themselves to strangers as residents of a particular village, harking back to family residence in the village that typically extends into the distant past. A family rooted in a particular village does not easily move to another, and even people who have lived in a city for a generation or two refer to their ancestral village as "our village."

Indian Villagers share use of common village facilities—the village pond (known in India as a tank), grazing grounds, temples and shrines, cremation grounds, schools, sitting spaces under large shade trees, wells, and wastelands. Perhaps, equally important, fellow villagers share knowledge of their common origin in a local and of each other's secrets, often going back generations. Interdependence in *rural* life provides a sense of unity among residents of a village.

A great many observances emphasize village unity. Typically, each village recognizes a deity deemed the village protector or protectress, and villagers unite in regular worship of this deity, considered essential to village prosperity. They may cooperate in constructing temples and shrines important to the village as a whole. Hindu festivals such as Holi, Dipavali (Diwali), and Durga Puja bring villagers together. In the north, even Muslims may join in the friendly splashing of colored water on fellow villagers in Spring Holi revelries, which involve villagewide singing, dancing, and joking. People of all castes within a village address each other by kinship terms, reflecting the fictive kinship relationships recognized within each settlement. In the north, where village exogamy is important, the concept of a village as a significant unit is clear. When the all-male groom's party arrives from another village, residents of the bride's village in North India treat the visitors with the appropriate behavior due to them as bride-takers—men greet them with ostentatious respect, while women cover their faces and sing bawdy songs at them. A woman born in a village in India is known as a daughter of the village while an in-married bride is considered a daughter-in-law of the village. In her conjugal home in North India, a bride is often known by the name of her natal village; for example, Sanchiwali (woman from Sanchi). A man who chooses to live in his wife's natal village—usually for reasons of land inheritance—is known by the name of his birth village, such as Sankheriwala (man from Sankheri).

Traditionally, villages in India often recognized a headman and listened with respect to the decisions of the *panchayat*, composed of important men from the village's major castes, who had the power to levy fines and exclude transgressors from village social life. Disputes were decided within the village precincts as much as possible, with infrequent recourse to the police or court system.

In present-day India, the government supports an elective *panchayat* and headman system, which is distinct from the traditional council and headman, and, in many instances, even includes women and very low-caste members. As older systems of authority are challenged, villagers are less reluctant to take disputes to court.

The solidarity of a village is always riven by conflicts, rivalries, and factionalism. Living together in intensely close relationships over generations, struggling to wrest a livelihood from the same limited area of land and water sources, closely watching some grow fat and powerful while others remain weak and dependent, fellow villagers are prone to disputes, strategic contests, and even violence. Most *villages* of India include what villagers call "big fish," prosperous, powerful people, fed and serviced through the labors of the struggling "little fish." Villagers commonly view gains as possible only at the expense of neighbors. Further, the increased involvement of villagers with the wider economic and political world outside the village via travel, work, education, and television; expanding government influence in *rural* areas; and increased pressure on land and resources as village populations grow seem to have resulted in increased factionalism and competitiveness in many parts of *rural* India.

Spread across 650,000 villages, with an average population of 1,100, *rural* villagers were long imagined by city dwellers as primitive, impoverished and irrelevant, something to drive past on the way to something else.

THE NRI AND INDIA'S RURAL ECONOMY

The total amount of FDI investments in India is estimated for 2007 is $ 15 billion. And we tout that fiigure proudly- and our stock market fluctuates on any variance from that figure too. Guess what NRI"s will remitt to India in the same period? A mind boggling $ 30 billion ! 60% of which goes into *Rural* India. Most consisting of small amounts for the maintanence of families left behind, or small investments. If the world bank is correct, every dollar remitted contributes 3 dollars to the GDP growth-which means that NRI's are contributing to growth of almost a $ 60 billon to India's *rural economy*.

Situation of the farmers was never good in india. The NRIs play a very vital role in *rural* development but yet it is not entirely visible because they remit money mainly in specific parts of India, i.e. Gujarat, & Kerela.. But a study of which parts the money is exactly remitted to can be very interesting. Or maybe the remitted money is so small for each transaction that it is consumed and not invested or maybe invested in cities.

Rural India is being neglected. However, it is the time that Enterprises look into *Rural* markets and develop the infrastructure accordingly. *Indian rural* market is pretty big. Look what Telecom companies have done in *Rural* India, now almost every *Indian* can afford a Phone. This creates economies of scale and millions of Jobs.

Suggestions for the development of Rural Indian market

(1) Empower the rural youth by providing them skilled/ unskilled jobs.

(2) strengthen the supply chain in agricutural sector, allow FDI in strengthening the infrastructure. (Kamalnath is pitching really hard).

(3) Government should take the complete control of rural education sector. It is high time we empower our rural youth and provide them with better education.

(4) Encourage entrepreneurial skills and provide a broad spectrum of investment base. If need is the mother of invention, we have the need to improve the quality of life in Rural India.

Seems like a bit of a policy, loan processes, land right, sometimes access problems.

Reminds us a bit of what Amartya Sen says about famine, and also may be understood what exactly the Bangladeshi banker who provides loans for rural people.

Rural Development is a must if India has to progress as a Nation. New Infrastructure projects should be spread across the length and breadth of the country to have a uniform growth everywhere and not just in the big cities. Here, the concept of "PURA" (Providing Urban Amenuties to Rural Areas) adocated by APJ Abdul Kalam is to be remembered. This would also prevent widespread migration to big cities like Mumbai, Delhi etc. which are already bursting at the seams.

The molestation of girls in Mumbai..more than any blame games attributed to traditional *Indian* culture, it is foremost to be blamed towards the direction that the *Indian* media including Bollywood has taken in the past few years..they are alienating the new generation from the grounded traditions of old in the guise of individual freedom which is nothing but inflation of ego putting individual before society. India is not ready to be as sexually explicit in media as the west, because it does not have the laws that persecute the violent outbursts of repression..in the west, these are controlled by laws, but the repression stays and morphsinto depression..so when output not equal to input, its trouble..so the input has to be balanced.

To put the scale of the remittances in perspective, consider this: money received by India through this route is roughly the same as the country's total estimated annual expenditure on defence, or about five times the estimated expenditure on education in 2007-08. Total income tax and wealth tax collections in the country are less than the remittances received. (legal-outside hawala. wonder how much would be the total). World Bank study estimates that the number of *Indian* immigrants is about 10 million.

Percentage of this money going to *rural Indian* is not high and whatever it is-its not even. example- Kerala and Gujarat are two states which get major share and in Bihar & east its almost nil.

NRIs pumping money into India is a good thing for India, there is no question about it, and the economic progress clearly reflects that.

NRIs are bidding for and buying farmlands and housing real estate for inflated prices and either squatting on that or just flipping the real estate, treating it like a stock market. This does not do any good to India and to the farmers-they cannot possibly compete with NRI dollars in procuring land. This leads to the artifical inflation of real estate market, as well as the fact that NRIs are NRIs-non-resident, so they don't develop the infrastructure much. Real estate should belong to the country & its residents as much as possible, so they can develop infrastructure and take it forward. There should be some amount of thinking in this area from politicians.

Kerala, for e.g, survives on NRI funds. being unfriendly to induustrial growth, it doesn't generate income. agricultural production is also zero-yet it is the most 'developed ' state in terms of health, education and the negligible % of BPL group, thanks to NRI's pumpimg funds into the state, rural areas in Kerala has medical facilities, educational institution, cyber cafes and departmental stores etc., like Goa.

RURAL DEVELOPMENT INSTITUTE

RDI is an international nonprofit organization working to secure land rights for the world's poorest people, those 3.4 billion chiefly rural people who live on less than $2 a day. Land rights represent the single greatest asset for the world's rural poor. For decades, RDI has used the law to bring land rights to the poor in a peaceful, fair and democratic manner. For 40 years, RDI professionals have worked with the governments of 40 developing countries, foreign aid agencies, and other partners to design and implement laws, policies, and programs that provide opportunity, further economic growth, and promote social justice. To date, RDI has helped provide land rights to more than 400,000,000 people.

China's 210 million agricultural households represent one out of every three farm families on the planet, and still comprise two-thirds of that vast country's population. While farmers are now better off than in the days of collective farming, many problems of rural poverty and a large gap between urban and rural incomes have persisted, and the issue of secure land tenure has remained central. RDI has worked with China's central policy-makers on rural land tenure issues since 1987, and is the principal foreign advisor in a current reform under which 85 million familes have received secure, 30-year land-use rights.

ORGANIC FARMING IN INDIAN RURAL ECONOMY

The role of Organic Farming in Indian *Rural Economy* can be leveraged to mitigate the ever-increasing problem of food security in India. With rapid industrialization of *rural* states of India, there has been a crunch for farmland. Further, with the exponential population growth of India, the need for food sufficiency has become the need of the hour. Furthermore, the overuse of plant growth inhibitor, pesticides and fertilizers for faster growth of agricultural produce is detrimental to human health and the environment as a whole. The proposition of Organic Farming in Indian *Rural Economy* holds good, as an alternative to arrest this problem. The introduction of the process of Organic Farming in Indian *Rural Economy* is a very new concept. The huge furor over the overuse of harmful pesticides and fertilizers to increase agricultural output has, in fact, catalyzed the entry of Organic Farming in Indian *Rural Economy*. The process of organic farming involves using of naturally occurring and decomposable matter for growth and disease resistance of different crops. The concept of organic farming in India dates back to 10,000 years and it finds its reference in many *Indian* historical books.

Agriculture was the main source of livelihood in India and the use of naturally occurring matters for increased productivity, disease resistance and pest control was always in use, since time in memorial. The use of oil cakes, cow dungs, neem leaves, etc. is still practiced in India to ward of pests and used as preservatives. The use of chemical fertilizer for increased productivity started from late 1850s. In India, the first use of chemical fertilizer for increased agriculture productivity started from 1906.

The main advantages of Organic Farming in Indian *Rural Economy* are as follows:

- Organic fertilizers are completely safe and does not produces harmful chemical compounds.
- The consumption of chemical fertilizers in comparison to organic fertilizers is always more, especially in unused cultivable lands.
- Moreover, chemical fertilizer needs huge quantities of water to activate its molecule whereas, organic fertilizers does not need such conditions.
- Further, chemical fertilizers almost always have some harmful effects either on the farm produce or on the environment.
- Furthermore, it can also produce harmful chemical compound in combination with chemical pesticides, used to ward-off harmful pests.
- It is estimated that there is around 2.4 million hectare of certified forest area for collection of wild herbs.
- The actual available area for cultivation of organic agriculture in India is much more than that is identified and certified so far.
- India has around 1,426 certified organic farms.
- India produces approximately 14,000 tons of output annually.
- It is estimated, that around 190,000 acres of land is under organic farming in India.
- The total annual production of organic food in India in the last financial year was 120,000 tons.

The *Indian* states involved in organic farming in India are as follows:

- Gujarat
- Kerala
- Karnataka
- Uttarachal
- Sikkim
- Rajasthan
- Maharashtra
- Tamil Nadu
- Madhya Pradesh
- Himachal Pradesh

The main organic agricultural products of India are as follows:

- Bajra-mustard-wheat
- Chilly
- Cereals-cereals
- Cereals-pulses
- Kholar
- Maize
- Ginger
- Soybean
- Large cardamom
- Passion fruit
- Dungarpur Pulses-cereals
- Bajra
- Mustard
- Til
- Wheat
- Nagour Guar-cumin
- Guar-wheat
- Moong

- Mustard
- Ganganagar Cotton
- Bhilwara Urd
- Jaisalmer Bajra
- Bharatpur Bajra and wheat
- Jhunjhunu Pulses and wheat
- Alwar Wheat and bajra
- Banswara Maize
- Cotton-grass
- Jaipur Guar

Organic farming is either really expensive or really cheap, depending on where you live and whether or not you are certified. Not only are the "natural" pesticides and fertilizers increasingly marketed by agribusiness as costly or costlier than their chemical counterparts, but proving you are an organic farmer requires certification, which is time-consuming and expensive. In the USA, converting to organic agriculture is a huge undertaking for commercial *farmers*, who have relied on chemical fertilizers and pesticides for many decades, but in *India*, the conversion is no less arduous, and far more ironic.

India's farmers are still mostly practicing organic methods, passed down for millenia. Organic fertilizer and natural pest control are the only tools available to most of these *farmers*, who have always lacked the financial resources to explore chemical solutions. But these *farmers*, whose produce is as organic as they come, cannot afford to pay the fees required to gain official certification.

As the international community adopts standards for organic agriculture, the challenges faced by *farmers* in the USA versus *farmers* in *India* in order to adapt are very different indeed. The danger is that the well-intentioned global move towards organic standards will make small organic *farmers* in countries like *India*, who have been never done anything but organic farming, no longer able to sell their crops.

In response to the $26 billion global market for organic foods, the Indian Central Government set up a National Institute of

Organic Farming in October 2003 in Ghaziabad, Madhya Pradesh. The purpose of this institute is to formulate rules, regulations and certification of organic farm products in conformity with international standards. The major organic products sold in the global markets include dried fruits and nuts, cocoa, spices, herbs, oil crops, and derived products. Non-food items include cotton, cut flowers, livestock and potted plants.

J.S. Mann, commissioner of Horticulture for the Union Agriculture Ministry, said, "The institute, set up as part of the national program for organic production, will have its offices across the country and is appointing certifying agencies for organic farm products for the domestic market."

The certifying agencies thus far named by the Centre include the APEDA (Agricultural and Processed Food Products Export Development Authority), the *Tea Board*, the *Spices Board*, the *Coconut Development Board* and the *Directorate of Cashew and Cocoa*. They will be accountable for confirming that any product sold with the new "*India* Organic" logo is in accordance with international criteria, and will launch major awareness and marketing campaigns, in *India* and abroad.

What's all the rush? Money, of course. Statistics are predicting that the global market that was only $17 billion in the year 2000 may touch the $31 billion mark by 2005– and *India*'s current share is only 0.001 per cent. In a survey called Land Area under Organic Management (SOEL-survey), *India* comes in 75th place in the world, alongside Cameroon. Officially, only 0.03 per cent of its land is slated to be under Organic

Agriculture–yet, in the same survey, the number of organic farms is listed as 5660, catapulting it to 16th place in the global organic map. What does this mean? Basically, most of *India*'s organic farms are not officially considered (or certified as) organic.

Most of *India*'s farms are "organic by default."

The irony and difficulty of the new governmental push for organic agriculture is that 65% of the country's cropped area is "organic by default," according to a study by Rabo *India*. By this somewhat degrading term they mean that small *farmers*, located mostly in the Eastern and North-Eastern regions of the country, have no choice except to farm without chemical fertilizers or pesticides. Though this is true in many cases, it is also true that a significant number of them have chosen to farm organically, as their forefathers have done for thousands of years.

Many have seen for themselves the effects of chemical farming-soil erosion and loss of soil nutrients, loss of nutrition in food, and human diseases resulting from the chemicals that inevitably seep into the water table, all the reasons for the urgent demand for organic foods and farming.

In 2002, according to Government statistics, from a total food production of over 200 million tonnes, the country produced only 14,000 tonnes of organic food products. *India* currently has only 1,426 certified organic farms.

This statistical discrepancy reveals that the weak link in the organic/economic chain is certification. Under current government policy, it takes four years for a farm to be certified as organic. The cost of preparing the report is a flat fee of Rs. 5000, and the certificate itself costs another Rs. 5000. While these costs are bearable for the new industrial organic greenhouses, they are equal to or more than an entire year's income for the average small farmer, if the costs of travel and inspection are included.

In the United States, an organic farm plan or organic handling plan must be submitted to a USDA - accredited private or state certification program. The plan must explain all current growing and handling methods, and any materials that will be used - in the present, and any future plans must be included as well. Records for the last five years must be presented. Land must be chemical-free for three years prior to harvest, so a conventional farmer cannot receive the organic label for the transitional years. This will generally mean a decrease in income– crops may be less plentiful than with conventional fertilizers and pesticides, and yet the higher price for organic products won't yet be possible. Many *farmers* cannot afford the transition, even if they want to.

One solution to the small farmer's dilemma of how to both certify and survive is that of community certification. At the

World Organic Congress, hosted last year by IFOAM (International Forum for Organic Agricultural Movements) in Victoria, Canada, the theme was "Cultivating Communities." The idea of community certification of organic farms was the main topic of discussion, a concept increasingly popular among farming communities worldwide who have become fed up with accreditation agencies.

In community certification, communities, on a non-profit basis, take charge of the certification process themselves. They evaluate the farmer's commitment to the stewardship of the soil, and examine from many angles whether the food is being grown in an environmentally sensitive way or not, rather than technical standards.

While community certification may be a viable solution on the local level, it is our opinion that, in the global marketplace, less than exact technical standards will never be enough for today's consumer-and, in today's largely poisoned environment, it shouldn't be, either. Furthermore, such "soft" guidelines can easily backfire on the *farmers* themselves, as a system not based on facts must be by definition subject to local politics, bribery, favoritism, etc.

India must find a way to keep the strict international organic standards intact if it wants to compete in the international market for organic foods–but is there a way to do it without leaving small *farmers* out in the cold? One obvious solution is for the government so eager to make *India* organic to subsidize these certification fees enough to make it a viable option for ordinary *farmers,* not just for neo-organic factory farms and greenhouses. Banks also could provide a more level playing field for small *farmers*– currently, almost all bank loans are for pure crop *farmers,* that is, monoculturalists. While many of these big-business *farmers* use harmful chemicals and processes, small *farmers* fertilizing their soil with recycled organic wastes are usually ineligible for insurance, much less state subsidies.

In the Hindu newspaper's annual environmental report, P.V. Satheesh, Director of the *Deccan Development Society,* writes, "It's a sobering thought that the *farmers* producing the best and cleanest food must pay extra to certify, instead of inorganic foods being certified as potentially bad for our health."

A rice field in *Tamil Nadu*. India is the second largest producer of rice in the world, and Tamil Nadu is the largest rice producing state in India.

Composition of India's total production (million tonnes) of foodgrains and commercial crops, in 2003–04.

India *ranks second* worldwide in farm output. *Agriculture* and allied sectors like *forestry, logging* and *fishing* accounted for 16.6% of the GDP in 2007, employed 60% of the total workforce and despite a steady decline of its share in the GDP, is still the largest economic sector and plays a significant role in the overall socio-economic development of India. *Yields* per unit area of all crops have grown since 1950, due to the special emphasis placed on agriculture in the five-year plans and steady improvements in *irrigation,* technology, application of modern agricultural practices and provision of agricultural credit and subsidies since *Green revolution in India.* However, international comparisons reveal that the average yield in India is generally 30% to 50% of the highest average yield in the world.

The low productivity in India is a result of the following factors:

- Illiteracy, general socio-economic backwardness, slow progress in implementing land reforms and inadequate or inefficient finance and marketing services for farm produce.
- The average size of land holdings is very small (less than 20,000 m^2) and is subject to fragmentation, due to land ceiling acts and in some cases, family disputes. Such small holdings are often over-manned, resulting in disguised unemployment and low productivity of labour.
- Adoption of modern agricultural practices and use of *technology* is inadequate, hampered by ignorance of such practices, high costs and impracticality in the case of small land holdings.

- Irrigation facilities are inadequate, as revealed by the fact that only 52.6% of the land was irrigated in 2003–04, which result in farmers still being dependent on rainfall, specifically the *Monsoon* season. A good monsoon results in a robust growth for the *economy* as a whole, while a poor monsoon leads to a sluggish growth.[57] Farm credit is regulated by *NABARD*, which is the statutory apex agent for *rural* development in the subcontinent.

India does have multiple farm insurance companies that insure wheat, fruit, rice and rubber farmers in the event of natural disasters or catastrophic crop failure. One notible company that provides all of these insurance policies is *agriculture insurance company of india* and it alone insures almost 20 million farmers. India has more than 500 farm insurance companies of various size that operate under the supervision of the *Ministry of Agriculture.*

THE PARADOX AND CHALLENGES OF INDIAN AGRICULTURE

Indian agriculture is facing a policy paradox. Although several forecasts of the 1990s predicted that India would be a large importer of grains in the years to follow, in fact from 2001 to 2004 India exported around 30 million tons of foodgrains. It was seeking primarily to liquidate its bulging grain stocks, which reached 63 million tons in July 2002. Whereas India's agricultural policy is still rooted in the goal of self-sufficiency in grains, contural products such as fruits and vegetables, livestock products, and fish. The policy environment is lagging behind the structural change occurring in India's consumption and production baskets.

On another front, foreign exchange reserves, which had reached a rock-bottom US$1.2 billion in July 1991, climbed to more than US$120 billion by the end of 2004. Nonetheless, despite comfortable food and foreign exchange reserves and reasonably high growth in gross domestic product (GDP) of about 6 per cent annually, India still has more than 250 million underfed people (below the poverty line) and high under umption patterns are changing fast toward high-value agricultural products such as fruits and vegetables, livestock products, and fish. The policy environment is lagging behind the structural change occurring in India's consumption and production baskets.On another front, foreign exchange reserves, which had reached a rock-bottom US$1.2 billion in July 1991, climbed to more than US$120 billion by the end of 2004. Nonetheless, despite comfortable food and foreign exchange reserves and reasonably high growth in gross domestic product (GDP) of about 6 per cent annually, India still has more than 250 million underfed people (below the poverty line) and high under employment. This situation reflects severe problems on the distribution front.

What are the Reasons Behind this Paradoxical Situation?

The answer presumably lies in the neglect of, as well as misallocation of resources in, agriculture and rural development, especially in the later phase of the reform process initiated in 1991. The average annual rate of growth in agriculture fell from more than 4 per cent per year during 1992/93 to 1996/97 to less than 2 per cent per year during the period 1997/98 to 2002/03, and it remains low.

What led to this dramatic decline in the growth of agriculture since 1997/98? How can it be revived? How can growth in agriculture and rural development diminish poverty quickly? To stimulate pro-poor agricultural growth and rural development, India will need to make some strategic choices. We propose action in five major areas that can help the government to accelerate agricultural growth and reduce poverty, malnutrition, and unemployment quickly and on a sustainable basis. All of these reforms can be achieved with due regard for the well-being of the country's rural poor.

Enhancing Pro-Poor Rural and Agricultural Investments and Cutting Subsidies

Since the early 1980s public investment in agriculture has experienced a secular decline, while input subsidies (on fertilizers, power, and canal irrigation) have been rising. In the early years of economic reforms, an attempt was made to arrest and reverse these trends, but this effort could not be sustained. As a result the gap between investments and subsidies kept widening.

Today input subsidies, together with food subsidies, amount to roughly five to six times the public investment in agriculture.

With a burgeoning subsidy bill and shrinking public investment, the growth impetus for agriculture has been declining. Private investment in agriculture has been increasing, yet it has not fully compensated for the loss from falling public investment.

The first strategic decision must be to raise the level of public investment in agriculture and in rural India. This move would also help unleash private sector investment, which complements public investment. The strategy should be to contain and target subsidies and plow the savings back into agriculture as investment. IFPRI research shows that investments in R&D have the highest impact on agricultural growth per million rupees invested. The rates of return to public investment in research have been as high as over 60 per cent, and in extension, over 50 per cent. India currently invests only about 0.5 per cent of its agricultural GDP in agricultural research, compared with 0.7 per cent in the developing countries as a whole and as much as 2–3 per cent in the developed countries. These figures suggest that government has been systematically underinvesting in a sector that offers a high social return and that there is considerable scope for diverting incremental outlays to priority areas in research.Investment in rural roads has the most potent effect on poverty alleviation, per million rupees invested, followed by investment in R&D. Across regions, the returns on each million rupees invested in the less-favored (rainfed) areas of western and southern India are now higher than in the irrigated tracts of the northwest. These rainfed areas were largely bypassed by the Green Revolution. Thus any investment in this region has a win-win potential in terms of both higher returns (efficiency) and equity. In R&D, India had a successful record of importing high-yielding seed varieties and adapting them to local conditions during the late 1960s and 1970s, an effort that led to the Green Revolution. Although there is still ample scope for increasing rice and wheat yields, especially in the water-abundant eastern belt, the Green Revolution has been stagnating in the northwest states of Punjab, Haryana, and western Uttar Pradesh, as well as in the southern states of Andhra Pradesh and Tamil Nadu. To keep pushing the production frontier outward, India must invest in new technologies and the institutions to accompany these technologies. The new agricultural technologies on the horizon are largely biotechnologies. Indian policymakers, scientists, and regulators have long supported the development of biotech nology (including genetic modification) that provides new crops favorable to India's climatic areas and is suitable for use by farmers in rural communities. One of the most important technologies in the Indian context is one that produces drought resistance. Developing biotechnology appropriately, however, will require effective research and reforms of the regulatory structure and process, duly recognizing the local and international debate on biotechnology, particularly regarding genetically modified (GM) crops. In this context, setting up a body like the National Biotechnology Regulatory Authority (NBRA) would enhance regulation of biotechnology in India. Investments in advanced crop technologies for Indian farmers will pay off only if there are accompanying investments in infrastructure. The connection of India's villages to information and communications technology is an important component of these initiatives. The private sector can be the key driving force, and many corporate giants have already entered rural areas with a view to expanding business. But public policy should facilitate these investments in rural areas by removing controls on private investment as well as by offering tax concessions for investing in rural areas, in order to improve poor communities' access to education, market information for farmers and other small businesses, and service information. Investing in appropriate institutions is as important as investing in agricultural R&D and infrastructure. Institutional changes are required to ensure greater transparency and accountability in implementing agencies. India faces endemic problems stemming from poor staff incentives and a lack of financial autonomy, accountability, and transparency in its public sector agencies. The best solution is likely to be selective privatization that takes into account both equity and efficiency considerations.

Public investment needs to be made more pro-poor and productive through decentralization. Community participation in constructing and maintaining rural infrastructure is crucial for the efficient operation of financial incentives and the establishment of a legal framework. The typical top-down approach followed so far in public investments will not give the desired results. Heavy participation of user groups and nongovernmental organizations (NGOs) in maintaining public infrastructure is required to turn the process of rural development from top down to bottom up.

Reforms with a Human Face: Addressing the Landless Poor

Reforms in the agricultural sector are an important step toward increasing growth rates in the Indian economy and thus reducing poverty sustainably. But many households are not in a position to share in economic growth because of their low asset base (for example, poor nutrition, low education, and few physical assets). Studies reveal that there is typically little mobility out of extreme poverty, and many households remain poor for generations.Indeed, low human capital status and an inability to build up a minimum physical asset base play a key role in the intergenerational transmission of poverty. Any credible, broad-based development strategy must therefore involve public policies aimed directly at promoting asset accumulation by chronically poor households. In addition, the labor productivity of the poor is currently impaired by nutrition problems, including "hidden hunger" in the form of micronutrient deficiencies. Agricultural research and production programs should focus on addressing these deficiencies through supplementation, fortification of foods (including complementary foods), and attention to making low-cost foods that are rich in micronutrients. India is home to a wide range of social safety net programs that together attempt to address the needs of poor households at various stages of the life cycle. For households with young children, the Integrated Child Development Scheme (ICDS) provides take-home food rations linked to acquiring nutrition guidance and crucial health care. To promote higher educational attainment, the Mid-Day Meals Program provides meals to children attending school. The Public Distribution System (PDS) provides subsidized food rations to poor households through a vast network of fair-price shops. A range of community public works programs (such as Jawahar Gram Samridhi Yojana or Employment Guarantee Schemes [EGSs]) provide employment to the poor during periods of economic downturn or during the slack agricultural season. The National Old-Age Pension program and the Annapurna program provide cash to destitute elderly households without alternative family support. These programs should be transformed from social assistance to social development programs that contribute directly to the creation of physical and social assets. Although safety net programs in India vary widely and absorb substantial public funds, their combined effectiveness is questionable. Rationed food subsidies are often poorly targeted, and corruption prevents much of the food from reaching the intended beneficiaries. For example, 53 per cent of India's rural poor live in three states (Bihar, Uttar Pradesh, and Madhya Pradesh), but their dependence on subsidized food through the PDS off-take is only between 5 and 10 per cent of their total cereal consumption—too little to make much difference in their food security. The costs associated with public distribution of food are also often unnecessarily high. There is a need to rationalize wages in public works programs, walking the line between too-high wages, which will result in leakage of transfers to nonpoor households, and too-low wages, which will undermine the very objective of the programs ,that is, poverty alleviation. These two considerations need to be balanced, in line with minimum wage regulation. In addition, high costs associated with managing the creation of assets through public works programs absorb scarce resources, and the resulting projects are often of low quality or never benefit the poor. The economic inefficiencies associated with financing these safety net and public works programs can also be substantial, as is the case with foodgrain support prices that distort production incentives. These different safety net programs are often poorly integrated, with some households receiving benefits from a number of sources and other poor households being completely excluded.

As a first step, existing social safety net programs in India need to be revisited to assess their targeting mechanisms, coverage, cost-effectiveness, and overall impact on poverty alleviation. Research at IFPRI, along with several studies in India, shows that programs like the EGS of Maharashtra to build rural infrastructure are more cost-effective in reaching the poor than is the untargeted PDS. These public works schemes need to be scaled up to build rural infrastructure, develop and preserve watersheds, undertake forestation, desilt canals, and so forth. Bangladesh's Food for Education (FFE) scheme and India's own ICDS show that targeted programs have been highly successful and are worth investigating. Under the FFE scheme, the poor family of the school-aged child gets a quantity of subsidized food as long as the child attends school. This program ensures higher attendance in village schools, especially of girls, and provides food security to the poor. Such a program may be worth implementing in India on a pilot basis. Achieving reforms for the landless poor requires developing and applying credible evaluation techniques that can then inform the design and implementation of programs. Given budget constraints and the extent of poverty in India, the country cannot afford to tackle the problem of assisting the landless poor without substantial improvements in the cost-effectiveness of the overall social safety net system. Fortunately, we have learned much from diverse experiences in several developing countries, and the wide variation in program performance across Indian states may also be a valuable source of lessons for future policy reforms.

Addressing the Water Challenge

Rapid growth in nonagricultural water demand, the unsustainable overdraft of groundwater, and a slowdown in the growth of water supply investments are leading to growing water shortages for agrculture in much of India. These shortages are likely to worsen in the coming years if business as usual continues, and the local impacts on agricultural employment and rural livelihoods could be severe. Concerted policy efforts, however, could significantly mitigate the negative effects of growing water shortages. The ultimate irrigation potential of the country is roughly 140 million hectares, of which not more than 70 per cent has been exploited. During the Ninth Five-Year Plan (1997–2002), irrigation grew at only about half of its target rate. Large investments would be required to complete several hundred irrigation schemes that have gone unfinished for years because of severe resource constraints. Additional resources for those projects nearing completion would bring high returns to investments already made. Part of the solution to water scarcity, however, lies outside of the irrigation sector. Increased investments in agricultural research could boost agricultural productivity to compensate for the diversion of water from agriculture to domestic and industrial uses. Crop research needs to target rainfed production as well as irrigated areas, taking pressure off the irrigated crops sector. In the domestic and industrial water sectors, improving both efficiency and equity through increased water prices would provide incentives for conservation, cover the costs of delivery, and generate adequate revenues to finance the needed growth in supplies and expanded coverage of clean piped water. At the same time,pressure on water transfers from agriculture would be reduced.Generalized domestic and industrial water subsidies need to be replaced with subsidies targeted to the poor. In the irrigation sector, water policy should be designed to induce investment in improved technology and conservation of water and to encourage diversification away from irrigated cereals into crops that give more value per unit of water. It is feasible to design and implement water pricing systems on the basis of water rights that would introduce positive incentives for efficient water use and crop diversification, recover operations and maintenance (O&M) costs, and protect and even increase farm incomes.

Water rights, combined with appropriate incentives, are essential for establishing rational water allocation because they provide users with the security to invest in water-saving tech nology and practices. Because of the large number of small farmers in Indian irrigation systems, in most cases it is preferable to assign water rights to water user associations rather than to individual farmers. A water brokerage system with a river basin authority, or an irrigation system that brokers water trades among irrigators and between irrigation and nonirrigation water uses, could establish incentives to use water efficiently without reducing farm incomes.

A base water right would be established at major turnouts to water user associations. The user group would be responsible for internal water allocation. A fixed base charge would be applied to the initial (historical) quantity, sufficient to cover O&M and longer-term asset replacement (depreciation) costs. For demand abov the base water right, a price equal to the value of water in alternative uses would be charged to users; for demand below the base right, the same price would be paid to the water user for not using the water. This system would facilitate the mutually agreed purchase and transfer of water to higher-valued uses. The promise of efficient water use and the allocation of water resources without harming the welfare of irrigators and other rural water users make the establishment of water rights, together with appropriate incentives, one of the highest priorities for water reform.

Toward High-Value Agriculture

Given sustained increases in per capita incomes of about 4 per cent per year during the past two decades, consumption patterns in India are changing away from cereals to high-value agricultural products. How fast has the consumption basket of an average Indian changed? Data from the National Sample Survey Organisation (NSSO) show that per capita consumption of cereals from 1977 to 1999, for example, declined from 192 to 152 kilograms per year in rural areas and from 147 to 125 kilograms in urban areas. The consumption of fruits, on the other hand, increased by 553 per cent, of vegetables by 167 per cent, of milk and milk products by 105 per cent, and of meat, eggs, and fish by 85 per cent in rural areas over the same period. Similar changes occurred in urban diets. These dramatic changes indicate a structural shift in Indian diets. Add to this the new export market opportunities for many of the same products, owing to trade liberalization, and there is a happy match between the demands of the market and the need for farmers to diversify into higher-value activities. Further, high-value agricultural products have higher employment elasticity and can be suitable for smallholders, if they can participate. In this new situation, more of the energies and resources of the agricultural sector can be unleashed to produce the kinds of high-value foods and products that are now in high demand by India's growing middle classes and urban dwellers and that have new export market opportunities. A reinvigorated agricultural and agribusiness sector could thus continue to be a major engine of income and employment growth for the country. Despite the tremendous opportunities ahead, success is not yet assured. Important challenges will need to be overcome. The first challenge is to further shift the government's priorities from heavy support and protection of food staples to promotion of agricultural diversification, processing, and commercialization. Simply put, most farmers are not going to get rich by growing cereals when there are already national surpluses, demand growth is slow, and world markets are glutted with the subsidized production of rich-country farmers. Farmers must shift into higher-value products to increase their incomes. A set of public policies and investments is required to fully unleash this new potential. This set must include additional public investment in the kinds of rural infrastructure and technologies needed for these new high-value activities, improvements in marketing and distribution systems for higher-value and more perishable foods, and further liberalization of the agroindustrial sector. The private business sector can and should play a dominant role in these higher-value market chains, and public policy must strengthen the enabling environment. This change will require a fundamental shift in thinking in many public agencies that are still geared toward the dominant role that the state played in the market chains for food staples during the Green Revolution era. Although some of the funding for these new investments will come from the private sector, new public investments are also needed. The needed funds might be obtained by reducing some of the huge subsidies that are still maintained on fertilizers, credit, and water for the food staples sector and that no longer serve a useful purpose. This could be a win-win strategy for farmers and the government and at the same time could contribute to national economic growth. The second challenge for the "new" high-value agriculture is to make it pro-poor. Left to market forces alone, the major beneficiaries of the new high-value agriculture will be mostly the larger and commercially oriented farms, as well as farms that are well connected to roads and markets. The majority of the 300 million or so poor people in India are rural people who depend on agriculture for their living, and many live in the less-favored regions. These people must not get left further behind during the next phase of India's agricultural development. Fortunately, there is great opportunity to guide the new high-value agriculture so that small farms and even many less-favored regions can be major participants. Achieving broad participation will require improving infrastructure and education in many less- favored regions and communities, ensuring that small farms get the technologies and key inputs they need, and promoting producer marketing organizations that can link small farmers to the new market chains (supermarkets, contractors, processors, exporters, and the like). Small farmers cannot do all of these things on their own, and the public sector, private sector, and NGOs all have important roles to play. Because high-value agriculture demands more working capital, which small farmers often lack, a major effort must be made to reform the rural credit delivery system to reach smallholders. Innovative institutions promoting vertical coordination between farms, firms, and forks (supermarkets) would reduce transaction costs and market risks and would also act as a conduit to funnel more credit into this venture, especially for smallholders. This system would help lay a foundation for globally competitive agriculture in which smallholders can also participate and prosper. Public policy can make a major contribution by facilitating farmer organizations, standardization, transparent food safety policies, and contract security between farmers and the processing and retail industry. A third challenge will be overcoming many of the environmental problems that now plague agriculture. Water scarcities will continue to grow, and farmers must learn to use less water and to be less polluting. Land degradation and deforestation must also be contained. A shift toward more diversified and higher-value farming systems will help, both because many of the new crops need less water and because, by increasing returns to land, small farmers will have less need to overexploit poor lands and soils. Although agriculture can make a significant contribution to growth, employment creation, and poverty reduction, on its own it will not drive the full economic transformation that is now possible for India. A fourth challenge, therefore, is for policymakers to find ways of accelerating growth in the service and manufacturing sectors, which will require continued economic liberalization and privatization

AGRICULTURE & RURAL DEVELOPMENTS

Irrigation, Food Processing, Fertilizers & Fisheries

A Saga of Success

From a nation dependent on food imports to feed its population, *India* today is not only self—sufficient in grain production, but also has a substantial reserve. The progress made by agriculture in the last four decades has been one of the biggest success stories of free *India*. Agriculture and allied activities constitute the single largest contributor to the Gross

Domestic Product, almost 33% of it. Agriculture is the means of livelihood of about two—thirds of the work force in the country.

This increase in agricultural production has been brought about by bringing additional area under cultivation, extension of irrigation facilities, the use of improved high yielding variety of seeds, better techniques evolved through agricultural research, water management, and plant protection through judicious use of fertilizers, pesticides and cropping practices.

Crops

The 1970s saw a multi-fold increase in wheat production that heralded the Green Revolution. In the next decade rice production rose significantly; in 1995-96, rice production was 79.6 million tons. Total grain production crossed 191 million tons in 1994-95, a big leap from 51 million tons in 1950-5 1. During the Seventh Plan, the average grain production was 155 million tons, 17 million tons more than the Sixth Plan average.

To carry improved technologies to farmers, a National Pulse Development Program, covering 13 states, was launched in 1986. The Special Food Production Program augmented efforts to boost pulse production further. In 1995-96, pulse production was 13.2 million tons. With some States offering more than the statutory minimum price, sugarcane production also received a boost, in 1995-96 a record 283.0 million tons was registered.

Irrigation

As efforts continued to increase the irrigation potential in the country, the last 40 years saw the gross irrigated area reach 8~ million hectares. Flood forecasting has become an important activity over the years. Over 500 hydrological stations collect and transmit data through 400 wireless stations for issuing forecasts for 157 sites. About 5000 forecasts are issued in a year with 94% accuracy. The country also receives international support, with the World Bank as a primary source, for developing the water resources. International cooperation is also envisaged in setting up a National Center for Information on Water and Power. As there is a broad seismic belt in the country, particularly along the Himalayan, the Kutch region and ports of Maharashtra, a scheme is being evolved to collect all data on seismic activity at various dam sites.

Fertilizers

The fertilizer industry in *India* has grown tremendously in the last 30 years. The Government is keen to see that fertilizer reaches the farmers in the remote and hilly areas. It has been decided to decontrol the prices, distribution and movement of phosphatic and potassic fertilizers. Steps have been taken to ensure an increase in the supply of non-chemical fertilizers at reasonable prices. There are 53 fertilizer quality control laboratories in the country. Since bio—fertilisers are regarded as an effective, cheap and renewable supplement to chemical fertilizers, the Government is implementing a National Project on Development and Use of Bio-fertilisers. Under this scheme, one national and six regional centers for organizing training, demonstrating programs and quality testing of bio-fertilisers has been taken up.

It was a challenging decision of the Government to take Bombay High gas through a 1,700-km pipeline to feed fertilizer plants located in the consumption centers of North **India**. However, the major policy which has ensured the growth of the fertilizer industry is the thrust on accelerating fertilizer consumption by fixing, on the one hand, low and uniform price for fertilizers, and on the other hand providing the manufacturers adequate compensation through the retention price and subsidy scheme. As expected, fertilizer nutrient demand has gone up from 0.29 million tons in 1960-61 to 13.9 million tons at the end of 1995-96, compared to 12.15MT during 1992-93.

Fisheries

Fish production achieved an all-time high of 4.9 million tons at the end of 1995-96. Programs that have helped boost production include the National Program of Developing Fish Seeds, Fish Farmers' Development Agencies and Brackish

Water Fish Farmers' Development Agencies. The Central Institute of Fisheries Nautical and Engineering Training trains the necessary manpower. To diversify fishing methods and introduce processed fish products on a semi-commercial scale, an Integrated Fisheries Project has been launched. A National Fisheries Advisory Board has also been established.

Food Processing

A Ministry of Food Processing *Industries* was established in July 1988 to ensure better utilization of farmers' output by inducting modem technology into the processing of food products, thus augmenting the income of farmers and generating employment opportunities in *rural* areas. A new seeds policy has been adopted to provide access to high quality seeds and plant material for vegetables, fruit, flowers, oil-seeds and pulses, without in any way compromising quarantine conditions. Initiatives have been taken to encourage private sector investment in the food processing industry.

Agricultural Research

The apex body for education, research and extension education in the field of agriculture is the Indian Council of Agricultural Research (ICAR), established in 1929. India's transformation from a food deficit to a food surplus country is largely due to ICAR's smooth and rapid transfer of farm technology from the laboratory to the land.

ICAR discharges its responsibilities through 43 research institutes, four national research bureaus, 20 national research centers, nine project directorates, 70 all-*India* coordinated research projects, and 109 Krishi Vigyan Kendras (farm science centers). Besides, the program of Agricultural Education is coordinated by ICAR with the curricula and other normative guidance given to the 26 Agricultural Universities and four National Research Institutes.

Oilseeds Production

A Technology Mission on Oilseeds was launched in 1986 to increase production of oilseeds in the country and attain self sufficiency. Pulses were brought under the Technology Mission in 1990. Before the Mission was launched in 1985-86, oilseed production was 10.83 million tons; during 1995-96, it was estimated at 22.42 million tons, which is a record. Soybean, rapeseed and mustard largely contributed the increase in production. Production of pulses has seen many ups and downs, which is expected to be checked under the Mission. The country grows mainly nine oilseeds, with groundnut, rapeseed and mustard accounting for 62% of total production. Lately, soybean and sunflower have shown major growth potential.

Drinking Water

A Technology Mission on Drinking Water and Related Water Management has been constituted to cover the residual problem villages and provide potable water at 40 liter per capita per day, and 70 liters per capita per day in desert areas inclusive of 30 liters for cattle. The Mission is tackling the problem through 55 mini-missions in project districts and countrywide problem oriented sub-missions. A Village Level Operation and Maintenance (VLOM) pump called *India* Mark-11 has been developed and is being exported to 40 countries. By March 31, 1993, over 79% of the *rural* and about 85% of the urban population was provided drinking water facilities.

2

RURAL MARKETING

Marketing plays a pivotal role in the growth of a country irrespective of size, population and the concepts are so interlinked that, in the absence of one, another virtually cannot survive. It is a historical fact that the development of marketing has always kept pace with the economic growth of the country. Both have experienced evolutionary rather than revolutionary change. The objective of modern marketing is to make profits through satisfying consumer's needs and wants. Hence, the marketers have to understand the real needs, wants, beliefs and attitudes of the consumers towards their products and services. Today, network marketing is a multi-billion dollar business. A number of companies have adopted this business model. It has grown into one of the driving forces of the 21st century economy. Network marketing is now regarded by many business leaders as the business for future. But this marketing method was misunderstood as a get rich-quick scheme. It is also too common for network marketer's world-wide to answer the legality and soundness of their business.

The rural sector, which encompasses about 70% of the total population, has an important role to play in the overall development of the country. Rural India is now undergoing a sea change resulting from the multi-pronged activities undertaken for overall development of villages. There is an indication of increasing prosperity in rural India. Prosperity in the rural areas has opened up new opportunities. It leads to certain definite increase in the demand for durable and non-durable goods. Also significant changes have been noticed in the buying and consumption pattern of the rural consumers, imbibing new ideas, attitude and way of life. As a result of the "Green Revolution", there is a socio-economic revolution taking place in Indian villages since last three decades. Increasing knowledge of fertilizers, water resources, pesticides, better quality seeds, modern farm equipments and methods of farming have changed the village for better. The per capita income of the farmers is on the increase and the manner in which they spend their disposable income has also changed. The rural market is not passive. It is vibrant and growing at a faster pace. It will soon exceed the urban market if this pace of development continues.

The villages have accepted the modern way of agriculture as a business but have also accepted modern living. Apart from food and consumable items, he is interested in buying small radios. televisions two wheelers mostly bicycles and motorcycles, wrist watches, cooking gas and furniture. Socio-economic changes in villages have led villagers to think of material well being. This change in the attitude of Indian farmer is sweeping across the countryside. The expanding rural market is important to the growth of economic development of India. The marketing focus is also changing towards villages. 'Go Rural' is the slogan of marketing gurus.

Prosperity in rural areas is very much reflected in the buying and consumption habits of rural folks. Their inclination to spend on the modern gadgets has increased as a result of their increase in purchasing power. This necessitates an appraisal of the rural marketing environment which is an outgrowth of various socio-economic and cultural forces. For evolving an appropriate marketing strategy, understanding the rural environment is quite essential. Recently attempts were made to define the distinct differences between the urban and the rural markers on the basis of the various socio-economic factors.

RURAL MARKETING–DEFINITION AND IMPORTANCE

Rural India comprises all places that are not urban. According to Thomen, the study of rural marketing comprises all the operations, and the agencies conducting them, involved in the movement of farm-produced foods, raw materials and their derivatives, such as textiles, from the farms to the final consumers, and the effects of such operations on producers, middlemen and consumers. This definition does not include the input side of rural marketing. Rural marketing is the study of all the activities, agencies and policies involved in the procurement of farm inputs by the farmers and the movement of rural products from the farms to the consumers. The rural marketing system is a link between the producer and the non-producer sectors. It includes the organization of agricultural raw materials supply to processing industries, the assessment of demand for producers' inputs and raw materials, and the policy relating to the marketing of farm products and inputs. According to the National Commission on Agriculture, rural marketing is a process which starts with a decision to produce a saleable farm commodity, and it involves all the aspects of market structure or system, both functional and institutional, based on technical and economic considerations, and includes pre and post harvest operations, assembling, grading, storage, transportation and distribution.

The importance of rural marketing cannot be over-emphasised. It is the base of industrialization as most of the raw materials are procured from rural marketing and agricultural products. Export Promotion Programme cannot be made successfully without developing and stimulating rural marketing system. India lives in villages as more than 72.7% of the population resides in villages. Rural marketing is the aggregation of agricultural development and the development of allied products. A country which is on the verge of development, India is making a number of policies and providing a number of facilities, privileges, incentives and subsidies in the rural sectors to develop the rural market. Agricultural marketing and rural marketing are interchangeably used. Rural marketing is a broad market comprising of rural industrialization, allied products and marketing of agricultural products which includes food processing industries.

The concept of Rural Marketing in India Economy has always played an influential role in the lives of people. In India, leaving out a few metropolitan cities, all the districts and industrial townships are connected with rural markets.

The rural market in India is not a separate entity in itself and it is highly influenced by the sociological and behavioral factors operating in the country. The rural population in India accounts for around 627 million, which is exactly 74.3 per cent of the total population.

The rural market in India brings in bigger revenues in the country, as the rural regions comprise of the maximum consumers in this country. The rural market in Indian economy generates almost more than half of the country's income. Rural marketing in Indian economy can be classified under two broad categories. These are:

- The market for consumer goods that comprise of both durable and non-durable goods
- The market for agricultural inputs that include fertilizers, pesticides, seeds, and so on

The concept of rural marketing in India is often been found to form ambiguity in the minds of people who think rural marketing is all about agricultural marketing. However, rural marketing determines the carrying out of business activities bringing in the flow of goods from urban sectors to the rural regions of the country as well as the marketing of various products manufactured by the non-agricultural workers from rural to urban areas. To be precise, Rural Marketing in India Economy covers two broad sections, namely:

- Selling of agricultural items in the urban areas
- Selling of manufactured products in the rural regions

Some of the important features or characteristics of Rural Marketing in India Economy are being listed below:

- With the initiation of various rural development programmes there have been an upsurge of employment opportunities for the rural poor.

RURAL MARKET BOOMING WITH BUSINESS PROSPECTS

Indian *rural* markets are expanding faster than urban ones. Interestingly, *rural India* accounts for 60 per cent of the total national demand. This segment is no more an inferior option of investment for big brands like ITC, Reliance, HLL, Godrej etc.

RURAL INDIA with its traditional perceptions has grown up over the years, not only in terms of income, but also in terms of thinking. The *rural* markets are growing at about two time faster pace than urban markets, not surprisingly, *rural India* accounts for 60 per cent of the total national demand.

According to a survey conducted by Mckinsey in 2007, *rural India* with a population of 630 million (approximately) would become bigger than total consumer *market* in countries such as South Korea or Canada in another 20 years and it will grow at least four times from its existing size.

Gone are the days when *rural* consumer went to nearby city to buy 'branded products and services'. The *rural* consumer is growing and this is an opportunity to grab the *market* share for all the global players in the *market*—whether it is into Fast Moving Consumer Goods (FMCG) sector or retail sector (either insurance or banking or for that sake any other sector).

The FMCG sector includes companies like Indian Tobacco Corporation (ITC), Godrej, Hindustan Lever Limited (HLL), Gujarat Cooperative Milk Marketing Federation (GCMMF-Amul) and Dabur *India* Limited. All these have shown a strong global presence in the *rural* sector and it can be said that all the FMCG companies should target the *rural* sector.

Some FMCGs products like toothpaste, hair oil and other like shampoos have done much better in the *rural* areas than the urban and the semi urban areas. It has been a phenomenon that the sales of many companies have gone up; Coca-Cola, Nestle and Godrej too have also reported better sales in *rural* areas.

The retail sector has a huge potential for growth as a study shows that opportunities in *rural* retail sector were estimated to be over $34 billion in the year 2007, which is expected to touch $43 billion by the year 2010. It can be seen from the *market* that companies like Reliance, Subhiksha are expanding in the *rural market*. ITC has launched its first *rural* mall 'Chaupal Sagar', which offers products ranging from FMCG to electronic appliance to automobiles. Indian Oil is planning to invest $ 189.10 in the *rural* areas during the financial year 2009.

Insurance sector has one of the biggest potential in the upcoming scenario and the fact lies in the statement that only eight to 10 per cent of the *rural* households are covered by life insurance. *Rural* investments are limited to their available option—post offices and a few limited *commercial banks rural* extension counters. The remaining 90 per cent offer a huge potential as such for the insurance companies. The *rural market* is vibrant and holds tremendous potential for growth of insurance business, particularly because of the strong saving habits. LIC has a target of selling four million policies in the current financial year.

Telecom sector is one of the booming sectors of the economy.

There are a large number of mobile subscribers in *India* and with the next 100 million to come from non-urban areas, many Indian mobile service providers are targetting the *rural market* with aggressive tariffs and low cost hand sets. In this regard Reliance Communication has targetted the *rural* segment by its 'Grameen programme' for *rural* subscribers. Spice Telecom is into the process of launching local *market* rates for the commodities across Karnataka to connect with *rural* customers. BSNL plans a $ 125.38 million to be spent on its *rural* infrastructure.

Consumer durable industry is also on the verge of making a foray into the *rural India* as it is all set to witness 12 per cent growth in the year 2008. Many companies like LG, Samsung are all set to put themselves into *rural* sector.

With *India* entering the globalisation mode and the *rural* revolution being governed by rising purchasing power, increased savings, changing consumer habits, there are sure and positive signs that a new dawn of *rural India* is going to come.

Dynamics of *rural* markets differ from other market types, and similarly *rural marketing* strategies are also significantly different from the *marketing* strategies aimed an urban or industrial consumer. There is growing importance of *rural* markets

The concept of *Rural* Marketing in India *Economy* has always played an influential role in the lives of people. In India, leaving out a few metropolitan cities, all the districts and industrial townships are connected with *rural* markets.

The *rural* market in India is not a separate entity in itself and it is highly influenced by the sociological and behavioral factors operating in the country. The *rural* population in India accounts for around 627 million, which is exactly 74.3 per cent of the total population.

The *rural* market in India brings in bigger revenues in the country, as the *rural* regions comprise of the maximum consumers in this country. The *rural* market in *Indian economy* generates almost more than half of the country's income. *Rural* marketing in *Indian economy* can be classified under two broad categories. These are:

- The market for consumer goods that comprise of both durable and non-durable goods
- The market for agricultural inputs that include fertilizers, pesticides, seeds, and so on

The concept of *rural* marketing in India is often been found to form ambiguity in the minds of people who think *rural* marketing is all about agricultural marketing. However, *rural* marketing determines the carrying out of business activities bringing in the flow of goods from urban sectors to the *rural* regions of the country as well as the marketing of various products manufactured by the non-agricultural workers from *rural* to urban areas. To be precise, *Rural* Marketing in India *Economy* covers two broad sections, namely:

- Selling of agricultural items in the urban areas
- Selling of manufactured products in the *rural* regions

Some of the important features or characteristics of *Rural* Marketing in India *Economy* are being listed below:

- With the initiation of various *rural* development programmes there have been an upsurge of employment opportunities for the *rural* poor

Over the years, marketers and researchers have realised that urban markets in India are fast reaching saturation levels and consequently *rural* markets in India have a huge untapped potential. As per NCAER projections, the number of middle and high income households in *rural* India is expected to grow.(by 2007 it was 111 million). Marketers are carefully examining the potentials of *rural* markets in India. The concept of *rural* markets in India is still in evolving shape, and the sector poses a variety of challenges. Although liberalization of the Indian *economy* began in 1991 and allowed *Indian* industry to be governed and led by market forces, there remain many restrictions that throttle *rural* development.

The *rural* market still remains regulated and controlled by the government to a great extent. There are government dictates that allow the sale of some varieties of farm produce only through government-owned mandis (markets)and there are crops that cannot move borders of the state they are grown in. These measures may have come into place to safeguard the interests of the farmers.

However, they are now passe and not in sync with current realities. Thus archaic regulations and half-hearted, hastily planned measures stifle the growth of the *rural economy* and need to be done away with, There are compelling reasons to reach out to the rural market for companies. The fast saturation of urban market presents the need to explore newer markets. The *rural* markets, however, remain unexplored because of high cost of telecom, infrastructure, diverse terrain, low affordability of the rural masses, etc.,

The services sector has arguably been the driver of India's growth process in recent years. The contribution of IT related services to this phenomenon is widely acknowledged and well documented.

Before gamboling into issues like where the Indian rural market stands and the opportunities for corporates to explore there... let's look at the definition of urban and rural India.

The Census defined urban India as - "All the places that fall within the administrative limits of a municipal corporation, municipality, cantonment board etc or have a population of at least 5,000 and have at least 75 per cent male working population in outside the primary sector and have a population density of at least 400 per square kilometer. Rural India, on the other hand, comprises all places that are not urban!"

Now for some facts and figures. The Indian rural market today accounts for only about Rs 8 billion (53 per cent - FMCG sector, 59 per cent durables sale, 100 per cent agricultural products) of the total ad pie of Rs 120 billion, thus claiming 6.6 per cent of the total share. So clearly there seems to be a long way ahead.

Time and again marketing practitioners have waxed eloquent about the potential of the rural market. But when one zeroes in on the companies that focus on the rural market, a mere handful names come to mind. Hindustan Lever Limited (HLL) is top of the mind with their successful rural marketing projects like 'Project Shakti' and 'Operation Bharat'. The lynchpin of HLL's strategy has been to focus on penetrating the market down the line and focusing on price point. Furthermore, activating the brand in the rural market through activities, which are in line with the brand itself, is what sums up HLL's agenda as far as the rural market is concerned informs MindShare Fulcrum general manager R Gowthaman. Amul is another case in point of aggressive rural marketing. Some of the other corporates that are slowly making headway in this area are Coca Cola India, Colgate, Eveready Batteries, LG Electronics, Philips, BSNL, Life Insurance Corporation, Cavin Kare, Britannia and Hero Honda to name a few.

We can safely say that until some years ago, the rural market was being given a step-motherly treatment by many companies and advertising to rural consumers was usually a hit and miss affair. More often than not, the agenda being to take a short-cut route by pushing urban communication to the rural market by merely transliterating the ad copy. Hence advertising that is rooted in urban sensitivities didn't touch the hearts and minds of the rural consumer. While, this is definitely changing, the process is slow. The greatest challenge for advertisers and marketers continues to be in finding the right mix that will have a pan-Indian rural appeal. Coca Cola, with their Aamir Khan ad campaign succeeded in providing just that.

Corporates are still apprehensive to "Go Rural." A few agencies that are trying to create awareness about the rural market and its importance are Anugrah Madison, Sampark Marketing and Advertising Solutions Pvt Ltd, MART, Rural Relations, O&M Outreach, Linterland and RC&M, to name a few. Also, the first four agencies mentioned above have come together to form The Rural Network. The paramount objective of the Network is to get clients who are looking for a national strategy in rural marketing and help them in executing it across different regions.

Interestingly, the rural market is growing at a far greater speed than its urban counterpart. "All the data provided by various agencies like NCAER, Francis Kanoi etc shows that rural markets are growing faster than urban markets in certain product categories at least. The share of FMCG products in rural markets is 53 per cent, durables boasts of 59 per cent market share. Therefore one can claim that rural markets are growing faster than urban markets," says Sampark Marketing and Advertising Solutions Pvt Ltd managing director R A Patankar.

Coca-Cola India tapped the rural market in a big way when it introduced bottles priced at Rs 5 and backed it with the Aamir Khan ads. The company, on its behalf, has also been investing steadily to build their infrastructure to meet the growing needs of the rural market, which reiterates the fact that this multinational has realised the potential of the rural market is going strength to strength to tap the same.

Clearly the main challenge that one faces while dealing with rural marketing is the basic understanding of the rural consumer who is very different from his urban counterpart. Also distribution remains to be the single largest problem marketers face today when it comes to going rural. "Reaching your product to remote locations spread over 600,000 villages and poor infrastructure - roads, telecommunication etc and lower levels of literacy are a few hinges that come in the way of marketers to reach the rural market," says MART managing director Pradeep Kashyap.

Citing other challenges in rural marketing, Patankar says, "Campaigns have to be tailor made for each product category and each of the regions where the campaign is to be executed. Therefore a thorough knowledge of the nuances of language, dialects and familiarity with prevailing customs in the regions that you want to work for is essential. The other challenge is the reach and the available means of reaching out to these markets, hence the video van is one of the very effective means of reaching out physically to the rural consumers."

The fact of the matter remains that when compared to the Indian urban society, which is turning into a consumerism society; the rural consumer will always remain driven by his needs first and will therefore be cost conscious and thrifty in his spending habits. "Decision-making is still conscious and deliberated among the rural community. But nevertheless, the future no doubt lies in the rural markets, since the size of the rural market is growing at a good pace. There was a time when market predictions were made on the basis of the state of the monsoon but this trend has changed over the years; there is a large non farming sector, which generates almost 40 per cent of the rural wealth. Hence the growth in the rural markets will be sustained to a large extent by this class in addition to the farmer who will always be the mainstay of the rural economy," affirms Patankar.

"Although the melting of the urban - rural divide will take a while, this is not for want of the availability of the means but for want of the rural consumer's mindset to change; which has its own logic, which is driven by tradition, custom and values that are difficult to shed," he points out.

Fulcrum's Gowthaman says, "The biggest impending factor or deterrent on rural monies going up is that there is a general sense of trying to benchmark cost per contact (CPC). The television CPC is going to anyways be cheaper to rural CPC and unless and until the volume-value equation turns the other way round, you will not be able to spend disproportionate monies in the rural market.

For HLL, a one rupee or a five rupee sachet or the Kutti Hamam (the small Hamam) helps in giving the consumers a trial opportunity. While it does help in generate volume but not in terms of values. "Till the time that volume - value equation is managed better, the CPC is preventing anybody to look at rural at a large scale activation programme," reiterates Gowthaman.

Ultimately, the ball lies in the court of rural marketers. It's all about how one approaches the market, takes up the challenge of selling products and concepts through innovative media design and more importantly interactivity.

Anugrah Madison's chairman and managing director RV Rajan sums up, "There is better scope for language writers who understands the rural and regional pulse better. I also see great scope for regional specialists in the areas of rural marketing - specialists like Event Managers, Wall painters, folk artists, audio visual production houses. In fact all those people who have specialised knowledge of a region are bound to do well, thanks to the demands of the rural marketers."

So the fact remains that the rural market in India has great potential, which is just waiting to be tapped. Progress has been made in this area by some, but there seems to be a long way for marketers to go in order to derive and reap maximum benefits. Moreover, rural India is not so poor as it used to be a decade or so back. Things are, sure, changing!

Rs 8 billion (53 per cent - FMCG sector, 59 per cent durables sale, 100 per cent agricultural products) of the total ad pie of Rs 120 billion, thus claiming 6.6 per cent of the total share. So clearly there seems to be a long way ahead.Time and again marketing practitioners have waxed eloquent about the potential of the rural market. But when one zeroes in on the companies that focus on the rural market, a mere handful names come to mind. Hindustan Lever Limited (HLL) is top of the mind with their successful rural marketing projects like 'Project Shakul and Operation Bharat'. The lynchpin of HLL's strategy has been to focus on penetrating the market down the line and focusing on price point. Furthermore, activating the brand in the rural market through activities, which are in line with the brand itself, is what sums up HLL's agenda as far as the rural market is concerned informs MindShare Fulcrum general manager R Gowthaman. Amul is another case in point of aggressive rural marketing.

Some of the other corporates that are slowly making headway in this area are Coca Cola India, Colgate, Eveready Batteries, LG Electronics, Philips, BSNL, Life Insurance Corporation, Cavin Kare, Britannia and Hero Honda to name a few.

"Improving the lives of the billions of people at the bottom of the economic pyramid is a noble endeavour.It can also be a lucrative one"

INDIAN RETAIL MARKET

The Indian retail market, which is the fifth largest retail destination globally, according to industry estimates, is estimated to grow from the US$ 330 billion in 2007 to US$ 427 billion by 2010 and US$ 637 billion by 2015. Simultaneously, modern retail is likely to increase its share in the total retail market to 22 per cent by 2010. India has one of the largest numbers of retail outlets in the world. Of the 12 million retail outlets present in the country, nearly five million sell food and related products.

Top retail companies in India like Pantaloons, Shoppers Stop, Westside, Ebony, etc. are on an expansion spree, spreading to Tier II and Tier III cities and towns. Tata's retail venture Westside, plans to open stores across 37 more cities. Many big names in international retail are also entering Indian cities.

- Wal-Mart's first front store is expected to be launched in August 2008, and the first wholesale, cash and carry, store is likely to open by December 2008, in Chandigarh.
- Rosebys, UK's largest home textile retail chain plans to spend US$ one billion for opening 700 outlets over the next 3 years.

- Marks & Spencer's already has 20 stores in various Indian cities.
- International sportswear major Reebok too has revealed its plans to open 230 stores for the footwear and apparel segments in 2008-09 in India touching the target of 850.

RURAL MARKETING IN INDIA

The concept of *Rural Marketing in India Economy* has always played an influential role in the lives of people. In India, leaving out a few metropolitan cities, all the districts and industrial townships are connected with *rural* markets.

The *rural* market in India is not a separate entity in itself and it is highly influenced by the sociological and behavioral factors operating in the country. The *rural* population in India accounts for around 627 million, which is exactly 74.3 per cent of the total population.

Defining Rural

Seventy per cent of India's population, or approximately 700 million people, live in *rural* areas (Moorthi, 2002). As of the 2000 census, this equates to just under 2.5 times the population of the U.S. A location is defined as *rural* if at least 75 per cent of the population is agrarian. With such a large number of potential consumers, it is clear why multinational corporations would like to successfully penetrate the *rural Indian market.Rural Income* With an average income equivalent to $42 per month ($504 dollars per year), *rural* Indians have a very low disposable income (Kripalani, 2002).Most *rural* homes have minimal storage space and no refrigeration. Very few people own or have access to cars. As a result, *rural Indian* purchasing habits tend to be of an "earn today, spend today" mentality. Rather than buying in bulk, which would mean paying more for a large quantity upfront, rural.

Indians tend to buy what they need for short segments of time (Dawar and C h a t t o p a d h y a y, 2002). These factors result in consumers buying pro d u c t s l o c a l l y, as well as on a daily basis. In addition to the fact that income levels are low, *rural* incomes also vary greatly depending on the monsoons. When a monsoon hits, this devastates the livelihood of most *rural* consumers because they are dependent on agricultural work for income. Corporations are also directly affected because this makes it difficult to predict demand (Kanaan, 2001).

Products and Uses

Before a company considers entering the *rural market*, understanding the types of products and packages that *rural* Indians typically use is crucial.For example, *urban Indian* consumers would typically use toothpaste for brushing their teeth, while most *rural* Indians prefer using tooth powder (Balu 2001). As a company seeking to enter India's *market* with an oral care product, this would be an important fact to know and consider during both the product and package development stages. Similarly, Hindustan Lever Ltd. (HLL), the *Indian* subsidiary of Dutch-based Unilever, discovered that *rural* Indians tend to use the same soap for washing everything from hair to their bodies to clothing (if they use any soap at all). Because HLL manufactures products including various soaps and detergents, HHL product and packaging development processes have taken this *rural* habit into account by designing all-in-one soaps (Balu, 2001).

By taking into account the low disposable incomes and the unique product and package needs of this *market,* consumer products that are designed and pack aged for this *market* have great potential.

Strategically Align with Industry

Another key aspect to consider is how and where to produce and package the product. There are several options when a company is attempt ing to strategically aligning with industry. Companies can partner with an existing *Indian* company, buy out a local *Indian* manufacturer of a similar product, or strictly import products into India while keeping manufacturing facilities elsewhere.

Ten years ago, foreign consumer products were scarce in India and only available to the affluent. Import restrictions prevented or severely hindered foreign consumer goods from entrance to India. With the economic lib eralization that ensued, foreign brands are now prevalent across India (Luce, 2002). Today, multinational corporations view emerging markets such as India as prime opportunities for growth. According to Shanthi Kanaan, writer for The Hindu, *rural* markets are growing twice as fast as the *urban* markets (2001).

With a *rural* population equal to just under 2.5 times the population of the entire United States as of the 2000 census, the potential consumer base isssu astounding. But generally speaking, success in India's *rural* markets for multinational corporations has been mediocre at best. It is from these struggles and failures, however, that multinational corporations seeking to enter the *rural Indian market* can learn how to do so more wisely. Kellogg's, is an excellent example of a company that has struggled in the *Indian market*. Kellogg's entered the *Indian market* in the mid-1990's. They had the intentions of finding a new *market*, which would consist of over a million people, many of whom did not eat cereal. What Kellogg's discovered was that they were introducing a completely new product category. This meant they would have to invest large sums of money to create new eating habits in consumers. The most common *Indian* breakfast consists of biscuits and tea (Dawar and Chattopadhyay, 2002). While Kellogg's was busy creating new eating habits, local competitors were able to snatch away portions of India's already small cereal *market* by introducing local cereal flavors at lower prices (Prahalad and Lieberthal, 2003). The unimpressive sales that followed in their first three years resulted in Kellogg's needing to completely realign their marketing to meet local needs as well as introduce a line of inexpensive breakfast biscuits.

Disappointments like this have caused companies who seek to enter the *rural Indian market* to reevaluate their entire approach.

Understand the Rural Market

With a population already in excess of one billion people, India has caught the eye of multinational corporations across the globe as a place of opportunity for exploring new markets. While India has portions of their popu lation that would be considered wealthy or middle class by Western standards, a much greater percentage of India's population is low income. As a result, they spend money, live, and use products differently than the countries where most multinational corporations originate (Prahalad Lieberthal, 2003). *Rural* areas, in particular, exemplify these differences. Understanding the characteristics that make the people and the *market* in *rural* India unique can help corporations to enter this *market* with success. The key characteristics define the term *rural,* determine the amount and flow of income, and determine the types of products and packages that are typically used in *rural* India.

Partnering

The first and best option for aligning with the *Indian* industry is for the multinational to partner with an *Indian* company that is already successfully producing and selling a similar type of product. In doing so, the new company can take advantage of the manufacturing facilities and distribution networks that are already in place rather than having to start from scratch. As a result of India's colonial experience when it was controlled by Britain, many Indians have "...a profound mistrust of foreign brands" (Luce, 2002). By creating a partnership with an *Indian* company plays down the foreign factor and helps to dispel some of this mistrust. Hindustan Lever is a multinational corporation that has found success with this method of aligning with industry. By partnering with local entrepreneurs who own and manage their own plants, Hindustan Lever is able to manufacture their products with minimal amounts of fixed capital. In these partnerships, the entrepreneurs agree to devote their plant's capacity to manufacturing only Hindustan Lever products (Prahalad and Liebethal, 2003).

Buy-Out

A second alternative for aligning a new industry to enter India's *rural market* is to buy out a local *Indian* manufacturer. As with partnering, buying out a local manufacturer gives a company the ability to capitalize on existing manufacturing facilities and distribution networks. The disadvantage is that *Indian* consumers may view this negatively. Coca-Cola is an example of a multinational corporation that tried buying out a local distributor. In 1992, Coca-Cola made its second appearance to the *Indian market*. In an attempt to eliminate its biggest competitor, Coca-Cola acquired Thumbs Up, the local *market* leader in cola. When Coca-Cola tried to exchange its own brand on the regular Thumbs Up distribution network, *Indian* consumers looked unfavorably upon Coca-Cola. The company has been struggling ever since (Luce, 2002).

Importing

Additionally, companies can enter India's *rural market* by importing products from manufacturing locations overseas. Importing has only been a viable means of getting consumer goods into India for just over ten years, when trade restrictions were eased (Luce, 2002). However, there are several disadvantages to this method of marketing to *rural* India. Without a manufacturing facility in India, a company has no ties to India's already challenging distribution network, thus making sales even more difficult. In addition, *Indian* consumers tend to feel more loyalty and trust toward locally made products. The afore- mentioned Thumbs Up and Coca-Cola scenario also illustrates this fact. Though Thumbs Up is a cola of lower quality that Coke, it is a locally made *Indian* brand that *rural* consumers can relate with. Consequently, Coca-Cola is third behind Pepsi and Thumbs Up in the *Indian* soft drinks *market* (Luce,2002). Partnering with or buying out an existing *Indian* company, as well as importing from overseas, are all viable ways to get packaged consumer goods into *rural* India. Based on the past experiences of multinational corporations entering the *market*, partnering is the most successful option.

Tackle the Distribution Networks

Distribution networks in emerging markets tend to be very unique and often times disjointed (Dawar and Chattopadhyay, 2002). India is no exception. Before a multinational corporation even considers entering India's *rural market*, it is important to first get an understanding of the current distribution system characteristics as well as the ways that the system is likely to change over time (Prahalad and Lieberthal, 2003). In doing so, a company can assess whether or not accurate and timely product distribution can be achieved without first investing in the distribution networks. Some of the characteristics unique to *rural* India's distribution networks include the modes of transportation used as well as the point of sale. Despite the challenges of the *rural Indian* distribution environment, there have been distribution successes from multinational corporations.

Modes of Transportation

Over three million retail outlets in India are reached by companies that produce packaged goods. Methods of transportation used include camels, bull-drawn carts, bicycles, trucks, and trains (Prahalad and Lieberthal, 2003). In addition, poor roads and unreliable electricity are two additional obstacles common to the distribution networks in *rural* communities (Kripalani, 2002). Though glass bottles are popular in India, breakage can be a serious problem when the glass is carried over bumpy roads in the back of a truck (Prahalad and Lieberthal, 2003). Companies must be prepared to design packages for their products that will be capable of withstanding these types of conditions.

Point of Sale

The retail establishment where most *rural* consumers purchase their day-to-day goods is at a kirana or street shop. These small open stalls line the streets and are approximately the size of a living room. Consumers purchase everything from bananas to razors at a kirana. With over 2.5 million kiranas throughout India's *rural* towns and villages, keeping store shelves stocked is one of the main challenges to consumer goods manufacturers (Bullis, 1997). In order to reach these local shops and establish a brand presence in them, companies need substantial amounts of working capital and a large committed sales force (Dawar and Chattopadhyay, 2002).

Success Stories

In spite of all the distribution challenges, there have been several multinational corporations that have experienced great successes in tackling the distribution networks. Hindustan Lever has been able to build a distribution network in India that directly serves 800,000 stores and uses wholesalers and distributors to reach another 3.5 million outlets (Dawar and Chattopadhyay, 2002). Not only does this help Hindustan Lever move products from manufacturing facilities to retail outlets, it also provides a large deterrent to potential competitors. In addition to the distribution networks that reach local stores in India, Hindustan Lever began using an experimental concept called Shakti distributors. They implemented this tactic in 2000 to get their products into some of the most remote *rural* areas (Balu, 2001). Douglas Bullis calls this a multilevel marketing system, where independent distributors sell products directly to consumers and earn a commission on the products they sell, plus for other distributors they recruit (1997). It is similar to the way Amway and Mary Kay distribute products in the U.S. Shakti distributors are *rural Indian* women who partner with Hindustan Lever to receive training in micro-business skills, which includes a Personal Digital Assistant (PDA) to access product prices. They pur chase HLL products at cost and sell them to their villages for a profit. This unique method of distribution gets products beyond the typical reach of HLL's distribution networks (Merchant, 2003). In spite of the unusual modes of trans portation and the challenge of supplying small kirana, creative distribution methods have produced success for several multinationals in the *rural Indian market*.

Create the Packaging Solution

When approaching the task of designing a package for the *rural Indian market*, all of the aforementioned factors must be considered. Multinational corporations that have been successful with marketing and packaging consumer products for *rural* India have taken time to research the target *market*. They built an insightful and unbiased understanding of the characteristics that make it unique (Prahalad and Lieberthal, 2003). As a result of this research, two of the most effective elements of a package designed for *rural* India include the size and visual communication. Material usage is also another important element for the packaging engineer to consider.

Think Small

Due to the fact that *rural* Indians have small disposable incomes and very little storage space, one of the most popular concepts to hit the *ruralmarket* has been sachets. Sachets are plastic pouches that contain approximately 20 milliliters (.68 oz.) of product (Bailay, 2003). Sachets were first introduced to India in the 1990's by an *Indian* company selling a 10-milliliter sachet of Velvette shampoo. Before the sachet, shampoo in India was only available in larger bottles, therefore limiting its sales success among people with small incomes (Moorthi, 2002). Sachets meet the needs of the *rural* consumer in several ways. Sachets are inexpensive, they occupy a small amount of space, and they allow consumers to experiment with new products that they may never have tried before (Bailay, 2003).

Coca-Cola is another company that has found success by thinking small. In a packaging change aimed directly at the *rural* and lower-income markets, Coca-Cola launched a new 200 mL (6.8 oz.) bottle for the equivalent of 10 cents in 2001 (Kripalani, 2003). After introducing the smaller size bottle, sales increased 34 per cent by the end of the first quarter in 2002 (Kripalani,2002). Packaging in smaller units clearly helps to increase the affordability of products for *rural Indian* consumers.

Visual Communication

The *rural* area is a *market* where large portions of the population are illiterate. So, when packaging consumer products for *rural* markets, companies must use prominent logo symbols and logo colors to assure that illiterate consumers will be able to recognize the products (Bullis, 1997). Therefore, communicating brand values through the package rather than with words becomes essential. Emotional Surplus Identity (ESI) is a concept that that uses the shape,color, and content of a package to differentiate a brand in the eye of a consumer. By creating a bond with the consumer through the package, companies are able to establish a relationship that encourages repeat purchases. Loud, bright colors are typically used on packages to differentiate a product from the others on the shelf and to create a lasting impression in a consumer's mind Another technique used by multinational corporations has been tailoring products, including changing brand names, to give them a *rural* image. In the eyes of the consumer, branded products are associated with quality and value. Nirma, the largest selling detergent in the world, found success in the *rural Indian market* by using unelaborate packaging to position their product as one that cleaned well yet was affordable (Bullis, 1997). While this technique is not the most eye-catching, it allows *rural Indian* consumers to experience the benefits of a branded product without requiring elaborate or expensive packaging on the part of the multinational corporation.

Material Usage

Cost is not only a factor that influences a consumer's decision. Multinational corporations also address cost when evaluating various packaging options. For example, meeting the needs of consumers by packaging p roducts in small quantities increases the packaging costs for a company in comparison to a large bottle of product. One way companies are able to keep the prices of sachet-type packages down is partially due to lower govern m e n t duties on small packs. In some instances, it can actually be cheaper for a consumer to purchase sachets rather than a bottle of product. For example, a 100-milliliter (3.4 oz.)

bottle of Pantene shampoo retails for 61 rupees where-as 100 milliliters worth of sachets sells for 40 rupees (88 cents) (Bailay, 2003).By thinking small, using pronounced colors and logos, and planning for material usage, multinationals can create packages that meet the needs of the rural *Indian* consumer.

With an approximate population of 700 million people, the *rural Indian market* is important for multinational corporations to tap. Although *rura l*ndians need to purchase consumer goods just as their Western counterparts do,*rural Indian* consumers have a different set of needs that must be met by both package and product. Spending time researching the *rural Indian* consumer as well as the *market* before diving in can help to prevent unnecessary struggles and failures. If the opportunity exists, partnering with an existing *Indian* company upon *market* entry can provide several key advantages to a company. Understanding the available distribution networks in *rural* India is crucial to making a successful entry into the *rural Indian market*. Packages need to be designed to withstand more distribution abuse due to poor roads and more primitive modes of transportation. Finally, when creating a package for *rural* India, small sizes allow consumers to try new products. It also caters to the fact that most *rural* Indians have low disposable incomes and little storage space at home. By applying these lessons that have been learned from multinational corporations in the past, the task of entering the *rural Indian market* should be promising.

The *rural* market in India brings in bigger revenues in the country, as the *rural* regions comprise of the maximum consumers in this country. The *rural* market in *Indian economy* generates almost more than half of the country's income. *Rural marketing* in *Indian economy* can be classified under two broad categories. These are:

- The market for consumer goods that comprise of both durable and non-durable goods
- The market for agricultural inputs that include fertilizers, pesticides, seeds, and so on

The concept of *rural marketing* in India is often been found to form ambiguity in the minds of people who think *rural marketing* is all about agricultural *marketing*. However, *rural marketing* determines the carrying out of business activities bringing in the flow of goods from urban sectors to the *rural* regions of the country as well as the *marketing* of various products manufactured by the non-agricultural workers from *rural* to urban areas. To be precise, *Rural Marketing* in India *Economy* covers two broad sections, namely:

- Selling of agricultural items in the urban areas
- Selling of manufactured products in the *rural* regions

Some of the important features or characteristics of *Rural Marketing* in India *Economy* are being listed below:

- With the initiation of various *rural* development programmes there have been an upsurge of employment opportunities for the *rural* poor. One of the biggest cause behind the steady growth of *rural* market is that it is not exploited and also yet to be explored.
- The *rural* market in India is vast and scattered and offers a plethora of opportunities in comparison to the urban sector. It covers the maximum population and regions and thereby, the maximum number of consumers.
- The social status of the *rural* regions is precarious as the income level and literacy is extremely low along with the range of traditional values and superstitious beliefs that have always been a major impediment in the progression of this sector.
- The steps taken by the Government of India to initiate proper irrigation, infrastructural developments, prevention of flood, grants for fertilizers, and various schemes to cut down the poverty line have improved the condition of the *rural* masses.
- "Improving the lives of the billions of people at the bottom of the economic pyramid is a noble endeavour. It can also be a lucrative one".

Rural retailing

With more than six people living in villages, *Indian rural* market has a huge potential to offer for retailing industry. 70% of India's population lives in 627000 villages in *rural* areas. According to the NCAER study, there are almost twice as many 'lower middle income' households in *rural* areas as in the urban areas.

- At the highest income level there are 2.3 million urban households as against 1.6 million households in *rural* areas.
- Middle and high-income households in *rural* India are expected to grow from 80 million to 111 million by 2007.
- In urban India, the same is expected to grow from 46 million to 59 million. Thus, the absolute size of *rural* India is expected to be double that of urban India.

The *rural* market accounts for half the total market for TV sets, fans, pressure cookers, bicycles, washing soap, blades, tea, salt and toothpowder, What is more, the *rural* market for FMCG products is growing much faster than the urban counterpart.

According to Hansa Research, a market research firm that has published a *Guide to Indian Markets 2006*, the penetration of consumer durables has risen sharply in *Indian* villages between 2000 and 2005. Color TV sales are up 200% and motorcycle sales are up by 77%. In absolute numbers, however, the penetration is still low. Coke, for instance, reaches barely 25% of the *rural* market. This means the upside potential is huge for companies that develop effective *rural marketing* strategies.

According to NCAER, the low penetration rates can be attributed to three major factors: low income levels, inadequate infrastructure facilities and different lifestyles. But income levels are going up, infrastructure is improving and lifestyles are changing. Almost a third of the *rural* population now uses shampoo compared with 13% in 2000, according to Hansa Research. Retail chains in *India* prefer tie-ups with *big farmers* that have irrigated farms. Small farms that are rain-fed are out of the reckoning.

Food Retail Chain

A study on the Food Retail Chain and Supermarket Evolution in *India* has shown that the [emerging] Food Retail Chains (FRCs) prefer to do business with *big* and medium *farmers* who own two to five hectares of land. As against this, the traditional or non-FRC businesses work with small *farmers* who own less than two hectares. Others in the organised food retail sector are Pantaloon, Mother Dairy, Margin Free Market, Dairy Farm, Metro Group, Adani, Bharti and Reliance. Foreign direct investment is permitted only in single brand retail and through franchise. The total retail sales are to the tune of Rs. 231281 million, while the share of food, grocery and tobacco is Rs. 175426 million, at the workshop jointly organised by the United States Department of Agriculture and the Indian Council of Agriculture Research under the Indo-US Agriculture Knowledge Initiative here on Saturday.

Table 1
Rural Share of Consumer Demand (%)

Category	*FY96*	*FY02*	*FY10E*
Scooters	33.1	39.4	39.9
Motorcycles	47.3	39.8	48.3
Mopeds	52.7	58.2	57.7
Cars/Jeeps	2.1	8.0	10.9
Automotive	37.9	36.0	37.9
TVs	54.0	54.5	44.2
Other Whitegoods	23.8	23.9	23.7
All Fans	50.0	56.9	56.7
Other low-cots items	58.1	60.1	61.3
Shampoos	27.2	31.9	33.0
Edible oils	64.3	67.1	62.9
Washing cakes	68.7	71.4	75.6

Source: NCAER

Some have formed *farmers* and vendors associations. However, they have not been able to penetrate the fruits and vegetable markets. Besides, their rejection rate is rather high, the cost of which is borne by the *farmers.* Presentations at the workshop showed that the FRCs were reluctant to offer low-interest credit to *farmers* or insurance to cover risks as part of the contract farming deals. They wanted the government to step in for this. There were suggestions for setting up regulated wholesale markets and consolidators on the western models to do away with intermediaries. "Restrictive laws" and lack of a legal mechanism to regulate the farmer-corporate/firm link were identified as the major bottlenecks in the setting up of food retail chains and supermarkets.

However, the basic question remains, whether the *rural* consumer is aware of the products, if yes, can he afford them? To answer these problems some of the largest MNCs like Hindustan Lever and LG electronics have established strong distribution network in the *rural* areas. 'Sachet' revolution has really changed the dynamics of the *rural* market. Now more and more companies are coming out with small packs of Rs.4-5 so that the *rural* consumer can easily afford the products. For instance, HLL introduced Lifebuoy soap for Rs 2 and coca-cola came out with an idea of returnable 200-ml glass bottle for Rs 5 for *rural* markets. Today, the corporate world has gone further from just introducing sachets or small packs for *rural* market. They are coming out with *'Rural malls'*. Chaupal Sagar is one of the first organized retail effort in the *rural* area. This is a venture by ITC. It extended its warehouse into a *rural* shopping-cum-information center to attend to the needs of *rural* consumer. The size of the mall is very small with just around 7,000 sq feet as compared to ordinary mall sizes in urban area. But it still offers everything - from toothpastes to televisions, hair oils to motorcycles, mixer-grinders to water pumps, shirts to fertilizers, whatever a *rural* consumer needs. ITC started its first *rural* mall in Sehore, Madhya Pradesh and is planning to expand its network by another 40 shopping malls across *rural* Madhya Pradesh and Uttar Pradesh alone and over to increase its *rural* outlets to 700 by 2013. Following the footsteps of ITC, DCM Sriram Consolidated Ltd. (DSCL) has opened Hariyali Bazaars in 2002 focusing mainly on agri products. These bazaars offer–

- *Quality Agri-Inputs:* Provides a complete range of good quality, multi-brand agri inputs like fertilizers, seeds, pesticides, farm implements & tools, veterinary products, animal feed, irrigation items and other key inputs like diesel, petrol at fair prices.

- *Financial Services:* Provides access to modern retail banking & farm credit through simplified and transparent processes as also other financial services like insurance etc.
- *Farm Output Services:* Farm produce buyback opportunities, access to new markets & output related services.
- *Other Products and Services:* Fuels, FMCG, Consumer Goods and Durables, Apparels etc.

So far, 70 "Hariyali" Stores have been set up in different states across India which would scale up to 200-250 in next year or two. Ranbaxy's Fortis Health World is tying up with Hariyali Kisan Bazaar to make entry into the *rural* market.

Hindustan Lever followed another way of reaching *rural* consumers. Its Project Shakti, (*rural* self-help group) is a classic example of involving women in the distribution network through empowering women. The project started in 2000 encourages women to sell its products who operate like a direct-to-home sales women. A typical Shakti distributor sell products worth Rs 10,000-15,000 (around $250) a month, which provide an income of Rs 700- 1,000 (around $25) a month on a sustainable basis. This business model has created history in the *Indian rural marketing*. According to media reports, Shakti distributors now account for 15% of the company's sales in *rural* India. By the end of 2007, HLL will have at least 10,000 Shakti dealers covering over a lakh villages. Amongst its latest plans, HLL is involving non-competing brands/ companies to be a part of its project. For instance, HLL approached ICICI Prudential and Max New York Life to sell their insurance policies through its 'shakti dealers'.

Godrej Agrovet Ltd is another company who initiated its *rural* retail business through 'Godrej Aadhaar'. These outlets offer *rural* households, the basic food, grocery, apparel, footwear to furniture, kitchenware and home appliances to value-added services including banking, postal services and pharmacy. Godrej is planning to setup atleast 1000 stores across the *rural* India in next five years.

Even India Oil is planning to tap the *rural* market, opening Kisan Seva Kendras across the *rural* areas to provide fuel and non-fuel-added services to *rural* consumer.

Taking a lesson or two from the corporate world even government is thinking big for *rural* areas. Government of Madhya Pradesh proposes to develop *Rural* Shopping Malls (RSM) across the state to cater to the needs of *rural* population. RSMs would act a two way supply chain. Apart from selling goods to the farmers these malls will buy farmers produce as well.

LG India- tripled the number of its retail & distributor outlets in *rural* areas from 2004 to 2006 The average price of its Sampoorna range of CTVs came down to about the price so competitive that, thereby bridging the gap between CTVs and other local B/W TVs.It also tapped local forms of entertainment like annual *haats* and fairs and made huge investments in infrastructure for distribution and marketing. *Consumer Goods companies must go the Rural Way*

- The *rural market* accounts for 60 per cent of new CTV buyers for LG
- The *rural market* for LG grew at 25 per cent over the last year, against a 15 per cent growth in *urban* areas.
- Sampoorna TVs sold in the *Indian* heartland and the semi-*urban* belts ,enforced a strong connection with India for LG.
- It connected very well with down the population strata.

RURAL INFRASTRUCTURE AND SERVICE COMMON (RISC)

India's economic growth and development is predicated to a large extent upon the development of its 700-million strong *rural* population. Currently, the majority of India's population lives in about 600,000 small villages and are engaged primarily in agriculture and related activities. Since a very large labor force in agriculture necessarily implies very low per capita incomes, a substantial portion of India's current agricultural labour force has to move to non-agriculture sectors for incomes in all sectors to go up. The challenge is to manage the transition of a large segment–perhaps even 80 per cent–of the *rural* population from a village-centric agricultural-based *economy* to a city-centric non-agricultural *economy*, and do so in a reasonable period.

Urbanization and Development

Economic growth is both a cause and consequence of urbanization. By urbanization is meant the dense aggregation of people into economically interacting units (cities and towns) of anywhere between 100,000 people and several million people. Cities are engines of economic growth because they give rise to economies of scale, scope, and aggregation. This is so because infrastructure – buildings, roads, power, telecommunications, water, sanitation, security, maintenance–can be provided economically to larger aggregations of people. Availability of low cost infrastructure in turn makes the availability of a wide range of services possible in cities as opposed to very small villages. It is the aggregation of supply and demand for economic goods and services (and therefore indirectly for infrastructural goods) which account for cities.

Constraints

A set of basic facts define the constraints within which the economic growth and development of India's *rural* population must be addressed. Fundamentally, they relate to resource constraints, the nature of infrastructure, and the future trajectory of the geographical distribution of the population.

First, people need access to a wide range of services which allow them to engage in economically productive activities. These services include, at a minimum, market access, educational, health, financial, entertainment, transportation, and communications. It is primarily these services which enhance life and livelihood, and with which any population is concerned with.

Second, the provision of services depend on the availability of infrastructure. Without the foundation of affordable infrastructure, affordable services cannot be provided.

Third, infrastructure investment is 'lumpy'–the average cost of provision of infrastructure is inversely related to the scale of the operation.

Fourth, if there were no limitations on the financial and other resources available for providing infrastructure, it would be possible to provide infrastructure at every village. Resource limitations preclude this option.

Fifth, even if the full set of infrastructure were provided at every village, they will not be commercially sustainable as the aggregate derived demand for the infrastructure will be insufficient to make them commercially viable. Clearly, subsidy of infrastructure for 600,000 villages is not an option considering resource constraints.

Finally, while the current geographical distribution of the *rural* population is into over half a million small villages, the future distribution is a much smaller number of much larger aggregations of people – if the desired future is one where the agriculture sector's share of GDP is to be significantly smaller relative to manufacturing and services sectors, and if the majority of the labor has to be engaged in non-agricultural activities. In other words, *the basic geographical structure of population distribution will eventually undergo a change,* whether one likes it or not.

Not Village-centric

It is therefore argued that 'village-centric' development is not feasible because of resource limitations and because people naturally tend to migrate out of villages to cities. Furthermore, it not desirable since a vibrant *economy* depends on the aggregation of the population into units much larger than a small village. In short, investing scarce resources into villages is short-sighted and uneconomical.

Based on the above considerations, a model for *rural* development has been conceived called RISC–*Rural* Infrastructure and Services Commons.

The RISC Paradigm

The RISC idea is to bring to the *rural* population the full set of services that are normally available only in urban locations. It works within the constraints of limited resources by focusing attention to and concentrating investments at specific locations to obtain economies of scale, scope, and agglomeration.

RISC follows the logical trend of moving away from vertically integrated institutions to one of horizontal segmentation and specialization. Thus, conceptually and operationally, a RISC has two levels: the lower one is *the infrastructure level* (I-level) which provides a reliable, standardized, competitively-priced infrastructure platform consisting of power, broadband telecommunications, and the physical plant (building, water, air-conditioning, sanitation, security). The I-level is achieved by the coordinated and cooperative investment of firms that specialize in the component activities.

The *user services level* (S-level) is above the I-level. Co-located at the S-level are firms that provide user services such as market making, financial intermediation, education, health, social services, governmental services, entertainment, logistics, etc. The presence of the I-level reduces the cost of the services and therefore the prices that the users face. Economies of scope and agglomeration are obtained by the presence of the variety of different service providers.

Given that *rural* populations are very poor, it is reasonable to expect that the aggregate demand of a single village for any single service will be very low. However, the aggregate demand for, say, a 100 villages for a single service could be significant. Aggregating the demand for many different kinds of services of the same 100 villages would translate into lot of services. These services would require infrastructural inputs which can be commercially and sustainably supplied. Thus, a RISC would supply to the needs of about 100 surrounding villages.

The total *rural* population of India can be covered by about 6,000 RISCs each servicing the needs of approximately 100,000 people. Further external economies of scale can be obtained by implementing a few thousand RISC locations across the *rural* landscape. Access to a RISC for any *rural* person would be only a 'bicycle commute' away.

Operationalizing RISC

The distinction between the I-level and the S-level becomes apparent at the operational level. The I-level is provided by a small number of firms which specialize in the provision of infrastructure. The essential requirement is that the investments from these various firms are coordinated. This resolves the 'coordination failure' generally associated with investments that are large, lumpy, which have large lead times in implementation, and have long pay-back periods. These can be private sector or public sector firms.

There is an element of planning in the creation of the I-level. But it is not a top-down, bureaucratic, government imposed centralized planning. It is coordinated investment in various components of the infrastructure so that they all make each other mutually viable. The role of the government is highest at this level.

The government has to facilitate the process of the creation of the I-level first through light-handed regulation. Second, it has to give required tax incentives to the firms. Third, the government may be required to facilitate investment though loan guarantees. Finally, it has to help with the acquisition of land required for the projects. The model does not require the government to directly fund any of the infrastructure.

The firms providing the infrastructure will be basing their investment decisions on adequate return on investment, of course. The infrastructure will be used by, and paid for, the firms which are at the S-level and which provide the services that the users demand.

The composition of firms at the S-level will be almost entirely market-driven. There will be two basic categories of services. First, services which the users are willing and able to pay for. This means that the benefits to the users of the services will be greater than the costs. These are the 'income-enhancing services' such as greater market access. Second, services which are not fully priced such as government services and those provided by NGO and charitable entities.

What RISC Does

RISC provides a signal to coordinate the activities of a host of entities: commercial, governmental, NGO's. It synchronizes investment decisions so as to reduce risk. It essentially acts as a catalyst that starts off a virtuous cycle of introducing efficient modern technology to improve productivity that increases incomes and thus the ability of users to pay for the services, and so on. It creates a mechanism that reduces transaction costs and therefore improves the functions of markets.

Therefore, RISC

- serves as a focal point for the bi-directional flow of information and materials within the *rural* areas
- clusters economic activities in specific *rural* locations by facilitating firms' businesses
- seeds urbanization and urbanize the *rural* population without socially costly *rural* to urban migration
- integrates the *rural economy* with the national and international *economy* and remove inefficiencies

By providing a full complement of services, RISC creates a 'mini-city' which seeds the formation of a city by drawing to it the population from the surrounding villages. Initially, those who need the services will commute to the RISC location but as time goes by, the area around a RISC will naturally evolve into a small city. RISC is the grain of sand around which the pearl of a city can develop.

Development of People, Not Villages

The economic development of the *rural* population, rather than the development of villages, is the goal. This requires that the population have access to services, which in turn requires the availability of infrastructure. Infrastructure investment is lumpy and cannot be economically provided at the scale appropriate to small villages which are the norm in *rural* India. Furthermore, looking to the future, the *economy* of present day *rural* India cannot continue to be dispersed into 600,000 villages. The population will have to migrate to a much smaller number of larger aggregations. These formation of these aggregations can be catalyzed by the coordinated investment of infrastructure, either in greenfield ventures or in existing locations where there is road or rail connectivity.

RISC is not an attempt at social engineering through centralized planning. Neither is it another model of Internet kiosk or telecenter. It aims to solve a problem by appealing to the profit motives of all participants, be they private sector, NGOs, or the public sector. The good that will surely come out of it can only be attributed to Adam Smith's invisible hand.

Characteristics of the Rural Market

India is a developing economy. Any economy consists of two sectors -the urban and the rural. In case of the developed western countries, the urban sector plays the most important role. The majority live in the urban areas. The urban sector also contributes the largest amount to the national income.

India, however, is predominantly rural in character. In 2001 about 72.2 per cent of India's population lived in the rural areas, consisting of 6.3 lakh villages. It is true with economic development and industrialization, urbanization also has progressed. But the rate of urbanization has been rather slow. In the beginning of this century about 11 per cent of the people lived in the urban areas. In 2001, this percentage has increased to 27.8. Thus India has been, and still is, a "land of villages".

This rural character of the Indian economy has far-reaching social, economic and political consequences. We shall discuss below some of the important characteristics of the rural economy of our country. The Indian rural market is much larger when compared to the urban market in terms of population and number of households. The rural market consists of about 100 million households with a population of about 620 million. But the rural areas are characterized by low per capital income, low literacy, average agricultural productivity, and low level of industrialization. These characteristics of rural India limit its-capacity for consumption of goods and services compared to any advanced and developed country. So far, these factors have inhibited the enthusiasm of marketing people to perform in rural areas. In recent times the scene has changed considerably due to the rapid progress achieved in agricultural development and allied activities–animal husbandry, sericulture, horticulture, pisciculture–and due to the encouragement of rural and cottage industries.

The potential for marketing of goods and services depends heavily on agriculture, since it is the main occupation in rural areas. The market for agricultural inputs–fertilizers, pesticides nad insecticides, tractors, lift irrigation equipments, hybrid and high yielding seeds- has been expanding over the years in rural areas as the India farming is fast becoming market–oriented, as opposed to subsistence farming earlier. The Indian farmer has been receptive to new technology, which helped in improving his standard of living.

Barring organizations manufacturing and marketing agricultural inputs, the rural market has remained a 'dark area' for those manufacturing and marketing consumables and consumer durables. Only a few established companies–Hindustan Lever, Lipton, Brooke Bond, TOMCO, Procter and Gamble–have been tapping the potential of the rural market for a long time. But these are exceptions.

Give the development which has taken place in rural areas under the Five Year Plans and other special programmes, today the rural market offers a vast untapped potential. Development programmes in the fields of agriculture and allied activities, health, education, communication, rural electrification, etc. have improved the life styles of rural populace and some market research agencies forecast that the rural demand will supersede the urban demand in the near future.

To successfully exploit the potential offered by rural market, there is a need to first understand the rural market not only in terms of households and population, but also their occupational pattern, income generation, marketing arrangements for agricultural produce, the process of rural and cottage industrialization, communication facilities, rural buyer behaviour, attitudes and beliefs of rural people and their aspirations.

Predominance of Agriculture Agriculture encompasses farming of crops and grazing of animals. It involves the production of food, animal feed and hide by organized nurturing of plants and animals.*Agri* stems from the Latin term *ager* (meaning field) and culture traces its roots from the Latin term *cultura* (meaning cultivation). Agriculture traces its roots from man's need of subsistence in ancient times and today a substantial amount of agricultural production is a large-scale commercial exploit.

- India is still an agriculture-based country and the agrarian sector contributes substantially to the GDP of India. Around seventy per cent of the *Indian* population still depends on agriculture and allied areas for livelihood.

A basic feature of India's rural economy is the predominance of agriculture. Although agriculture makes up just a fifth of India's economy, two-thirds of the population make a living from the land.

The occupational structure of India is indicative of a UDC. Agriculture provides employment to about two-thirds of the total working population. At the beginning of this century, the agricultural sector absorbed 71.7 per cent of the total labour force; this proportion went up to 76.0 per cent in 1921. This indicated a deterioration in economic condition, deindustrialization and ruralisation of the economy. Since then, there was a slow decline in this proportion, although the percentage of working population engaged in agricultural in 1971 was more than that in 1901. The industrial sector and the tertiary sector did not show any significant change over the years. The 1981 population census however, for the first item registered a significant decline in the proportion of labour force engaged in agriculture, this process gathered some further momentum in the subsequent decades–presently 58 per cent of the labour force is estimated to be engaged in this sector. This is an indication of economic progress and structural change that is gradually taking place.

Predominance of agricultural is reflected in the following factors. Agriculture provides subsistence to the vast masses living in the country-side. Agriculture constitutes the backbone of the rural life. Agriculture influences the occupational structure of the country. Agricultural absorbs any growth in labour force. This explains why the percentage of population engaged in agriculture has remained more or less static since the beginning of this century. Again, about 35 per cent of our exports consist of agricultural products. The performance of this sector to a large extent influences the performance of the economy as a whole.

It would be seen that over the period the primary sector's share has fallen by 40 per cent, while those of the secondary and tertiary sectors have increased. This trend is projected to go further in wake of liberalization of the economy.

Table 2
Percentage Contribution to Increase

(in GDP_{FC})

	1951-52 to 1960-61	*1961 – 62 to 1970 -71*	*1971- 72 to 1980-81*	*1981 – 82 to 1990-91*	*1992-93 to 1996-97*	*1997-98 to 2005-06*
Primary	45.2	35.1	27.2	24.2	20.3	13.0
Secondary	23.7	26.5	25.6	28.6	30.9	23.1
Tertiary	31.3	38.4	47.2	47.2	48.8	63.9
Total	100.0	100.0	100.0	100.0	100.0	100.0

This trend of the declining share of a agriculture in the national income is broadly in consonance with the conclusions derived by the development economists; what is, however, amazing is the fact that the rate of change has been rather slow. In spite of nearly five and a-half decades of planned development, the agricultural sector continues to hold the dominant place. (In the poorer State agriculture's contribution to the domestic product is close to 40 per cent.) This, in turn, indicates two things as follows:

The growth of secondary and tertiary sectors has been relatively slow as compared to what has been expected in the initial stages of growth. The Indian economy still holds out a vast potential for growth by developing secondary and tertiary sectors.

Figure 1: Percentage Share of a Agriculture in GDP

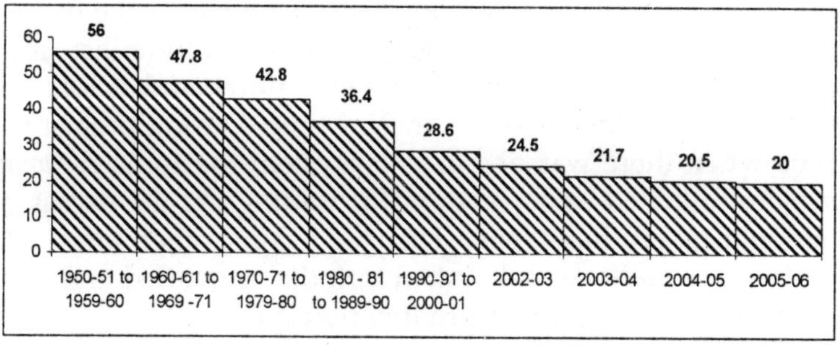

Whatever it is, the situation as it obtains presently requires that more of available resources should be devoted to the development programmes in the agricultural sector, as it is this sector that continues to have great potential for reducing poverty and hunger in the rural sector. For every additional rupee generated through agricultural production in India, the existing economical linkages can add other three rupees to the income of the rural economy. It is important to raise the productivity and level of output in this sector, which in turn means that agricultural must make an incremental contribution to the growth rate of the economy despite a diminishing land frontier. This is one simple truth that has to be accepted by our plan framers.

Major Source of Livelihood: Agriculture has been and is a major source of livelihood in India. Over the years , the size of labour force dependent on agriculture is heavy. Globally, smallholder agriculture accounts for a large share of agricultural production and almost 85% of all farms in developing countries are of less than two hectares. In India too, similar size accounts for 85% of the farms, about two-fifths of foodgrains production and most of the share in livestock production.

The Rural Economy in India is wholly agriculture based and it is of tremendous importance because it has vital supply and demand links with the other *Indian* industries. Agriculture is the main stay of the *Indian economy,* as it constitutes the backbone of *rural* India which inhabitants more than 70% of total *Indian* population. The fertility of the soil has augmented the success of agriculture in India. Further, *Rural Economy* in India has been playing an important role towards the overall economic growth and social growth of India. India has been predominantly an agriculture-based country and it was the only source of livelihood in ancient time. During prehistoric time when there was no currency system the India *economy* system followed barter system for trading i.e. the excess of agricultural produce were exchanged against other items. The agriculture produce and system in India are varied and thus offers a wide agricultural product portfolio.

Today, the *rural economy* in India and its subsequent productivity growth is predicated to a large extent upon the development of its 700-million strong *rural* population. The agricultural *economy* of India is drafted according to the needs of *rural* India since majority of the population lives in about 600,000 small villages. In India, agriculture accounts for almost 19% of *Indian* gross domestic products (GDP). The *rural* section of *Indian* population is primarily engaged with agriculture, directly or indirectly. The Ministry of Agriculture, the Ministry of *Rural* Infrastructure, and the Planning Commission of India are the main governing bodies that formulate and implements the policy related to *rural economy* in India and its subsequent development for the overall growth of the *Indian economy.*

The main agricultural products that controls the fate of the *Rural Economy* in India are as follows:

- *Food Grains*-Rice, Wheat, Pulses, Cereals, Corn, Maize, Rice Bran Extractions, Sorghum, Soy meal, Suji, Parmal, Lentils, Jowar, Bajra, Chick pea.
- *Fruits and Nuts*-Cashew Kernels, Cashew Nut, Cashews, Almonds, Roasted Dry Fruits, Peanuts, Groundnut, Walnut Kernels, Walnuts, *Indian* Peanuts, HPS Groundnuts.
- *Fruits*-Bananas, Beans, Cherry, Cucumbers, Dried Fruits, Dried Truffles, Carrots, Lemon, Mandarins,

Mango steens, Meslin, Shallots, Apples, Asparagus, Grapes, Oranges, Gherkins, Turnips, Oranges, Papaya, Pineapple.

- *Vegetables*–Potatoes, Bitter gourd, Stripe Gourd, Pumpkin, cauliflower, Cabbage, Tomato, Onion, Green Pepper, Drum Sticks, Lady's finger, Banana, Papaya, Spinach, Cucumber, Mushroom, Mushroom Spawn, Radiata.
- *Seeds, Buds, Plantation and Related Products*-Basil Seed, Cumin seeds, Dill Seed, Buds, Celery Seed, Hybrid Seeds, Sesame Seeds, Sesbania Seed, Sunflower Seeds, Mustard Seeds, Oil Seeds, Plant Products, Plantation, Plants, Psyllium Seed, Fennel Seed, Fenugreek Seed, Herb Seeds, Tamarind Seed, Vegetable Seeds.
- *Spices*-Black Pepper, Chilli Powder, Chillies, Cinnamon, Cloves, Coriander Powder, Cumin, Curry Powders, Dry Ginger, Dry Red Chilly, Cardamom, Anise, Salt, Onion Powder, Pepper, Fenugreek, Clove, Ginger, Turmeric, Turmeric Powder.
- *Tea and Coffee*-Black Tea, Coffee, Coffee Beans, Darjeeling Teas, Assam Teas, Instant Coffee, Leaf Coffee, Leaf Tea, Packaged Tea, Green Tea, CTC Teas
- *Tobacco and Tobacco Products*-Beedi, Betel nut Leaves, Betel nut, Bidi Leaves, Chewing Tobacco, Cigarettes, Arecanut, Jarda, Scented Tobacco, Smoking Tobbacco, Snuff, Opium, Pan, Chatni, Pan Masala, Gutkazarda, Zafrani Zarda
- Cotton, Rubber, Jute etc.

Glimpses of Rural Economy of India

- A target of Rs 225,000 crores for farm credit has been set for the financial year 2007-2008.
- 50 lakh new farmers have been brought under the banking system.
- Agricultural Insurance to facilitate agricultural loans to the farmer.

- Allocation for the *Rural* Infrastructure Development Fund to be increased substantially.
- In the financial year 2006-07, 35 projects were successfully completed.
- Additional irrigation of 900,000 hectares has been targeted in the financial year 2007-2008.
- For better farm yields modern farming techniques has been set up.
- Direct disbursement of subsidy to *rural Indian* farmers has been arranged through a pilot program.

Underdeveloped Nature of Agriculture

Although agricultural plays such a vital role in India's rural economy, yet it is in an unprogressive stage. It is in a depressed state. Heavy dependence of population on agriculture leads to low productivity. Agricultural productivity is also proved from the fact that although about 69 per cent of the working population is engaged in agriculture, yet it hardly contributes 20 per cent of national income.

It is true since the sixties, some regions of the country have been benefited by the Green Revolution. Improved methods of cultivation have raised agricultural productivity. But an average cultivation still uses very little capital in cultivating his land. He practices old, traditional methods of farming.

Dichotomy

However, one may witness the presence of a sort of dichotomy in the rural areas. Some progressive farmers in the rural areas have taken recourse to scientific cultivation. They have an access to the various institutional sources of credit. They also make use of the various assistance provided by the Government. But the majority of the small and marginal farmers still follow the traditional methods. This decreased pockets of affluence in the rural areas. The gap between the rich and poor farmers has widened, leading to growing tension. Such dualism is present not only in a particular region. Introduction of modern farm techniques has widened inter-State economic differences as well.

Occupation Pattern

Industrial plant in a *rural* area near *Jodhpur,* Rajasthan. Industrial growth in India has provided increase employment opportunities across India.

Agricultural and allied sectors accounted for about 57% of the total workforce in 1999–2000, down from 60% in 1993–94. While agriculture has faced stagnation in growth, services have seen a steady growth. Of the total workforce, 8% is in the organised sector, two-thirds of which are in the public sector. The NSSO survey estimated that in 1999–2000, 106 million, nearly 10% of the population were unemployed and the overall unemployment rate was 7.32%, with *rural* areas doing marginally better (7.21%) than urban areas (7.65%).

For a vast majority of the rural population, the main occupation is agriculture and allied activities. Table 2 gives the distribution of rural population as per their occupation pattern.

About half of the rural population owns lease land to cultivate it for their livelihood. Another 37 per cent are dependent on these cultivators for jobs as agricultural labourers. Thus, a total of 77 per cent of rural population solely depend upon land only for their living and land is the source of their income. There are others, constituting a small proportion, who are engaged in business like petty shop-keepers or itinerant merchants, and salary earners like teachers, health workers, and village level officials. The implication of this type of occupations pattern is that the income generation in rural areas entirely depends upon how the land is used, what crops are cultivated, how much is marketed, how much is consumed and the marketing arrangements for the production. If the rainfall is adequate, weather conditions are favorable and appropriate technology is available of the rural areas prosper as it has happened in states like Punjab, Haryana and Western Uttar Pradesh. If the weather is unfavourable, the rural income suffers a great deal, as it often happens in drought prone areas. So, the disposable income in the hands of rural people is very much conditioned by the status of agriculture and other allied activities.

Table 3
Occupation Pattern

Occupation	*Proportion of Rural Population (%)*
Agriculture	50
Agricultural Labour	27
Business	10
Non Agricultural Labour	9
Salary Earners	2
Not gainfully Employed	2
Total	100

The above occupations pattern can be observed when seen in terms of households also. There are about 100 million households in rural areas, out of which 72 per cent are cultivating households and another 15 per cent are agricultural labour households. Whichever way it is looked at, the fact is that, land-based activities are the main sources of income of rural population.

The Occupational structure in some of the State has undergone a marked change. The all-India trends, however, conceal the different types of changes taking place in the industrial distribution of workers in different States. In Kerala, Tamil Nadu, Maharashtra and Bengal the proportion of working population engaged in industries and services has gone up. It Rajasthan and Orissa, however, there has been an opposite development, the proportion in agriculture having increased and that in industries and services having decreased. About other States no definite trend has emerged.

The population of a country can be divided into workers and non-workers. The workers again are engaged in some job or occupation. If some work as farmers, others work in factories. Some work as teachers, doctors, engineers. Others work in banks or insurance companies. Broadly all occupations or industries in which the labour force of a country earn its living are divided into three major groups. These are:

(a) Primary occupations: Agriculture, animal husbandry, forestry, fishery, etc., belong to this category. They are called as primary as they produce goods which are basic necessities for the human beings. Nature also plays an important role in these occupations.

(b) Secondary occupations: Manufacturers in small and large scale industry or construction, etc., are the examples of secondary occupations.

(c) Tertiary occupations: Services in transport, communications, banking and personal services of different types are included within this category.

The working population of a country are engaged in these occupations. The distribution of working population among these three types of occupation is known as the "Occupational structure" or "occupational pattern". The occupational structure of the population indicates the economic progress of a country. In a less developed economy a large percentage of the population is engaged in primary occupation such as agriculture , forestry, etc. As the country develops more and more people shift to secondary occupations. In a still highly advanced country, a very small portion of the population is dependent on agriculture.

Literacy Level

Table 4 presents the literacy level of males and females in rural and urban areas respectively.

Table 4
Literacy Levels

	Literacy Level in Percentage						
	1971		*1981*		*1991*		*2001*
Sex	*Rural*	*Urban*	*Rural*	*Urban*	*Rural*	*Urban*	
Male	34	61	41	66	58	81	75.85
Female	13	42	18	48	31	64	54.16
All	24	52	30	57	45	73	65.38

Given the distribution of rural and urban population, it can be seen that the number of literates in rural areas are more than those in urban areas. In the year 1991, even though the urban literacy level was high at 73 per cent, the number of literates in urban areas was around 157 million persons as opposed to about 279 million literate persons in rural areas. The same can be observed for the year 1981 also, when the urban literates were 91 million and rural literates were 152 million. It is also interesting to note that the increase in the number of literate persons in 1981-91 was about 66 million in urban areas, while it was about 127 million in rural areas during the corresponding period.

The literacy rate has its implication in communication with the rural population. It appears that communication should not prove a hurdle, provided appropriate means are chosen. Today, television has proved to be an effective medium for communication with the rural masses. The telecasting network in the country today covers about 93 per cent of the population. Assuming that the entire urban population is covered by telecast network, which is only about 26 per cent, then nearly 67 per cent of the rural population is covered by television. Thus, television reaches a larger segment of rural population than any other form of mass media. Though radio is also very popular, people like to see to believe.

The number of empirical studies have demonstrated a positive relationship between education and the level of economic development. To quote the World Bank, "Developing countries with high literacy rates have tended to grow faster, even after allowances are made for difference in incomes and physical investment, and they have had higher physical investment rates",

According to the census definition, a person is deemed as literate if he or she can read and write with understanding in any language. A person who can merely read by cannot write is not literate. Any person who is not literate according to the above definition of literacy, is an illiterate person.

Gross Economic Inequalities

Not only there is widespread poverty in the rural areas, one may further notice gross inequalities in the distribution of wealth and income. For instance, the majority of the rural people do not possess any assets worth the name. The poorest 30 per cent hardly hold 2 per cent of the total assets in the rural areas. Whereas the top 10 per cent of the families own more than 50 per cent of the total assets. The unequal distribution of land also is a testimony of massive rural poverty. Thus at the top, 3 per cent hold about 26 per cent of the total land. At the bottom about 72 per cent of the farmers hold only 23 per cent of land area. Out of this again 55 per cent hold area less than one hectare of land each. This unequal distribution of land ownership has further widened economic inequalities. As the rich have large tracts of land, they can carry on scientific and improved cultivation. The poor are deprived of enjoying the benefits of new farm technology due to the small size of their holdings.

Table 5
Distribution of Land in 1976-77

Categories of Holdings	*Size Group*	*Percentage No. of Holdings*	*Percentage of Total Area*
Marginal	Less than 1 Hect.	54·54	10·66
Small	1·0-2·0 Hect.	18·06	12·76
Semi-Medium	2·0-4·0 Hect	14·29	19·80
Medium	4·0-10·0 „	10·06	30·33
Large	10 Hect. & Above	3·05	26·45
	Total	100	100

At present there are about 3 crore small and margial farmers and I crore other farmers. Globally, smallholder agriculture accounts for a large share of agricultural production and almost 85% of all farms in developing countries are of less than 2 hectares. In India too, similar size accounts for 85% of the farms, about two-fifths of foodgrain production and most of the share in livestock production According to the state agriculture department, there are about six million small and marginal *farmers* in Karnataka. Unlike other states, *farmers* in Karnataka get loans at four per cent interest from cooperative banks. The interest subsidy of two per cent is borne by the state governmentAccording to the state agriculture department, there are about six million small and marginal *farmers* in Karnataka. Unlike other states, *farmers* in Karnataka get loans at four per cent interest from cooperative banks. The interest subsidy of two per cent is borne by the state government According to the state agriculture department, there are about six million small and marginal *farmers* in Karnataka. Unlike other states, *farmers* in Karnataka get loans at four per cent interest from cooperative banks. The interest subsidy of two per cent is borne by the state government

Low Rate of Saving and Capital Formation

Saving and capital formation depends on income. As the majority of the rural people are poor they lack any capacity to save. The rural rich have some capacity to save. But they spend lavishly on unproductive activities. This has adversely affected the rate of capital formation in the rural areas.

Inequalities in Income Distribution

One of the critical problems facing India's *economy* is the sharp and growing regional variations among India's different states and territories in terms of per capita income, poverty, availability of infrastructure and socio-economic development.

The five-year plans have attempted to reduce regional disparities by encouraging industrial development in the interior regions, but industries still tend to concentrate around urban areas and port cities. After liberalization, the more advanced states are better placed to benefit from them, with infrastructure like well developed ports, urbanisation and an educated and skilled workforce which attract manufacturing and service sectors. The union and state governments of backward regions are trying to reduce the disparities by offering tax holidays, cheap land, etc., and focusing more on sectors like tourism, which although being geographically and historically determined, can become a source of growth and is faster to develop than other sector.

There is the prevalence of gross inequalities in the Indian Economy. The World Bank, in its World Development Report, 2006, has revealed that the richest 20 per cent took 41.6 per cent of the total income and the poorest 20 per cent received only 8.9 per cent of the total income distribution.

Income distribution in India matches that of most developed countries, where there is a "40:40:20 pattern", that is, top 20 per cent of the population earns 40 per cent of the income, the middle 40 per cent get the other 40 per cent, with the poorest 40 per cent getting merely 20 per cent of the income share. Following the opinion of Simon Kuznets , we may anticipate a worsening of income distribution as growth picks up momentum in the Indian economy.

The extent and magnitude of inequalities of income in India can be studies on the basis of available data relating to: (1) income distribution, (2) consumption expenditure, and (3) distribution of savings in the country.

The data relevant to income distribution is contained in a number of studies carried out to measure the extent of inequalities. Table 6 summarises the results of a few of these studies. A conclusion common to all the studies is: the gross inequalities of income exist in India, notwithstanding a marginal fall in the share of top.

What is more, inequality of wealth has been consistently higher than even income inequality. The Ginni Coefficient of wealth distribution has been around 0.65.

Similarly, distribution of savings originating in the household sector also brings out the fact of inequalities in income distribution. According to NCAER, the bottom 70 per cent save 6 per cent of that total while the top 10 per cent save 68 per cent and the top 5 per cent save 50 per cent. In particular, the lowest 45 per cent of the urban people saved 4 per cent, while the top 10 per cent saved 56 per cent.

Pressure on Land

India is an agricultural country. But the rapid growth of population has put a severe pressure on land. The majority of the work force depend on agriculture, industrial development is not adequate to provide employment to the increasing population. This compels people to depend on agriculture.

As the pressure of population on land increased, plots of land were divided and subdivided. This is known as the problem of subdivision and fragmentation of land. The average size of holdings has come down. The number of large operational holdings has declined. Adoption of improved

Table 6
Different Estimate of Inequalities of Income in India (Per cent)

Source	*Ahmed Bhattacharya*	*NCAER*	*World Bank*	*World Bank*	*World Bank*	*World Bank*	*World Bank*	*World Bank*	*World Bank*
Period covered	(1964-65)	(1964-65)	(1975-76)	(1983)	(1989-90)	(1992)	(1994)	(1997)	(1999-00)
Share of top 10 per cent	31.4	33.5	33.6	26.7	27.1	28.4	25.0	33.5	–
Share of bottom 20 per cent	7.5	7.50	7.0	8.1	8.8	8.5	9.2	8.1	8.9
Lorenz Ratio	0.372	0.39	–	–	–	–	–	–	–

Source: Pramit Chaudhri: The Indian Economy, Poverty and Development, 1978, P. 199; World Development Report, 2006.

techniques of cultivation becomes difficult. This has affected agricultural productivity. Unemployment and disguised unemployment also increased.

Rapid growth of population has led to a decline in the per capita availability of cultivable land. This has come down from 0.47 hectare in 1951 to 0.29 hectare in 1976. The per capita net sown area is hardly 0.22 hectare. For the rural population per capita availability of land was 0.37 hectare.

This fall in per capita availability of land has led to several consequences. First, due to limited size of the holding, the farmer's choice of crops is limited. He gives top priority to the production of foodgrains and does not want to assume any risk. This affects agricultural development. Besides, this has also led to an increase in the number of agricultural labourers. Between 1971 and 1978, the number of agricultural labourers. has double from 32 million to 65 million. Increases in the number of agricultural labourers will increase the number of poor and weak in the society. Rural unemployment will rise. There will be a rural exodus towards the cities.

Disguised Unemployment

It refers to unemployment which is 'hidden', i.e., not open for anyone to see. A number of persons who may apparently be employed may not be contributing anything to production. In technical jargon, the disguised unemployed are those who are so numerous, relative to the resources, that the marginal productivity of labour over a wide range is zero, if not negative.

This situation obtains exclusively, or predominantly, in the agricultural sector, where family labour and non-wage employment predominate.

Unemployment, underemployment and disguised unemployment result from the fact that labour in the UDCs is relatively abundant in relation to capital and the productivity of labour is usually low in most UDCs in comparison with such productivity in the developed countries. Low productivity in the UDCs is the result of mixed factors like (a) paucity of capital and other resources, (b) backward technology, (c) lack of proper education, etc.

Unemployment

Unemployment in India is characterized by chronic underemployment or disguised unemployment. Government schemes that target eradication of both poverty and unemployment (which in recent decades has sent millions of poor and unskilled people into urban areas in search of livelihoods) attempt to solve the problem, by providing financial assistance for setting up businesses, skill honing, setting up public sector enterprises, reservations in governments, etc. The decreased role of the public sector after liberalization has further underlined the need for focusing on better education and has also put political pressure on further reforms.

Summarisation of the changes in unemployment and underemployment:

- An increase in the current daily status unemployment rate in three of the four population segments, with urban women as the sole exception,
- The increase in the daily status unemployment rate has been the steepest for rural males (29 per cent): an increase which could well be due to a change in the status composition of the work force (a rise in the proportion of casual labouer and a reduction in the share of the self-employed) and a conversion of underemployment of the erstwhile self-employed into open unemployment of the casual labourers;

  a reduction in the unemployment rates on the usual principal status for the educated in almost all the four population segments; and, an increase in self-perceived underemployment captured by the 1990s, in the proportion of usual status workers who had not sought,

  However, much of this is reflected in an increase in additional work. the proportion of usual status workers who sought additional work on "Some days" rather than on "most days". Also, even among those adding to the proportion of workers who sought additional work on "most days", the principal reason was the need to supplement income rather than lack of work per se.

Rural Unemployment

In the rural economy, both unemployment and under-employment exist side by side and the distinction between them is by no means sharp.

In the rural areas, increasing population implies an increasing pressure on land. This pressure on land has resulted in an increase in the number of agriculturists, and this has largely contributed to the problem of unutilized labour of disguised unemployment in the agricultural sector.

Large labour force accumulates around primary occupations and the general inelasticity of occupational structure also prevents any large movement away from these in periods of slack demand. This leads to seasonal unemployment also. Seasonality is by far the problem of 'inelasticities of the time–pattern of primary production'. The incidence of seasonal unemployment may vary from region to region and even within the same region over different seasons depending on climate, the cropping pattern and the socio-economic factors, and affect different sections of the rural population differently due to the periodic entry into and withdrawal from the labour force.

To sum up, rural unemployment scene in India is largely characterized by the existence of underemployment, seasonal unemployment and disguised unemployment. Urban unemployment is characterized by the existence of both open unemployment, which in turn is an offshoot of rural unemployment itself, and the educated unemployment.

A major economic problem faced by the country is that of unemployment. There was a backlog of unemployment. The bulk of this unemployment is concentrated in the rural areas. As the majority of the rural people do not have sufficient land, agriculture cannot provide them year long engagement. So there is large scale seasonal unemployment.

But an important aspect of the rural unemployment problem is that it is often disguised. There are no alternative sources of employment. Agriculture thus is the main vocation. But agriculture cannot fruitfully absorb the increasing number of people who fall back of land. The number of people engaged in agriculture is more than what is necessary to carry on cultivation. Thus, there is surplus labour engaged in agriculture. They are physically employed but economically unemployed. This type of unemployment is known as disguised unemployment. Even if this surplus labour is withdrawn total agricultural production will not be affected.

The presence of disguised unemployment in the rural areas makes a special case for rural industrialization. inferior training and skill, and (e) poor health and nutrition. Unemployment is the major cause of widespread poverty in the UDCs.

The key results are:

An increase in the current daily status unemployment rate in three of the four population segments, with urban women as the sole exception. The increase in the daily status unemployment rate has been the steepest for rural males (29 per cent): an increase which could well be due to a change in the status composition of the work force (a rise in the proportion of casual labourers and a reduction in the share of the self-employed) and a conversion of the underemployment of the erstwhile self-employed into open unemployment of the casual labourers; ii. a reduction in the unemployment rates on the usual principal status for the educated in almost all the four population segments; and, iii. an increase in self-perceived underemployment captured by a reduction, over the 1990s, in the proportion of usual status workers who had not sought additional work. However, much of this is reflected in an increase in the proportion of usual status workers who sought additional work on "Some days" rather than on "most days". Also, even among those adding to the proportion of workers who sought additional work on "most days", the principal reason was the need to supplement income rather than lack of work.

Rural Employment Generation Programme (REGP)

On the basis of recommendation of the High Power Committee report, submitted in May 1994, headed by the then Prime Minster of India, the KVIC launched Rural Employment Generation Programme (REGP) with effect from 1st April, 1995 for generation of two million jobs under the KVI sector in the rural areas of the country. The term rural areas has been defined under the KVIC Act, 1956 as under:

Any area classified as village as per the revenue records of the state, irrespective of population.

It also includes an area classified as town, provided its population does not exceed 20,000 as per 1991 census.

Similarly, the term village industries has been defined as "any industry located in rural area which produces any goods or renders any service with or without the use of power and in which the fix capital investment per head of artisan or worker does not exceed Rs. 50,000 or such other sum as may be specified by Central Government from time to time". All activities which do not appear in the negative list circulated by KVIC are eligible for financing under the scheme.

MAIN OBJECTIVES

To generate employment in rural areas.To develop entrepreneurial skill and attitude among rural unemployed youth.To achieve the goal of rural industrialization.To facilitate participation of financial institutions for higher credit flow to rural industries.

SALIENT FEATURES OF THE SCHEME

The scheme is applicable to all village industries project set up in rural areas.

The eligible agencies under the scheme are (i) individuals (rural artisans/entrepreneurs) (ii) institutions cooperative societies, Trusts & SHGS for projects upto Rs. 25.00 lakhs.

Partnership Firms Private/Public Limited companies, Joint ventures, Jt. Borrowers, Co-obligators of HUF are not eligible under the Scheme.

Under this programme, capital subsidy in the form of margin money is provided at the rate of 25% of the project cost upto Rs. 10 lakhs and 10% on the balance project cost upto Rs. 25 lakhs.

In case of weaker section beneficiary viz. SC/ST/OBC/ Women/Physically Handicapped/Ex-servicemen and for Hill border and Tribal Areas, North Eastern Region, Sikkim, Andaman & Nicobar Islands, Lakshadweep, Margin Money grant will be at the rate of 30 per cent of the remaining cost of the project. Cost of land should not be included in the project cost.

Under the scheme, the borrower is required to invest his own contribution of 10 per cent of the project cost. In case of SC/ST and other weaker section borrowers, the beneficiary's contribution will be 5% of the project cost.

Banks will sanction 90 per cent of the project cost in case of general category borrowers and 95 per cent of the project cost to the weaker section beneficiaries/institutions and disburse full amount of the loan. After the sanction of the credit facility by the Bank branch, eligible amount of Margin Money will be kept in Term Deposit of two years in the account of the borrower at the leading bank branch, which will be credited to the borrower's loan account after a period of two years from the date of first disbursement of loan.

IMPLEMENTATION

Presently KVIC is implementing REGP through:

- All Public Sector Banks,
- All regional Rural Banks,
- Co-operative Banks approved by the State/U.T., KVIBs, Private Commercial Banks approved by the state KVIBs; and
- Other Financing Institutions of State & Central Government as approved by KVIC.

Sponsorship: Sponsoring of Project by any agency is not mandatory. However, KVIC's State/Regional Offices and State KVI Boards/DIC may sponsor the project if approached.

EDP Training: Once the project is sanctioned by financing branch of the Bank, before releasing the second installment of loan, beneficiary is to be imparted 3-day training arranged by the State/Regional Director.

STATUS AND PROGRESS OF REGP

During the year 2004-05, the number of projects financed was 23,453 as against the 24,747 number of projects financed in the previous year. Further in Employment Generation through the Scheme, the Andhra Pradesh stood at No. 1 followed by Uttar Pradesh, Rajasthan, Madhya Pradesh, West Bangal and Haryana.

(a) ***Flow of Funds:*** For extending support to the entrepreneurs for providing margin money and other backward forward linkages, an amount of Rs. 292.40 crore was released to meet the margin money claims of the entrepreneurs and another Rs. 3.48 crore for the purpose of arranging backward, forward linkages for the REGP units in the Country. The banks which include the nationalized commercial banks as well as cooperative banks, extended financial assistance of about Rs. 665.21 crores which helped the entrepreneurs to establish the units.

(b) ***Categorywise Distribution of Projects:*** The number of projects sanctioned (category-wise) during 2004-05 are as under:

Table 7
Distribution of Rural Projects

Category	*No. Projects*
Scheduled Castes	2696
Scheduled Tribes	1760
O.B.Cs.	5531
Minority Community	1743
Ex-Servicemen /physically handicapped	577
General	11146
Total	*23453*
Women	6229

From the above table, it may be seen that the percentage in each category to the total number of projects was fairly good for all the categories i.e. for Scheduled castes it 11.50%, for Scheduled Tribes 7.50%, OBCs 23.58%, Women Entrepreneurs 26.56% and Others which include ex-servicemen, Physically handicapped, hill and border areas 2.46%.

(c) ***Cost-wise Range of REGP Projects:*** Though the units that have been set up differ from State to State with respect to size and industry, the financing pattern shows that there has been a distribution of all type of industries with respect to project cost e.g. the share of projects upto 1.00 lakh was 23.41%, Rs. 1.00 lakh to Rs. 5.00 lakh was 50.04%, Rs. 5.00 Lakh to Rs. 10.00 lakhs was 17.61% and 10.00 lakhs to Rs. 25.00 lakh was 8 94%. This shows that the number of small projects on the whole was on the higher side.

(d) ***Industry-wise Development:*** The KVIC has broadly classified all village Industries into 7 groups and care is taken to see that the development in all industries is according to the availability of local needs, raw material, technical competency and the market requirement. The maximum number of units established was in the Agro and Food Processing followed by the services sector.

(e) ***Physical Performance of REGP:*** During the year 2004-05, a total of 23453 projects have been financed under the scheme generating 530025 number of employments. A sum of Rs. 292.40 crores have been utilized as margin money for this period. The State-wise performance under the scheme for the year 2004-05 is given at Table 9. The cumulative figures in respect of number of projects financed, cumulative employment generated, and cumulative margin money utilizes under the REGP scheme till 31.03.2005 are given at Table 10, Table 11 and Table 12, respectively.

(f) ***Backward and Forward Linkages:*** The KVIC provided financial assistance to its State Offices as well as the State Khadi and Village Industries Boards for establishing backward and forward linkages of the entrepreneurs/institutions. Under this, an amount of Rs. 347.58 lakh was released which was utilized for organizing 92 Nos. of workshops, 209 Nos. awareness

camps, 71 Nos. of exhibitions, 67 Nos of Bankers Meeting organized. 11525 No. of persons trained under Entrepreneur Development Programmes (EDPs) and 5156 No. of units were physically verified during the year 2004-05.

Table 8
Progress Made Under REGP During 2004-05-State-wise Performance

State/Ut	*No. of Projects*	*Margin Money Utilized (Rs. lakh)*	*Employment Generated*
Andhra Pradesh	1988	3394.19	66463
Arunachal Pradesh	43	66.03	1219
Assam	1658	1277.42	25768
Bihar	254	281.69	5049
Goa	138	88.90	1670
Guajrat	376	530.55	8581
Haryana	1140	2142.25	35691
Himachal Pradesh	469	584.55	12256
Jammu & Kashmir	922	657.72	9406
Karnataka	934	1063.83	19478
Kerala	914	1027.95	16434
Madhya Pradesh	1361	2125.71	40539
Maharashtra	1773	1439.17	25040
Manipur	102	73.66	1313
Meghalaya	146	196.03	3789
Mizoram	162	257.48	5180
Nagaland	151	204.46	3851
Orissa	991	863.05	15241
Punjab	864	1834.63	30665
Rajasthan	1537	2064.33	38287
Sikkim	139	1147.28	3227
Tamilnadu	925	214.14	19159
Tripura	233	3596.64	3994
Uttar Pradesh	2210	1999.62	64900
West Bengal	2584	165.78	36581
A & N Island	6	4.16	93
Chandigarh	8	21.45	188
Delhi	9	8.09	144
Pondichery	7	9.05	146
Jharkhand	240	1000.91	6855
Chattisgarh	656	320.60	18347
Uttaranchal	513	578.63	10471
Total	23453	29239.95	530025

Table 9
Number of Projects Financed Under REGP Upto 31 March 2005 Since Its Inception

State/ Ut	*Number of Projects Financed*
Andhra Pradesh	14858
Arunachal Pradesh	422
Assam	3865
Bihar	1100
Goa	2439
Guajrat	1474
Haryana	6249
Himachal Pradesh	2374
Jammu & Kashmir	7556
Karnataka	14093
Kerala	9341
Madhya Pradesh	19884
Maharashtra	21684
Manipur	840
Meghalaya	3293
Mizoram	1070
Nagaland	4941
Orissa	4157
Punjab	10467
Rajasthan	27434
Sikkim	286
Tamilnadu	6741
Tripura	666
Uttar Pradesh	17725
West Bengal	19807
A & N Island	422
Chandigarh	156
D. & N. Haveli	15
Delhi	228
Lakshdweep	10
Pondichery	956
Jharkhand	1058
Chattisgarh	1787
Uttaranchal	2307
Total	209705

NEW INITIATIVES

For smooth implementation of the programme, following new initiatives were taken by KVIC during the year 2004-05:

- Decentralisation of the implementation of the scheme by making payment of margin money through State Offices and State KVI Boards.
- Fixation of targets for projects and Margin Money for all field offices based on Rural Population of the State.
- Financing of units based on coir as raw material is allowed.
- Financing of auto-rickshaws in Andaman and Nicobar Islands, house boat, shikara and tourist boat in Jammu and Kashmir are also allowed under rural transport, keeping in view the special requirement of these States.
- For providing information/guidance to the new entrepreneurs, REGP helping counters are opened in all the field offices of the KVIC and the State KVI Boards.
- 346 number of model branches of Public Sector Banks are identified. They are provided margin money in advance on quarterly basis.
- Training to all KVIC/KVIB's field offices staff are provided to acquaint them with the implementation of the programme.
- Extensive publicity programme was made through workshops, awareness camps, exhibitions etc.

Table 10
Employment Oprotunities Generated Under REGP Upto 31 March 2005 Since Its Inception

States	*Numbers*
Andhra Pradesh	268821
Arunachal Pradesh	6336
Assam	56387
Bihar	15764
Goa	22184
Gujarat	16648
Haryana	139031
J & K	59562

Contd.

States	Numbers
Him.Pradesh	57256
Karnataka	176030
Kerala	150934
M.P.	218191
Maharashtra	210734
Manipur	15755
Meghalaya	28806
Mizoram	18700
Nagaland	93714
Orissa	45799
Punjab	147653
Rajasthan	313496
Tamilnadu	86439
Tripura	15167
U.P.	332871
West Bengal	170478
Sikkim	5512
A & N. Island	2718
Chandigarh	1295
D & N. Haveli	303
Delhi	4681
Lakshdweep	173
Pondicherry	12121
Chattisgarh	50336
Jharkhand	21566
Uttaranchal	39774
Total	2805235

Table 11

Margin Money Utilised Under Regp Upto 31 March 2005 Since Its Inception

States	*Margin Money Utilized (Rs. lakh)*
Andhra Pradesh	11116.45
Arunachal Pradesh	270.37
Assam	2693.66
Bihar	669.84
Goa	976.09
Gujarat	905.94
Haryana	7603.78
J & K	2162.45
Him.Pradesh	3881.72
Karnataka	11251.72
Kerala	10014.30

Contd.

States	*Margin Money Utilized (Rs. lakh)*
M.P.	8832.78
Maharashtra	8478.11
Manipur	1793.36
Meghalaya	985.31
Mizoram	1689.81
Nagaland	1562.76
Orissa	2555.08
Punjab	9336.00
Rajasthan	13485.41
Tamilnadu	4656.17
Tripura	612.24
U.P.	18221.53
West Bengal	6463.43
Sikkim	314.06
A & N. Island	148.45
Chandigarh	89.77
D & N. Haveli	18.59
Delhi	178.61
Lakshdweep	49.42
Pondicherry	72.70
Chattisgarh	2827.17
Jharkhand	1001.40
Uttaranchal	2268.
Total	137186.8 0

The Indian economy has been passing through the trajectory of high growth for several years. The overall Gross Domestic Product (GDP) is estimated to grow at 8.4 per cent, with the agriculture and allied sector projected to bounce back with 3.9 per cent growth during 2005-06. The Government has also been consolidating its fiscal position, creating a conducive climate for investment activities. Investment demand in the economy is picking up, reflecting the growing dynamism in the industrial sector. The exports have also assumed vibrancy. Thus, the Indian economy as a whole is poised for still higher growth in the coming years.

DISTRIBUTION OF VILLAGES IN INDIA

Bottom Heavy Cluster among Villages

68 % of the villages in India are below the 1000 Population.

- Marketers overlooking the same.
- Reaching out to these villages critical to exponential growth.
- Bottom Cluster with greater than 2000 Population slowly saturating.

Generation Challenge

The Top tier villagers walk , talk & Think like any other man.

- Servicing him is an absolute mandate
- Beefing up the supply chain critical to reaching out to these masses.
- *Rural* centric public distribution, transport and sound communication essential.

Source: NCAER.

Rural Below Poverty Line Decreasing

10 % improvement in 10 Yrs.

- *Rural* Fast Catching up with *Urban*
- Has a rippling effect on the overall Below Poverty Line of India
- *Rural* overall fairing better than *Urban* India

Source: NCAER

Untapped Rural Potential

- 600,000 villages with 700 mn people
- >50% of total GDP from rural India
- Nearly 50% of Very rich + Well off households in rural India.

Rural India

- Electricity Shortage – Sporadic Power Supply
- Acute Water Shortage.
- Poor Transportation availability.
- Consumer Finance Options Can we make energy saving products?? Can we give him a washing machine which

consumes less water?? Can we give him access to buying products near by his location??

The Challenge

- Set up of a Life style Research Team which would analyze the needs & preferences of the consumer , In-depth..
- Understand at length his comfort levels in terms of what he wants and what he would spend for what he wants..
- Make products and service available for him to suit his needs & Preferences..
- Have a deep pocket network to make products available for him at a close proximity from where he is.

The Solution

The Road Map–4 Point Mantra
Regional Marketing Approach
Deep Channel Penetration
Sophisticated & Deep After sales Service
Rural Centric Marketing Promotions
Rural Market is the key to survival in India

Regional approach in marketing is required.

Increased Channel Networking which Resulted in an increased *Rural Market* Reach
Network/Channel Development–The key to improving *Rural* reach.

RURAL MARKET - A WORLD OF OPPORTUNITY

Gone are the days when a rural consumer went to a nearby city to buy"branded products and services". Time was when only a select household consumed branded goods, be it tea or jeans. There were days when big companies flocked to rural markets to establish their brands. Today, rural markets are critical for every marketer - be it for a branded shampoo or an automobile. Time was when marketers thought van campaigns, cinema commercials and a few wall paintings would suffice to entice rural folks under their folds. Thanks to television, today a customer in a rural area is quite literate about myriad products that are on offer in the market place. An Indian farmer going through his daily chores wearing jeans may sound idiotic. Not for Arvind Mills, though. When it launched the Ruf & Tuf kits, it had created quite a sensation among the rural folks as well within few months of their launch.

Trends indicate that the rural markets are coming up in a big way and growing twice as fast as the urban, witnessing a rise in sales of hitherto typical urban kitchen gadgets such as refrigerators, mixer-grinders and pressure cookers. According to a National Council for Applied Economic Research (NCAER) study, there are as many 'middle income and above' households in the rural areas as there are in the urban areas. There are almost twice as many 'lower middle income' households in rural areas as in the urban areas. At the highest income level there are 2.3 million urban households as against 1.6 million households in rural areas. According to Mr. D. Shivakumar, Business Head (Hair), Personal Products Division, Hindustan Lever Limited, the money available to spend on FMCG (Fast Moving Consumer Goods) products by urban India is Rs. 49,500 crores as against is Rs. 63,500 crores in rural India.

As per NCAER projections, the number of middle and high income households in rural India is expected to grow from 80 million to 111 million by 2007. In urban India, the same is expected to grow from 46 million to 59 million. Thus, the absolute size of rural India is expected to be double that of urban India. The study on ownership of goods indicates the same trend. It segments durables under three groups- (1) necessary products-Transistors, wristwatch and bicycle, (2) Emerging products-B&W TV and cassette recorder, (3) Lifystyle products-CTV and refrigerators. Marketers have to depend on rural India for the first two categories for growth and size. Even in lifestyle products, rural India will be significant over next five years.

At a recent seminar in Chennai on 'rural marketing for competitive advantage in globalised India', organised by Anugrah Madison Advertising Pvt Limited, marketing pundits have echoed that a sound network and a thorough understanding of the village psyche are a SINE QUO NON for making inroads into rural markets. The price-sensitivity of a consumer in a village is something the marketers should be alive to. Rural income levels are largely determined by the vagaries of monsoon and, hence, the demand there is not an easy horse to ride on. Apart from increasing the geographical width of their product distribution, the focus of corporates should be on the introduction of brands and develop strategies specific to rural consumers. Britannia Industries launched Tiger Biscuits especially for the rural market. It clearly paid dividend. Its share of the glucose biscuit market has increased from 7 per cent to 15 per cent.

Effective Communication

An important tool to reach out to the rural audience is through effective communication."A rural consumer is brand loyal and understands symbols better. This also makes it easy to sell look-alike", says Mr. R.V Rajan, CMD, Anugrah Madison Advertising. The rural audience has matured enough to understand the communication developed for the urban markets, especially with reference to FMCG products. Television has been a major effective communication system for rural mass and, as a result, companies should identify themselves with their advertisements. Advertisements touching the emotions of the rural folks, it is argued, could drive a quantum jump in sales.

There is a need to differentiate the brand according to regional disparities. The differentiation may not necessarily be in terms of product content. It may also be in terms of packaging, communication or association with the brand.

The brand has to be made relevant by understanding local needs. Even offering the same product in different regions with different brand names could be adopted as a strategy. At times it is difficult to pass on an innovation over an existing product to the rural consumer unlike his urban counterpart-like increased calcium or herbal content or a germ-control formula in toothpaste.

According to Mr. Shivakumar, HLL, the four factors which influence demand in rural India are-access, attitude, awareness and Affluence. HLL has successfully used this to influence the rural market for its shampoos in sachets. The sachet strategy has proved so successful that, according to an ORG - MARG data, 95 per cent of total shampoo sales in rural India is by sachets. The company had developed a direct access to markets through wholesale channel and created awareness through media, demonstration and on ground contact. This changed the attitude of the villagers. Today, the young and the educated in the villages are already large in number. And this number is increasing. Already, 40 per cent of all those graduating from colleges are rural youth. They are the decision makers and are not very different in education, exposure, attitudes and aspirations from their counterparts at least in smaller cities and towns.

District Marketing

Since marketing is to target the growing segments, Mr. Francis Xavier, Managing Director, Francis Kanoi Marketing Research, wants to see the urban-like village dweller as an urbanised person from the districts. The village then becomes a location or a suburb of a district. And the district becomes the basic geographical entity. Since the urban-like populations in the villages are taken as a part of the district, they will represent the dominant part of the market in most of the districts. This will compel the kind of attention that it deserves. A districts perspective removes the complexities, heterogeneity, access and targetability that have hindered rural marketing initiatives. He feels that rural marketing requires every element of marketing including product, pricing, packaging, advertising, and media planning to have the rural customer as the target. And, this becomes possible when we have districts marketing as a separate entity.

Rural Vs Urban

People crowded like sardines into cities. Rickshaws, bikes, cars, trucks, camel and oxcarts, cows and people taking up every bit of open space so that as a pedestrian The reality is that India is farm country. One of their proudest accomplishments of the past 30 years is their "Green Revolution". Which because of good political stewardship and the introduction of new varieties of crops, fertilizers and soil maintenance, India has raised its output of wheat by leaps and bounds. Now the lands are producing much more and famine is only a historical memory. It went from a beggar nation depending on America's excess wheat, left over from farm subsidies, to a donor nation which was able to give to Ethiopia and Vietnam during their famines in the 80's. One reads that during this time of growth farmers were actually seen as rich. Something that is hard to imagine as an American. Land is a great resource in a growing country that needed to be fed.

The majority of India's 1.2 billion people are *rural*, but the scales are tipping as more and more people are moving to the cities where jobs are being created. The population of Delhi, Mumbai and Calcutta are exploding. With no housing, people are forced to live out on the sidewalks and sleep there too. You see people asleep on any flat surface including the mediums of main roads. Delhi's population grew by a staggering 46% between 1991 and 2001 to almost 14 million.

The *rural* versus *urban* contrasts show themselves in many ways. Cities are filled with billboards advertising cell phones, clothes and stores and traversed by many people dressed in western dress yet only a few kilometers outside of town things totally change. One drives from the land where cars and smog are taking over the roads. The rich are even beginning to drive SUVs and taking them up ancient alleyways that were built for pedestrians and only have room for them too.

Right of way in India is basically given to the vehicle or person who moves first and so those snarls get to be a real mess with no logical thought about how to clear the path. Bikes, people and motorcycles keep pushing through any open space while beeping their horns the whole way. (India is not a place for the faint hearted!)

In the countryside, people live in mud huts in very modest circumstances. Their only vehicles are their feet or perhaps a camel cart or oxcart. Their heads are their best carrier of freight which means women with multiple brass jugs balanced on top of their heads are seen in every direction.

While the Green Revolution brought wealth to the *rural* lands, the new IT boom is mostly only affecting the *urban* centers. It's a boom of the educated and the *rural* areas are worried that they are being left behind. The hope is that the money from the IT boom will be spent to help the *rural* people. They need electricity, education, healthcare and roads and there is some evidence that these things are coming. According to books, India is rapidly reducing its poverty levels but according to my eyes it's very hard to believe. The only signs of modern progress are new wells that seem to be newly placed along the roads. According to the New Yorker there were two million wells in India thirty years ago; today, there are twenty-three million.x Predictions are that India will end extreme poverty by 2010 or 2015 (less than a dollar a day), which means lift one third of their society (350 million people) onto a new playing field. While it is hard to believe, change is definitely in the air and everything here is in flux so maybe real progress is even being made in the countryside.

Urban Market

The Census defined urban India as - "All the places that fall within the administrative limits of a municipal corporation, municipality, cantonment board etc or have a population of at least 5,000 and have at least 75 per cent male working population in outside the primary sector and have a population density of at least 400 per square kilometer.

India today is experiencing a major economic transformation. Within a little over two decades, it has transformed itself from a 'developing nation' to a nation with a rapidly growing, diverse, service-led economy. It is largely India's fast developing urban areas, which are spurring this growth.

With more disposable incomes and changing mindsets, urban Indians are spending like never before. A large segment of Indian consumers today consists of well educated, young couples with double incomes who are keen on premium, branded products. The new urban consumer has complex needs and looks forward to constant changes and new products.

With socio-economic changes greatly impacting urban India, the result is creation of many new markets and a further expansion of the existing ones. The forthcoming developments in India's urban markets are also poised to create major opportunities for the Indian and multi-national companies alike.

A country without infrastructure is like a body without a backbone('Undoing The Urban Tangle', BW,10 November 2008). The commercial capital of India (Mumbai) is struggling to provide basic infrastructure to its population and the story is no different in other metros, namely Bangalore, Kolkata and Delhi. The attraction of setting in metropolitan cities has resulted in pressure on existing city infrastructe. The management authorities of the local governments should plan and construct new cities keeping sustainability in mind. For instance, lack of infrastructure in Munbai has led to mass migration to Navi Mumbai. We dream about being on a par with Shanghai in the near future, but to attain that the local governments have to be a little more proactive.

Increasing Urbanisation: Report by UNFPA

India is getting urbanised at a faster rate than the rest of the world and, by 2030, 40.7 per cent of the country's population will be living in urban areas, according to a report by the United Nations Population Fund (UNFPA).

With better job opportunities and higher wages, States like Maharashtra and Tamil Nadu are witnessing rapid urbanisation as compared to Bihar and Assam, which are least urbanised. UNFPA's India representative Nesim Tumkaya disagrees that that rural migration was driving urbanization, 'Urbanisation is happening more due to the natural rate of population growth than increased migration.'

Among factors contributing to urbanisation, the report gives 61 per cent weight to the natural increase in the urban area, 22 per cent to rural to urban migration and 17 per cent to reclassification of rural areas as urban.

India's urban population is second largest in the world, higher than the total urban population of all countries put together barring China, USA and Russia. In terms of population, Mumbai (fifth) and Delhi (sixth) figure among the world's top ten cities (and Kolkata is the 12th).

States/Union Territories

Among all the States and Union territories, the National Capital Territory of Delhi is most urbanized with 93 per cent urban population followed by Union territory of Chandigarh (89.8 per cent) and Pondicherry (66.6 per cent).

Among the major States, Tamil Nadu is the most urbanized state with 43.9 per cent of the population living in urban areas followed by Maharashtra (42.4 per cent) and Gujarat (37.4 per cent).

Maharashtra takes the lead in terms of absolute number of people living in urban areas with 41 million persons i.e. 14 per cent of India's total population. Uttar Pradesh accounts for about 35 million, followed by Tamil Nadu's 27 million. The country's total urban population on 1st March 2007 was 285 million.

City-size Distribution

Over the years, the city–size distribution of urban population has shifted significantly in favour of metropolitan cities which now account for approximately one–third of India's total urban population. Another one-third is accounted for by cities in the population range of 100,000 and one million.

Going by the 2001 census, the number of metropolitan cities with a million-plus population has risen to 35. These include Greater Mumbai. Kolkata, Delhi, Chennai, Bangalore, Hyderabad, and Ahmedabad.

According to the United Nations Department of Economic and Social Affairs, there will be 70 cities with a million-plus population by 2030, which would have close to half of the total urban population. Also, the mega cities of today will continue to grow and, by 2015, the top six mega cities are expected to have 84 million residents.

Cities: Contribution and Potential

Cities hold tremendous potential as engines of economic and social development, creating jobs and generating wealth through economies of scale. At present, the contribution of India's urban sector to its gross domestic product (GDP) is in the range of 50-60 per cent. By 2011, this share is expected to increase to 65 per cent. However, this higher contribution depends on the availability and quality of urban infrastructure like power, telecom, roads, water supply, mass transport and civic amenities.

Government Initiatives

In this context, enhancing the productivity of urban areas is now central to the policy pronouncements of the Ministry of Urban Development. Accordingly, the government has been enacting various measures to ensure that the growth in cities is sustained and augmented through the high productivity for country's economic growth. Some of these measures include:

- Allowing up to 100 per cent foreign direct investment (FDI) under the automatic route in townships, housing, built-up infrastructure and construction-development project (which would include–but not be restricted to–housing, commercial premises, hotels, resorts, hospitals, educational institutions, recreational facilities, city and regional level infrastructure), subject to fulfillment of certain conditions.
- The National Urban Information System (NUIS) Scheme launched in March, 2006 to develop GIS databases for 137 Indian towns/cities.
- Tax exemption in case of bonds issued by Municipal/ Local Governments.
- Encouraging citywide reforms and restructuring so as to ensure that cities are managed efficiently and become creditworthy (to attract private finance) which

will enable them to prepare long term plans for infrastructure investments and implement poverty alleviation programs.

- The Jawaharlal Nehru National Urban Renewal Mission (JNNURM) to encourage reforms and fast-track planned development of identified cities.

Real Estate

The Indian real estate sector is witnessing a revolution, driven by the rapid urbanisation and booming economy. Growing at a blistering 35 per cent, the realty sector is estimated to be worth US$ 15 billion. The face of Indian cities is changing fast with state-of-the-art malls, office spaces and residential areas being developed by domestic as well as foreign investors. Global players have lined up investments to the tune of US$ 10 billion with the industry also attracting international architects and planners. It is also the second largest employing sector in India. Prominent domestic players in this sector include DLF, Omaxe Ltd, Puravankara Projects Ltd, Housing Development and Infrastructure Ltd, etc while prominent foreign players include Emaar Properties (Dubai), IJM Corp (Malaysia), Lee Kim Tah Holding (Singapore) and Salim Group (Indonesia

India today is experiencing a major economic transformation. Within a little over two decades, it has transformed itself from a 'developing nation' to a nation with a rapidly growing, diverse, service-led economy. It is largely India's fast developing urban areas, which are spurring this growth. With more disposable incomes and changing mindsets, urban Indians are spending like never before. A large segment of Indian consumers today consists of well educated, young couples with double incomes who are keen on premium, branded products. The new urban consumer has complex needs and looks forward to constant changes and new products.

With socio-economic changes greatly impacting urban India, the result is creation of many new markets and a further expansion of the existing ones. The forthcoming developments in India's urban markets are also poised to create major opportunities for the Indian and multi-national companies alike.

Branded Goods

The urban Indian is becoming increasingly brand conscious. According to experts the market for branded luxury goods in India is projected to grow from US$ 3.5 billion now to US$ 30 billion by 2015. Today, apart from electronic gizmos and fancy cars, apparel, jewellery, accessories, luxury watches, cosmetics, perfumes, food items are just a few names that figure in urban India's continuing love affair with foreign brands. With international brands like Tommy Hilfiger, Esprit and Puma growing well over 100 per cent, many others are also planning to foray into the Indian retail market. Calvin Klein is the most frequently bought brand with over a third (34 per cent) of Indian consumers buying it at some point. However, Gucci was the most coveted foreign brand, for people who could afford it. Gucci has 2 stores, Calvin Klein has 4, whereas, Tommy Hilfiger plans to open 23 points of sale by the end of this fiscal. Home grown apparel brands are growing in popularity too. The latest Global Lifestyle Monitor, India survey conducted by Cotton Council International (CCI) says that while small, independent clothing stores still account for a majority of garments shopping in India at 36 per cent, the figure has dropped from 64 per cent in 2003. And for departmental stores like Shoppers Stop and Life Style, the preference has risen from three per cent in 2003 to 17 per cent in 2008, as has for multi-brand stores like Planet Fashion from six per cent in 2003 to 16 per cent in 2008.

Mobile Phone

The mobile phone market is largely driven by India's urban consumers, though it is increasingly making inroads into the rural markets as well. According to data from the Telecoms Regulatory Authority of India (TRAI), India had 261 million mobile phone subscriptions at the end of March 2008, making it the world's second largest cellular market in numerical terms after China. Wireless connections now outnumber the 39 million fixed line phones in India by a seven to one ratio.

Direct Selling

The year 2008 is likely to witness intense competition among direct selling companies in India, which are vying for a pie in the US$ 11.6 billion segment. The industry is poised to grow 10 times more than the existing rate.

- Mumbai-based Image Multitrade Private Ltd is planning to launch new corporate initiatives through a subsidiary called Image Lifestyle to foray into the retail mall segment in Mumbai, Pune, Bhubaneshwar, Nagpur, Kolhapur, Bhopal, and Jabalpur, among others. Further, plans are also on the anvil to tie up with retail majors such as LG Electronics and Subhiksha.
- Amway India is planning to add 100 more branches and two lakh distributors, mostly in Tier II and Tier III cities. Amway has entered the nutraceutical business with an aim to reposition the brand in Indian urban centres and is looking at a 20 per cent growth in turnover at US$ 222.43 million in 2008.
- In a span of 12 years in India, Swedish direct selling major Oriflame Cosmetics has 12 offices in various cities, supplies in 1,261 cities, and is planning to cover more areas in the country.

Entertainment

Due to the need for leisure and de-stressing, fun is a very serious business in India's urban centres. The repertoire is wide, from TV to music, cinema to reading, outings to retail therapy, fitness and even religion. This also includes new age engagements like gaming and net-based activities. Indian Media and Entertainment industry has the potential to touch US$ 200 billion by 2015.

The number of radio and TV channels is increasing rapidly.

- Starting as only a metro phenomenon initially, FM channels have proliferated small towns too. There are now over 260 FM stations, out of which nearly 200 are operational.
- The spawning of multiplexes in Indian has spread to tier II and III cities like Ludhiana, Lucknow, Moradabad, Indore, Nashik, Aurangabad, Kanpur and Amritsar. Big players in the segment are Adlabs, Cinemax, Inox, Fame, PVR Cinemas.

Wellness

Presently, the Indian health and wellness market, estimated at US$ 4.6 billion, is booming with a year-on-year growth of over 25 per cent. Thanks to rising awareness and growing consciousness among urban Indians, there is a big niche for products that can enable freedom from stress, and the ill-effects of a sedentary lifestyle. Yoga, aroma-treatment, spas, nature-therapy, weight loss clinics, organic farming and the like are becoming popular with urban Indians and businesses are stepping in to satisfy this burgeoning need of the consumers. Cashing on this awareness, a wide range of products has inundated the market.Wellness centres are providing a healthy holistic experience. "The idea of wellness has been clearly understood by the elite class of population for sometime now." says Organic India's Saurabh Tiwari.Many other retail giants like Reliance Retail and the Birla group are also joining hands with wellness experts.

Restaurants

Indians are moving beyond the usual burger-pizza routine supported by the likes of McDonalds, KFC and Pizza Hut. With world cuisine at their doorsteps, urban Indians are indulging their taste buds like never before. Irish, Korean, Chinese, Mexican, Italian, Australian and Filipino fare are on offer from the labels that are looking to set up shops in malls, multiplexes, and residential areas of metro cities. At stake is US$ 2.3 billion restaurant market in India, which is growing at

28 per cent a year. New names entering the market are US-based Bennegan's, Panban International, South Korean fast-food franchise operator Genesis and US-based Mark Pi. Philippines-based fast-food firm Jollibee Foods Corp and Australia's Sumo Salads are seriously considering the Indian market.

E-commerce

Broadband Internet connections hit 3.9 million at the end of March 2008.

The increase in the PC and internet penetration along with the growing preference of Indian consumers to shop online has given a tremendous boost to e-tailing-the online version of retail shopping. According to the Indian Marketing Research Bureau (IMRB) and Internet and Mobile Association of India (IAMAI), the e-tail market is estimated to grow by 30 per cent to US$ 273.02 million in 2007-08, from US$ 210.01 million in 2006-07.

A new niche segment has emerged in this sector-on-demand personalisation of products. Online start-ups like Myntra, Dilsebol and Pringoo are some of the first movers in this area, which provide products, which are customised according to the client's demand.

Opportunities and Challenges

Urban India is well on its way to becoming a major world market. While major cities will drive the urban market; niche cities will also provide opportunities to industry players. Discretionary spending and consumption will increase as people move beyond basic necessities. Other than meeting the huge challenge emerging due to the rising services standards demanded by citizens, business models will need to adopt new strategies to mould and educate new consumers about their products, in order to establish brand loyalty. MNCs aiming at volume markets will have to continuously innovate with new features and products in order to appeal to discerning urban consumers.

Union Budget

3 Crore small and marginal farmers to benefit from Chidambaram's Largesse

To give a boost to the agricultural sector, the scheme of Debt Waiver and Debt Relief for *farmers* has been announced by the Finance Minister, Shri P Chidambaram.

All agricultural loans distributed by scheduled commercial banks, regional rural banks and cooperative credit institutions upto March 31, 2007 and overdue as on December 31, 2007 will be covered under Debt Waiver and Debt Relief scheme.For *marginal farmers* and *small farmers* there will be a complete waiver of all loans that were overdue on December 31,2007 and which remained unpaid until February 29,2008. In respect of other *farmers,* there will be a One Time Settlement (OTS) scheme for all loans that were overdue for the above period. Under the OTS, a rebate of 25% will be given against payment of the balance of 75%.

Agricultural loans which were rescheduled and are restructured during 2004-06 as per the RBI guidelines will also be eligible for a waiver or an OTS on the same pattern.

The implementation of the Debt Waiver and Debt Relief scheme will be completed by June 30, 2008. Upon being granted debt waiver or signing an agreement for debt relief under the OTS, the farmer would be entitled to fresh agricultural loans from the banks.

Three crore *small* and *marginal farmers* and one crore other *farmers* will benefit from the scheme. The total value of overdue loans being waived is estimated at Rs.50,000 crores and the OTS relief on the overdue loans is estimated at Rs. 10,000 crores

Besides government initiatives, the budget for the fiscal year 2007-08 proposes the following:

- The Centre's budgetary allocation to JNNURM has increased from US$ 1.13 billion in 2006-07 to US$ 1.23 billion in FY 2007-08.
- Urban local bodies have been allowed to issue tax-free bonds through State Pooled Finance entities formed to raise funds for the 'group of' urban local bodies'.

- Under Plan B of the Eleventh Plan a share has been allocated to urban infrastructure and water resources from the additional resources of US$ 1.73 billion that the Centre plans to generate through better tax administration.
- Allocation for the Rajiv Gandhi Drinking Water Mission has been enhanced from US$ 1.15 billion in 2006-07 to US$ 1.44 billion in 2007-08.
- Provision for Total Sanitation Campaign has been increased from US$178.17 million in 2006-07 to US$ 232.61 million in 2007-08.

Source: Press Information Bureau.

Investment

To meet the huge growth in the urban population and better service standards demanded by citizens, cities and towns will require large investments in these areas. For example, the total investment required in urban transport in India during the next five years is estimated at US$ 29.5 billon. Similarly, according to the World Bank, India will need US$ 37 billion over the next decade to give city dwellers access to safe water and sanitation.

To meet this present and expected demand for investment, government has been tapping various sources to channel investment in to these services. It has been providing support through budgetary allocation. Also, various external agencies have shown an interest to participate in this programme.

Significantly, India is to be the recipient of two loans–totaling US$ 620 million–from the Asian Development Bank to improve rural roads and basic urban services in the two States of Jammu & Kashmir and Madhya Pradesh.

Similarly, India and Japan formalized their agreement to work closely on urban development by signing a Memorandum of Understanding in May 2007. The Japan Bank for International Cooperation (JBIC) has already loaned over US$ 1.36 billion for the Delhi Mass Rapid Transit System and additional assistance for new corridors under Delhi Metro Phase II and other metro projects are under discussion.

Also, the Government is talking to the World Bank to set up an urban infrastructure fund for making available easy loans for city development programmes, to the tune of US$ 500 million. India stands next to China in terms of both funds lent and the number of lending operations to the urban sector.

The private sector is also not lagging behind. Both domestic and foreign players have evinced a keen interest in exploiting the opportunities within the growing urban population. This is particularly true for the country's real estate sector. Prominent domestic players in this sector include DLF, Omaxe Ltd, Puravankara Projects Ltd, Housing Development and Infrastructure Ltd, IVR Prime Urban Developers Ltd and Kolte Patil Developers Ltd. Prominent foreign players include Tishman Speyer Properties LP, Emaar Properties (Dubai), IJM Corp (Malaysia), Lee Kim Tah Holding (Singapore) and Salim Group (Indonesia).

There have also been instances of public private partnership to provide for urban service. For example, the Confederation of Indian Industry (CII) and the government of Tamil Nadu will work together on urban development initiatives such as transportation, traffic management, the development of the urban corridor, city beautification and restoration of water bodies.

OCCUPATIONAL STRUCTURE IN INDIA

Table 13 given below indicates the pattern of occupational distribution in India, since the beginning of this century.

About 70 per cent of our population has been engaged in the agricultural sector, since 1901. In actual terms, agriculture now absorbs a larger number of people than in the past. Within the agricultural sector again the percentage of people engaged in allied activities such as animal husbandry and fishery, etc., is very small. The proportion of agricultural labourers in this sector has gone up.

Definite changes have taken place in the industrial and tertiary sectors since independence. The number of industrial workers is going up. Similarly more and more people are getting employed in banks, schools, trades, business, etc. But all this has failed to make any sufficient impact on the occupational structure of the country. The occupational structure of India reveals the underdeveloped nature of the economy.

Table 13: below presents data relating to India's occupational structure since the beginning of the present century.

Table 12
Occupational Distribution of Working Population(Percentage)

Sector	*1901*	*1921*	*1951*	*1971*	*1981*	*1991*	*1999-00*
Primary	71.7	76.0	72.1	72.1	68.7	65.0	60.4
Secondary	12.6	10.5	10.7	11.2	13.5	15.0	15.8
Tertiary	15.7	13.5	17.2	16.7	17.8	20.0	23.8

Source: Census of India, 1981, and 1991. For 1999-2000 NSSO 55 Round and 59th Round (2005).

Table 13
Estimates of Population and Work Force by Gender and Rural-Urban Location: All-India 1993-94 - 1999-2000

(in '000)

Population Segment	*Estimates of Population as on*		*Estimates of Usual Status (PS+SS) Work Force as on*		*Usual status (PS+SS) Crude Worker Population Ratios (Per 1000)*	
	1.1.94	*1.1.2000*	*1.1.94*	*1.1.2000*	*1993-94*	*1999-2000*
Rural Males	338,628	370,761	187,266	196,874	553	531
Rural Females	317,881	348,104	104,265	104,083	328	299
Rural Persons	656,509	718,865	291,531	300,957	444	419
Urban Males	124,930	148,853	64,964	77,106	520	518
Urban Females	112,566	136,367	17,337	18,955	154	139
Urban Persons	237,496	285,220	82,301	96,061	347	337
All Areas: Males	463,558	519,614	252,230	273,980	544	527
All Areas: Females	430,447	484,471	121,602	123,038	283	254
All Areas: Persons	894,005	1,004,085	373,832	397,018	418	395

Notes:

1. Estimates of total Male and Female Population as on 1.1.94 and 1.1.2000 (the mid-points of Survey year 1993-94 and 1999-2000) are obtained by

interpolation from Population Census estimates for 1st March 1991 and 1st March 2001, which are (in '000): Males: 1991=439,230, 2001: 531,277; and Females: 1991: 407,072 and 2001: 495,738. RGI, Census of India 2001, Paper 1 of 2001, Provisional Population Total, March 2001.

2. The rural-urban split of the male and female population for 1993-94 are assumed to be same as given in Visaria (1998) and for 1999-2000 are obtained by interpolation from estimates for 1st March 1999 and 1st March 2000 contained in RGI (1996).

3. Crude Worker-Population ratios on the usual (principal plus subsidiary status) for rural males, rural females, urban males and urban females are drawn from, respectively, Sarvekshana, vol. 20, no. 1, July-September 1996 for 1993-94 and, Report on Employment-Unemployment in India 1999-2000, Key Results, NSS 55th Round, July 1999-2000, December 2000.

Table 14

India:Age Specific Usual Status (PS+SS) Worker Population Ratios By Rural Urban Residence and Gender 1983 to 1999-2000Age-Group

Age-Group	*Rural Males*				*Rural Females*			
	1983	*1987-88*	*1993-94*	*1999-2000*	*1983*	*1987-88*	*1993-94*	*1999-2000*
5-9	25	23	11	6	23	24	14	7
10-14	238	190	138	91	224	182	141	96
15-19	644	600	577	503	433	399	364	304
20-24	884	872	859	844	483	465	456	409
25-29	963	959	957	950	540	523	525	491
30-34	985	982	983	979	577	577	585	555
35-39	987	986	989	984	606	596	608	579
40-44	982	979	987	983	611	610	606	586
45-49	980	978	983	980	589	580	594	566
50-54	957	959	970	953	526	523	542	515
55-59	921	928	942	929	476	459	467	450
60+	662	668	699	639	227	218	241	218
All	543	539	553	531	330	323	328	299
	(564)	(546)			(346)	(333)		

Age-Group	*Urban Males*				*Urban Females*			
	1983 -88	*1987 -94*	*1993 -2000*	*1999*	*1983 -88*	*1987 -94*	*1993*	*1999-2000*
5-9	7	5	5	3	7	3	5	2
10-14	106	85	66	49	64	65	45	36
15-19	398	355	356	314	144	146	123	105
20-24	710	674	674	658	182	185	180	155
25-29	913	914	904	883	222	223	224	194
30-34	964	969	964	960	290	272	301	235

Contd.

Age-Group	*Urban Males*				*Urban Females*			
	1983 -88	*1987 -94*	*1993 -2000*	*1999*	*1983 -88*	*1987 -94*	*1993*	*1999-2000*
35-39	981	981	983	975	290	309	301	285
40-44	978	983	981	974	305	308	320	283
45-49	972	973	973	969	283	306	317	267
50-54	939	938	942	935	269	268	286	262
55-59	837	845	856	809	230	234	226	207
60+	508	480	442	402	124	123	113	94
All	510	506	520	518	146	152	154	139
	(538)	(526)			(155)	(159)		

Note: Figures in parentheses show the crude WPRs that would have been observed if the age distribution of the surveyed population in 1983 and 1987-88 had been the same as was reported by the 1993-94 survey.

Sources: For 1983, and for age-standardised WPR for all ages for 1983 and 1987-88: P. Visaria, "Employment and Work force in India: Implications for National Income Estimates", mimeo, July 1998.
For 1987-88, Sarvekshana, Spl. No. September 1990.
1993-94: Sarvekshana Vol. 20, no. 1, 68th Issue, July-September 1996.
For 1999-2000: NSSO: Employment and Unemployment in India 1999-2000 Key Results NSS 55 Round July 1999-June 2000, December 2000.

(Figures with in brackets relate to share (per 1000) of the occupation-group to the corresponding total workers in all occupations). Summary of results derived from the table: First, revisions based on the Provisional Population Totals from the 2001 Population Census raises the rate of growth of aggregate work force between 1994 and 2000 to a little over 1 per cent per annum with only a marginal reduction in the absolute size of female work force in rural areas. Second, while the decline in worker-population ratios in the younger age-groups between 1993-94 and 1999-2000 represents a continuation of a longer-term trend reflecting a beneficial rise in student-population ratios, in the 25 and above age-groups the decline in WPRs in the 1990s is getting exaggerated by the fact that, in a number of cases, the 1993-94 levels are outliers when seen against the WPRs from the earlier quinquennial Surveys. In other cases, either the variations are by and large within margins of sampling fluctuations (rural and men in the age-

Table 15
Industrial Distribution of Total (Rural plus Urban) Work Force: All India: 1961, 1993-94 and 1999-2000

Industry Division / Group	*1961*		*1993-94*		*1999-2000*	
	No. of Workers ('000)	*Share (per 1000)*	*No. of workers ('000)*	*Share (Per 1000)*	*No. of workers ('000)*	*Share (Per 1000)*
0. Agriculture, Forestry & Fishing	143,282	759	238,682	638	237,786	599
00-01. Crop production & Plantations	138,637	735	217,220	581	215,751	543
02. Livestock	3,684	20	16,936	45	16,141	41
03. Agricultural Services	NIL	NIL	1,850	5	3,769	9
04-06. Logging, Forestry & Fishing	952	5	2,696	7	2,125	5
1. Mining & Quarrying	919	5	2,676	7	2,263	6
2+3+97. Mfrg+Repair Services	17,906	95	43,218	116	48,296	122
Of which: Food Products	2,126	11	4843	13	5,409	14
Beverages & Tobacco	1,124	6	4,410	12	4,925	12
Textiles & Products	6,553	35	10,335	28	10,480	26
Wood, Products & Furniture	2,175	12	4,295	11	5,367	14
Leather, Fur & Products	704	4	730	2	1,081	3
Non-metallic Mineral Products	1,504	8	3,134	8	3,485	9
Metal Products & Parts	944	5	1,638	4	2,276	6
Repair Services	366	2	3,362	9	4,203	11
4. Electricity, Gas & Water	257	1	1,394	4	1,048	3
5. Construction	2,768	15	12,127	32	17,618	44
6. Trade, Hotels & Restaurants	8,171	43	28,459	76	37,128	94

Contd.

Industry Division / Group	*1961*		*1993-94*		*1999-2000*	
	No. of Workers ('000)	*Share (per 1000)*	*No. of workers ('000)*	*Share (Per 1000)*	*No. of workers ('000)*	*Share (Per 1000)*
Retail Trade	6871	36	21,384	57	28,887	73
Hotels & Restaurants	805	4	3,436	9	4,600	12
7. Trspt, Storage +Communication	3,262	17	10,757	29	14,757	37
8. Finance, Insurance, Real Estate & Business Services	542	3	3,653	10	4,924	12
9. Community, Social & Personal Services	11,571	61	32,866	88	33,200	84
Of which: Public Admn + Defence	3,394	18	10,349	28	10,589	27
Education + Research	1,811	10	6,513	17	8,554	22
Medical & Health	645	3	1,966	5	2,522	6
Community Services	593	3	1,125	3	1,055	3
Personal Services	4,490	24	10,654	28	9,429	24
Total Work Force	188,676	1000	373,832	1000	397,018	1000

groups between 30 and 49) or, as in the case of both rural and urban women, they largely reflecting declines in work participation on the subsidiary status. Third, the reduction in the number of workers in the agriculture and allied activities is more modest than indicated in our earlier and is seen to be concentrated among women workers. Fourth, a misclassification of the work force in repair services earlier had: (i) exaggerated the growth of work force in the Trade, Hotels and Restaurants sector; (ii) moderated the growth in employment in the Manufacturing sector; and, (ii) exaggerated the decline in the share of the Community, Social and Personal Services (taken as a group) in the total work force. Fifth, seen in relation to the industrial distribution of the work force in 1961, the *pace* of decline in the share of agriculture (and parallely, gains in the shares of other sectors) has been faster between 1994 and 2000 relative to the change between 1961 and 1994. Sixth, a noteworthy change during the 1990s has been the reduction in the absolute number of workers in personal services by over 1.2 million in the aggregate. Given that this segment has been traditionally low-productivity-low income-perworker sector, this reduction in the size and share of the personal services sector must be viewed as a positive development in the employment situation in the nineteen nineties. Seventh, in terms of occupation structure, despite a sizeable reduction of such workers in the total work force, India still remains a land of Farmers, Fishermen, Hunters and Loggers. At the other end of the skill spectrum, Professional and Technical Workers and Administrative, Executive and Managerial Workers together formed less than 7 per cent of the work force at the beginning of the year 2000. Eighth, revisions in the estimates of work force consequent on the 2001 Population Census have tended to dampen the growth in labour productivity (relative to our earlier estimates). While the re-allocation of repair-service workers to the Manufacturing sector accentuated the dampening of labour productivity growth, it has raised the labour productivity growth in the Trade, Hotels and Restaurants and the Community, Social and Personal services sectors. Ninth, a wide spread growth in *real* average daily

Table 16

Industrial Distribution of Rural Work Force: All India: 1961, 1993-94 and 1999-2000

Industry Division /Group	*1961*	*1993-94*	*1999-2000*			
	No. of Workers ('000)	*Share (per 1000)*	*No. of workers ('000)*	*Share (Per 1000)*	*No. of workers ('000)*	*Share (Per 1000)*
0. Agriculture, Forestry & Fishing	139,622	861	228,551	784	229,440	762
00-01. Crop production & Plantations	135,360	834	209,269	718	209,375	696
02. Livestock	3,452	21	15,328	53	14,843	49
03. Agricultural Services	NIL	NIL	1,665	6	3,520	12
04-06. Logging, Forestry & Fishing	805	5	2,289	8	1,702	6
1. Mining & Quarrying	708	4	1727	6	1494	5
2+3+97. Mfrg+Repair Services	10,379	64	21,711	74	24,062	80
Of which: Food Products	1466	9	2998	10	3104	10
Beverages & Tobacco	677	4	3,021	10	3,496	12
Textiles & Products	3,659	23	4892	17	5,130	17
Wood, Products & Furniture	1,649	10	2,998	10	3,694	11
Leather, Fur & Products	493	3	188	0.6	197	0.7
Non-metallic Mineral Products	1120	7	2,310	8	2,698	9
Metal Products & Parts	475	3	562	2	891	3
Repair Services	111	1	1,311	4	1772	6
4. Electricity, Gas & Water	79	0.5	562	2	394	1
5. Construction	1309	8	6930	24	10,005	33
6. Trade, Hotels & Restaurants	3572	22	12,486	43	13,700	46

Contd.

Industry Division /Group	*1961*	*1993-94*	*1999-2000*			
	No. of Workers ('000)	*Share (per 1000)*	*No. of workers ('000)*	*Share (Per 1000)*	*No. of workers ('000)*	*Share (Per 1000)*
Retail Trade	3217	20	9823	34	10,920	36
Hotels & Restaurants	266	2	1437	5	1,795	6
7. Trspt, Storage +Communication	914	6	4,224	14	6404	21
8. Finance, Insurance, Real Estate & Business Services	96	0.6	853	3	984	3
9. Community, Social & Personal Services	5567	34	14,487	50	14,475	48
Of which: Public Admn + Defence	1272	8	3,496	12	3,764	13
Education + Research	1026	6	3,268	11	4,099	14
Medical & Health	286	2	771	3	799	3
Community Services	324	2	666	2	498	2
Personal Services	2378	15	5247	18	5,014	17
Total Work Force	162,246	1000	291,531	1000	300,957	1000

Table 17

Industrial Distribution of Female Work Force: All India: 1961, 1993-94 and 1999-2000

Industry Division /Group	*1961*	*1993-94*	*1999-2000*			
	No. of Workers ('000)	*Share (per 1000)*	*No. of workers ('000)*	*Share (Per 1000)*	*No. of workers ('000)*	*Share (Per 1000)*
0. Agriculture, Forestry & Fishing	51,022	857	94,065	774	92,212	749
00-01. Crop production & Plantations	50,030	841	81,013	666	79,130	643
02. Livestock	822	14	11,855	97	11,074	90
03. Agricultural Services	NIL	NIL	784	6	1449	12
04-06. Logging, Forestry & Fishing	170	3	433	4	559	5
1. Mining & Quarrying	172	3	580	4	389	3
2+3+97. Mfrg+Repair Services	4857	82	11,500	95	12,510	102
Of which: Food Products	785	13	1353	11	1317	11
Beverages & Tobacco	380	6	3,019	25	3,676	30
Textiles & Products	2404	40	3624	30	3479	28
Wood, Products & Furniture	582	10	1129	9	1147	9
Leather, Fur & Products	67	1	87	0.7	114	0.9
Non-metallic Mineral Products	416	7	798	7	900	7
Metal Products & Parts	53	1	35	0.3	180	1
Repair Services	8	0.1	35	0.3	38	0.3
4. Electricity, Gas & Water	9	0.1	52	0.4	38	0.3
5. Construction	308	5	1648	14	2057	17
6. Trade, Hotels & Restaurants	865	15	3919	32	5253	43
Retail Trade	799	13	3122	26	4228	34

Contd.

Industry Division /Group	1961	1993-94	1999-2000			
	No. of Workers ('000)	Share (per 1000)	No. of workers ('000)	Share (Per 1000)	No. of workers ('000)	Share (Per 1000)
Hotels & Restaurants	53	0.9	556	5	834	7
7. Trspt, Storage +Communication	74	1	329	3	446	4
8. Finance, Insurance, Real Estate & Business Services	11	0.2	433	4	474	4
9. Community, Social & Personal Services	2188	37	9136	75	9662	79
Of which: Public Admn + Defence	103	2	1248	10	1157	9
Education + Research	341	6	2322	19	3290	27
Medical & Health	153	3	624	5	853	7
Community Services	45	0.8	173	1	199	2
Personal Services	1373	23	4422	36	3925	32
Total Work Force	59,505	1000	121,602	1000	123,038	1000

Table 18

Occupational Distribution of Work Force by Rural-Urban Residence: All-India, 1961-1999-2000 (in '000s)

	1961			*1993-94*			*1999-2000*		
NCO 1968 Divisions	*Rural*	*Urban*	*Total*	*Rural*	*Urban*	*Total*	*Rural*	*Urban*	*Total*
0-1. Professional & Technical and Related Workers	1689 (10)	1547 (59)	3236 (17)	6516 (22)	7191 87)	13707 (37)	5984 (20)	8590 (89)	14574 (37)
2. Administrative, Executive & Managerial Workers	764 (5)	1048 (40)	1812 (10)	2415 (8)	4717 (57)	7132 (19)	4179 (14)	8039 (84)	12218 (31)
3. Clerical & Related Workers	1046 (6)	2820 (107)	3866 (21)	3497 (12)	7573 (92)	11070 (30)	4053 (13)	8480 (88)	12533 (32)
4. Sales Workers	3244 (20)	3632 (138)	6876 (37)	11635 (40)	13681 (166)	25316 (68)	11716 (39)	15856 (165)	27572 (69)
5. Service Workers	2815 (17)	2743 (104)	5558 (30)	5331 (18)	7421 (90)	12752 (34)	7117 (24)	9219 (96)	16336 (41)
6. Farmers, Fishermen, Hunters, Loggers & Related Workers	134329 (830)	3261 (124)	137590 (731)	227763 (781)	10152 (123)	237915 (636)	226762 (753)	8885 (92)	235647 (594)
7,8,9: Production and Related Workers, Trspt Eqpt. Operators and Labourers	18052 (111)	11234 (427)	29286 (156)	34370 (118)	31564 (384)	65934 (176)	41148 (137)	36993 (385)	78141 (197)
All Occupations	161,939	26,285	188,224	291,529	82,299	373,826	300,959	96,061	397,021

average wage earnings of casual labourers, not being affected by the changes in the size and structure of the work force, continues to remain valid. Further, except for rural females engaged in manual work in other agricultural work (other than cultivation) and for manual work in agriculture as a whole, the evidence from the NSS Employment-Unemployment Surveys offers no support at all for the hypothesis of a slow down in the rate of growth of average daily wage earnings of adult casual labourers during the 1990s relative to that between 1983 and 1994. Finally, at the all-India level, the results of the 55th Round Employment-Unemployment confirms that the poverty ratios have indeed declined over the 1990s. However, at the level of individual states, the results are more mixed. While in eight out of fifteen major States, poverty ratios have indeed declined over the 1990s, in seven others it has remained either unchanged or have even increased. In all-cases, even at the all-India level, the order of decline (wherever that has materialised) in the poverty prevalence rates revealed by the Employment-Unemployment Survey has been significantly smaller than that revealed by the 55th Round Consumer Expenditure Survey.

3

RURAL AND AGRICULTURAL MARKETING

The rural market is made up of two broad areas:

(a) The market for consumption goods both consumer conveniene and shopping and durable goods.

(b) The market for agriculture inputs and other investment goods such as tractors etc.

Not surprisingly the entire demand potential for manufactured good that exists in the rural areas has been largely untapped. Not even a fraction of the rural market has been serviced by the industries in the organized sector. But that does not in any way lessen the importance of rural market as the following factors will indicate:

1. Size of the Rural Market: An analysis of National Sample Survey-data shows that of the total expenditure on manufactured consumer goods, 75 per cent is spent in rural India. The percentage remained almost unchanged since 1950-61. Though per capita consumption and expenditure on manufactured consumer items is low in rural areas, the market is approximately three times larger. On the assumption that all persons or families above the poverty line form the market for some branded consumer goods, this market has a size of 42 million households. If we take Punjab, Rajasthan, Gujarat and Andhra, the target market of 72 million people is largest numerically than France, U.K.or West Germany.

2. *Rural Target Population:* Wealth distribution in rural India is uneven and the top 12 per cent of the farmer's land holdings account for 37 per cent of cultivated area. Further, NSS data show that the top 10 per cent of the rural population accounts for above 37 per cent of the expenditure on consumer goods. Not surprisingly the potential market is at the top of the spectrum. However, with the increasing spread of the rural income, consumer goods are expected to make substantiál penetration into the lower income strata by the normal percolation effect. Then there is an increasing cross flow of population between urban and project town centres which act as conducts for cross flow of products and ideas thus supplementing the demand for such products.

3. *The Market for Agricultural Inputs:* There is a very rapidly expanding demand for agricultural inputs in rural market. This is borne out by the increased compound rate of growth in the off take of agricultural inputs like Pesticides, Tractors, Pumps and tubwells.

A recent survey in Andhra, Punjab and Haryana revealed that over 90 per cent of the farmers interviewed felt that they should use more and more new farm practices. The study established that in these areas the farmers are eager to use newer agricultural technology for improving profits and are prepared to take calculated risks.

4. *Rural Market in Value Terms:* For non-food consumption items the size and the value of the market has increased as estimated by NSSO & CSO. In real terms however, the growth has been very modest at 2.5 per cent per annum due to a number of factors such as.

(a) Lack of concerted effort by the organized sector to perpetrate the rural market.

(b) Averages are misleading in this type of analysis as peak opportunities which occur in certain pockets may not be fully realized.

(c) If the market for consumer products is considered as a whole it overshadows the opportunities that exist for selected products which may be growing at a much faster rate.

5. ***Helpful in the Food Processing Industry:*** India is a land of agricultural, horticulture, sericulture which produce a number of varieties of foodgrains, fruits, vegetables, commercial crops and flowers. The government of India making its efforts to develop the food processing industry while giving a number of benefits including tax benefits, incentives, subsidies, transportation and marketing facilities.

Food manufacturers or processors are primarily engaged in adding form utility to raw farm products. Wheat is milled into flour, livestock is converted into meal products, fruits and vegetables are canned or frozen. These firms play a vital role in transforming bulky, raw perishable farm products into storable, concentrated, and more appealing good products. Food processors occupy a strategic position in the food industry. Through the purchase of farm commodities, their activities are closely linked to farmers. As the source of many food product innovations and as the major brand advertisers in the food industry, they are also in close contact with consumer markets. Punjab, Himachal Pradesh and Jammu & Kashmir are the main producers of fruits and vegetables, in south Gujarat, Kerala and Karnataka, Maharashtra are the producer of coconut, groundnut, bananas, cashew-nuts and certain other products like tea and coffee. Government is developing food processing industries in these states., which is being responded as per the expectations. Fisheries, Meat products and other eatable are also much appreciated and preferred.

6. ***Sources of Rural Purchasing Capacity:*** Following are the factors which contribute to purchasing capacity in rural areas:

(a) Marketable Agricultural Surplus and rural/urban terms of trade: So far as manufactured consumer goods are concerned, regression analysis indicates that there is a 0.7 per cent rise in consumption for every one per cent increase in marketable surplus of foodgrains. As the surplus is increasing every year, there will be increasing purchasing capacity with farmers.

(b) Remittances: The traditional remittances from within the country are now being supplemented in several states by

remittances from overseas. The total inward remittances in the state of Kerala have increased significant. This creates new consumption and purchasing patterns.

(c) Government Expenditure: Investments in food control and irrigation facilities will be around Rs. 20,000 crores in 2007-2008 and central sector outlay for rural development and associated programme will be Rs. 14000 crores. These will generate income, and increased purchasing power of rural areas can be expected to support consumption of manufactured items. Further, these investments are expected to augment the income generation process from land in future years, which in turn, will accelerate the growth of rural markets. The investment proposed during the 10th plan higher for developing village and khadi industries is of higher order. Thus too will encourage the income generation process.

(d) Dispersal of Industry: The investment in the development of back-ward areas will greatly speed up the income generation process in rural areas.

7. Increase in Farm Income: As efficient marketing system ensures higher levels of income for the farmers by reducing the number of middlemen or by restricting the commission on marketing services and the malpractices adopted by them in the marketing of farm products. An efficient system guarantees the farmers better prices for farm products and induces them to invest their surplus in the purchase of modern input so that productivity and production may increase. This again results in an increase in the marketed surplus and income of the farmers. If the producer does not have an easily accessible market-outlet where he can sell his surplus produce, he has little incentive to produce more. The need for providing adequate incentives for increased production is therefore very important, and this can be made possible only by streamlining the marketing system.

8. Optimization of Resource Use and Output Management: *An efficient* rural marketing system leads to the optimization of resource use and output management. An efficient marketing system can also contribute to an increase in the marketable surplus by scaling down the losses arising out of inefficient processing, storage and transportation. A well-designed system of marketing can effectively distribute the available stock of modern inputs, and thereby sustain a faster rate of growth in the rural sector.

9. Helpful in Economic Development: Rural marketing plays an important role not only in stimulating production and consumption, but in accelerating the pace of economic development. Its dynamic functions are of primary importance in promoting economic development. For this reason, it has been described as the most important multipler of rural development. The development of an efficient marketing system is important in ensuring that scarce and essential commodities reach different classes of consumers. Marketing is not only an economic link between the producers and the consumer; it maintains a balance between demand and supply. The objectives of price stability, rapid economic growth and equitable distribution of goods and services cannot be achieved without the support of an efficient marketing system.

The rural marketing system plays a dual role in economic development in countries whose resources are primarily agricultural. Increasing demands for money with which to purchase other goods leads to increasing sensitivity to relative prices on the part of the producers, and specialization in the cultivation of those crops on which the returns are the greatest, subject to cultural, ecological and economic constraints. It is the marketing system that transmits the crucial price signals. On the land, and in order to sustain non-agricultural development, resources have to be diverted from the agricultural sector–physical resources to guarantee supplies of food and raw materials for the agro-industry and financial resources for investment of non-from economy as well as for re-investment and financial resources for investment in agricultural.

10. Employment: The marketing system provides employment to millions of persons engaged in various activities, such as packaging, transportation and processing. Persons like commission agents, brockers, traders, retailers, weigh-men, hamals and regulating staff are employed in the marketing system. A number of employees are working in the marketing system which is three their system ranging from primary marketing society, central marketing committee and state marketing board. Side by side cooperative marketing system provides employments to a number of employees. Storages, warehousing, transportations and middlemen, provide employments to a number of prospects.

11. Creation Utility: Marketing is productive, and is as necessary as the farm production. It is, in fact, a part of production itself, for production is complete only when the product reaches a place in the form and at the time required by the consumers. Marketing adds cost to the product; but, at the same time, it adds, utilities to the product. The following four types of utilities of the product are created by marketing:

(a) Form Utility : The processing function adds form utility to the product by changing the raw materials into a finished form. With this change, the product becomes more useful than it is in the form in which it is produced by the farmer. For example, through processing, oilseeds are converted into oil, sugarcane into sugar, cotton into cloth and wheat into flour and bread. The processed forms are more useful than the original raw materials.

(b) Place Utility: The transportation function adds place utility to products by shifting them to a place of need from the place of plenty. Products command higher prices at the place of need than at the place of products because of the increased utility of the product.

(c) Time Utility: The storage function adds time utility to the products by making them available at the time when they are needed.

(d) Possession Utility: The marketing function of buying and selling helps in the transfer of ownership from one person to another. Products are transferred through marketing to persons having a higher utility from persons having a low utility.

12. Contribution to National Income: Marketing activities add to the nation's gross national product and net national product. An estimate indicate that 14% of the gross national product comes from the rural sector and 11% is derived from rural industries. Moreover, there are number of activities which are called allied activities to rural sectors. They are also giving a reasonable contribution to the national net worth.

13. Better Living: The marketing system is essential for the success of the development programmes which are designed to uplift the population as a whole. Any plan of economic development that aims at diminishing the poverty of the agricultural population, reducing consumer food prices, earning more foreign exchange or eliminating economic waste has, therefore, to pay special attention to the development of an efficient marketing for food and agricultural products.

14. Price Signals: All efficient marketing system helps the farmers in planning their production in accordance with the needs of the economy. This work is carried out through price signals. The government is announcing the minimum support price of the agricultural produce every year and also emphasising the importance of a particular farm products. For examples during the past 5 years the government is stimulating the farmers to produce more commercial crops like Sugar cane, soyabean, sunbean, groundnut, tobacco and tobacco products, sericultures products, fruits and vegetables, cotton and oilseeds. To fetch a good price the farmers are directed to produce as per the requirements of the economy. This paves a way for the development of rural industralisation and hence, the development of rural market.

15. Adoption and Spread of New Technology: The marketing system helps the farmers in the adoption of new scientific and technical knowledge. Past experiences shows that our rural areas were totally under-developed and under utilised because of the lack of mechanisation of agriculture. With the advancement of technology, mechanization, introduction of high yielding varieties, development of fertilizer and pesticides and proper government policy the agriculture production has increased to a greater extent which is the back bone of rural industries.

16. Widening of Markets: A well–knit marketing system widens the market for the products by taking them to remote corners of the country, i.e. to areas far away from the production points. The widening of the market helps in increasing the demand on a continuous basis, and thereby guarantees a higher income to the producer.

17. Growth of Agro-based Industries: An improved and efficient system of rural marketing helps in the growth of agro-based industries and stimulates the overall development process of the economy. Many industries depend on agriculture for the supply of raw materials. So many producers have installed their industrial units near the village side and are also interested to install the units in the rural areas so as to minimize the transportation cost, easily availability of raw materials and some benefits which are specially mean for rural producers. So growth of agro based industries constitute one of the most important segment of rural marketing.

PROBLEMS OF AGRO-BUSINESS

In addition to existing problems, there are the possibilities of new emerging problems which any business will have to attend. Along with problems of shortages, we have the problem of plenty in certain products. Many of the rural produces are perishables having life of one day to one year. Accordingly sales and consumption has to take place. The Green Revolution has helped us to be self reliant in foodgrains and what is required is to keep it up and maintain a balanced growth of different requirements.

Rural people are aware of problems like lesser rains, more rains, one non-seasonal rains, electricity shortage, poor roads, middlemen expoitation etc. Some of them cope up with this and some leave it on God's wish. The policymakers, agriculture universities, bigger farmers and government bodies continue to strive for progressive for a more prosperous India. Some of the emerging problem are discussed as under.

(i) Agro-Inputs: The usage of HYV seeds, fertilizers and pesticides requires qualitative and quantitative improvement. This has to be done by counselling training and persuading the farming community. There are financial facilities for these activities which farmers must use to grow more and grow better quality produce.

(ii) Roads and Transports: Roads of approach to rural areas and their link to towns and cities are very bad. This is an age old problem which needs to be attended to by Panchayat and State governments. Most of the roads are meant for bullock carts and pedestrians. About seventy per cent of rural roads are not motorable. This needs serious attention of the State government. Even where tar roads are made, the quality of workmanship is very poor.

The cooperatives and big farmers must do some arrangement of transportation by tempos and trucks. The traditional movement of goods through bullock carts is too slow and quantity being moved is small. To be in tune with the modern world and its speed, we must switch over to automobiles in a much bigger way than it is now.

The rail service, though used for long distance movements, is only a supplementary effort to improve. It cannot be the main transport as most of the villages are away from railway lines. Air service is used only for flower exports and some high value commodities.

(iii) Inadequate Training of Farmers: The education and training to farmers is far from adequate. Increasing productivity per man per acre, changing of crop pattern, use of quantity and quality of fertilizers and pesticides are the areas which need to be improved a lot. Certain factors are within limitations of farmers. Some others are environmental factors. Thus, there is more need to train, re-train and enlighten the rural people on many facts of agricultural production and marketing.

(iv) Abnormal Growth of Certain Commodities: Farmers have the habit of copying the success of friends, relatives and try to grow the same crop. This leads to excess production of a particular crop and lesser production of other crops. This problem becomes very severe if the crop is of shorter life and early consumption is essential. For example, in the year 1992, many farmers around Mandy (Karnataka) grew sugarcane to cater to the sugar factories. The growth of output was so huge that thousands of tones of sugarcane was left uncut as factories could not accommodate the excess availability. Finally, the crop was left to dry as even cutting and transport cost could not be covered. This shows even a good crop in excess is a perishable waste. A similar situation pertained to the excess growth of tomatoes, potatoes and onion on different occasions. Neither they get price nor buyers. The time, investment, effort and the crop becomes a waste thus setting in demoralization.

This problem of excess produce will not be severe in case of durable like rice, wheat, jowar etc. Where only lesser price will be available but the total waste situation does not happen as in the case of sugarcane.

(v) Grading/classification of agricultural production: Grading of agricultural production enables to get fair price for the quality. This is part of their business activities and many farmers, especially small and marginal farmers do not do grading and sell their goods in a hurry to overcome debts.

For any rural product, grains, fruits, flowers and seeds, the gradation has to be done based on quality, size, taste and variety. Only after this, the packing has to be done. This simplifies marketing and getting appropriate price in the market. Consumers also will be happy to see uniform grade of product in their purchase.

INTERNATIONAL DEVELOPMENT ENTERPRISES (INDIA)

For most, *small* and *marginal farmers* are either 'recipients of charity' or at best, 'beneficiaries'. Divulging from the oft-repeated charity mode of the past trends' IDEI views the *small* and *marginal farmers* as potential customers. This innovative givers to enabler approach to development marks the beginning of a dynamic growth in the socio-economic development of the marginalized farming segment.

Consequently, a notable achievement has been the utilisation of donor funds for the establishment of a penetrative delivery mechanism ie., a commercial marketing channel ensuring the availability of its products at the village level.

In essence, IDE *(India)'s* model for sustainable development involves bridging gaps at various levels:

- *Between technological inventions in research institutions and their adaptations to suit the needs of small and marginal farmers:* IDE *(India)* identifies such technological innovations from across *India* and the world, and modifies them to cater to the needs and affordability of *small farmers.*

- *Between availability of low-cost technologies and generating awareness about them among small farmers based in remote villages*: IDE *(India)* employs innovative promotional techniques to generate awareness about IDE *(India)'s* products among the *marginal farmers.*
- *Between demand for IDE (India)'s products and their supply to small farmers in rural areas:* We develop and nurture the commercial marketing channel and the NGO network to ensure the accessibility of our products in the remotest corners of the country.

PEOPLE BENEFITED AND NEED FOR TECHNOLOGY

IDEI has worked towards reducing poverty in *India* by helping the rural poor increase their agricultural productivity and income through the use of affordable and sustainable technologies. IDEI has helped empower more than 450,000 rural poor and enable them to progress from subsistence agriculture to *small*-scale commercial farming, thus beginning an upward spiral out of poverty.

In *India* ,70% of farming population consists of *small* and *marginal farmers* cultivating land less than 1 hectare in size, average size of which decreases by half every 15 years due to the rapid population growth. Today nearly 60% of the *farmers* belong to *marginal* category with an average of 0.4 ha land. Agriculture in *India* is mainly rain fed and majority of the *farmers* have little access to alternate source of irrigation. These poor *farmers* are still dependent on the vagaries of the monsoons to sustain their livelihoods. Thus no availability of affordable, dependable irrigation devices is a major factor behind increasing number of *farmers* being drawn into the poverty spell.

Major parts of Eastern *India* comprising the sub-Himalayan Terai belt and the Brahmaputra valley have a very high water table. However, the nature and cost of the technology limits independent access to groundwater for irrigation. In these areas IDEI promotes the use of a manually operated water-lifting device for irrigation called the treadle pump. While Diesel pumps existed for decades to cater to big *farmers,* and traditional means were being employed by smaller *farmers* which were cumbersome, there was a huge gap in the market that needed technology which was affordable yet efficient to fulfill the need of *small farmers.* TP technology taps exactly that segment of *small* landholders having little to invest other than their labour.

The Treadle pump is a waterlifting foot operated device that can irrigate *small* plots of land in regions that have high water table. It is a low cost system , simple in design and easily manageable and appropriately answers the irrigation need for the *small farmers.* Till date 325000 *small* and *marginal farmers* have adopted the technology in north east *India.*

Similarly in the semi arid regions the need is to prevent overexploitation of precious resources like soil and water by alternative irrigation techniques which not only use the resources better but also result in increased production levels. But these technologies are expensive and out of the reach of the poor *farmers.*

More than 70% of Indian *farmers* are *small* scale operators cultivating plots less than one hectare. They are largely constrained due to the absence of simple and low cost technologies suited to *small* plots which can be managed by themselves. The present technologies are expensive and fit for use in large fields for big *farmers.* Thus the systems needed to be technically less esoteric so that the *farmers* could easily manage it and set it up themselves. Learning practical lessons from grassroots practitioners -the *farmers,* IDEI embarked upon the innovative adaptations of low cost systems catering to the needs of the smaller *farmers,* bringing in more flexibility , simplicity and affordability. IDEI promoted drip kits cost almost 80% cheaper than the conventional drip kits and thus bring about a shift from subsistence farming to higher value production farming doubling the income of the poor *farmers* and greatly enhancing household food security.

The drip irrigation technology and Treadle Pump technology frees the farmer from the limitations of rain fed farming, enabling him to grow wider variety of crops, cultivate all the year round, higher cropping intensity and do priority farming. Good irrigation technologies and agricultural practices coupled with enhanced participation of the poor in the markets is the key to income generation. Income dimension is important because it has the potential to buffer the poor communities against the stresses and shocks they encounter.

IDEI promotes affordable drip irrigation technologies (ADITI) in the form of packaged and ready-to-use kits such as bucket kit, drum kit, and customized systems which are used by *farmers* for growing both horticulture crops and cash crops and till date have been successfully adopted by 85,000 *small* and *marginal farmers.*

4

RURAL POPULATION IN INDIA

India's population has been increasing at a very fast rate. During the four decades 1961-2001, India's population increased at an anuual average rate of about 2.2 per cent and even currently is increasing at about 1.8 per cent. This is to be contrasted with zero per cent in Portugal, Germany and the U.K., and between 0 and 1 per cent in all other industrialised countries. Apparently, the population growth rate is very high and it is on top of a very large population base that India has. As a consequence, the absolute annual increase in India's population is being estimated at about 17 million. i.e., India is adding daily about 50,000 new guests all through the year, 365 days of it.

Here, it should be noted that this large population will require a wide a range of consumable and durable goods, and services. At the same time the need of the rural areas does not automatically guarantee a market, unless it is backed by income and the resultant purchasing power.

LOCATION OF RURAL POPULATION

One of the deterrents for marketing men to exploit the rural market potential has been, the vastness of the rural market in term of areas covered and the location of the rural population. It is much easier to cater to the needs of urban population because of their concentration, but it is very difficult in the case of rural population because of their widespread nature.

Table 1
Rural Population in India

Year	*Rural Population in Million*	*Proportion %*	*Urban Population in Million*	*Proportion %*	*Total in Million*
1951	298.2	82.4	62.8	17.6	361
1961	360.0	82.0	78.9	18.0	439.2
1971	439.0	79.8	109.1	20.2	548.1
1981	523.8	76.7	159.5	23.3	683.3
1991	628.7	74.3	217.6	25.7	846.3
2001	742	72.2	285	27.8	1027

The whole waban population is located in about 3,119 places like metros, cities and towns, while the rural population is about three times the urban population, their places of location is several times greater.

From the tables, it can be seen that the rural population is distributed in about 5,57,137 villages unlike the urban population. This apart, it should also be noted that the villages are not uniform in size. Near by 48 % of the villages have a population of less than 500 persons or about 100 households, which is probably of no consequence for marketing men. This may be acceptable since the proportion of population covered by these 48 per cent of village account for only about 12 per cent. Yet is should be borne in mind that the people of these villages also have land and cultivate and generate some income. Thus, the location of villages throw a challenge to marketing men. This phenomenon is not true for the whole country and there are wide variations among the different states. In states with high irrigation facilities and fertile lands, the concentration of population is more when compared to states with low irrigation facilities and lack of arable land.

RURAL–URBAN DISTRIBUTION

While there has been a progressive increase in the number as well as the proportion of people residing in urban areas during the last few decades, India continues to be predominantly rural. The urban population increased by 41 per cent during 1941-51. Even if we discount this rate because of the influx of refugees after the partition of the country by knocking off the influx, the urban growth rate during the decade was 35 per cent which increased to 36.91 per cent during 1981-91 but slowed down to 30.7 per cent during 1991-2001. The percentage of urban population in total population has gone up from 17.1 per cent in 1951 to 25.72 per cent in 1991 and 27.8 per cent in 2001, and is further projected to go to up to 32 per cent in 2011, and 36.2 per cent in 2026.

Inter-State variations may also be observed. Tamil Nadu is the most urbanized state with 43.9 per cent of the population living in the urban areas. The share of urban population in total population is more than 30% in States like Goa, Gujarat, Karnataka, Maharashtra, and Mizoram while it is between 20% and 30% in other States like Uttar Pradesh, Andhra Pradesh, Haryana, Jammu and Kashmir, Kerala, Madhya Pradesh, Manipur, Punjab, Rajasthan and West Bengal.

Table 2

Current Population

India	1,139,560, 57
World	6,777,772,16

Rural-Urban Distribution of Population-India and States/Union Territories: 2001

		Population			
*India/State/ Union Territory**	*T/R/U*	*Persons*	*Males*	*Females*	*Per cent Urban Population*
INDIA	T	1,027,015,247	531,277,078	495,738,169	27.78
	R	741,660,293	381,141,184	360,519,109	
	U	285,354,954	150,135,894	135,219,060	
*State/Union territory**					
Jammu & Kashmir	T	10,069,917	5,300,574	4,769,343	24.88
	R	7,564,608	3,925,846	3,638,762	
	U	2,505,309	1,374,728	1,130,581	
Himachal Pradesh	T	6,077,248	3,085,256	2,991,992	9.79
	R	5,482,367	2,754,251	2,728,116	
	U	594,881	331,005	263,876	
Punjab	T	24,289,296	12,963,362	11,325,934	33.95

Contd.

India/State/ Union Territory*	T/R/U	Population Persons	Males	Females	Per cent Urban Population
	R	16,043,730	8,500,647	7,543,083	
	U	8,245,566	4,462,715	3,782,851	
Chandigarh*	T	900,914	508,224	392,690	89.78
	R	92,118	56,837	35,281	
	U	808,796	451,387	357,409	
Uttaranchal	T	8,479,562	4,316,401	4,163,161	25.59
	R	6,309,317	3,143,380	3,165,937	
	U	2,170,245	1,173,021	997,224	
Haryana	T	21,082,989	11,327,658	9,755,331	29.00
	R	14,968,850	8,017,622	6,951,228	
	U	6,114,139	3,310,036	2,804,103	
Delhi*	T	13,782,976	7,570,890	6,212,086	93.01
	R	963,215	533,219	429,996	
	U	12,819,761	7,037,671	5,782,090	
Rajasthan	T	56,473,122	29,381,657	27,091,465	23.38
	R	43,267,678	22,394,479	20,873,199	
	U	13,205,444	6,987,178	6,218,266	
Uttar Pradesh	T	166,052,859	87,466,301	78,586,558	20.78
	R	131,540,230	69,096,765	62,443,465	
	U	34,512,629	18,369,536	16,143,093	
Bihar	T	82,878,796	43,153,964	39,724,832	10.47
	R	74,199,596	38,510,686	35,688,910	
	U	8,679,200	4,643,278	4,035,922	
Sikkim	T	540,493	288,217	252,276	11.10
	R	480,488	255,386	225,102	
	U	60,005	32,831	27,174	
Arunachal Pradesh	T	1,091,117	573,951	517,166	20.41
	R	868,429	453,560	414,869	
	U	222,688	120,391	102,297	
Nagaland	T	1,988,636	1,041,686	946,950	17.74
	R	1,635,815	846,651	789,164	
	U	352,821	195,035	157,786	
Manipur	T	2,388,634	1,207,338	1,181,296	23.88
	R	1,818,224	923,428	894,796	
	U	570,410	283,910	286,500	
Mizoram	T	891,058	459,783	431,275	49.50
	R	450,018	233,718	216,300	
	U	441,040	226,065	214,975	
Tripura	T	3,191,168	1,636,138	1,555,030	17.02
	R	2,648,074	1,359,288	1,288,786	
	U	543,094	276,850	266,244	
Meghalaya	T	2,306,069	1,167,840	1,138,229	19.63
	R	1,853,457	939,803	913,654	

Contd.

India/State/ Union Territory*	T/R/U	Population Persons	Males	Females	Per cent Urban Population
	U	452,612	228,037	224,575	
Assam	T	26,638,407	13,787,799	12,850,608	12.72
	R	23,248,994	11,983,157	11,265,837	
	U	3,389,413	1,804,642	1,584,771	
West Bengal	T	80,221,171	41,487,694	38,733,477	28.03
	R	57,734,690	29,606,028	28,128,662	
	U	22,486,481	11,881,666	10,604,815	
Jharkhand	T	26,909,428	13,861,277	13,048,151	22.25
	R	20,922,731	10,660,430	10,262,301	
	U	5,986,697	3,200,847	2,785,850	
Orissa	T	36,706,920	18,612,340	18,094,580	14.97
	R	31,210,602	15,711,853	15,498,749	
	U	5,496,318	2,900,487	2,595,831	
Chhatisgarh	T	20,795,956	10,452,426	10,343,530	20.08
	R	16,620,627	8,290,983	8,329,644	
	U	4,175,329	2,161,443	2,013,886	
Madhya Pradesh	T	60,385,118	31,456,873	28,928,245	26.67
	R	44,282,528	22,975,256	21,307,272	
	U	16,102,590	8,481,617	7,620,973	
Gujarat	T	50,596,992	26,344,053	24,252,939	37.35
	R	31,697,615	16,289,423	15,408,192	
	U	18,899,377	10,054,630	8,844,747	
Daman & Diu*	T	158,059	92,478	65,581	36.26
	R	100,740	63,576	37,164	
	U	57,319	28,902	28,417	
Dadra & Nagar Haveli*	T	220,451	121,731	98,720	22.89
	R	169,995	91,887	78,108	
	U	50,456	29,844	20,612	
Maharashtra	T	96,752,247	50,334,270	46,417,977	42.40
	R	55,732,513	28,443,238	27,289,275	
	U	41,019,734	21,891,032	19,128,702	
Andhra Pradesh	T	75,727,541	38,286,811	37,440,730	27.08
	R	55,223,944	27,852,179	27,371,765	
	U	20,503,597	10,434,632	10,068,965	
Karnataka	T	52,733,958	26,856,343	25,877,615	33.98
	R	34,814,100	17,618,593	17,195,507	
	U	17,919,858	9,237,750	8,682,108	
Goa	T	1,343,998	685,617	658,381	49.77
	R	675,129	339,626	335,503	
	U	668,869	345,991	322,878	
Lakshadweep*	T	60,595	31,118	29,477	44.47
	R	33,647	17,196	16,451	
	U	26,948	13,922	13,026	

Contd.

India/State/ Union Territory*	T/R/U	Population Persons	Males	Females	Per cent Urban Population
Kerala	T	31,838,619	15,468,664	16,369,955	25.97
	R	23,571,484	11,450,785	12,120,699	
	U	8,267,135	4,017,879	4,249,256	
Tamil Nadu	T	62,110,839	31,268,654	30,842,185	43.86
	R	34,869,286	17,508,985	17,360,301	
	U	27,241,553	13,759,669	13,481,884	
Pondicherry*	T	973,829	486,705	487,124	66.57
	R	325,596	163,586	162,010	
	U	648,233	323,119	325,114	
Andaman & Nicobar Islands*	T	356,265	192,985	163,280	32.67
	R	239,858	128,837	111,021	
	U	116,407	64,148	52,259	

Notes:

1. The total, rural and urban population of India includes the estimated total, rural and urban population of entire Kachchh district, Morvi, Maliya-Miyana and Wankaner taluks of Rajkot district, Jodiya taluka of Jamnagar district of Gujarat state and estimated total and rural population of entire Kinnaur district of Himanchal Pradesh where population enumeration of Census of India, 2001 could not be conducted due to natural calamities.
2. The figures of total, rural and urban population of Himachal Pradesh state have been arrived at after including the estimated total and rural population of entire Kinnaur district where population enumeration of Census of India, 2001 could not be conducted due to natural calamity.
3. The figures of total, rural and urban population of Gujarat state have been arrived at after including the estimated total, rural and urban population of entire Kachchh district , Morvi, Maliya-Miyana and Wankaner taluks of Rajkot district, Jodiya taluka of Jamnagar district where population enumeration of the census of India, 2001 could not be conducted due to natural calamity.

Table 3
Distribution of Villages in India

Population	No. of Villages	% of Total
Less than 200	114267	18%
200-499	155123	24.30%
500-999	159400	25.00%
1000-1999	125758	19.70%
2000-4999	69135	10.80%
5000-9999	11618	1.80%
10000 and above	3064	0.50%
Total	638365	100%

Bottom Heavy Cluster among Villages

68% of the villages in India are below the 1000 Popln.

- Marketers overlooking the same
- Reading out to these villages critical to exponential growth.
- Bottom Cluster with greater than 2000 Popl. slowly saturating.

Logistics-The 3rd Generation Challenge

The Top tier villagers walk, talk & think like any other man.

- Servicing him is an absolute mandate.
- Beefing up the supply chain critical to reaching out the these masses.
- Rural centric PDS, Transport and sound communication essential.

Table 4
Location and Concentration of Rural Population

Population Range (No. of Persons)	*Number of Villages*	*Proportion*
Less than 200	1,20,073	21.55
200 to 499	1,50,722	27.05
500 to 999	1,35,928	24.40
1000 to 1999	94,486	16.96
2000 to 4999	46,892	8.42
5000 to 9999	7,202	1.29
10,000 and above	1,834	0.33
Total	5,57,137	100.00

Source: Census of India.

Table 5
Location and Concentration of Urban Population

Population Range (No. of Persons)	*Number of Towns*
10,00,000 and above	8
5,00,000 to 9,99,999	9
1,00,000 to 4,99,999	134
50,000 to 99,999	219
20,000 to 49,999	652
10,000 to 19,999	987
5,000 to 9,999	820
Less than 5,000	290
Total	3119

INCOME GENERATION

The occupation pattern dictates the pattern of income generation also.

Table 6
Income Generation in Rural Areas

Sources of Income	*Proportion to Total*
Agriculture	59
Agricultural Wages	16
Business and Craft	9
Non Agricultural Wages	7
Salaries	3
Current Transfers	2
Others	4
Total	100

Seventy five per cent of income generation in rural areas is from agriculture and agriculture-related activities. This is logical, as the major occupations is agriculture. This further confirms the earlier statement that the prosperity of rural areas depends upon the status of agriculture and related activities. Therefore, the development of rural market, to a large extent, depends upon the progress of agriculture.

The following results are available from latest survey of the NCAER.

Urban incomes growing at 3.2% a year, rural incomes at 4.5% a year.

- 1994-95: Rural income 55-58% of Urban
- 2001-02 Rural income 63-64 % of Urban
- 2004-05: Rural income 66% of Urban income (estimated)

Rural middle class growing at 12%, in Urban areas it is increasing at 13%

- 2001-02: 35% of India's 60 million middle class in villages.
- 2009-10: 33% of India's 154 million middle class in villages (Middle class: annual household earning Rs. 2 lakh–10 lakh).

It would mean that the fruits of economic reforms are finally getting filtered down to rural areas.

The sources of income by occupation groups both in rural and urban sectors are summarized in Table 7 below:

Table 7
Sources of Income by Occupation Groups
(Percentage distribution)

Occupation Group	*Urban*	*Rural*
Farming	1.72	35.37
Non-farming	20.74	11.16
Salary	54.07	17.42
Agricultural Wage	0.74	20.29
Non-agricultural wage	4.94	7.56
Others	17.78	8.20
All sources	100.00	100.00

Source: Basanta K Pradhan *et al.*: "Rural–Urban Disparities", *EPW*, Vol. XXXV, No.29, July 21,2000.

Farm tools for agricultural productivity, which still remain outdated, need to be modernised. "Small and marginal farmers constitute 78 per cent of the farming community in India. These farmers can be spared of the drudgery they are suffering from generations if science and technology helps them in increasing crop productivity

SHARE OF THE ORGANISED AND UNORGANISED SECTORS

Another way to look at the structural change in the income is to look at the organisational pattern of the economy.

The NAS divides the economy into two sectors: organized sector which is identified with a modern market economy and unorganized sector or traditional economy. The unorganized sector is defined to include "all unincorporated enterprises and household industries- other than organized ones and which are not regulated by any of the Acts.

EXPENDITURE PATTERN

The expenditure patterns of the rural and urban areas are presented in Table 8. The National Sample Survey Organisation conducts consumer expenditure surveys in the country. The latest data available for 45th round conducted during July '89 to June '90 are presented in the table. Usually, the expenditure data is presented 'expenditure group-wise' for different items under two major headlings-food items and non-food items. The figures are the value of consumption of different items per person per month.

Table 8
Value of Consumption Per Person Per Month

Items	*Rural (in Rs)*	*Urban (in Rs)*
Cereals	45.38	42.34
Gram	0.40	0.59
Cereal Substitutes	0.24	0.22
Pulses	8.31	10.04
Milk and milk products	18.35	29.53
Edible Oils	9.10	14.60
Meat, Eggs and Fish	6.84	11.42
Vegetables	10.25	14.65
Fruits and Nuts	3.23	6.87
Sugar	6.34	7.78
Salt	0.33	0.38
Spices	4.88	6.00
Beverage and Others	8.13	21.04
Total Food Items	121.78	165.46
Pan, Tobacco and Intoxicants	6.69	7.57
Fuel and Light	14.44	19.26
Clothing	12.15	19.86
Footwear	1.63	2.61
Miscellaneous goods and services	27.80	55.89
Durable Goods	4.33	15.38
Rents	0.57	11.40
Taxes and Cess	0.03	0.57
Total Non-food Items	67.68	132.54
Total Consumer Expenditure	189.46	298.00

Source National Sample Survey: 45th Round (July 89 to June 90), *Sarvekshana*, Vo. 16, No. 1, pp. S216–S217.

From the table certain interesting inference can be drawn. The total expenditure on food items is of the order of Rs. 9,07,505 million in rural areas as opposed to Rs. 4,26,887 million in urban areas. Approximately the expenditure incurred by rural areas is double that of urban areas. Similarly, the expenditure on non-food items in rural areas is about 1.5 times the expenditure in urban areas. For example consider foot wear, which is about 1.8 times the urban expenditure.

Category do not spend any amount on foot-wear, while the families in higher expenditure classes spend as much as their urban counterparts. Similarly the rural expenditure on durable goods is about Rs. 32,267 million, whereas the urbanites spend Rs. 39,680 million. Here again, the difference will be low per capita consumption in rural areas and higher per capita consumption in urban areas. In addition, the demand in urban areas may be for superior durable goods like automobiles, washing machines, quartz watches, televisions, etc. while in rural areas bicycles, mopeds, electrical goods, hand wound watches, etc. are in demand. The rural areas demand cheaper and long-lasting products.

From the above data it appears that the rural areas are not lagging far behind the urban areas in demand for food and non-food items.

We may further look at the pattern of final consumption expenditure. Bulk of the income is still being spend on food items, as is natural in a UDC. The fact that the quality of food-intake too has been poor leading to serious malnutrition among a large section of population can be established with the help of a number of indicators,

- heavy bias in favour of cereals and cereal substitutes.
- a fall in the expenditure during the last five and a-half decades on such items as milk and milk products, meat, egg and fish- the sources of animal – based proteins,
- consumption of fruits, vegetables and roots accounting for only an insignificant proportion of total expenditure.

Per Capita oil consumption which is generally accepted as a criterion for level of living is very low in India, a mere 0.6 barrels as against the world average of 4.5 barrels and 24 barrels in USA, 16.5 barrels in Japan and 14.4 barrels in South Korea. Per capita consumption of polymers in India is mere 3.6kg.

per annum against the world average of 24.6kg. These are all manifestations of a low standard of living. No wounder, in a recent survey of 20 countries conducted by The Economist, India was the last country any foreigner would want to live in. Coefficient of consumption expenditure has been around 40.40 in urban areas and somewhat lower in rural areas.

5

RURAL POVERTY IN INDIA

Though the middle class has gained from recent *positive economic developments, India* suffers from substantial *poverty*. According to the new World Bank's estimates on poverty based on 2005 data, India has 456 million people, 41.6% of its population, living below the new international poverty line of $1.25 (PPP) per day. The World Bank further estimates that 33% of the global poor now reside in India. Moreover, India also has 828 million people, or 75.6% of the population living below $2 a day, compared to 72.2% for Sub-Saharan Africa.

On the other hand, the Planning Commission of India uses its own criteria and has estimated that 27.5% of the population was living below the *poverty line* in 2004–2005, down from 51.3% in 1977–1978, and 36% in 1993-1994. The source for this was the 61st round of the National Sample Survey (NSS) and the criterion used was monthly per capita consumption expenditure below Rs. 356.35 for rural areas and Rs. 538.60 for urban areas. 75% of the poor are in rural areas, most of them are *daily wagers*, self-employed householders and landless labourers. Although Indian economy has grown steadily over the last two decades, its growth has been uneven when comparing different social groups, economic groups, geographic regions, and rural and urban areas.

Wealth distribution in India is fairly uneven, with the top 10% of income groups earning 33% of the income. Despite significant economic progress, 1/4 of the nation's population earns less than the government-specified *poverty threshold* of $0.40/day. Official figures estimate that 27.5% of Indians lived below the national poverty line in 2004-2005. A 2007 report by the state-run National Commission for Enterprises in the Unorganised Sector (NCEUS) found that 25% of Indians, or 236 million people, lived on less than 20 rupees per day with most working in "informal labour sector with no job or social security, living in abject poverty."

Income inequality in India *(Gini coefficient:* 32.5 in year 1999-2000) is increasing. In addition, India has a higher rate of malnutrition among children under the age of three (46% in year 2007) than any other country in the world.

CAUSES OF POVERTY IN INDIA

Slums next to high-rise commercial buildings in *Cochin,* Kerala. Despite India's recent "economic miracle", continued dependence of large sections of Indian populace on agriculture for livelihood has increased *income inequality* levels.

There are at least two main schools of thought regarding the causes of poverty in India.

The Developmental View

Colonial Economic Restructuring

Jawaharlal Nehru noted, "A significant fact which stands out is that those parts of India which have been longest under British rule are the poorest today." The Indian economy was purposely and severely *deindustrialized* (especially in the areas of textiles and metal-working) through colonial privatizations, regulations, *tariffs* on manufactured or refined Indian goods, *taxes,* and direct seizures. In 1830, India accounted for 17.6% of global industrial production against Britain's 9.5%, but by 1900 India's share was down to 1.7% against Britain's 18.5%. (The change in industrial production per capita is even more extreme due to Indian *population growth).*

Not only was Indian industry losing out, but consumers were forced to rely on expensive (open monopoly produced) British manufactured goods, especially as barter, local crafts and subsistence *agriculture* was discouraged by law. The agricultural raw materials exported by Indians were subject to massive price swings and declining terms of trade.

Mass Hunger

British policies in India exacerbated weather conditions to lead to mass *famines* which, when taken together, led to between 30 to 60 million deaths from *starvation* in the Indian colonies. Community grain banks were forcibly disabled, land was converted from food crops for local consumption to *cotton, opium, tea,* and *grain* for export, largely for animal feed.

In summary, deindustrialization, declining terms of trade, and the periodic mass misery of man-made famines are the major ways in which colonial government destroyed development in India and held it back for centuries.

The Neoliberal View

- *Unemployment* and *underemployment,* arising in part from protectionist policies pursued till 1991 that prevented high foreign investment. Poverty also decreased from the early 80s to 1990 significantly however
- Lack of property rights. The right to property is not a fundamental right in India.
- Over-reliance on agriculture. There is a surplus of labour in agriculture. Farmers are a large vote bank and use their votes to resist reallocation of land for higher-income industrial projects. While services and industry have grown at double digit figures, agriculture growth rate has dropped from 4.8% to 2%. Neoliberals tend to view food security as an unnecessary goal compared to purely financial economic growth.

  There are also a variety of more direct technical factors:
  - About 60% of the population depends on agriculture whereas the contribution of agriculture to the GDP is about 18%
  - High population growth rate, although demographers generally agree that this is a symptom rather than cause of poverty.

And a few cultural ones have been proposed:

- The *caste system,* under which hundreds of millions of Indians were kept away from educational, ownership, and employment opportunities, and subjected to violence for "getting out of line." British rulers encouraged caste privileges and customs, at least before the 20th century.

Despite this, India currently adds 40 million people to its middle class every year. Analysts such as the founder of "Forecasting International", *Marvin J. Cetron* writes that an estimated 300 million Indians now belong to the middle class; one-third of them have emerged from poverty in the last ten years. At the current rate of growth, a majority of Indians will be middle-class by 2025. Literacy rates have risen from 52 per cent to 65 per cent in the same period.

HISTORICAL TRENDS IN POVERTY STATISTICS

The proportion of India's population below the poverty line has fluctuated widely in the past, but the overall trend has been downward. However, there have been roughly three periods of trends in income poverty.

1950 to mid-1970s: Income poverty reduction shows no discernible trend. In 1951, 47% of India's rural population was below the poverty line. The proportion went up to 64% in 1954-55; it came down to 45% in 1960-61 but in 1977-78, it went up again to 51%.

Mid-1970s to 1990: Income poverty declined significantly between the mid-1970s and the end of the 1980s. The decline was more pronounced between 1977-78 and 1986-87, with rural income poverty declining from 51% to 39%. It went down further to 34% by 1989-90. Urban income poverty went down from 41% in 1977-78 to 34% in 1986-87, and further to 33% in 1989-90.

After 1991: This post-economic reform period evidenced both setbacks and progress. Rural income poverty increased from 34% in 1989-90 to 43% in 1992 and then fell to 37% in 1993-94. Urban income poverty went up from 33.4% in 1989-90 to 33.7% in 1992 and declined to 32% in 1993-94 Also, NSS data for 1994-95 to 1998 show little or no poverty reduction, so that the evidence till 1999-2000 was that poverty, particularly rural poverty, had increased post-reform. However, the official estimate of poverty for 1999-2000 was 26.1%, a dramatic decline that led to much debate and analysis. This was because for this year the NSS had adopted a new survey methodology that led to both higher estimated mean consumption and also an estimated distribution that was more equal than in past NSS surveys. The latest NSS survey for 2004-05 is fully comparable to the surveys before 1999-2000 and shows poverty at 28.3% in rural areas, 25.7% in urban areas and 27.5% for the country as a whole, using Uniform Recall Period Consumption. The corresponding figures using the Mixed Recall Period Consumption method was 21.8%, 21.7% and 21.8% respectively. Thus, poverty has declined after 1998, although it is still being debated whether there was any significant poverty reduction between 1989-90 and 1999-00. The latest NSS survey was so designed as to also give estimates roughly, but not fully, comparable to the 1999-2000 survey. These suggest that most of the decline in rural poverty over the period during 1993-94 to 2004-05 actually occurred after 1999-2000.

In summary, the official poverty rates recorded by NSS are (Table 1).

Table 1

Year	*Round*	*Poverty Rate (%)*	*Poverty Reduction per year(%)*
1977-78	32	51.3	
1983	38	44.5	1.3
1987-88	43	38.9	1.2
1993-94	50	36.0	0.5
1999-00	55	26.9	7.4
2004-05	61	27.5	0.8

HISTORY OF ATTEMPTS TO ALLEVIATE POVERTY

Since the early 1950s, government has initiated, sustained, and refined various *planning* schemes to help the poor attain self sufficiency in food production. Probably the most important initiative has been the supply of basic commodities, particularly food at controlled prices, available throughout the country as poor spend about 80 per cent of their income on food.

OUTLOOK FOR POVERTY ALLEVIATION

Eradication of poverty in India can only be a long-term goal. Poverty alleviation is expected to make better progress in the next 50 years than in the past, as a trickle-down effect of the growing middle class. Increasing stress on education, reservation of seats in government jobs and the increasing empowerment of women and the economically weaker sections of society, are also expected to contribute to the alleviation of poverty. It is incorrect to say that all poverty reduction programmes have failed. The growth of the middle class (which was virtually non-existent when India became a free nation in August 1947) indicates that economic prosperity has indeed been very impressive in India, but the distribution of wealth is not at all even.

After the liberalization process and moving away from the socialist model, India is adding 60-70 million people to its middle class every year. Analysts such as the founder of "Forecasting International", Marvin J. Cetron writes that an estimated 390 million Indians now belong to the middle class; one-third of them have emerged from poverty in the last ten years. At the current rate of growth, a majority of Indians will be middle-class by 2025. Literacy rates have risen from 52 per cent to 65 per cent during the initial decade of liberalization (1991-2001)

CONTROVERSY OVER EXTENT OF POVERTY REDUCTION

While total overall poverty in India has declined, the extent of poverty reduction is often debated. While there is a consensus that there has not been increase in poverty between 1993-94 and 2004-05, the picture is not so clear if one considers other non-pecuniary dimensions (such as health, education, crime and access to infrastructure). With the rapid economic growth that India is experiencing, it is likely that a significant fraction of the rural population will continue to migrate toward cities, making the issue of urban poverty more significant in the long run.

Economist *Pravin Visaria* has defended the validity of many of the statistics that demonstrated the reduction in overall poverty in India, as well as the declaration made by India's former Finance Minister *Yashwant Sinha* that poverty in India has reduced significantly. He insisted that the 1999-2000 survey was well designed and supervised and felt that just because they did not appear to fit preconceived notions about poverty in India, they should not be dismissed outright. *Nicholas Stern*, vice president of the *World Bank*, has published defenses of the poverty reduction statistics. He argues that increasing globalization and investment opportunities have contributed significantly to the reduction of poverty in the country. India, together with China, have shown the clearest trends of globalization with the accelerated rise in per-capita income.

A 2007 report by the state-run National Commission for Enterprises in the Unorganised Sector (NCEUS) found that 77% of Indians, or 836 million people, lived on less than 20 rupees per day (*USD* 0.50 nominal, *USD* 2.0 in PPP), with most working in "informal labour sector with no job or social security, living in abject poverty."

A study by the McKinsey Global Institute found that in 1985, 93% of the Indian population lived on a household income of less than 90,000 rupees a year, or about a dollar per person per day; by 2005 that proportion had been cut nearly in half, to 54%. More than 103 million people have moved out of desperate poverty in the course of one generation in urban and rural areas as well. They project that if India can achieve 7.3% annual growth over the next 20 years, 465 million more people will be spared a life of extreme deprivation. Contrary to popular perceptions, rural India has benefited from this growth: extreme rural poverty has declined from 94% in 1985 to 61% in 2005, and they project that it will drop to 26% by 2025. Report concludes that

India's economic reforms and the increased growth that has resulted have been the most successful anti-poverty programmes in the country.

Deoki Nandan Education Trust Inc (DNET) is a 100% volunteer-run 501(c)3 tax-exempt nonprofit organization incorporated in the Commonwealth of Virginia that aims to bring education to poor children in rural India.

THE PROBLEM

India's rural areas have been left behind in the wake of high growth in cities like Bangalore and Hyderabad. One cause of rural poverty is the inability for children in rural areas to obtain basic education. While schools do exist in rural India, many children are not able to attend because they are needed instead to earn money for their families by working in factories or fields. Without a foundation of basic education, these children are trapped in a life of hard labor and barely sustainable wages.

Our Solution

DNET programs select students who are not able to attend school due to financial reasons. A DNET program monitor in the field pays tuition, provides books and uniforms, and assures that the children meet attendance and performance requirements in school. In addition, the children's families receive a stipend to relieve the students of the need to work. See the *Programs* section for more detailed information.

MISSION STATEMENT

Article 26 of the *Universal Declaration of Human Rights* states "Elementary education shall be compulsory." In the impoverished rural areas of northern India, however, basic education often falls by the wayside as families struggle to earn their daily meals. By providing scholarships, books, and uniform donations, the Deoki Nandan Education Trust strives to ensure that all Indian children have access to education.

Rural Poverty

A large numbers of India's people live in abject poverty. 14.3% of the population earned less than $1 a day in 2005 down from 33.3% in 1990. According to the new World Bank's estimates on poverty based on 2005 data, India has 256 million people, 21.6% of its population, down from 60% in 1981 living below the new international poverty line of $1.25 (PPP) per day. The World Bank further estimates that 13% of the global poor now reside in India. Moreover, India also has 228 million people, or 20.6% of the population living below $2 a day, compared to 72.2% for Sub-Saharan Africa.

Wealth distribution in India is improving since the liberalization and with the end of the socialist rule termed as the license raj. While poverty in India has reduced significantly, official figures estimate that 27.5% of Indians still lived below the national poverty line in 2004-2005. A 2007 report by the state-run National Commission for Enterprises in the Unorganised Sector (NCEUS) found that 65% of Indians, or 750 million people, lived on less than 20 rupees per day with most working in "informal labour sector with no job or social security, living in abject poverty."

Since the early 1950s, successive governments have implemented various schemes, under *planning,* to alleviate poverty, that have met with partial success. All these programmes have relied upon the strategies of the *Food for work* programme and *National Rural Employment Programme* of the 1980s, which attempted to use the unemployed to generate productive assets and build *rural* infrastructure. In August 2005, the *Indian parliament* passed the *Rural Employment Guarantee Bill,* the largest programme of this type in terms of cost and coverage, which promises 100 days of minimum wage employment to every *rural* household in 200 of *India's 600 districts.* The question of whether economic reforms have reduced poverty or not has fuelled debates without generating any clear cut answers and has also put political pressure on further economic reforms, especially those involving the downsizing of labour and cutting agricultural subsidies.

India defines its poverty line at roughly Rs. 15 a day. The new World Bank poverty line is $1.25 or Rs. 53 per day. The ugly feature of the rural economy of India is its widespread poverty. According to World Bank criteria, the number of poor in India is 456 million. It is the largest figure in the world. That is 42% of the population, down from 60% in 1980. While India's economic growth has helped alleviate poverty by 19% between 1990 and 2005, globally poverty rates declined 38%. During the first planning period there was larger in the number of poor people in the country. In 1973 the total number of people living below the poverty line was estimated at 123 million. The number rose to about 317 million by 1979-80. on the Plan. Of the total rural population about 51 per cent were poor. Out of 317 million poor people in the country 260 million lived in the rural areas. In other words, more than 80 per cent of the total number of poor were living in the rural areas.

During the Sixth Plan due to the serious efforts of the Government, the number of people living below the poverty line declined. Still in 1985 about 40 per cent of the total rural population lived below the poverty line.

Poverty in the rural areas is thus deep and universal. This massive poverty leads to squalor, disease, hunger, ill-health, malnutrition and general degradation of human life. About 28 per cent of the rural population suffered from chronic malnutrition.

In the rural areas poverty is concentrated among the landless labourers, small and marginal farmers, artisans and cottage workers.

India defines its poverty line at roughly Rs. 15 a day. The government says this is enough to maintain a 2,200 calorie diet required to prevent death. The new World Bank poverty line is $ 1.25 or Rs. 53 per day. This nearly doubles the number of poor in India from the government's official figure of 280 million to 456 million. That is 42% of the population, down from 60% in 1980. According to World Bank report, about 600 million i.e. about 55% of India's population live in povertys. India has the largest number of poor in the world. A higher poverty bar will make India look bad, but the truth is most

Indians do live in appalling conditions. So, poverty-eradication initiatives must be strengthened. The calorie-based measure used by National Sample Survey to measure poverty may be inadequate, but it is more suitable than the World Bank's system. For that, the poverty line should be redefined to cover other basic needs such as healthcare, shelter, electricity and education. This will broaden our focus to improve overall living standards of people below the poverty line. A higher bar also factors in inflation that has taken place in recent months.

Hile India's economic growth has helped alleviate poverty by 19% between 1990 and 2005, globally poverty rates declined 38%.

The Planning Commission has now conceded that in addition to the officially recognized population below the poverty line, there are at least another 25 per cent of the population "who consider themselves poor and deserving of government help". Poverty is measured by the international poverty line of below a dollar a day. On the basis of recommended nutritional requirements of 2,435, rounded as 2,400 calories per person per day for rural areas and 2,095 rounded as 2,100, calories for urban areas (incidentally these are also the world standards). The logic in using calorie intake as a yardstick of poverty is simple: the poor spend between 60% and 80% of their income on food. The average calories requirement is estimated by taking into account the population composition by age, sex and occupation categories, together with the corresponding recommended calorie norms by the Indian Council of Medical Research. In rupees the poverty line is the mid-polar of the expenditure class in which the calories needs are satisfied. (This has also been termed as the "food energy method"). On this basis, the cut-off point turns out to be Rs. 228.00 and Rs. 264.00 for rural and urban areas respectively at 1992-93 prices. For a household of five member, the poverty line has been fixed at an annual income of Rs. 13,680 in rural areas and Rs. 15,840 in urban areas.The percentage of population below the poverty line, called the head-count ratio, in 1972-73, 1977-78,1987-88,1993-94 and 1999-2000 with the above cut-off points is shown in Table 2.

Table 2
The Percentage of Population below the Poverty Line

	1972-73	*1977-78*	*1987-88*	*1993-94*	*1999-2000*	*2007*
Rural	54.10	51-20	39.09	37.27	27.09	21.0
Urban	41.20	38.20	38.20	32.36	23.62	14.6
All-India	51.50	48.30	38.86	35.97	26.10	19.2

It would be seen from Table 19 that according to the Planning Commission about one-forth (26 per cent) of India's total population, i.e., about 260 million, live below the poverty line-an incidence of poverty worse than even in Black Africa. India's First Social Development Report 2006 confirms these estimates.

Inter-state Variations: Poverty, however, is not equitably distributed throughout the country. The states are not an undifferentiated sack of potatoes, there are apples and oranges too.

Among the states, in percentage terms, Orissa has the dubious distinction of having the highest proportion (47.15%) of its population living below the poverty line. It is followed by Bihar which has 42.60 per cent of its population categorized as poor. In third place is Madhya Pradesh where 37.443 per cent of the population is poor; Sikkim (36.55) and Tripura (34.44 per cent) come next.

But in terms of sheer numbers, it is Uttar Pradesh which tops the list with around 5.3 crore people below poverty line. Bihar, with about 4.3 crore of the country's poor occupies the second place, followed by Madhya Pradesh (3 crore), Maharashtra (2.2 crore), West Bengal (2.1 crore), Orissa (1.7 crore) and Andhra Pradesh (1.2 crore).

Bihar, Jharkhand, Chattisgarh, Uttaranchal, M.P., Rajesthan and U.P. account for 51 per cent of the country's poor. If Assam, Orissa, West Bengal and some Union Territories are added, these states would account for over 70 per cent of the poor in the country.

Among the states where the number of poor is small, is Jammu and Kashmir (3.46 lakh). Himachal Pradesh too has merely 5.12 lakh people categorized as poor.

Despite a marginal reduction in the number of days worked by male workers-per usual (ps+ss) Status worker-and the reduction in crude worker-population ratios, the sizeable and broad-based growth in average daily wage earnings in real terms and the rise in the number of days worked by female worker was adequate to raise real average wage earnings per capita at over 2.5 per cent per annum in both rural and urban India over the period 1993-94 to 1999-2000

At the all-India level, the results are clear and unambiguous. Except in respect of girl children in urban India, there is a definite and unambiguous decline in the proportion of population in households that lie below the poverty line. The same holds true, in terms of the proportion of households below the poverty, for all the types of households distinguished by reference to their principal means of livelihood. Particularly significant is the 7.5 percentage point decline in the incidence of poverty for agricultural labour households and a 6 percentage point decline for other labour households. There is a clear and sizeable decline in the poverty prevalence ratios among agricultural labour households and other labour households would survive any adjustment for use of a 365-day reference period for durables etc. according to the NSS 55th Round Survey.

By the same token, the decline in the incidence of poverty in the self-employed households is much less striking. Equally important to note is the fact that, the order of decline in the proportion of population below the poverty line (between 2 and 3 percentage points) is much less than what has been claimed on the basis of the 55th Round Consumer expenditure survey.

Financing Anti-poverty Programmes

Subsequently in the Eighties financing anti-poverty programmes (loans-cum-subsidy schemes) exclusively for the benefit of the weakest amongst the weaker sector beneficiaries amongst *rural* poor gained momentum. Thus began a period of directed *credit*, during which *credit* was directed towards the so-called weaker sectors. The most important new scheme of this phase was the Integrated *Rural* Development Programme (IRDP), a scheme for the creation of productive income bearing assets among the poor through the allocation of subsidized *credit*. Initiated as a pilot project in 1978-79, it was extended to all *rural* blocks of the country in 1980. Despite certain weaknesses in the programme in its implementation, IRDP played an important role in the 1980s in that it gave new access to millions of *rural* households to the formal banking system and increased levels of purchasing power in *rural* India significantly.

There are various other *rural* development schemes in many of which *Banks* have a significant role to play. Some of them are listed below:

- Jawahar Gram Samridhi Yojana
- Swarnjayanti Gram Swarozgar Yojana (SGSY)
- Jawahar Rozgar Yojana
- Employment Assurance Scheme (EAS)
- Indira Awaas Yojana
- Ganga Kalyan Yojana
- Supply of Improved Toolkits to *Rural* Artisans (SITRA)
- *Rural* Sanitation Programme
- Accelerated *Rural* Water Supply Programme (ARWSP)
- Drought Prone Areas Programme (DPAP)
- Desert Development Programme (DDP)
- Integrated Wastelands Development Programme (IWDP)
- *Rural* Water Supply Programme
- Million Wells Scheme
- National Watershed Development
- Pradhan Mantri Gramodaya Yojana (PMGY)
- Scheme for Land Development
- Pradhan Mantri Gram Sadak Yojana (PMGSY)
- Training of *Rural* Youth for Self-Employment (TRYSEM)

- Agricultural and *Rural* Debt Relief Scheme
- Food for Work Programme
- Self Help Groups
- Sampoorna Grameen Rozgar Yojana (SGRY).

Overall, at the all-India level, the results of 55th Round the Employment-Unemployment Survey confirms the direction of change: the prevalence of poverty has indeed declined over the 1990s. However, the order of decline is much less than that indicated by the 55th Round Consumer Expenditure Survey.

Table 3
Percentage of Households Below Poverty Line

Household/Type	*1993-94*	*1999-2000*
Self-employed in agriculture	27.81	24.12
Self-employed in non-agriculture	29.68	27.0
Agricultural Labour	54.49	46.96
Other Labour	35.21	29.24
Others	23.64	18.38
All	35.24	31.48

Source: Results on Employment-Unemployment in India, 1993-94 and 1999-2000, NSS 55th Round July 1999-June 2000.

Poverty in India is reducing but it is still a major issue. *Rural* Indians depend on unpredictable agriculture incomes, while *urban* Indians rely on jobs that are, at best, scarce.

Since its independence, the issue of *poverty* within India has remained a prevalent concern. According to the common definition of *poverty*, when a person finds it difficult to meet the minimum requirement of acceptable living standards, he or she is considered poor.

Millions of people in India are unable to meet these basic standards, and according to government estimates, in 2007 there were nearly 220.1 million people living below the *poverty* line.

Nearly 21.1% of the entire *rural* population and 15% of the *urban* population of India exists in this difficult physical and financial predicament. The following chart presents the *poverty* situation:

Figure 1

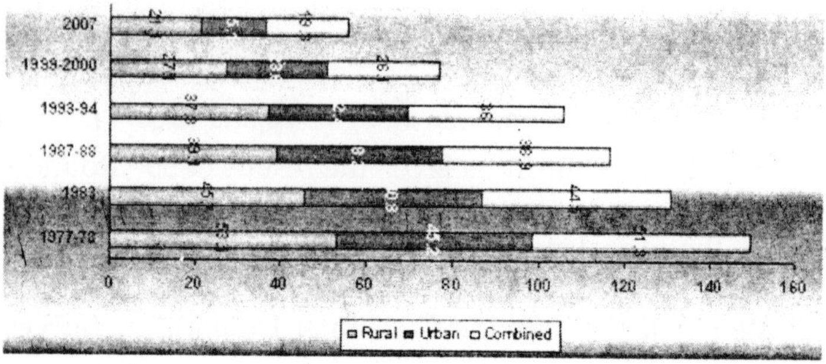

The division of resources, as well as wealth, is very uneven in India–this disparity creates different *poverty* ratios for different states. For instance, states such as Delhi and Punjab have very low *poverty* ratios. On the other hand, 40-50% of the populations in Bihar and Orissa live below the *poverty* line.

The *poverty* ratios illustrated here are divided in two types: *urban* and *rural*. Specific reasons for *poverty* vary in the *urban* and *rural* settings.

A number of factors are responsible for *poverty* in the *rural* areas of India. *Rural* populations primarily depend on agriculture, which is highly dependant on rain patterns and the monsoon season. Inadequate rain and improper irrigation facilities can obviously cause low, or in some cases, no production of crops.

Additionally, the Indian family unit is often very large, which can amplify the effects of *poverty*. Also, the caste system still prevails in India, and this is also a major reason for *rural poverty* – people from the lower casts are often deprived of a number of facilities and opportunities. The government has planned and implemented *poverty* eradication programs, but the benefits of all these programs have yet to reach the core of the country.

The phenomenal increase in the city populations is the main reason for *poverty* in the *urban* areas of India. A major portion of this additional population is due to the migration of the *rural* families from villages to cities. This migration is mainly caused by poor employment opportunities in villages. This situation is exacerbated by the fact that there are few job opportunities in the *urban* areas of India.

Since 1970, the Indian government has implemented a number of programs designed to eradicate *poverty*, and has had some success with these programs. The government has sought to increase the GDP through different processes, including changes in industrial policies. There is also a Public Distribution System, which has been somewhat effective so far. Other programs include the Integrated *Rural* Development Programme, Jawahar Rozgar Yojana, the Training *Rural* Youth for Self Employment (TRYSEM) and to the credit of the government, other on-going initiatives.

High poverty levels are synonymous with poor quality of life, deprivation, malnutrition,illiteracy and low human resource development.The eradication of poverty has been an integral component of the strategy for economic development in India. The Planning Commission has been estimating the incidence of poverty at the national and state level using the methodology contained in the report of the Expert Group on Estimation of Proportion and Number of Poor (Lakdawala Committee) and applying it to consumption expenditure data from the large sample surveys on consumer expenditure conducted by the NSSO at an interval of approximately five years. On this basis, comparable estimates of poverty are available at national and state level from 1973-74 to 1999-2000. According to the latest large sample survey data on consumer expenditure made available by the National Sample Survey Organisation (NSSO) from its 55th Round Survey (July 1999-June 2000), the poverty ratio on a 30 day recall basis, is estimated at 27.09 per cent in rural areas, 23.62 per cent in urban areas and 26.10 per cent for the country as a whole. The incidence of poverty expressed as a percentage of people living below the poverty line has witnessed a steady decline from 55 per cent in 1973-74 to 36 per cent in 1993-94 and 26 per cent in 1999-2000. (Table 4). Though the poverty ratio declined, the number of poor remained stable at around 320 million for a fairly long period of two decades, (1973-1993), due to a countervailing growth in population. The latest estimates for 1999-2000 reveal a significantly reduced number of poor, at about 260 million out of a total population of 997 million.10.6 Poverty at the national level is estimated as the weighted average of state-wise poverty levels. The poverty ratio is estimated from the state-specific poverty lines and the distribution of persons by expenditure groups obtained from the NSS data on consumption expenditure. The state specific poverty ratios at the national and state levels are listed at Table 5. State-wise poverty ratios have witnessed a secular decline from 1973-74 to 1999-2000. Though poverty has declined at the macro-level, rural–urban and inter-state disparities are visible. The rural poverty ratio is still relatively high in Orissa, Bihar and the North Eastern States. In Orissa, Madhya Pradesh, Bihar and Uttar Pradesh, the urban poverty ratios were in the range of 30.89 to 42.83 per cent in 1999-2000. The combined rural and urban poor make up 47.15 per cent of Orissa and 42.60 per cent of Bihar. For the states of Madhya Pradesh, Sikkim, Arunachal Pradesh and Assam the combined poverty ratios in 1999-2000 were in the range of 33.47 to 37.43 per cent. There has been a significant reduction in poverty during the period in Kerala, Jammu & Kashmir,Goa, Lakshdweep, Delhi, Andhra Pradesh, Gujarat, Tamil Nadu, Karnataka, West Bengal and Andaman and Nicobar Islands. Thus, while some states such as Punjab and Haryana have succeeded in reducing poverty by following the path of high agricultural growth,

Table 4
Poverty in India

Year	*All India Number (mn)*	*Poverty Ratio (%)*	*Rural Number (mn)*	*Poverty Ratio (%)*	*Urban Number (Mn)*	*Poverty Ratio (%)*
1973-74	321	54.9	261	56.4	60	49
1977-78	329	51.3	26.4	53.1	65	45.2
1983	323	44.5	252	45.7	71	40.8
1987-88	307	38.9	232	39.1	75	38.2
1993-94	320	36.0	244	37.3	76	32.4
1999-2000	260	26.1	193	27.1	67	23.6

Source: Planning Commission.

Table 5
State-wise Poverty Line-2004-05

Rs. Percapita month

State	*Rural*	*Urban*
Andhra Pradesh	292.95	542.89
Assam	387.64	378.84
Bihar	354.36	435.00
Chhattisgarh	322.41	560.00
Delhi	410.38	612.91
Goa	362.25	665.90
Gujarat	353.93	541.16
Haryana	414.76	504.49
Himachal Pradesh	394.28	553.77
Jammu&Kashmir	391.26	451.24
Jharkhand	366.56	599.66
Karnataka	324.17	559.39
Kerala	430.12	570.15
Madhya Pradesh	327.78	665.90
Maharashtra	362.25	528.49
Orissa	325.79	466.16
Punjab	410.38	559.63
Rajasthan	374.57	547.42
Tamil Nadu	351.86	558.62
Uttar Pradesh	365.84	483.26
Uttarakhand	478.02	637.67
West Bengal	382.82	449.32
Dadra & Nagar Haveli	362.25	665.90
All India*	356.30	538.60

* The Poverty Line (implicit at all-India level is worked out from the expenditure Class-wise distribution of persons (based on Uniform Recall Period- consumption, i.e. consumption data collected from 30-day recall period for all items) and the poverty ratio at all India level. The poverty ration at all-India level is obtained as the weighted average of the state-wise poverty ratio.

Note: State specific poverty lines identified by the Expert Group and updating them to 2004-05 prices using the consumer price index of agricultural labourers (CPIAL) for rural poverty lines and consumer price index for industrial workers (CPIIW) for urban poverty lines.

Source: Planning Commission.

others have focussed on particular areas of development e.g.Kerala has focussed on human resource development, West Bengal on vigorous implementation of land reform measures and empowerment of Panchayats, and Andhra Pradesh on direct public intervention in the form of public distribution of foodgrains.

Table 6
Percentage of Population Below Poverty Line

	Rural		*Urban*	
States	*1993-94 – 1999-00*		*1993-94 1999-00*	
All India	39.36	36.35	30.37	28.76
Andhra Pradesh	27.97	25.48	35.44	32.28
Assam	58.28	61.78	10.13	12.45
Bihar	64.41	58.85	45.03	45.10
Gujarat	28.62	26.22	28.86	21.70
Haryana	30.52	14.86	13.40	13.79
Karnataka	37.73	38.50	32.40	24.55
Kerala	33.95	26.50	28.20	31.89
Madhya Pradesh	36.93	39.35	46.02	46.29
Maharashtra	50.21	50.00	33.52	32.16
Orissa	59.12	62.67	36.99	34.27
Punjab	17.61	14.24	6.79	6.74
Rajasthan	25.92	15.01	30.60	24.36
Tamil Nadu	37.27	39.37	37.83	29.82
Uttar Pradesh	39.08	29.87	34.23	36.39
West Bengal	54.15	56.16	20.97	16.74

Source: *Sarvekshana*, Vol. 20, No.1, July-Sept 1996, Draft Report No. 458 (55/10/2).

Results on Employment-Unemplyment in India, 1993-94 and 1999-2000, NSS 55th Round July 1999-June 2000.

IMPORTANT POINTS ABOUT POVERTY IN INDIA ARE:

(i) In respect of rural areas in six States (Assam, Karnataka, Madhya Pradesh, Orissa, Tamil Nadu and West Bengal) *the poverty prevalence ratios in 19992000 are higher* than in 1993-94 while in Maharashtra, there has been virtually no change in the poverty ratios between 1993-94 and 1999-2000. At the all-India level, and in eight of the fifteen major States, rural poverty

Table 7
Proportion of Population in BPL Households by Gender, Age and Rural-Urban Location All-India: 1993-94, 1999-2000

	1993-94		*1998-99*		*1999-2000*	
	Rural	*Urban*	*Rural*	*Urban*	*Rural*	*Urban*
Rural Males	45.43	34.45	38.66	42.31	31.17	35.55
Rural Females	46.85	36.08	39.96	45.64	32.63	37.34
Rural Persons	46.10	35.25	39.36	43.89	31.90	36.35
Urban Males	37.44	25.09	29.14	36.42	23.57	27.68
Urban Females	39.69	27.69	31.69	39.41	25.53	29.83
Urban Persons	38.51	26.33	30.37	37.84	24.51	28.76
Males	43.62	31.95	36.26	40.98	29.07	33.52
Females	45.22	33.96	37.94	44.25	30.76	35.47
Persons	44.37	32.96	37.13	42.54	29.90	34.42

Source: 1993-94: Results on Employment Situation in India, Fifth Quinquennial Survey, NSS 50th Round (July 1993-June 1994), *Sarvekshana*, Vol. 20, No. 1, July-September 1996.

1999-2000: Results on Employment-Unemployment in India, 1999-2000, NSS 55th Round, July 1999-June 2000.

prevalence ratios have declined over the 1990s. Of these eight states, except in three States (Andhra Pradesh, Bihar and Gujarat) where the decline in poverty ratios is less than 10 per cent (of the 1993-94 value), the decline has been sizeable: ranging from 19 per cent in Punjab to 51 per cent in Haryana;

(ii) In urban areas, a decline in poverty ratios is seen in eight of the fifteen states - besides all-India. Among these eight states (Andhra Pradesh, Gujarat, Karnataka, Maharashtra, Orissa, Rajasthan, Tamil Nadu and West Bengal) the order of decline was less than 5 per cent in Maharashtra and between 5 and 10 per cent in Andhra Pradesh and Orissa. In the other five states, the decline ranged between 20 and 25 per cent of the 1993-94 levels. As for the other seven states, the poverty ratios remained more or less unchanged in Bihar, Haryana, Karnataka, and Punjab, while in Uttar Pradesh, the increase was of the order of 6 per cent. In two states, Assam and Kerala, the poverty ratios increased by more than 13 per cent between 1994 and 2000. *Overall, the confirmation that we obtained from the Employment-Unemployment that, at the all-India level the prevalence*

of poverty in India had indeed declined over the 1990s is not uniformly present across all the major States. While in a majority of the 15 States analysed (albeit a majority of one) poverty ratios have indeed declined between 1993-94 and 1999-2000, in both the rural and the urban areas, in seven States poverty ratios have either remained unchanged or have even increased over the 1990s. This above result is, of course, in sharp contrast to the results of an across-theboard and sharp reduction in poverty obtained from the 55th Round Consumer Expenditure Survey. The only effective way of resolving this conflict of results from the two Surveys is to track the consequences of the two sources of non-comparability (with the 1993-94 Survey) that remain: (I) the use of an abridged consumer expenditure schedule in the 55th Round Employment-Unemployment Survey; and, (ii) the use of a 365-day reference period in respect of expenditure on durables as well as certain items of miscellaneous expenditure. At the all-India level, the combined effect of a reduction in the number of days worked in year (for males) and the growth in real daily wage-earnings to show a significant growth over the 1990s in average wage-earnings on a per capita basis (despite a reduction in worker-population ratios) and argued that such a result was consistent with a reduction in poverty at the all-India level. A parallel analysis at the level of individual states would offer another approach to resolve the conflicting results from the 55th Round Consumer Expenditure and Employment-Unemployment Surveys. The draft report on the 55th Round Employment-Unemployment Survey, by providing the data on average daily wage earnings of casual wage labourers at the level of individual States, has provided one key component for this exercise. However, in the absence of parallel, processed data from the 1993-94 Survey it is not possible to carry out the analysis presently.

PEOPE BELOW POVERTY LINE DECREASING

- 10% Improvement in 10 years
- Rural fast catching up with urban
- Has a rippling effect on the overall BPL of India
- Rural overall fairing better than Urban India

The World Bank's definition of the *poverty line,* for under developed countries, like *India,* is US$ 1/day/person or US $365 per year. As per this definition, more than 75% of all Indians are, probably, below the *poverty line!*

As per the Government of *India, poverty line* for the urban areas is Rs. 296 per month and for rural areas Rs. 276 per month, i.e. people in *India* who earn less than Rs. 10 per day. As per GOI, this amount will buy food equivalent to 2200 calories per day, medically enough, to prevent death. At this level of earning, even in a poor country like *India,* survival on Rs. 10 per day is a nightmare! This actually translates to Rs. 3650 per year or US $ 75 per year.

On what basis have our planners decided this definition of "*Poverty Line*"? Does it mean that the person will get enough food to stay alive? How and where is he or she supposed to cook it? What about the minimum needs in education, housing, health services, clothing,and other basic necessities? Are we supposed to live on pavements and sleep under trees from birth till death?

The minimum wages in *India,* vary from state to state and city to city, and average Rs. 1000 - 1250/month or Rs. 12,000 - 15,000/yr. Or US $ 250 - US $ 300/yr. India's per capita is US $ 440 per year. (China's is US $ 990).

If *India* could provide Roads, Electricity, TV's and Telephones in every village, it would improve, education, health, family planning, agriculture, animal husbandry, GDP and reduce migration from vllages to cities.

*Cost of employee = salary & wages + all allowances including housing + perks + retirement benefits.

PER CENT OF POPULATION LIVING UNDER THE POVERTY LINE

Though the middle class has gained from recent *positive economic developments, India* suffers from substantial *poverty.* According to the new World Bank's estimates on *poverty* based on 2005 data, *India* has 456 million people, 41.6% of its population, living below the new international *poverty line* of $1.25 (PPP) per day. The World Bank further estimates that

33% of the global poor now reside in *India*. Moreover, *India* also has 828 million people, or 75.6% of the population living below $2 a day, compared to 72.2% for Sub-Saharan Africa.

On the other hand, the *Planning Commission* of *India* uses its own criteria and has estimated that 27.5% of the population was living below the *poverty line* in 2004–2005, down from 51.3% in 1977–1978, and 36% in 1993-1994. The source for this was the 61st round of the National Sample Survey (NSS) and the criterion used was monthly per capita consumption expenditure below Rs. 356.35 for rural areas and Rs. 538.60 for urban areas. 75% of the poor are in rural areas, most of them are *daily wagers*, self-employed householders and landless labourers. Although Indian economy has grown steadily over the last two decades, its growth has been uneven when comparing different social groups, economic groups, geographic regions, and rural and urban areas.

Wealth distribution in India is fairly uneven, with the top 10% of income groups earning 33% of the income. Despite significant economic progress, 1/4 of the nation's population earns less than the government-specified *poverty threshold* of $0.40/day. Official figures estimate that 27.5% of Indians lived below the national *poverty line* in 2004-2005.[9] A 2007 report by the state-run National Commission for Enterprises in the Unorganised Sector (NCEUS) found that 25% of Indians, or 236 million people, lived on less than 20 rupees per day with most working in "informal labour sector with no job or social security, living in abject *poverty*."

Income inequality in *India* (*Gini coefficient:* 32.5 in year 1999-2000) is increasing. In addition, *India* has a higher rate of malnutrition among children under the age of three (46% in year 2007) than any other country in the world.

HUNGER: MAJOR THREAT IN 33 COUNTRIES

The 2008 Global Hunger Index (GHI) shows that the world has made slow progress in reducing food insecurity since 1990, with dramatic differences among regions and countries. In the nearly two decades since 1990, some regions—South and Southeast Asia, the Near East and North Africa, and Latin America and the Caribbean—have made significant headway in improving food security. Nevertheless, the GHI remains high in South Asia. The GHI is similarly high in Sub-Saharan Africa, where progress has been marginal since 1990.

The GHI level in the world as a whole remains serious. The countries with the most worrisome hunger status and the highest 2008 GHI scores are predominantly in Sub-Saharan Africa, with the Democratic Republic of Congo, Eritrea, Burundi, Niger, and Sierra Leone at the bottom of the list. Several dozen countries in various regions have GHI scores categorized as low. Hunger is closely tied to poverty, and countries with high levels of hunger are overwhelmingly low- or low-middle income countries. Sub-Saharan Africa and South Asia are the regions with the highest GHI scores and the highest poverty rates.

The recent advent of higher food prices has uneven effects across countries, depending on a range of factors, including whether countries are net importers or exporters of food. Among the countries for which the GHI is calculated, net cereal importers, for example, greatly out-number exporters, implying that many more countries combating hunger are likely to suffer from higher prices than benefit from them. Higher food prices have also caused violent and nonviolent protests in dozens of countries.

In this context of higher food prices, prospects for improving food and nutrition security do not appear favorable, given that at least 800 million people were food insecure even before the food price crisis hit. Higher food prices cut into poor households' food budgets, with particularly serious risks for undernourished infants and children. High prices also reduce the amount of food aid that donors can supply with a given amount of funds. Combating the food crisis will require more food aid for poor people; much greater investments in agriculture, especially the small farm sector; more investment in social protection programs and social sectors like education and health; reforms to create a fair world trading system;

changes to biofuel policies; measures to calm global food markets; better data collection and improved monitoring of the food and nutrition situation; and more support for non-governmental organizations that work on behalf of poor people in developing countries. the world is making slow progress in reducing food in-security. Given that the Millennium Development Goals are benchmarked against the year 1990, the GHI also tracks change since then. In the nearly two decades since 1990, some regions–South and Southeast Asia, the Near East and North Africa, and Latin America and the Caribbean—have made significant headway in improving food security. Nevertheless, the GHI remains high in South Asia. The GHI is at a similarly high level in Sub-Saharan Africa, where progress has been marginal since 1990. Food prices appear likely to remain high in the near term, leading to food and nutrition insecurity for poor people around the globe (von Braun *et al.* 2008). Particularly worrisome is the potential effect of the food price crisis on poor children. Rising food prices may prevent even more poor households from providing pregnant mothers and infants and young children with adequate nutrition, an outcome that can have irreversible long-term consequences for children's future health and productivity.

Overcoming these challenges to food security and nutrition will require actions to address emergency food needs as well as steps to improve longer-term agricultural productivity and strengthen safety nets. In this risky and changing environment, the GHI can be useful in highlighting key trends and the geographic areas of greatest vulnerability.

1. the prevalence of underweight in children under the age of five (indicating the proportion of children suffering from weight loss and/or reduced growth); and
2. the mortality rate of children under the age of five (partially reflects the fatal synergy between inadequate dietary intake and unhealthy environments). 969 million people live on less than US $ 1 a day and 17% of those live on less than US $0.50 a day.

Table 8
Some Facts about India

Earnings of Diffrent Types of Employees in India	*Converted into Rs./month*
Average cost of employee* in Air-*India*	Rs. 53,000
Average cost of employee* in MARUTI UDYOG	Rs. 24,000
Average cost of employee* in the MUMBAI MUNICIPAL CORP.	Rs. 16,000
Minimum starting salary in the FIRE Dept. in Mumbai	Rs. 7,000
Average earning of an Indian - US$ 440 per year or about (This is based on a GDP of US$ 440 billion and 1 billion people)	Rs. 1,727
Minimum earning required, as per WORLD BANK, to live at above *poverty line*, for underdeveloped countries like India, China etc, about US$ 1.0 per day or US$ 30 per month	Rs. 1,410
MINIMUM WAGES, as per Government of *India*, for all the States, about Rs. 40 to 60 per day per person, average about Rs. 50 per day. For 25 days per month	Rs. 1,250
POVERTY LINE definition, as per Government of *India*, see below for explanation, at Rs. 10 per day, per person, approx.	Rs. 300
Other related & relevant data	In millions, people
Number of people, in *India*, who are below poverty line	About 300 million (30 Cr.)
Number of people, in *India*, who work in the organized Public Sector, i.e. with the Central and State Governmen	About 19 million (1.9 Cr.)
Number of people, in *India*, who work in the organized Private Sector	About 8 million (0.8 Cr.)
Number of people, in *India*, who work in the unorganized Sector	About 320 million (32 Cr.)
Number of people, in *India*, who are unemployed approximately	About 321 million (30 Cr.)
Number of JOBS which need to be created every year, to fulfill the aspirations of the people of *India*	About 10 million/yr. (1 Cr.)
Number of people BORN every year in *India* (China is only 10 million per year	About 27 million/yr. (2.7 Cr.)
Number of people, in *India*, who are below 35 years of age	About 700 million (70 Cr.)

Poverty leads to undernutrition and food insecurity by limiting poor people's access to food. At the same time, because undernourished people are less productive and child malnutrition has severe, per manent consequences for physical and intellectual development, hunger can lead to or help entrench poverty. Thus poverty and hunger can become entwined in a vicious cycle, and levels and trends in these indicators can be expected to be similar. Indeed, the table on page 20 shows that countries with high levels of hunger are overwhelmingly low- or low-middle-income countries. All countries with extremely alarming levels of hunger are low-income countries. Rising food prices intensify the Hunger Crisis

Due to the sheer size of the population living in poverty, India is strategically significant in the global efforts to alleviate poverty and to achieve the Millennium Development Goal of halving the world's poverty by 2015. Microfinance has been present in India in one form or another since the 1970s and is now widely accepted as an effective poverty alleviation strategy. Over the last five years, the microfinance industry has achieved significant growth in part due to the participation of commercial banks. Despite this growth, the poverty situation in India continues to be challenging.

THE POVERTY LINE IS A STARVATION LINE

The *poverty line* in *India* measures only the most basic calorie intake, recording not nutrition but only the satiation of hunger. At present the *poverty line* stands at Rs 368 and Rs 559 per person per month for rural and urban areas, just about enough to buy 650 grams of foodgrains every day. A nutritious diet itself would cost around Rs 573 per capita per month, let alone the cost of securing other basic needs. When such an inclusive measure of *poverty* is used, as many as 68-84% of Indians would qualify as poor

> *"I have learnt to seek my happiness by limiting my desires rather than in attempting to satisfy them."*
>
> *John Stuart MilL*

When defining *poverty* in *India,* the Planning Commission seems to be taking J S Mill quite literally. For decades it has followed a limited definition of *poverty*. The official *poverty line* in *India* is based only on calories and accounts for little else but the satiation of hunger. It would have been more accurate to call it the "starvation *line*".

This limited definition has allowed successive governments to claim great achievements in the percentage reduction of *poverty,* though very little absolute reduction in the number of poor. Using an expanded definition that factors in other basic human needs, minimum living standards and access to public services, a majority of Indians are, in fact, still extremely poor.

How *India* defines *poverty* will determine the nature and content of public policy related to eliminating *poverty*. A discussion of the definition of *poverty* in *India* is also relevant to an international audience because the one-dollar-a-day *poverty line* adopted by the United Nations borrows substantially from the Indian *poverty line.*

DRAWING THE LINE

The idea of defining *poverty* in terms of a *poverty line* was first proposed during the Indian Labour Conference in 1957. A Working Group under the Planning Commission then stipulated a calorie-based *poverty line* of Rs 20 per person per month. In 1979, a Task Force was assigned by the Planning Commission to reconsider this definition of *poverty*. After much deliberation, it too fixed a *poverty line* largely based on calories. It delineated Rs 49 and Rs 57 per person per month as rural and urban *poverty* lines respectively at 1973 prices. This *poverty line* continues to be used to this day except for adjustments based on inflation. In 1999-2000, the *poverty* lines after adjusting for inflation were Rs 327 and Rs 454 in rural and urban areas respectively. As of December 2005, these figures stand at approximately Rs 368 and Rs 559 per person per month for rural and urban areas.

This official *poverty line* in *India* is, however, woefully unsatisfactory. Apart from factoring in about 650 grams of foodgrains every day, the *line* makes little provision for the other essentials of life such as health, shelter and clothing. The average Indian does not have access to these basic needs. Such conditions point to the absurdity of India's aspiration of joining the league of developed nations by 2020.

It is striking to note that despite what is obviously a low threshold of *poverty*, in 1973 nearly 55% of the population or 321 million people were below the *poverty line* (see Table 8). In 1993, even after 20 years of the State trying to alleviate *poverty*, the number of poor remained at almost the same level, at 320 million. By 2004, the number declined to about 250 million.

However, this is hardly an achievement, as the rate of decline of *poverty* since 1973 has been at a dismal 0.81% per annum. Considering that the economy grew at over 5% over the same period, such a low rate of decline of *poverty* is unacceptable. It is not surprising that the Planning Commission and the government prefer not to talk about these figures and instead dwell on the fact that the percentage of poor has declined to 26%. Many experts dispute even this claim. They suggest that this "decline" is the result of statistical jugglery and not actual fact.

Table 9
Percentage and Number of Poor in India since 1973

Year	*Percentage of Poor*	*Number of Poor (millions)*	*Annual Real Rate of Decline in the Number of Poor ^*
1973-74	54.9 %	321	4.0
1977-78	51.3 %	329	- 0.59 %
1983	44.5 %	323	0.31 %
1987-88	38.9 %	307	1.25 %
1993-94	36.0 %	320	- 0.70 %
1999-00	26.1 %	260	3.40 %

* As per the Expert Group Methodology

^ A negative rate of decline means the number of poor increased

Source: National Institute of Rural Development (2004); *Rural Development Statistics*, 2002-03.

BROADENING THE VISION

If Vision 2020 of a developed *India* is to become a reality, a proper definition of *poverty* is vital. By that time, the State needs to ensure that every citizen not only gets at least two adequate and wholesome meals a day, but also has access to all the basic amenities required to lead a modestly comfortable life with dignity. The present inadequate definition of *poverty* has ensured that all the policies aimed at alleviating *poverty* aim much too low by focussing on eliminating hunger rather than eliminating *poverty* as a whole.

A good example of this is the National Rural Employment Guarantee Scheme (NREGS), which guarantees one able-bodied member of each family work at a wage of Rs. 60 a day. Even if this person works on all 30 days of a month, he/she earns only Rs. 1,800. For a family of five, that amounts to Rs 360 per person, which is exactly what the rural *poverty line* is right now. Therefore, even a scheme released with as much fanfare as the NREGS at best only ensures that each person in the family consumes a certain quantity of foodgrains. It guarantees little else. Moreover, the guarantee is only for 100 days in a year, leaving the poor to fend for themselves for the rest of the 265 days.

The present ceiling on *poverty* is so low that even if the government were to hand out enough money to each poor family to buy enough food to be just above the official *poverty line*, it would only cost around Rs 570 billion per year. This amount is only 25% of what it costs to maintain the entire bureaucracy of *India* (around Rs. 2,270 billion every year).

The sad fact remains that despite a conveniently low notion of *poverty* adopted by the government, one in every four Indians is poor. This is abysmal, but the truth is that the situation is much worse. When we develop a *poverty line* based on all basic needs, we find that over two-thirds of the Indian population is *poverty*-stricken.

THREE PROBLEMS WITH THE POVERTY LINE

As we have argued, the definition of *poverty* based just on the caloric norm is unacceptable. Many persons who are above the *poverty line* may in fact be getting less than the stipulated daily calories. In addition, despite the increase in agricultural production, the per capita availability of cereals is about the same since 1981, whereas the per capita availability of pulses has declined from 37.5 grams in 1981 to 28.2 grams in 2003.

Therefore, the present official *poverty line*, which was only supposed to ensure a certain calorie intake, fails even on that single front. The *line* is based on the norm that the average person in urban and rural *India* should be able to consume between 2,100 to 2,400 calories. In 1979, when the *poverty line* was formed, this was indeed the case. However, currently (1999-2000), people who are just above the official *poverty line* do not meet this norm. This group consumes an average of 1,868 calories in rural areas and 1,912 calories in urban areas. Therefore, these groups fall short of the caloric norm by 22% in rural areas and 9% in urban areas.

Secondly, the current caloric standard is not only an inadequate norm, it is also an insufficient nutritional norm. Firstly, the caloric standard set by the Planning Commission is a glaring under-stipulation. The Indian Council of Medical Research (ICMR) prescribes 3,800 calories for an adult male doing heavy activity and 2,925 calories for an adult female carrying out heavy activity. This makes it clear that for the millions of poor unskilled wage labourers in *India* who do heavy manual labour every day, a stipulation of 2,100-2,400 calories in urban and rural areas is grossly insufficient.

More significantly, it is important to go beyond a simple caloric standard, because the body also needs proteins, fat, minerals, iron and vitamins. Nutrition deficiency is a leading cause of disease. According to the UNICEF, "Malnutrition limits development and the capacity to learn. It also costs lives: about 50% of all childhood deaths are attributed to malnutrition." A nutritious diet is a fundamental need of the human body and this must not be ignored when formulating a *poverty line*.

Thirdly, as argued above, the *poverty line* not only ignores important nutritional needs but also the other basic needs of life: shelter, clothing, healthcare, sanitation, drinking water and equal opportunity education.

In 1979, when the present *poverty line* was defined, the expenditure on non-food items of the group of people who consumed over 2,100-2,400 calories in urban and rural areas was calculated. In addition to the total expenditure on calories, this non-food expenditure was also included in the *poverty line*. However, such a method is akin to suggesting that whatever the poor spend on non-food items is "enough".

Instead, one needs to analyse what is consumed through non-food expenditure and verify whether it meets the basic needs of a human being. Therefore the amount of non-food expenditure for a poor person should be based on norms, not on behaviour. For example, the latest national sample survey on consumer expenditure shows that those who are just above the *poverty line* in rural *India* spend only around Rs 8 per month on medical care. This is grossly insufficient.

REDEFINING POVERTY IN INDIA

The argument that India's *poverty line* needs to be substantially redefined is not a new one. Even the Planning Commission recognises this urgent need. Despite this "recognition" no new norms exist. Most of these norms can be derived scientifically, so the only plausible explanation for why the *poverty line* has not been redefined can be that raising the *poverty* bar higher will compound the task of India's policymakers and economic planners. It therefore remains at a ridiculously low level to enable claims of achievement and to avoid deployment of resources to areas and people who deserve them the most.

The Centre for Policy Alternatives has attempted to outline a new *poverty line*. It used the Cost of Basic Needs (CBN) approach to set norms for all basic needs and then attribute a cost to achieving that norm. We derived a new *poverty line* by adding up these costs. This is a more inclusive definition than the calorie-based *poverty line*.

As much as 68.5% of India's population is below this more inclusive *poverty line*. That is over two-and-a-half times the present official *poverty* rate of 26.1%. The situation in rural *India* is worse, with over 84% of the people below this more realistic *poverty line*.

We calculated that the total expenditure to live a life with the minimum basic needs of nutrition, healthcare, clothing, shelter etc. comes to about Rs. 840 per month per person in *India.* This is almost twice the current urban *poverty line* for the country. Table 10 shows the details of this cost calculation.

Table 10
Cost of Basic Needs

Basic Need	*Cost Per Capita Per Month (Rs.)*
Nutritious diet	573
Healthcare	30
Electricity consumption	35
Kerosene consumption	20
Clothing	17
Miscellaneous expenditure	164
Total*	840

* The total is Rs 839. We round it off to Rs 840 for convenience.

Source: Calculated using various sources. For details, refer to 'Redefining *Poverty*: A New *Poverty Line* for a New *India*' at *www.cpasind.com* .

Table 11
Poverty Ratio Using a Holistic Poverty Line

Area	*Percentage*
Rural	84.6
Urban	42.4
Weighted average	68.8

Calculated using GoI (2001a): *NSS Report No. 454: Household Consumer Expenditure in India , 1999-2000— Key Results* , NSSO, New Delhi ; GoI (2005b): "Statistics, Index Numbers", Labour Bureau, October 2005; and a *poverty line* of Rs. 840.

Although the *poverty line* of Rs 840 per month is more inclusive of the basic needs of human life, it still only partially reveals the true state of *poverty* in *India.* There are some basic needs that cannot be quantified in monetary terms. Therefore, in addition to the *poverty line,* a proper definition of who is poor should also include "access parameters". Some of the crucial parameters that must be included in the definition of *poverty* are:·

- 37.7% of Indian households do not have access to a nearby water source.
- 49% do not have proper shelter.

- 69.5% do not have access to suitable toilets.
- 85.2% of Indian villages do not have a secondary school. 43% of Indian villages are not connected to an all-weather road.

Therefore, as we define it, a person is poor in *India* if he or she has a monthly per capita expenditure that is less than Rs 840 or does not have access to drinking water, proper shelter, sanitation, quality secondary education or an all-weather road with public transport.

RAISING THE BAR

The present definition of *poverty* grossly misrepresents the real situation. It is inappropriate to use a simple caloric measure as the yardstick. The responsibility of the state exceeds this manifold. *India* needs to upgrade the concept of food security to that of nutritious food security. In addition, it should also be the right of every Indian citizen to have access to safe shelter, sanitation, healthcare, education and clothing. When planning policy for the poor, these benchmarks should be the target.This *poverty line* should be separately calculated for each state to account for regional differences in taste, clothing requirement, housing requirement, and others. It is also important to understand that the norms of basic needs and what may be regarded as luxuries, evolve over time. If one tap in a bathroom is considered a minimum norm now, in a few years, as more and more households fulfil this norm, the norm may be upgraded to include a flush toilet; or, by 2020, piped gas for cooking may become the norm. To account for such changes in established norms, the *poverty line* should be updated every five years. The present *poverty line* is updated only to account for an increase in prices. In the long run this distorts the picture of *poverty.India* needs to urgently revisit its concept of *poverty*. The present unrealistically low *poverty line* only serves the purpose of making the government and its development efforts-or the lack of it-look good. If the State is as committed to addressing the ills of *poverty* as it claims to be, it should start by redefining the *poverty line*. This will ensure that the government gets its priorities straight and is able to target policy effectively.Based on our proposed *poverty line* of Rs. 840 per month, the State should try to ensure that a typical household of five people is able to earn around Rs. 50,000 per year, or about Rs. 4,200 per month. This family should have access to a sturdy house with basic amenities such as a toilet connected to a sewerage system and electrical fittings. Access to water should be within 10-15 metres if not, ideally, within the home. The children of the family should be able to access their constitutional right to education. Moreover, the State needs to go beyond offering an accessible school and ensure that the schooling guarantees each student equal opportunities in life. Such a household, where the most fundamental of needs are met, should be the minimum ideal that the State must aim for. This calls for a paradigm shift in the sphere of development policy in *India.* The shift is overdue and imperative.

In respect of rural areas in six States (Assam, Karnataka, Madhya Pradesh, Orissa, Tamil Nadu and West Bengal) *the poverty prevalence ratios in 19992000 are higher* than in 1993-94 while in Maharashtra, there has been virtually no change in the poverty ratios between 1993-94 and 1999-2000.

At the all-India level, and in eight of the fifteen major States, rural poverty prevalence ratios have declined over the 1990s. Of these eight states, except in three States (Andhra Pradesh, Bihar and Gujarat) where the decline in poverty ratios is less than 10 per cent (of the 1993-94 value), the decline has been sizeable: ranging from 19 per cent in Punjab to 51 per cent in Haryana;

ii. In urban areas, a decline in poverty ratios is seen in eight of the fifteen states - besides all-India. Among these eight states (Andhra Pradesh, Gujarat, Karnataka, Maharashtra, Orissa, Rajasthan, Tamil Nadu and West Bengal) the order of decline was less than 5 per cent in Maharashtra and between 5 and 10 per cent in Andhra Pradesh and Orissa. In the other five states, the decline ranged between 20 and 25 per cent of the 1993-94 levels.

As for the other seven states, the poverty ratios remained more or less unchanged in Bihar, Haryana, Karnataka, and Punjab, while in Uttar Pradesh, the increase was of the order of 6 per cent. In two states, Assam and Kerala, the poverty ratios increased by more than 13 per cent between 1994 and 2000.

Data from the National Survey of Families and Households are used by the University of Nebraska-Lincoln to compare the psychological well-being of the rural and urban poor. Overall, the urban poor are higher in perceived health than the rural poor, although no differences are apparent in happiness or depression. Significant interactions are present between rural/urban poverty and sex, race, and family status. The psychological well-being of poor African Americans is higher in rural than urban areas, whereas the well-being of poor whites is higher in urban than rural areas. This trend is especially pronounced for depression among males. In addition, single men without children have especially high depression scores in rural areas, whereas married women without children have especially low depression scores in urban areas. The results are interpreted in terms of the environmental quality of inner-city neighborhoods and attitudes toward poverty in urban and rural communities.

ECONOMIC FREEDOM NEEDED TO ALLEVIATE POVERTY AROUND THE WORLD

Robert A. Lawson is professor of economics and George H. Moor Chair in the School of Management at Capital University in Ohio. He is co-author of Economic Freedom of the World: 2002 Annual Report, produced jointly by the Fraser Institute and the Cato Institute.

Both as an ideology and as a practical system, communism has utterly failed to deliver the goods. Eastern European nations are now rushing to become members of the European Union, and China is undertaking market-oriented reforms. Cuba and North Korea stand as the last remaining communist stalwarts.

One would think that this failure of communist central planning would have unleashed a groundswell of support for its main ideological alternative: economic freedom or market capitalism. But as the anti-globalization protestors in Seattle and at last week's G8 meeting in Canada demonstrate, economic freedom still has a long way to go to win over the hearts and minds of many people.

Robert A. Lawson is professor of economics and George H. Moor Chair in the School of Management at Capital University in Ohio. He is co-author of Economic Freedom of the World: 2002 Annual Report, produced jointly by the Fraser Institute and the Cato Institute.

These protesters believe that free markets lead to widespread poverty, greater gaps between the rich and the poor, and environmental degradation. Only strong government planning through trade tariffs, expansive welfare states, and strict labor and environmental rules can protect the poor of this world from the ravaging forces of the market. These people are dead wrong.

A new study, co-authored by James Gwartney and myself, was recently released by a consortium of think tanks, which includes the Cato Institute in the United States. This publication, Economic Freedom of the World: 2002 Annual Report, presents an economic freedom index for 123 countries. Based on 37 data components drawn from a multitude of sources, this index measures the degree to which nations are pursing policies consistent with economic freedom or market capitalism. To score highly on this index, a nation should have low government spending and taxes, sound property rights and legal system, sound money, liberal trade policies, and few government regulations. Economic freedom means that each individual plays the primary role in his economic life, not the government or central plan.

The most economically free nation in the world remains Hong Kong followed by Singapore and the United States. The rankings of other major economies are the United Kingdom (4th), Canada (8th), Germany (15th), Japan (24th) Taiwan (30th), France (38th), Mexico (66th), and India (73rd). Most of the lowest ranked nations are in Africa and Latin America. Botswana has the best record for an African nation, tied for 38th with six other nations including France and South Korea. Chile, with the best record in Latin America, was tied with three other nations at 15th. Three former communist countries are in the bottom 10: Russia (116th), Ukraine (119th), and Romania (114th) all did worse than communist China (101st). Data for North Korea and Cuba are not available.

The study also shows that economic freedom is strongly linked with both higher levels of income and faster rates of economic growth. The people living in the top one-fifth of the most free countries enjoy an average income of $23,450 and a growth rate in the 1990s of 2.56 per cent per year; in contrast, the bottom one-fifth in the rankings had an average income of just $2,556 and a -0.85 per cent growth rate in the 1990s.

That economic freedom leads to more and faster wealth creation is no longer a controversial argument. But what of the argument that market capitalism leaves the poor behind? In fact, the poor gain a lot from economic freedom. The share of income going to the poorest 10% of the population is completely unrelated to economic freedom. But poor people are much better off with economic freedom. The poorest 10% of the population have an average income of just $728 in the least free countries compared with over $7000 in the most free countries. Simply put, it is much better to be poor in a free, rich country than an unfree, poor country.

Free people live longer too. The life expectancy of people living in the most free nations is fully 20 years longer than for people in the least free countries. This is quite literally the difference between knowing your grandchildren or not.

Other studies confirm that environmental quality is likely to be enhanced as poor countries become wealthy enough, through economic freedom, to invest in environmental amenities like water treatment plants.

People who are concerned about poverty and environmental issues around the globe must realize that economic freedom and the resulting economic prosperity, not oppressive government taxation and regulation, represent the best hope for the poor and the environment alike.

Also of interest

In general, the states, which were under the zamindari regimes, had experienced relatively ineffective agrarian and land reforms and thereafter marginal impact of the green revolution, have been losers.

Despite a marginal reduction in the number of days worked by male workers-per usual (ps+ss) Status worker-and the reduction in crude worker-population ratios, the sizeable and broad-based growth in average daily wage earnings in real terms and the rise in the number of days worked by female worker was adequate to raise real average wage earnings per capita at over 2.5 per cent per annum in both rural and urban India over the period 1993-94 to 1999-20005. This result was consistent with a decline, over the same period, in poverty ratios in both rural and urban India. However, given the fact that the results of the 55th Round Consumer Expenditure are still mired in controversies regarding possible "contamination" of results with a 30-day reference period by the simultaneous convassing of expenditure details on a 7-day reference period, it would be useful to examine the evidence on this issue from the Employment-Unemployment Surveys. For reasons discussed in the Introductory section, such an exercise would be valuable despite the residual problems of comparability (with the results of the 1993-94 survey) that would still remain. At the all-India level, the results are clear and unambiguous. Except in respect of girl children in urban India, there is a definite and unambiguous decline in the proportion of population in households that lie below the poverty line. The same holds true, in terms of the proportion of households below the poverty, for all the types of households distinguished by reference to their principal means of livelihood. Particularly significant is the 7.5 percentage point decline in the incidence of poverty for agricultural labour households and a 6 percentage point decline for other labour (Annual wage-earnings per capita (at constant 1993-94 prices) for 1993-94 and 1999-2000 imply an average growth at 2.35 per cent per annum. The estimates of poverty prevalence rates based on the NSS 55th Round Employment-Unemployment Survey show a reduction of close to eight percentage points in the proportion of agricultural labour households below the poverty line.) households. There is a clear and sizeable decline in the poverty prevalence ratios among agricultural labour households and other labour households would survive any adjustment for use of a 365-day reference period for durables etc. in the NSS 55th Round Survey. By the same token, the decline in the incidence of poverty in the self-employed households is much less striking. Equally important to note is the fact that, the order of decline in the proportion of population below the poverty line (between 2 and 3 percentage points) is much less than what has been claimed on the basis of the 55th Round Consumer expenditure survey.

Overall, at the all-India level, the results of 55th Round the Employment-Unemployment Survey confirms the direction of change: the prevalence of poverty has indeed declined over the 1990s. However, the order of decline is much less than that indicated by the 55th Round Consumer Expenditure Survey.

IS THE ABOVE CONCLUSION ALSO VALID FOR THE MAJOR STATES INDIVIDUALLY?

To answer this question, we present in Table 12, estimates of poverty prevalence ratios for all-India and 15 major States for 1993-94 and 1999-2000 based on the size distribution now available from the 55th Round Employment-Unemployment Survey..

i. In respect of rural areas in six States (Assam, Karnataka, Madhya Pradesh, Orissa, Tamil Nadu and West Bengal) the poverty prevalence ratios in 1999-2000 are higher than in 1993-94 while in Maharashtra, there has been virtually no change in the poverty ratios between 1993-94 and 1999-2000.At the all-India level, and in eight of the fifteen major States, rural poverty prevalence ratios have declined over the 1990s. Of these eight states, except in three States (Andhra Pradesh, Bihar and Gujarat) where the decline in poverty ratios is less than 10 per cent (of the 1993-94 value), the decline has been sizeable: ranging from 19 per cent in Punjab to 51 per cent in Haryana;ii. In urban areas, a decline in poverty ratios is seen in eight of the fifteen states-besides all-India. Among these eight states (Andhra Pradesh, Gujarat, Karnataka, Maharashtra, Orissa, Rajasthan, Tamil Nadu and West Bengal) the order of decline was less than 5 per cent in Maharashtra and between 5 and 10 per cent in Andhra Pradesh and Orissa. In the other five states, the decline ranged between 20 and 25 per cent of the 1993-94 levels. As for the other seven states, the poverty ratios remained more or less unchanged in Bihar, Haryana, Karnataka, and Punjab, while in Uttar Pradesh, the increase was of the order of 6 per cent. In two states, Assam and Kerala,the poverty ratios increased by more than 13 per cent between 1994 and 2000. Overall, the confirmation that we obtained from the Employment-Unemployment that, at the all-India level the prevalence of poverty in India had indeed declined over the 1990s is not uniformly present across all the major States. While in a majority of the 15 States analysed (albeit a majority of one) poverty ratios have indeed declined between 1993-94 and 1999-2000, in both the rural and the urban areas, in seven States poverty ratios have either remained unchanged or have even increased over the 1990s. This above result is, of course, in sharp contrast to the results of an across-theboard and sharp reduction in poverty obtained from the 55th Round Consumer Expenditure Survey. The only effective way of resolving this conflict of results from the two Surveys is to track the consequences of the two sources of non-comparability (with the 1993-94 Survey) that remain:

(i) the use of an abridged consumer expenditure schedule in the 55th Round Employment-Unemployment Survey; and,

(ii) the use of a 365-day reference period in respect of expenditure on durables as well as certain items of miscellaneous expenditure.,At the all-India level, the combined effect of a reduction in the number of days worked in year (for males) and the growth in real daily wage-earnings to show a significant growth over the 1990s in average wage-earnings on a per capita basis (despite a reduction in worker-population ratios) and argued that such a result was consistent with a reduction in poverty at the all-India level. A parallel analysis at the level of individual states would offer another approach to resolve the conflicting results from the 55th Round Consumer Expenditure and Employment-Unemployment Surveys. The draft report on the 55th Round Employment-Unemployment Survey, by providing the data on average daily wage earnings of casual wage labourers at the level of individual States, has provided one key component for this exercise. However, in the absence of parallel, processed data from the 1993-94 Survey it is not possible to carry out the analysis presently.We may now summarise our principal results. First, revisions based on the Provisional Population Totals from the 2001Population Census raises the rate of growth of aggregate work force between 1994and 2000 to a little over 1 per cent per annum with only a marginal reduction in the absolute size of female work force in rural areas. Second, while the decline in worker-population ratios in the younger age groups between 1993-94 and 1999-2000 represents a continuation of a longer-term trend reflecting a beneficial rise in student-population ratios, in the 25 and above age groups the decline in WPRs in the 1990s is getting exaggerated by the fact that, in a number of cases, the 1993-94 levels are outliers when seen against the WPRs from the earlier quinquennial Surveys. In other cases, either the variations are by and large within margins of sampling fluctuations (rural and men in the age-groups between 30 and 49) or, as in the case of both rural and urban women, they largely reflecting declines in work participation on the subsidiary status.

(iii) The reduction in the number of workers in the agriculture and allied activities is more modest than indicated in our earlier and is seen to be concentrated among women workers.Fourth, a misclassification of the work force in repair services earlier had:

- (i) exaggerated the growth of work force in the Trade, Hotels and Restaurants sector;
- (ii) moderated the growth in employment in the Manufacturing sector; and,

(iii) exaggerated the decline in the share of the Community, Social and Personal Services (taken as a group) in the total work force.

(iv) in relation to the industrial distribution of the work force in 1961,the pace of decline in the share of agriculture (and parallely, gains in the shares of other sectors) has been faster between 1994 and 2000 relative to the change between 1961 and 1994.

(v) a noteworthy change during the 1990s has been the reduction in the absolute number of workers in personal services by over 1.2 million in the aggregate.Given that this segment has been traditionally low-productivity-low income-perworker sector, this reduction in the size and share of the personal services sector must be viewed as a positive development in the employment situation in the nineteen nineties.

(vi) in terms of occupation structure, despite a sizeable reduction of such workers in the total work force, India still remains a land of Farmers, Fishermen, Hunters and Loggers. At the other end of the skill spectrum, Professional and Technical Workers and Administrative, Executive and Managerial Workers together formed less than 7 per cent of the work force at the beginning of the year 2000.

(vii) revisions in the estimates of work force consequent on the 2001Population Census have tended to dampen the growth in labour productivity (relative to our earlier estimates). While the re-allocation of repair-service workers to the Manufacturing sector accentuated the dampening of labour productivity growth, it has raised the labour productivity growth in the Trade, Hotels and Restaurants and the Community, Social and Personal services sectors.

(viii) the result in our earlier paper of a wide spread growth in real average daily average wage earnings of casual labourers, not being affected by the changes in the size and structure of the work force, continues to remain valid. Further, except for rural females engaged in manual work in other agricultural work (other than cultivation) and for manual work in agriculture as a whole, the evidence from the NSS Employment-Unemployment Surveys offers no support at all for the hypothesis of a slow down in the rate of growth of average daily wage earnings of adult casual labourers during the 1990s relative to that between 1983 and 1994. Finally, at the all-India level, the results of the 55th Round Employment-Unemployment confirms that the poverty ratios have indeed declined over the 1990s. However, at the level of individual states, the results are more mixed. While in eight out of fifteen major States, poverty ratios have indeed declined over the 1990s, in seven others it has remained either unchanged or have even increased. In all-cases, even at the all-India level, the order of decline (wherever that has materialised) in the poverty prevalence rates revealed by the Employment-Unemployment Survey has been significantly smaller than that revealed by the 55th Round Consumer Expenditure Survey. Clearly, there is scope for further work in terms of tracking the consequences for poverty of the two remaining sources of non-comparability with the results of the 1993-94 Survey.

NOTES

(1) Estimates of total Male and Female Population as on 1.1.94 and 1.1.2000 (the mid-points of Survey year 1993-94 and 1999-2000) are obtained by interpolation from Population Census estimates for 1st March 1991 and 1st March 2001, which are (in '000): Males: 1991=439,230, 2001: 531,277; and Females: 1991: 407,072 and 2001: 495,738. RGI, Census of

India 2001, Paper 1 of 2001, Provisional Population Total, March 2001.

(2) The rural-urban split of the male and female population for 1993-94 are assumed to be same as given in Visaria (1998) and for 1999-2000 are obtained by interpolation from estimates for 1st March 1999 and 1st March 2000 contained in RGI (1996).

(3) Crude Worker-Population ratios on the usual (principal plus subsidiary status) for rural males, rural females, urban males and urban females are drawn from, respectively, Sarvekshana, vol. 20, no. 1, July-September 1996 for 1993-94 and, Report on Employment-Unemployment in India 1999-2000, Key Results, NSS 55th Round, July 1999-2000, December 2000.inferior training and skill, and (e) poor health and nutrition. Unemployment is the major cause of widespread poverty in the UDCs. Before examining the evidence from the 55th Round Employment:

Unemployment Survey on the issue of changes in the poverty-prevalence rates over the 1990s, it would be useful to summarise the changes in unemployment and under employment drawing on our earlier paper. The key results are:

(i) An increase in the current daily status unemployment rate in three of the four population segments, with urban women as the sole exception. The increase in the daily status unemployment rate has been the steepest for rural males (29 per cent): an increase which could well be due to a change in the status composition of the work force (a rise in the proportion of casual labourers and a reduction in the share of the self-employed) and a conversion of the underemployment of the erstwhile self-employed into open unemployment of the casual labourers;ii. a reduction in the unemployment rates on the usual principal status for the educated in almost all the four population segments; and,

(ii) an increase in self-perceived underemployment captured by a reduction, over the 1990s, in the proportion of usual status workers who had not sought additional work. However, much of this is reflected in an increase in the proportion of usual status workers who sought additional work on "Some days" rather than on "most days". Also, even among those adding to the proportion of workers who sought additional work on "most days", the principal reason was the need to supplement income rather than lack of work.

6

SMALL SCALE INDUSTIRES & AGRO AND RURAL INDUSTRIES

ROLE AND FUNCTIONS

The Ministry of Small Scale Industries & Agro and Rural Industries is the Nodal Ministry for policy formulation, promotion, development and protection of small-scale industries. It also monitors the implementation of these policies. The Ministry was created on the 14th October, 1999. This puts the SSI sector in focus.

The Ministry of Small Scale Industries & Agro and Rural Industries designs and implements the policies through its field organisations for promotion and growth of small and tiny enpterprises, including the coir industries. The Ministry also coordinates with other Ministries/Departments on behalf of the Small-Scale Industries (SSI) sector.

The rural industry continues to play a significant role in the expansion of employment, improvement in productivity and earnings, and poverty reduction in many non-industrialized countries; this is particularly the case in India.

Large-scale *rural* unemployment is one of the major factors that drives most underdeveloped and developing countries to growth. Generally, these economies suffer from the problem of a high *rural* population that is dependent mainly on agriculture for their livelihood. A large part of this population can be substantially utilised in non-farm activities without affecting the agricultural output.

The linking factor between economic development and poverty alleviation in any economy is employment generation. As a greater proportion of the *rural* people in *India* is below the poverty line, any intervention geared towards poverty alleviation must focus on bucolic *India.* The urban areas have better employment opportunities and the poverty in those areas is not as serious as in the *rural* areas. Therefore, effective measures need to be taken to reduce *rural* poverty. In this context, it is important to note that the promotion of the agricultural sector alone will not be enough to achieve the desired results, as it can not absorb the abundant labour force in the *rural* areas and can not attain a high economic growth rate.

Labour being the most abundant resource of the *rural* areas, any programme for *rural* employment generation must maximise its productive use. Also the experiences of many advanced countries demonstrate that industry is an engine of growth. Thus, taking into account the these issues and the extent of poverty prevailing in *rural India,* the creation of employment opportunities through *rural* industrialisation for a faster growth rate of *rural* areas is essential.

The role of industry in *rural* economy is very obvious. The Indian *rural* economy is suffering from mass poverty, which is a consequence of unemployment and the resultant disparities of income and wealth. *Rural industries* are labour-intensive by their very nature. These *industries* provide the maximum employment per unit of capital invested; the labour-capital ratio in these *industries* is higher than that of in large-scale *industries.* A corollary of higher employment potential of *rural industries* is the higher output capacity per unit of capital. Just as a labour-surplus economy tries to maximise the employment potentiality of available capital resources, it also tends to maximise the output potentiality of available capital resources. *Rural industries* with a higher output-generating capacity per unit of capital offer a very useful technique of growth to the developing agrarian economies.

The Indian Agriculture Industry is on the brink of a revolution that will modernize the entire food chain, as the total food production in *India* is likely to double in the next ten years.

As per recent studies the turnover of the total food market is approximately Rs.250000 crores (US $ 69.4 billion) out of which value-added food products comprise Rs.80000 crores (US $ 22.2 billion). The Government of *India* has also approved proposals for joint ventures, foreign collaborations, industrial licenses and 100% export oriented units envisaging an investment of Rs.19100 crores (US $ 4.80 billion) out of which foreign investment is over Rs. 9100 crores (US $ 18.2 Billion). The agricultural food industry also assumes significance owing to India's sizable agrarian economy, which accounts for over 35% of GDP and employs around 65 per cent of the population. Both in terms of foreign investment and number of joint-ventures/foreign collaborations, the consumer food segment has the top priority. The other attractive features of the indian agro industry that have the capacity to lure foreigners with promising benefits are the deep sea fishing, aqua culture, milk and milk products, meat and poultry segments.

Excellent export prospects, competitive pricing of agricultural products and standards that are internationally comparable has created trade opportunities in the agro industry. This further has enabled the Indian Agriculture Industry Portal to serve as a means by which every exporter and importer of *India* and abroad, can fulfill their requirements and avail the benefits of agro related buy sell trade leads and other business opportunities.

This Indian agro industry revolution brings along the opportunities of profitable investment and agriculture-industry-*india*.com provides you the B2B platform with agro related *catalogs, trade leads, exporters & importers directory* etc. that help you make your way to profit easy.

To lead yourself to the destination of profit through the Indian Agriculture Industry, know maximum about the *EXIM policy, programs & schemes, price policy, seed policy* and *statistics* at the Indian agro portal and harvest benefits from *India*, world's second largest producer of food and a country with a billion people. From canned, dairy, processed, frozen food to fisheries, meat, poultry, food grains, alcoholic beverages & soft drinks, the Indian agro industry has dainty areas to choose for business.

DIFFERENT ORGANISATIONS

Development Commissioner Small Scale Industries (DC SSI)

The Office of the Development Commissioner (Small Scale Industries) also known as Small Industries Development Organisation (SIDO) is an attached office of the Department which assists the Ministry in formulation and implementation of policies and programmes for promotion and development of the Small Scale Sector. It inter-alia provides comprehensive range of common facilities, technology support service, marketing assistance through its network of 28 Small Industries Service Institutes, 30 branch Institutes, 2 Extension Centres, 4 regional Testing Centres, One Production Centre and 10 Field Testing Stations.

National Small Industries Corporation (NSIC)

The National Small Industries Corporation Limited is a public sector undertaking set up by the Government of India in 1955 to promote, aid and foster the growth of small scale industries in the country. NSIC helps the small scale industries through its various schemes such as hire purchase, equipment leasing, marketing domestic as well as export, raw material assistance, single point registration, etc. Under the hire purchase, NSIC supplies both indigenous and imported machines on easy hire purchase terms to SSI units.

Small-Scale Industry Board

The SSI Board, under the chairmanship of Minister Incharge, Ministry of SSI & ARI provides a forum for interaction among its members in order to facilitate co-ordination and inter-institutional linkages and to render advice to the Government on various policy matters and development of the small-scale sector. The term of the Small Scale Industries Board is two years.

The Board was last constituted on 26th September, 1998 with 93 members besides the Chairman.

Evolution and Development of SSI Policy

The Industrial Policy measures announced in 1991 contained a special thrust on the promotion and strengthening of Small, Tiny and Village Industries. Under the package of measures announced, the investment limit for tiny industries was raised to Rs. 25 lakhs million and locational conditions were withdrawn . in 1997, there was a major upward revision in the investment limit in Plant and Machinery for the purpose of defining SSI and Tiny Sector units. The limit was brought up to Rs. 3 crore. But now, has been brought down to Rs. One crore recently in December, 1999.

Performance

The steady growth of small-scale industries has been one of the most significant features of planned economic development. The small-scale sector has grown phenomenally during the last three decades and the sector has played and has potential to play a vital role in the fulfillment of our socio-economic objectives. The total number of small-scale units in the country in 1998-99 was 31.21 lakh, compared to 30.14 lakh in 1997-98. Value of production of small-scale units in 1998-99 aggregated to Rs. 5,27,515 crore.

Table 1

No. of Units, Production, Employment and Exports in SSI Sector

Year	*No. of SSI Units (in lakhs)**	*Production (Rs. Crores)*	*Employment (in lakhs)**	*Export (Rs. Crores)*
1993-94	23.84	2,41,648	139.38	25,307
1994-95	25.71	2,93,990	146.56	29,068
1995-96	27.24	3,56,213	152.61	36,470
1996-97	28.57	4,12,636	160.00	39,248
1997-98	30.14	4,69,377	167.20	44,436
1998-99	31.21	5,27,575	171.58	49,481

*10 lakhs = 1 million

Source: Annual Report 1999-2000, Ministry of SSI&ARI, Government of India.

The volume of employment in the small scale stood at 171.6 lakh as of end-March 1999. Exports from the SSI Sector accounted for about 35 per cent of the country's total exports. In 1998-99, SSI exports valued at Rs. 49,481 crore, increased by 11.4 per cent over 1997-98.

SMALL SCALE INDUSTRIES

In the literature on industrial economics the definition of small scale industry varies. The problem of defining a small scale unit is not only present in India. Such a problem has arisen in the past in the foreign countries as well.

A Small industry may be functionally defined as a segment of manufacturing industry carried out in relatively small establishments. According to Eugene Staley and Richard Morse a small industry stands for all manufacturing activity carried on in relatively small establishments. A small industry, thus, may be a factory as well as non-factory establishment. Such a definition is not very appropriate. The small industries are not the miniature large scale industries. They have a significance of their own. They are established in accordance with the unutilised physical and human resources.

The Fiscal Commission defined a small scale industry as one "which is operated mainly with hired labour normally numbering 10 to 50 hands."

The Director General of Supplies and Disposals held that the small scale industries are those which do not ordinarily employ more than 100 persons without power or 50 persons with power and working capital of less than Rs.5 laksh. Here, the emphais is on the size of employment. In the foreign countries also the definition of a small scale unit is influenced by the volume of employment. The criterion of size of employment, however, was more or less deceptive, because the figures relating to persons employed was purely arbitrary.

In course of time, the small scale units were being defined on the basis of the size of investment in machinery and equipment, instead of the criterion of the size of employment.

Two main approaches to the definition of small scale industries may be noticed; although definitions on other consideration also are possible. One approach takes into account the size of employment and the other, the size of capital investment.

In India, in the beginning the definition was based on the size of investment as well as size of employment. But today the Indian definition is based on the size of investment in plant and machinery alone. Such an approach has a defect. To enjoy the various facilities provided by the Government, the manufacturers may deliberately prefer to keep small. It prevents the small units from growing larger and more modern. But India is a labour-surplus and capital–scarce country. The policy of the Government is to encourage employment. So a definition based on the limitation on capital investment irrespective of the number of persons employed seems to be appropriate.

DIFFERENCE BETWEEN SMALL SCALE AND COTTAGE INDUSTRIES

The small scale and cottage industries have some characteristics of their own. The differences between the two arise from the characteristics of these industries. The difference between the two sectors is often misleading. The following difference between the two sectors may be noted.

(1) Cottage and small scale industries may also be distinguished on the basis of the technique of production applied. In a cottage industry the emphasis is on manual labour, although some tools and equipments are used. There is the predominant use of manual processes. In a small scale industry there is greater use of machinery. Mechanical process predominate. The cottage industries are usually technically backward. The technology of the small scale industries is more modern.

(2) Capital investment in the cottage industries is very less in comparison to that of the small scale industries. The maximum limit of capital investment in fixed assets has been raised to Rs.35 laksh on the part of the small scale industries.

(3) The scope of the cottage industry is narrower than that of the small scale industry. In a cottage industry the volume of production is small. Its market also is small. The distinction between the two is based on the geographical covering for deriving inputs and selling output.

(4) Another distinction between the two may be made in terms of the working place. In a cottage industry production is usually conducted at the place of residence of the artisan. It is usually a household industry. But a small industry operates in a separate workshop. It is a non-household unit.

(5) Cottage industries are mostly producers of consumer goods. Small scale industries may or may not be the exclusive producers of consumer goods. Nowadays a large variety of intermediate goods and industrial components, such as cycle parts, auto parts, T.V. components, etc., are produced in the small scale sector.

(6) Cottage industries are rural in character. Small scale industries have an urban bias. Such industries are usually set up in and around metropolitan areas. Nowadays various incentives are provided to disperse the small scale industries to the backward and rural centres.

TYPES OF RURAL INDUSTRIES

Cottage Industries

Characteristics of Cottage Industries

Cottage industries in India have certain features. While describing the cottage industries, P.N.Dhar and H.F.Lydall mention that cottage industries are almost entirely household enterprise (employing little or no hired labour), most of them derive their raw materials from local sources and they sell most of their products in local markets. They are, in sum, small scale, rural localized and technically backward."

1. ***Hereditary:*** Very often the cottage industries are hereditary in character. The secrets of the trade are handed down from generation to generation. So cottage industries are also known as household industries.

2. ***Household :*** Production is mostly conducted at the place of residence of the artisans.

3. ***Small Scale:*** In cottage industries production is on a small scale. The market also is small.

4. ***No or Little Power is used:*** The operations involve mostly manual labour. In the past, therefore, very little power was used in these industries. In the recent times, however, electricity is increasingly used by the cottage industries.

5. ***Technically Backward:*** These industries use traditional methods. They use old and outdated equipments.

6. ***Rural:*** These industries are mostly localized in the rural areas.

7. ***Negligible Capital Investment:*** Cottage industries are capital light. They need very little capital.

8. ***Decentralised Nuture:*** Usually the cottage industries are scattered throughout the country. Some types of activities, however, may be partially localized; such as, sericulture, bell-metal industry, coir making, hosiery products, etc. Such localization is influenced by the availability of raw materials, tradition, skilled labour, etc.

9. ***Local Market:*** The products of the cottage industries are supposed to have a local market. However, in the recent the Government have taken several measures to extend the market of handicrafts, handloom, silk, coir products, etc. The foreign markets also are being explored.

10. ***Family Labour:*** Cottage industries usually are managed by family labour, very little or no outside labour is used. These industries can engage women and children. There is no fixed hours of work. Hence, cottage industries are highly suitable as subsidiary sources of employment.

Cottage industries are also known as village or household industries. Cottage industries consist of traditional cottage and household enterprises. They use traditional methods to make traditional products. These industries are located in rural areas, mostly in households. They are carried on wholly or primarily with the help of family labour. They need very little capital. The required capital is usually provided by the household itself. Sometimes the capital may also be supplied by the moneylenders or financial institutions. Most of them use local resources as raw materials. The products are usually sold in the local markets. These cottage industries are usually classified into the following five categories:

(a) Khadi and Village Industries.

(b) Handlooms.

(c) Handicrafts.

(d) Sericulture, and

(e) Coir industry

The Planning Commission held that cottage industries are mainly rural in character and are generally associated with agriculture involving operations mostly by hand and are carried on in the home either as a whole-time or part time occupation, primarily with the help of members of the family.

The Report, of the Fiscal Commission (1949-50) defined cottage industry as one which is operated mainly or primarily with the help of the members of the family, either as a whole-time or part-time occupation.

Dr. R.V.Rao has favoured the definition of a cottage industry, put forth by the Director General of Supplies and Disposals. According to this definition "a cottage industry is one which is carried on in a place which is not a factory for the purpose of Factories Act of 1948; that is, an industry which is carried on wholly or primarily with the help of the members of the family, for a whole or part-time occupation."

Recent interest on *rural industries* derives from recognition of the limits of agriculture and organised manufacturing sector in employment generation especially during the post-liberalisation period in *India*. Historically, industrial development of the West and the East present contrasting pictures of *rural industries.* One, the linearity model founded on the historical experience of the West, holds that development implies a movement away from traditional subsistence production in *rural* areas to modern industrial production in urban centres. The other, the East Asian Experience has shown that the growth potential of *rural* industries is considerable given the under-utilisation of the physical labour and the entrepreneurial ability of *rural* people. A combination of putting out system and subcontracting system-along with modern factory and industrial cooperatives-has persisted in the *rural* manufacturing sector even in the era of economic liberalisation. We find differential capital endowments and socio-economic constraints of *rural* artisans reflecting extensive division of labour, specialisation and fragmentation of the labour process. These do not satisfy the requirements of the linearity model founded in advanced capitalist countries.

Most people living in the rural areas of the country draw their livelihood from agriculture and allied sectors. Accordingly, the strategy of the Government has been to improve the economic and social conditions of the underprivileged sections of the rural population with emphasis on agricultural production and also the non-farm sector to promote productive employment opportunities, by integrating traditional production infrastructure, skills and locally available raw material.

The rural non-farm sector in India has been growing in aggregate size and increasingly contributing to rural income generation. The growing pace of international trade and globalisation presents both opportunities and challenges for the Indian economy, including the small enterprises sector, which consists of small scale, agro & rural industries and service/business entities.

Recognising that long-term development of Indian economy depends critically on the effective exploitation of the productive potential of the rural non-farm sector and development of village industries, the Ministry of Agro and Rural Industries (MoARI) was set up in September, 2001. This was done with the objectives of facilitating coordinated and focused policy formulation and effective implementation of programmes, projects, schemes, etc., for improving supply chain management, enhancing skills, upgrading technology, expanding markets and capacity building of the entrepreneurs/artisans and their groups/collectives.

ORGANISATION OF THE MINISTRY

The Ministry deals with the khadi and village and coir industries through the *Khadi and Village Industries Commission (KVIC)* and the *Coir Board* and coordinates implementation of two countrywide employment generation programmes, namely, the *Rural Employment Generation Programme (REGP)* and the *Prime Minister's Rozgar Yojana (PMRY)* with the cooperation of State Governments, Reserve Bank of India (RBI) and other banks.

Khadi and Village Industries Commission

The Khadi & Village Industries Commission (KVIC), established by an Act of Parliament, is a statutory organization engaged in promotion and development of khadi and village industries for providing employment opportunities in the rural areas, thereby strengthening the rural economy. The KVIC has been identified as one of the major organisations in the decentralised sector for generating sustainable rural non-farm employment opportunities at low per capita investment. It undertakes activities like skill improvement, transfer of technology, research & development, marketing, etc., in the process of generating employment/self-employment opportunities in the rural areas.

The KVIC is a statutory organisation established in 1957 by an Act of the Parliament. It plays a pivotal role in the strengthening of the rural economy by promoting and developing Khadi and Village Industries. The objectives of the KVIC include skill improvement, employment generation in rural areas, transfer of technology, rural industrialisation and promotion self-reliance among the people and to build up a strong rural community base.

The functions of the KVIC are to plan, promote, organise and assist in implementation of programmes for the development of khadi and village industries. The KVIC operates through 30 State/UT KVI Boards, 4969 registered institutions and 30,129 cooperatives, 188 departmental units and 15,441 sales outlets

The Khadi and Village Industries Commission (KVIC) is a statutory body established by an Act of Parliament (No. 61 of 1956, as amended by act no. 12 of 1987 and Act No.10 of 2006. In April 1957, it took over the work of former All India Khadi and Village Industries Board

Khadi and Village Industries are highly suitable iThe Khadi and Village Industries Commission (KVIC statutory body established by an Act of Parliament (No. 61 of 1956, as amended by act no. 12 of 1987 and Act No.10 of 2006. In April 1957, it took over the work of former All India Khadi and Village Industries Boarden a rural setting. They provide an instrument for helping people below the poverty line. They help in solving the social and economic problems, through decentralization of industries. Our principal economic problem is unemployment and underemployment of a large section of rural population. Agriculture has been unable to solve this problem. We have to seek practical remedies. The practical solution lies in a greater expansion of the primary, subsidiary and industrial activities. Thereby a large part of the population could be absorbed in non-agricultural operations. India is still land of villages. So the rural areas should be the center-pieces of any economic programme.

Besides, by taking part in production activities in the rural industries the artisans derive job satisfaction. Rural industries also promote national integration. When all are working, the feeling of high and low will be eliminated.

The Central Government has allotted Rs.700 crore as grant to the KVIC. (The Hindu dated 30-11-2008) The Centre had received a loan for the same amount from the Asian Development Bank(ADB) for helping KVIC institutions across the country.

Khadi

Khadi is defined as "cloth woven in India on handlooms from yarn spun by hand from cotton, silk or a mixture of these fibres." Khadi is a hundred per cent village industry. Hand spinning has been one of the oldest cottage industries in the country. Its raw material is cotton. It is grown and spun in the village. It is also woven by the villagers. To Gandhiji, therefore, Khadi was a symbol of economic freedom and equality. Charkha became the symbol of Swadeshi movement. According to him Khadi was "the sun of the village solar system". Everybody gained by adopting it.

Gandhiji was a staunch supporter of Khadi. To him the charkha was the sun around which revolved all other arts and crafts. Charkha was not only a source of subsidiary occupation to the farmer, it was an instrument of emancipation. Khadi was the symbol of freedom. Gandhiji supported khadi not only on economic grounds. Khadi was related to cultural and spiritual values of the nation. It was true khadi was costlier than mill made cloth. But the merits of khadi are too significant and too numerous.

Khadi has a number of advantages. Hand spinning is one of the oldest cottage industries in India. People are familiar with hand spinning in every part of the country. Hand spun and woven cloth from India established a world reputation even in the distant past. "The handlooms and spinning wheel were pivots of Indian society." It was only during the British period that khadi gradually lost its ground. It could not withstand the competition from the cheap mill-made cloth.

The technology improvement programme of the K.V.I.C. has the following objectives:

(a) It should enable the workers to earn living wages.

(b) It should improve the productivity, scale and quality.

(c) As far as possible the technology should utilize local raw materials.

(d) It should use non-conventional sources of energy

(e) It should reduce drudgery.

As a result of constant efforts, the K.V.I.C has developed a number of tools, machines, equipments and process in the extensive field covered by the K.V.I.C.

The Commission also provides marketing assistance to these industries. It has a network of 13,000 sales outlets throughout the country, which sell the products of khadi and village industries. Besides, the Commission has about 3,700 Khadi Gramodyog Bhandars and a number of emporia.

In our Five Year Plans also improvement of technology of the rural industries has always been emphasized. Improvement in productivity is an important objective of our Five Year Plans. Our Plan rightly emphasizes that "the traditional skills of rural artisans require upgradation to higher technical levels for improving their competitiveness.

The Khadi and Village Industries Commission has worked consistently for the improvement of technology by the rural industries. It set up several research institutes. The Commission launched the science and technology programme in 1975 to introduce and transfer the improved appropriate technology. A Science and Technology Directorate was created in order to coordinate the various activities of research and development. To guide and monitor the science and technology programme of the commission, a standing committee on science and technology has been sup up. Various national laboratories and technical and engineering institutions are represented in the committee. The committee also created an instrumentation cell for the speedymanufacture and fabrication of improved tools and implements.

The KVIC has developed and introduced a number of improved technologies in Khadi and village industries. The Commission is making constant efforts to update the technology.

In addition to these measures some incentives and relaxation may be necessary for the adoption of improved technology in KVIC programme. Mr.J.L.Choudhury, Director (Science and Technology), made the following suggestions:

(1) Licensing could be used to regulate the expansion, establishment and location of industries.

(2) Regulating the force of machinery, materials and choice of technology.

(3) Providing tax incentives and concessions and fiscal differentiation.

(4) Direct investment by Government.

(5) Package of extension services, supply and purchasing facilities and preferential treatment in purchase by Government.

Programme for the Development of Khadi and Village Industries

The Khadi and village industries enjoy a crucial position in the Indian economy. Gandhiji advocated khadi and village industries as a part of the Swadeshi Movement in 1925. In the same year All-India Spinner's Association was set up. The All-India Village Industries Association was started in 1935 to promote khadi and village industries.

The K.V.I. Commission at present covers khadi and 25 special village industries. The Commission operates as an apex organization. There are 26 state Khadi and Village Industries Boards, about 1,100 registered institutions and 30,000 industrial co-operatives through which the porgrammes of the K.V.I.C are implemented. The activities of the K.V.I.C cover about 13 lakh villages.

The khadi and village industries face innumerable problems. Accordingly, these industries need close attention from the Government. Every effort must be made to solve their problems. So in the beginning of the First Five Year Plan, the Planning Commission felt the necessity of an all –India organization which would look to the problems of these industry. In January 1953, the Government of India set up the All-India Khadi and Village Industries Board. The Board was responsible for the preparation and execution of the various programmes for the development of these industries. The Board, however, faced certain difficulties in practice. To remove these difficulties the Khadi and Village Industries Commission was set up under an Act of Parliament on 1st April, 1957.

The Commission is also constantly engaged in improving tools and equipments through research and field trials. Under the new 20 point programme emphasis has been put on the up gradation of technology. In fact research and development activities have been going on in this sector for the last 57 years. There is a Research Centre for cotton khadi at Ahmedabad. Research Centres for Silk and Muslin are located at Malda (W.B) and Trichur (Kerala). The Central Bee-keeping institute was established at Pune in 1962. The Bio-gas Research Centre at Kora Kendra, Mumbay, set up by the K.V.I.C., is engaged in research work for the improvement of bio-gas technology. Besides, there are the central village Pottery Training and Research Institute at Khanapur in Karnataka, improving various types of pottery wheels and new designs of kilns. There are also Research and Training Centre in palm gur industry at Madras and Central Research and Training Centre for neo-edible oils and soap at Nasik.

The Commission was responsible for planning, organising and implementing programmes for the promotion and development of these industries. The Commission provides financial assistance towards working capital, for production sales. It also provides assistance for capital expenditure in land, building, workshed, tools and implements, etc. The rate of interest charged is usually low at one to four per cent. The Commission provides management grant to new institutions, technical assistance grant and promotional grant in the form of sales, rebate, etc. It provides training for rural artisans engaged in the production of khadi and village industries.

Advantage of Khadi

(1) Khadi requires less capital, training and technical skill.

(2) The necessary raw materials can be procured locally and are inexpensive.

(3) It can solve the problem of unemployment and under employment.

(4) It is ideal as a subsidiary occupation, as spinning can be done even during spare time.

(5) There is very little physical exertion in spinning. Hence, even women, children and elderly people can

take part in spinning. Thus spinning has a place of its own in a joint-stock family.

(6) Marketing of Khadi is not difficult. For clothing has a universal demand.

(7) It does not create the problem of environmental pollution.

(8) Spinning gives a sense of fulfillment and cultural satisfaction.

Progress

Remarkable progress has been made by the khadi and village industries in India under the K.V.I.C.

An analysis of these figures would indicate that employment in these industries has not grown in the same proportion as the growth in production or earnings. Over the last 25 years if production has gone up by 2566% and earnings by 1678%, employment has gone up by only 183%. This shows that the benefits from the various K.V.I. programmes have been monopolized by a limited number of influential persons. The benefits have not been shared by a vast number of workers and artisans. It is, therefore, essential to pay special attention to the employment generation aspect of these industries.

The benefits of the K.V.I.C. have not gone to all the States equally. In some of the traditional States, the khadi and village industries have fared much better than in others. Causes for the failure of these industries should be ascertained and removed. Orissa's performance in this respect is not very encouraging.

Besides, these industries provide for more of part-time employment than full time employment. This proves that these industries play an important role as a subsidiary source of income to the rural people. Special measures have to be taken to convert these industries as a source of full-time occupation.

Employment in cotton khadi industries was rather discouraging. Hence, it is suggested to encourage the production of woolen and silk khadi. Introduction of muslin khadi and ploy-vastra also would be in keeping with the changing taste of the people.

In Orissa, the Khadi and Village industries Board has been restructured. For implementing different programmes the Board receives financial assistance from the K.V.I.C. "the Board has undertaken a massive drive for promotion and development of 21 village industries in selected villages of the State with a view to providing employment to at least 50 families in each block". Facilities to these artisans are given in the form of training, supply of free tools, loans and subsidies, etc., under I.R.D.P. and TRYSEM Schemes.

Till now khadi and village industries have suffered due to low level of technology. This kept the volume of production and earnings at a lower level. In the recent years, research and development activities in cottage and village industries have tremendously gone up. The research programmes aim at the evolution of appropriate technology to increase productivity and earnings in these industries. Important achievement have been made in Charkha technology, palm products, eri and tassar, silk, muslin khadi and non-edible oils, etc.

Again, within the scope of the K.V.I.C some village industries have done much better than others. Village oil units, gur and khandsari industries and gobar gas plants, etc., have grown at a faster rate. So, special attention should be paid for the promotion of other industries, such as non-edible oils, soap, leather and tanning industries, pottery articles, fancy articles made of bamboos and canes, processed food, etc. There should be a diversification of activities to create more and more of employment opportunities. In fact, in 1979 the KVIC introduced new programmes for rapid expansion of cottage match industry, non-edible oils and soap industry and village leather industry.

The KVIC follows a training programmes of its own. It has its own multi-industrial or unitary training centres at convenient places. The Commission also finances institutions and co-operatives imparting such training. Under the KVIC training programme lakh of persons were trained.

The expansion of training facilities and creating a vast manpower of skilled labour is a hard task. Certain suggestions may be put forth in this regard:

(a) The training must be imparted by qualified persons.
(b) Many composite training centres should be set up to meet the increased demand.
(c) Appropriate technology should be used in the training centres for imparting training.
(d) Design centres should be set up in all the States.
(e) There should be proper coordination in the training facilities in the States,
(f) The training facilities should be mass-oriented.

A substantial number of people of the weaker and disadvantaged sections and women are engaged in khadi and village industries. So special efforts should be made so that the developmental programmes of the KVIC would benefit these sections of the people. Similarly, people of the hill, border and backward areas also should receive special attention. At present the KVIC's pattern of assistance has a liberal element of grant for these areas. In the employment coverage through the KVIC, the share of these people is to go up to considerably by the end of the Eleventh Plan.

Our Five Year Plans visualize a big leap in employment and production in this sector. A large section of the traditional khadi and village industries artisans not yet covered by the KVC programmes are to be brought within the fold of the KVIC. Efforts will be made to ensure fuller employment in their present occupation. Efforts should be made to prevent displacement from the existing activities.

The employment target for the KVIC is 23.31 lakhs in khadi and 40.52 lakhs in village industries. Thus a total of 63.83 lakh people are proposed to be engaged in these industries, both on a full time as well as part time basis. It is expected that total production of khadi would be 320 million square meters, valued at Rs.460 crores. The value of total production under the village industries is expected to be Rs. 2,400 crores.

Employment Generation Schemes

The Ministry of Agro and Rural Industries (MoARI) implements two nation-wise employment generation programmes, namely, *Rural Employment Generation Programme (REGP)* and *Prime Minister's Rozgar Yojana (PMRY)*. Both these programmes are credit-linked subsidy schemes, which are implemented through commercial banks. While the REGP is implemented by the KVIC, the PMRY is implemented by the State Governments through the District Industries Centres (DICs).

Government has recently launched the Scheme of Fund for Regeneration of Traditional Industries (SFURTI) under which 100 traditional industry clusters (of khadi, village industry and coir) would be taken up for comprehensive development over 5 year. The KVIC and the Coir Board are the nodal agencies for the Scheme, which will be the first comprehensive initiative for regeneration of the khadi and village industries sector, based on the cluster development methodology. The *guidelines for the SFURTI* have been issued on 3.10.2005. All State Governments/Union Territories have been asked to send their proposals for cluster development to this Ministry for consideration/approval. A Core Group under the chairmanship of Secretary (SSI & ARI) has been constituted on 13.01.2006 with the following composition to assist the Scheme Screening Committee for examining the proposals received in the Ministry for cluster development:

Secretary (SSI & ARI)	Chairman
AS & DC (SSI)	Member
AS & FA	Member
Adviser (VSE), Planning Commission	Member
CEO, KVIC	Member
Secretary, Coir Board	Member
Shri Mukesh Gulati, UNIDO	Member
Shri R.C.M. Reddy, IL & FS	Member
Shri Dinesh Awasthe, Director, EDI	Member
Principal Secretary (College and SSI), West Bangal	Member
Addl. Chief Secretary (Industries) Assam (representing NER)	Member

Coir Board

The coir industry is a labour-intensive and export-oriented industry. It uses a by-product of coconut, namely, coir husk.

The Coir Board, a statutory body established under the Coir Industry Act 1953, looks after the promotion, growth and development of the coir industry, including export promotion and expansion of the domestic market. The Coir Board implements a number of schemes, which include assistance for participation in exhibitions, training for skill development and assistance under Mahila Coir Yojana, training, financial assistance for modernisation of existing units, undertaking R&D activities, etc.

The Coir Board is an autonomous statutory body established by an Act of the Parliament under the Coir Industry Act, 1953 (45 of 1953) for the overall development of the Coir Industry. The Board consists of a Chairman and 30 members representing various interests like growers of coconut, producers of husks and coir yarn, manufacturers of coir products, dealers in coir, coir yarn, coir products, three members of the Parliament; two from Lok Sabha and one from the Rajya Sabha, representatives of Governments of principal coconut growing States etc.

The Headquarters of the Board is located at Cochin. There are three Regional Offices one each at Bangalore, Visakhapatnam and Pollachi for promoting the development of the coir industry primarily in the brown fibre sector. The Central Coir Research Institute (CCRI) at Alleppey, Kerala and the Central Institute of Coir Technology (CCIT), Bangalore are engaged in research and development. The Coir Board has established 33 showrooms and Sales Depots in important cities in the country for promoting sale and consumption of coir products in the domestic markets.

The coir industry in India is mainly localized in Kerala. Gradually the coir industry is fast developing in other States as well, namely, Tamilnadu, Karanataka and Andra Pradesh and Orissa. In other States its progresss has been quite limited.

The Board took various measures to facilitate the growth of co-operatives in the industry. Steps were also taken to introduce mechanization and upgrade the technology. The Central Coir Research Institute was set up in 1954 for carrying on research on coir products. The National Coir Training and

Design Centre was set up at Alleppy to impart training to artisans and other supervisory staff. Long term training courses in advanced coir technology also are organised.

The industry was in a depressed state in Kerala. The industry was in the grip of middlemen. When the First Year Plan started, steps were taken to reorganize the industry on co-operative lines. Consequently, a number of husk societies, coir co-operative societies and central marketing societies were set up in the State. The Coir Board was established as a statutory body in 1954. It undertake activities for the promotion of coir industry. It also facilitates marketing both within as well as outside the country.

The programme for the development of coir industries in Orissa includes organization of primary coir co-operatives, basic as well as advanced training to coir artisans, development and production of designs of various coir products in the State. The State Apex Co-operative Society looks after the procurement and supply of fibre yarn and marketing of the finished products.

As a result of the development schemes 29 Coir Co-operative Societies with 1,153 members have been organized in the State till 1982-83

A SHORT NOTE ON RURAL INDUSTRIES IN INDIAN ECONOMY

The Ministry of Agro and *Rural Industries* (MoARI) in *India* was established in September, 2001 with the aim to develop the *Rural Industries* in the Indian Economy. The main objectives of this initiative were to ameliorate the supply chain management, upgrade skills, introduce innovative technologies and expand markets of the entrepreneurs and artisans. A wide range of programs, schemes, projects and policies have been formulated to carry out various activities in the *rural* sector in *India*. Also, the Government of *India* has also ensured employment generation program in the *rural* regions under *Rural* Employment Generation Program (REGP) and the Prime Minister's Rozgar Yojana (PMRY) in association with of State Governments, Reserve Bank of *India* (RBI) and other banks.

Some of the major sectors in rural economy of India have been listed below:

Rubber Business in India

Rubber is one of the significant commercial crops in *India*. Rubber Industry in *India* has accounted for a production of 6.49 lakh tons for the year 2006. Places in *India* where rubber is cultivated include areas of southwest Konkan and Malabar Coast in Kerala and in some areas of Tamil Nadu.

The *Rubber Business in India* is one of the oldest industries in the country. Rubber has been one of the most important commercial crops in India. Rubber is an important commodity in our day-to-day life. Rubber is also an important contributor to the rural development. With the rubber business on the rise again, the rubber cultivators have a bright future.

Rubber Business in India-Important points

- The Rubber Business in India is on the rise at present.
- The production of rubber in the year 2006 was 6.49 lakh tonnes.
- The consumption of rubber in the year 2006 was 7.18 lakh tonnes.
- The rubber business in India has huge potentials but the it needs to the improve the techniques of production.
- In order to encourage export of natural rubber, the Rubber Board of India provides subsidy on export.
- The Government subsidy on the export of natural rubber is one of the most disputed matter pertaining to the rubber business in India.

Rubber Business in India-Areas of cultivation

- Traditional Regions: Natural rubber is cultivated in the remote areas of southwest Konkan and Malabar coast, in Kerala and the Kanyakumari District of Tamil Nadu.

- Non-traditional Regions: Natural rubber is also cultivated in the remote coastal areas of Karnataka, Konkan region of Maharashtra, Goa, remote regions of Orissa and Andhra Pradesh, Andaman and Nicobar Islands, and the Northeastern States.

Rubber Business in India-Climate and Soil

- The rubber cultivation requires humid climate.
- The average annual rainfall should be around 2000-4500 mm.
- The temperature should be around warm to very warm.
- Both the south west monsoon and the north east monsoon helps in the rubber cultivation.
- The soil where the rubber is grown is mainly lateritic in nature, but some of the cultivation is also done on alluvial soils and red soils that are well drained, porous, and acidic in nature.

Rubber Business in India-Production Natural Rubber

- Production of Ribbed Smoked Sheet (RSS) in September 2007 was 45905 metric tonnes.
- Production of Solid Block Rubber in September 2007 was 8660 metric tonnes.
- Production of Latex Concentrates in September 2007 was 6800 metric tonnes.
- Production of Pale Latex Crepes in September 2007 was 100 metric tonnes.

Rubber Business in India-Consumption Natural Rubber

- Consumption of Ribbed Smoked Sheet (RSS) in September 2007 was 53305 metric tonnes.
- Consumption of Solid Block Rubber in September 2007 was 10880 metric tonnes.
- Consumption of Latex Concentrates in September 2007 was 6150 metric tonnes.

- Consumption of Pale Latex Crepes in September 2007 was 205 metric tonnes.

Rubber Business in India-Export and import

- The export of Natural Rubber till September 2007 was 980 metric tonnes.
- The import of Natural Rubber till September 2007 was 9381metric tonnes.

Fisheries in Rural India

The fish production rate in *India* has witnessed a remarkable growth since 1995-96. The National Program of Developing Fish Seeds, Fish Farmers' Development Agencies and Brackish Water Fish Farmers' Development Agencies have been the major contributors to the growth in fisheries in *rural India*. A diversified range of fishing methods along with processed fish products have been introduced in the Indian *rural* market through an Integrated Fisheries Project.

Poultry Business in India

Poultry Business is one of the major contributors to the growing economy of *rural* and semi-urban *India*. *India* has witnessed a remarkable growth in the egg and poultry meat industry in the recent period. States of Andhra Pradesh, Karnataka, Kerala and Tamil Nadu contribute to around 45 per cent of the total egg production in *India* whereas the eastern and central parts of *India* contribute to around 20 per cent of the same. *India* is the seven largest poultry producer all over the world.

The *Poultry Business in India* is a very old practice and this food industry is one of the important contributors to the economy of rural and semi-urban India. As per the reports, the Indian poultry industry has contributed around US $ 229million, to the gross national product and is witnessing steady growth till the current fiscal year. Further, the report also envisages a strong growth for the egg and poultry meat industry of India, both in urban and rural India, in the next two decades. The current scenario of poultry business in India is encouraging because India ranks seventeenth in the world poultry production index. Further, India is the fifth largest producer of eggs and ninth largest producer of poultry meat amongst all the countries. The poultry industry of India produced over 34 billion of eggs and around 600,000 tons of poultry meat in the financial year 2004. The market research report of the poultry business in India found that egg consumption rate in India has grown at a much faster pace, than the consumption of poultry meat. Moreover, with the continual rise in purchasing power capacity, the rate of consumption is estimated to triple by the end of the year 2020.

The average per capita poultry meat consumption in India increased from 0.69 to 1.28 kg and the total egg consumption is estimated to touch 106 billion in 2020 from 34 billion in 2000. Furthermore, the poultry meat consumption is estimated to increase from 687 million kg to 1,674 million kg. Presently, the Poultry Business in India produces around 37 billion of eggs and 735,000 tonnes of poultry meat. The Indian states of Andhra Pradesh, Karnataka, Kerala and Tamil Nadu cumulatively produces around 45 % of the India's egg production while the eastern and central parts of India account for about 20% of egg production. Further, the four southern states of India have per capita consumption of 57 eggs and 0.5 kg of broiler meat while the central and eastern states of India has per capita consumption of 18 eggs and 0.13 kg of broiler meat.

The structure of India's poultry industry is varied and small-scale producers account for the bulk of production while large-scale producers accounts for a growing share of output in some regions. The Poultry Business in India now employs around 1.6 million people among which around 80 % are directly employed, while the rest 20 % is engaged with its allied areas like in feed, pharmaceuticals, equipment, and other services as required by the poultry industry. Moreover, this sector also involves an additional workforce of around 1.6 million, primarily engaged with in marketing and sales of poultry products. India exports poultry products like table-eggs, meat, live birds, egg powder and frozen yolk. The total value of exports was around Rs. 5 billion at the end of the financial year 2000 and the numbers have risen steadily from there on.

Although, the Indian poultry industry is on a rise due to modern practice method of poultry farming but a major section of the industry still suffers from some bottlenecks, like the following:

- Lack of proper basic infrastructure like storage facility, transport, cold storage chains
- Fluctuations in the price of poultry products due to absence of proper storage facilities
- Unorganized and inefficient marketing system
- Interference of many market intermediaries
- Availability of proper nutritious feed in absence of corn or maize, which constitutes the bulk of broiler feed
- Lack of proper disease knowledge of the fowls.

Tobacco Business in India

India is one of the most predominant producers as well as consumers of tobacco in *India.* It ranks third in terms of tobacco production around the world. Tobacco leaves are highly exported in the overseas countries which has accounted for a 99 per cent increase in the revenue from exports.

Tobacco Business in India is important for the economic development of the country. The tobacco contributes to the major portion of gross domestic product of India. It also helps in the rural economic development. Tobacco and tobacco products are exported to different countries and helps in earning stronger foreign currencies.

Tobacco Business in India-Major points

- India ranks third in the production of tobacco in the world
- India is even one of the largest consumers of tobacco and tobacco based products
- The yearly production of tobacco in India is 5,80,000 metric tonnes

- Nearly 12 lakh people are involved in the cultivation of tobacco in India
- Tobacco and tobacco products consists of cigarettes, bidis, zarda, cigars, etc
- Bidi manufacturing is the largest cottage industry in India
- Nearly 5 million people are involved in the commercial operation pertaining to tobacco
- Tobacco is consumed by smoking of cigars, hukka, bidis, cigarettes, by chewing of zarda, pan masala, tobacco leaves, etc

Tobacco Business in India-Areas of cultivation

- Northern Black Soils (NBS): Tobacco is grown on the black soils in the districts of Karimnagar, Khammam, East and West Godavari, and Warangal.
- Central Black Soils (CBS): Tobacco is grown on the black soils in Guntur and Krishna districts of Andhra Pradesh and Maharashtra's Gadchiroli district, by the means of rain water. The average produce is nearly 1100 Kgs per hectares.
- Southern Black Soils (SBS): Tobacco is grown on the black soils in Prakasam and Nellore districts near the Coromondal coast Southern India. The area cultivated is nearly 30,000 hectares.
- Southern Light Soils (SLS): Tobacco is grown on the light soils in Nellore and Prakasam districts. The area cultivated is nearly 58,000 hectares.
- Northern Light Soils (NLS): Tobacco is grown on the light soils in East and West Godavari and in the parts of Khammam districts. The area cultivated is nearly 18,000 hectares.
- Eastern Light Soils (ELS): Tobacco is grown on the light soils in Vijayanagaram of Andhra Pradesh and the Rayagada sector of Orissa.The area cultivated is nearly 700-800 hectares the average production is 1 M.Kgs.

- Karnataka Light Soils (KLS): Tobacco is grown on the light soils in Mysore, Shimoga, Chikkamagalore, Davangere, Hassan, Coorg, and Chitradurga districts of Karnataka. It is a monsoon crop.

Tobacco Business in India-Revenue

- The contribution of the excise duty on cigarettes to the total revenue is 8.8 %
- The excise duty on cigarettes was levied at a rate 10%, which was later reduced to 8.8 %
- The contribution of the excise duty on other tobacco products such as bidis, cigars, etc, to the total revenue is 3.3%

Tobacco Business in India-Exports

- The domestic consumption of tobacco is very high
- The export of tobacco depends on the demand for the same in the country
- The highest export earnings pertaining to tobacco comes from tobacco leaves
- The earnings from the export of cigarettes has declined by 76%
- The earnings from the export of tobacco leaves has increased by 99%

Jute Business in India

Jute is one of the most prime products in terms of exporting to the overseas nations and it brings in maximum foreign exchange earnings. The delta of the river Ganges in West Bengal is perfect for jute cultivation. A wide range of gunny bags, shopping bags, handicrafts, carpets, and many more other items are made from Jute.

Jute Business in India is one the major foreign exchange earner for the country. The India is one of the leading producers of jute. The delta of the river Ganges in West Bengal is the ideal place for the cultivation of jute in India. Jute is one of the most popular natural fibers next only to cotton. Jute is used for a variety of uses such as gunny bags, shopping bags, handicrafts, carpets, etc.

Jute Business in India-Facts

- Jute is the is called the 'golden fiber'
- India is the largest cultivator of jute in the world
- Nearly 85% of the total jute production in the world takes place in the Ganges delta
- With the present improvements in the method of jute cultivation, India has huge scope in the future
- India has the potential to be the largest exporter of jute in world
- Jute is growing to be the most wanted bio-degradable replacement for plastic packing material
- India is the biggest consumer of jute and jute products
- India is also the largest world wide manufacturer of jute products

Jute Business in India-Cultivation

- The jute takes around four months to grow
- The jute plants are harvested at the time they start flowering
- The stalks are cut off and soaked in water for 20days and this process is called retting
- The jute cultivation requires warm temperature ranging from 35 to 38 degree centigrade
- Jute needs plenty of rainfall during the sowing period

Jute Business in India-Strengths

- India has international standard research and development provisions for cultivation of jute, designing machineries, and product development
- The stringent quality control or the implementation of 'total quality control' is one of the factors for the success of the Jute Business in India

- Jute and various jute products are being exported for nearly 100 years
- India has the capability of manufacturing different types of jute product as per the customers need
- India has infrastructure such as shipping facilities, harbor, ports to support the jute business in India
- The Jute manufacturers in India have the capacity to meet the global demand for jute products.

Jute Business in India-Areas of cultivation

- The delta of Ganges River is the best place for the cultivation of Jute, and it is further divided in to three regions.
- Jat Area (Brahmaputra Alluvium): The jute is grown in the parts of Assam, Meghalaya, and Tripura. This region receives deposit of
- silts from the floodwater of Brahmaputra and the soil is acidic in nature. This is called the Jat type jute, which is commercially the best quality jute in India.
- District Area (Ganges Alluvium): The jute is grown in parts of West Bengal along the river Ganges. This jute is called as the
- District Jute and there are two types of it, namely Soft District Jute and Hard District Jute.

Jute Business in India-Products

- Hessian
- Sacks and Gunny bags
- Yarn
- Carpet Backing Cloth
- Food Grade Jute products
- Jute Soil Saver
- Hand and Shopping bags
- Gift and Novelty Items
- Home Furnishing
- Handicraftss

Horticulture Business in India

India has a diverse soil and climate which provides a promising opportunity for horticulture. Some of the crops cultivated in the horticultural sector comprise of fruits, vegetables, root and tuber crops, flowers, ornamental plants, medicinal and aromatic plants, spices, condiments, plantation crops and mushrooms.

Sericulture Business in India

Sericulture is one of the *rural* based agro *industries* in *India*. Silk production activity has accounted for a total income from export production of more than USD 600 million. Sericulture offers agro based, ecologically and economically sustainable activity for the poor, small and marginal farmers which also include women. 60 per cent of the pre-cocoon and post-cocoon sector activities are carried out by women.

Sericulture is another type of cottage industry widely practiced in the country. It is related to the production of silk. Silk is said to be the "queen of fibres". Silk has been popular for its strength and beauty the world over. China has been the traditional seat of Sericulture. China, Japan, Russia and South Korea are the principal producers of silk. India is the second largest producer of silk. India produces all the four varieties of silk, namely, mulberry, tasser, eri and muga.

Sericulture can play a crucial role in the rural economy of the country. So it can serve as a subsidiary source of employment to the farmers. It an serve as a spare time occupation. Even women and children can find enagement in sericulture.

Climate conditions in many parts of the country are suitable for silk worm rearing. R.V. Rao mentions certain special feature of mulberry sericulture. It is possible to raise five to six crops a year. It, thus, serves as a source of recurring cash returns to the farmers. Once set up, a mulberry garden continues for 10 to 12 years. Even women and children can attend to the rearing of the worms. Mulberry can withstand irregular rainfall and can be cultivated both in the rainfed and irrigated areas.

Most important of all, sericulture affects three sections of the economy, namely, agriculture , industry and commerce. In the socio-economic structure of the country also sericulture has an importance of its own. Silk is considered to be a symbol of purity. There is widespread use of silk clothings on religious and other festive occasions.

Karnataka, West Bengal and Jammu and Kashmir have been the traditional areas of mulberry sericulture. Orissa, Bihar, M.P. and Assam are famous for the production of tasser. Of late mulberry sericulture is being practiced in other States as well; such as Andhra Pradesh, Tamilnadu, U.P., Orissa, and the North Eastern region.

Since independence, the Government have taken several steps for the promotion of sericulture in the country. In 1949 the Central Silk Board was set up. The Board carries on a number of activities for the development of sericulture, covering all varieties. It particularly concentrates on research, training, production of basic seed, etc. The Board established two Tassar, and a Regional Research Station for Muga. Besides, a number of regional research sub-stations are attached to each major research institute. Due to research it has been possible to produce high grade bivoltine raw silk in the traditional silk producing areas. Average per hectare productivity of mulberry silk increased to 28.2 kg by the end of 1982-83.

The Silk Board has taken steps to establish two more Regional Research Stations and 10 Research sub- stations– cum-extension centres for mulberry sericulture. About 70 scientific and technical personnel were trained during 1982-83. In addition, the Central Sericulture Research and Training Institute, Mysore, availed of the services of five Japanese experts. An International Centre for Training and Research in tropical sericulture has been set up at Mysore, under the Indo-Swiss Technical Co-operation programme.

The area under mulberry production is about 1.70 lakh hectares today.

At the end of the Seventh Five Year Plan in 1989-90, the production of raw silk went up to 100 lakh kg. This increase in production is achieved through extension of area under sericulture, as well as increase in productivity. Sericulture is expected to provide employment to about 24 lakh pensions. In 1980 only 16 lakh persons were employed. Export earnings from silk went up to Rs. 140 crores by the end of the Seventh Plan from Rs. 49 crores in 1979-80.

Till now the emphasis has been on mulberry sericulture. In the recent years the Government have adopted various measures for the development of non-mulberry silk such as tassar, eri, muga, etc., as well.

Orissa has a rich tradition in sericulture. The State mainly grows tassar, other varieties of silk like mulberry and eri also are grown in the State.

The revised target for the Sixth Plan was 60,000 kg., with 20,000 beneficiaries under tasser and 9,000 kg. with 1,800 beneficiaries under eri. The area under mulberry is negligible. By 1985, the employment potential of sericulture in the State is of 25,000 persons.

Sericulture is recognized as a village-based industry providing employment to a sizable section of the population in India. Sericulture encompasses activities including mulberry farming, silkworm rearing, reeling, twisting dyeing, weaving, etc., is elemental in uplifting the rural folk through provision of adequate employment and income from the time immemorial. Though Sericulture is considered as a subsidiary occupation due to significant breakthrough in the technological innovations, it has been possible to take it up on an intensive scale for generating potential income and year round employment.

India is the second largest producer of silk in the world with an annual silk production of around 18,475 MT annually (Central Silk Board, 2007). All the four known types of silk, Viz. Mulberry, Eri, Muga and Tasar are produced in India. Mulberry silk is the most popular variety in India, contributing more than 87% of the Country's silk production. Export potential of this sector is promising as silk production in Japan is declining and that of China which is the largest silk producer in the world, is stagnant or declining.

Due to the prevalence of favourable climatic conditions, mulberry is grown mainly in five states, viz., Karnataka, Andhra Pradesh, Tamil Nadu, West Bengal and Jammu & Kashmir. Collectively these five states account for 97 per cent of the total area under mulberry cultivation and 95 per cent of raw silk production in the country. Karnataka is the principal silk producing state in the country, which accounts for about 58 per cent of the total mulberry raw silk production.

It can be noticed from Table 2 that the sericulture sector at the stage of raw silk production is capable of employing up to 6 million jobs annually. Sericulture occupies a unique position in India economy and assumes more importance in alleviating the problems of the rural poor. It is highly suitable in the context of diversification of farm enterprises with a possible integration and capacity to generate attractive income. There are only a few other farm enterprises that can match sericulture for providing employment to rural poor. Sericulture provides employment for 506.20 man-days per annum per acre (Lakshmanan et al, 1998). The above features have attracted the policy makers to propagate sericulture enterprise as a suitable answer to rural unemployment and low per capita income.

Being a rural based labour intensive industry, sericulture is ideally suited for improving the social and economic standards of the rural poor. In many of the government-sponsored programmes, sericulture has retained a dominant place as an essential tool for rural development. As the activities in sericulture are capable enough to engage the households year round, the enterprise has been often considered under various employment programmes. As a result sericulture is being intensively promoted in traditional states like Karnataka, Andhra Pradesh, Tamil Nadu. J&K and West Bengal.

India is the second largest produces of raw silk in the world next only to China. With a contribution of nearly 18,475 Mt of raw silk, the production of pure silk fabric accounts to nearly 150 million sq. meters per year. Out of the total fabric produced 60-70 per cent of the soft silk constitute handloom silk. Special types of silk viz., Crepe, Georgette and Chiffon etc., contribute around 10-12 per cent of the total silk fabrics. Out of the annual raw silk production, there exists a huge domestic demand, as the consumption rate is highly elastic. This has resulted in creating a larger gap in production. The domestic consumption has been estimated to reach 25000 MT annually in the coming years.

Performance of Sericulture

I. Income earnings: The net incomes derived from one hectare of mulberry sericulture and other important crops were assessed. The annual cost and returns were estimated based on the economic performance of individual and sequence of crops (Table 3). It was clearly brought out from the analysis that the net return derived from practicing sericulture was highest (Rs. 62,730.00) followed by sugarcane (Rs. 35,700). The sequence of paddy followed by paddy could realize Rs. 32,607.00/ hectare/year with a next best alternative sequence of paddy followed by "Ragi" (Rs. 27,975.00).

This clearly indicated that the enterprise sericulture hastened the chances of earning a highest net income when compared to other operative farm enterprises. Sugarcane considered a keep competing crop to mulberry sericulture, stood as next highest enterprise for income generation. The sequence of paddy followed by paddy formed another option for higher income earning. Hence as a provider of income, mulberry sericulture was found to be more lucrative than any other farm enterprises.

II. Employment potential: Mulberry sericulture has been termed as one of the essential tools for rural development, due to its impact on the engagement of labour for year round employment. The enterprise sericulture is a provider of year round employment.

A critical analysis of the employment potential through sericulture revealed that, the labour employed was up to the tune of 569 mandays and 450 women days per hectare per year (Table 4). It revealed that, the engagement of hired labour was to the tune of 285 man days and 204 women days per hectare per year. Thus it revealed that there was an engagement of both Men and Women equitability.

Table 2
Year-wise Area, Production and Labour Employment in Sericulture

Particulars	*Years* 2001-01	2005-06	% Change
Area under mulberry (lakh ha)	2.16	1.92	-11.11
Production of raw silk (Tonnes)	15857	18475	+16.51
Employment (Million)	5.40	6.03	+11.66

Table3
Cost and Returns from Mulberry Sericulture as Compared to Its Competitive Crops

(Value in Rs./ha/year)

Particulars	*Paddy - Paddy*	*Paddy - Ragi*	*Sugar Cane*	*Mulberry Sericulture*
Total cost	32730.00	23684.00	42925.00	120870.00
Total recurs	65337.00	51479.00	78625.00	183600.00
Net returns	32607.00	27795.00	35700.00	62730.00

Tabe 4
Pattern of Labour Employment in Sericulture
(No. of Days/Hectare/Year)

Type of Labour	*Cultivation of Mulberry Silkworm Rearing*							
	Own	*Hired*	*Own*	*Hired*	*Own*	*Hired*	*Total*	*Own to Hired Ratio*
Male	152	143	132	142	284	285	569	1.01
Female	30	124	216	80	246	204	450	0.82
Total	182	267	348	222	530	489	1019	0.92
Male to female ratio	0.20	0.87	1.65	0.56	0.87	0.71	0.79	

Table 5
Generation of Net Farm Income and Employment through Important Sericulture –Crop Combination in the Farmers' Field

Particulars	*Net Farm Income (Rs/ha/yr)*	*Employment (Mandays/ ha/yr)*
Field crops + Sericulture	76725.95	894
Field crops + Sericulture + Livestock	70515.18	809
Field crops + Sericulture+ Plantation crops	67315.18	769
Field crops + Sericulture + Vegetable crops	78515.18	861
Field crops + Sericulture+ Livestock + Plantation crops	65564.68	746
Field crops + Sericulture + Livestock + Vegetable crops	76564.68	825
Field crops + Sericulture + Livestock + Vegetable crops + Plantation crops	70581.18	778

Table 6
Energy Use Pattern in Sericulture and Other Competing Crops

	Crops							
	Rice		*Ragi*		*Sugarcane*		*Sericulture*	
Particulars	*Energy Used*	*% Share*	*Energy Used*	*% Share*	*Energy Used*	*% Share*	*Energy Used*	*% Share*
Labour (MJ/ha)	6507.2	18.97	3214.4	21.55	7071.68	'5.59	13141	19.41
Machinery (MJ/ha)	5253	15.31	2491	16.70	6148	13.55	12452	18.39
Irrigation (MJ/ha)	562	1.64	234	1.57	791	1.74	845	1.25
Material (MJ/ha)	21980	64.08	8975	60.18	31350	69.11	41255	60.94
Total energy (MJ/ha)	34302		14914		45361		67693	
Crop yield (Qt/ha)	51		24		850		15.3	
Gross income (Rs/ha)	32351		18647		78625		183600	
Energy to generage 1 rupee income (MJ)	1.06		0.80		0.58		0.37	

Men and Women equitability. The activity wise labour employment also suggested that, there was an equitable employment of both men and women in both cultivation of mulberry leaf and rearing of silkworm activities. The over all male to female ratio was found to be 0.79 indicating that, the engagement of men and women labour are almost equal. The employment potential of sericulture is thus a phenomenon of greater importance in the farm sector.

A further analysis of the data suggested that, with the integration of sericulture with other farm enterprises of economic importance could yield higher net returns (Table 5). With the integration of sericulture with important activities like raising field crops, live stock and vegetable crops could reap highest net farm income per hectare per year. The highest of all the combinations was through integrating sericulture with field crops and vegetable crops with a net farm income of Rs. 78515.18 per hectare per year, followed by sericulture with field crops (Rs. 76725.95/hectare/year) and sericulture with a combination of field crops, livestock and cultivation of vegetable crops (Rs. 76564.68/hectare/year). The other combination of enterprises remained at a slightly lower level of realizable income. The employment potential of the integration of these enterprises also proved to be significantly high. The employment potential of the combination of sericulture with field crops was the highest with 894 man days per hectare per year.

Thus as a provider of income and employment the enterprise sericulture as found to be more lucrative than other farm enterprises. the usefulness of this sector because of the gainful year round employment thus eliminates the risk of seasonal employment and migration of rural labour force to urban areas.

III. Energy use pattern: Energy is derived from a number of sources like animate (manpower, draught power), chemical (fertilizer, pesticide) and commercial (Diesel and electricity) etc. There are however, wide variations in the level and pattern of energy use among various crops. Energy requirements for the production of major crops in the study area viz, rice, sugarcane, 'ragi' and silk cocoon are presented in Table 6.

The energy used in the production of different crops revealed that the material inputs used in production in the form of seeds, chemical fertilizers, pesticides, disinfectants (used in sericulture) were used to a maximum possible extent. Fertilizer was found to be the most important sources of energy in terms of contribution to total energy, while the relative contribution of other energy inputs varied among different crops. Since channel irrigation was the major source of irrigation, the electrical energy requirement was considerably reduced.

Further there existed much scope for mechanization in place of engagement of human labour for effective conservation of energy. The extent of energy required to earn a rupee of income was the least in case of mulberry sericulture with only 0.37 MJ/rupee earned, followed by sugarcane (0.80 MJ/rupee earned) and paddy (1.06 MJ/rupee earned). This clearly suggested that, sericulture in spite of the number of activities employed, requirement of the energy for the production is considerable less. Hence, it is evident that, the enterprise sericulture is going to be the most demanding activity in the coming days, Sericulture thus exists as a promising enterprise for lucrative income, employment and an effective component of energy conservation. The enterprise once termed as part of the subsistence economy of India, today has been considered to be the most vital economic activity in the generation of income and employment in the rural sector. Though known for the production of value added lustrous silk, the generation of employment through the various processes involved has been vital. Labour component in sericulture was found to be highly productive than any other enterprises. With the steep increase in the agricultural wages in the rural areas, considerable thinking to employ this resource legitimately has to be made.

The thrust on engagement of rural women in sericulture activities makes the enterprise more promising. Currently sericulture is the only enterprise which is employing rural women to a maximum possible extent. Sericulture also forms one of the essential components of an effective integrated farming system combination of which, leads to profit maximization. Lastly, with the depleting energy resources, the farm sector has to look for the alternative sources of energy. Conservation of important sources of energy is possible by practicing sericulture. Policies governing the use of important energy resources are to be directed towards the encouragement of effective utilization of inputs in production

Tea Business in India

The tea business has been ruling Indian economy for the past 170 years. The chief areas of tea production in *India* include *rural* hills and backward areas of Northeastern and southern states like Assam, West Bengal, Tamil Nadu and Kerala. *India* mainly manufactures tea variants such as CTC, Orthodox tea and green tea. The *Wheat Business in India* is one of the major contributors to the rural business and economy. Wheat is one of the major agricultural produce of the country. At present Indian is the second largest producer of wheat in the world. With the onset of the green revolution and other developments in the agricultural sector, the Wheat Business in India was given a major boost.

The *Tea Business in India* is nearly a 170 years old practice. This agro-based industry is a very important contributor to the economy of India. The main axis of tea business in India is located along the rural hills and backward areas of Northeastern and southern states like Assam, West Bengal, Tamil Nadu and Kerala. Further, the regions, which are associated with small time tea business in India, are Karnataka, Tripura, Himachal Pradesh, Uttaranchal, Arunachal Pradesh, Manipur, Sikkim, Nagaland, Meghalaya, Mizoram, Bihar and Orissa.

The process of tea cultivation in India requires specific climatic and as well as soil conditions, which is prevalent only in the aforesaid areas of India. The tea business in India is mainly based on cultivation of tea variants like CTC, Orthodox tea and green tea. There is a huge demand for green tea in developed countries for its rich aromatic flavor and medicinal properties. The trend of green tea consumption is also on the rise in India due to rise in purchasing power capacity and overall living standards of Indian.

In India, tea is an essential item of domestic consumption and is the mostly consumed beverage. Further, tea is the cheapest beverage amongst all the beverages that are available in India and it is very popular amongst all sections of India society. The Indian tea industry engages around 20 lakh of workers, directly and they mainly represents the under privileged sections of the India society. The Tea Business in India registered a total turnover of Rs.8000 crore in the financial year ended 31st March 2006- 2007.

Some notable facts about the tea industry of India are as follows:

- There are 1655 registered tea manufacturers in India
- A total of 2008 registered tea exporters controls the export of tea from India

- The total number of registered tea buyers in India is 5148
- There are nine tea auction centers in India
- The Tea Business in India had witnessed phenomenal rise till the independence of India. The growth story of the Indian tea industry continued till the early 1970s and then it fell dramatically. United Kingdom was one of the largest and most important buyer of Indian tea but with the steady rise of Kenyan tea industry the market of Indian tea fell dramatically since, it exported same quality of tea at a discount. Until the 1991, USSR was the largest buyer of Indian tea but again with the disintegration of the Soviet Union the Indian tea industry went for a toss. Further, the Indian tea industry suffered loss due to emergence of China, Vietnam, Indonesia, Sri Lanka and Kenya as cheap tea exporters. Today, the major competitors to all Indian tea varieties are China (green tea), Sri Lanka (orthodox), Kenya (CTC), Indonesia (orthodox) and Vietnam.

During the early 1950s, around 79 million Kg or about 31% of total production of tea was retained for domestic market consumption and the trend changed dramatically to 771 million Kg or about 81% of total production of 956 million Kg of tea in 2006. Today, the tea business in India is an important source for earning foreign exchange. Over the last decade, the Indian tea industry registered a substantial growth with respect to the overall production of Indian tea, due to ever increasing size of its domestic market.

Wheat in India-Facts

- Wheat plays an important part in the Indian food economy
- It is one of the most important staple foods, covering almost the whole country
- Wheat is consumed in different forms such flour for bread, chapattis, pasta, semolina, noodles, etc.

- Nearly 70 million tonnes of wheat is produced in India every year
- The wheat production in India contributes to about 12% of the global wheat production
- Wheat is cultivated in India as a rabi crop, i.e., sown in October and harvested in May

Wheat Business in India-Growth promotional factors

- The use of high yielding variety of crops, better irrigation techniques, etc
- The price stability of the wheat though a major part of the produce is controlled by the private merchants
- The use of organic fertilizer in order to remove the ill effects so far caused by the synthetic manure
- The rapid rural development has contributed to the increase in the wheat produce

Wheat Business in India-Areas of cultivation

- Wheat production in India is divided into five parts
- North-Western Plains Zone: Plains of Haryana, Punjab, Northern Rajasthan, Jammu and western Uttar Pradesh
- North Eastern Plains Zone: Eastern Uttar Pradesh, West Bengal, Meghalaya, Arunachal Pradesh Assam, Manipur, Orissa, Nagaland, Mizoram, Bihar, Tripura, and Sikkim
- Central Zone: South Eastern Rajasthan, Madhya Pradesh, Gujarat, and Bundelkhand plateau in Uttar Pradesh
- Peninsular Zone: Maharashtra, Karnataka, Andhra Pradesh, and Tamil Nadu
- Northern Hill Zone: Hilly areas of Kashmir, Uttar Pradesh, Assam, West Bengal, Himachal Pradesh, and Sikkim.

Wheat Business in India-Irrigation

- The wheat cultivation requires four to six irrigations
- The first irrigation is for the crown root origination
- The second and the subsequent irrigations are provided at the time of tillering, flowering, and so forth

Wheat Business in India-Exports

- The decline in the U.S. wheat production provides huge scope for the export of wheat cultivated India
- The dry conditions of the region of western Asia during the winter has decreased the production of wheat and India has huge opportunities for export of wheat
- The export of wheat highly depend on the domestic consumption of the cereal
- The wheat grains can be exported to the other countries if the supply exceeds the demand, i.e. production is more than the consumption
- The export of wheat in India faces the problem of price. The price of a tonne of wheat in India is \$10-\$20 more than the international price
- In order to increase the export, the technology pertaining to the agriculture has to be developed further
- The lack proper processing facilities, storage space, transportation system, value chain, etc, disfavors the export of wheat from India
- The absence of well formulated export policy on wheat
- The lack of proper quality control is also hampering the export of wheat from India

The *Oil Seeds and Edible Oil Business in India* is one of the important providers to the growth of the Indian economy. Edible oil is an important ingredient in the cooking. It is widely used as a cooking medium.

Oil Seeds and Edible Oil Business in India-Edible Oils

- Groundnut oil
- Sunflower oil
- Corn oil
- Mustard oil
- Rapeseed oil
- Soybean oil
- Safflower oil
- Lin seed oil
- Sesame oil
- Castor seed oil
- Niger seed oil
- Cottonseed oil
- Coconut oil
- Rice bran oil

Oil Seeds and Edible Oil Business in India-Facts

- India is one of the biggest cultivators of oil seeds in the world
- The oil seed production in India is mostly saturated in southern and central districts
- The oil seed cultivating states are Gujarat, Andhra Pradesh, Madhya Pradesh, Rajasthan, and Karnataka
- The oil seed cultivation comprises of nine main oil seeds mustard or rapeseed, linseed, groundnut, safflower, sunflower, soybean, sesame, niger seed, and castorseed
- The Coconut oil from coconut copra comes under the category of plantation crops
- Groundnuts, mustard and soybean provides to almost 85% of the total oil seed cultivation in India

Oil Seeds and Edible Oil Business in India-Production of oilseeds

- Groundnut production in the 1997-98 was 8.90 in million tonnes

- Lin seed production in the 1997-98 was 0.30 in million tonnes
- Sesame seed production in the 1997-98 was 0.80 in million tonnes
- Soybean production in the 1997-98 was 5.90 in million tonnes
- Rape Seed production in the 1997-98 was 6.70 in million tonnes
- Sunflower production in the 1997-98 was 1.50 in million tonnes
- Niger seed production in the 1997-98 was 0.20 in million tonnes
- Safflower production in the 1997-98 was 0.40 in million tonnes
- Castor seed production in the 1997-98 was 0.08 in million tonnes.

Oil Seeds and Edible Oil Business in India-Exports

- Groundnuts exported in the year 1998 was 80000 metric tonnes
- Sesame seed exported in the year 1998 was 50000 metric tonnes

Oil Seeds and Edible Oil Business in India-Imports

- Though the production of oil seeds have increased, there is still a deficit in the domestic demand and supply of oil seeds
- The domestic supply of oil seeds in India is more than 5 million tonnes whereas the demand is more than 10 million tonnes
- The Central Government permits liberal import of oil seeds in order to avoid any scarcity
- With the onset of the liberalization policy, the import policy pertaining to the edible oils was transformed
- The import duty on edible oils used in the manufacturing of vanaspati was raised by 50%

- The under performing vanaspati manufacturing units was not included in this revision
- The duty was increased to 85% in case of the refined oils, apart from refined mustard oil and refined soybean oil
- The Special Additional Duty (SAD) was imposed at a rate of 4% on the import of edible oils.

REGENERATION OF TRADITIONAL INDUSTRIES

Some of our traditional industries, namely coir, handloom, handicrafts, sericulture, leather, pottery and other cottage industries not only contain great potential for growth and exports, but are integral for the maintenance of our cultural heritage. Accordingly, a Fund for the Regeneration of Traditional Industries, with an initial allocation of Rs.100 crore will be set up. The details, including mechanism for utilization of the fund will be worked out in consultation with the industries concerned.

Ministry/Department Concerned

Ministry of Agro & Rural Industries

Action Taken: The Government has approved a scheme titled the "Scheme of Fund for Regeneration of Traditional Industries (SFURTI) , for holistic development of traditional cluster of Khadi, Coir and Village Industries including leather and pottery. It is proposed to take up development of hundred clusters (25 Khadi, 50 Village Industries and 25 Coir clusters) over the next five years (beginning 2005-06). For implementation of the scheme a detailed office memorandum (O.M.) has been issued on 03.10.205.

Target Date for implementation: The implementation of the scheme has already started in 2005-06. Please see the link SFURTI on left side for more details.

AGRO-INDUSTRIES

"The *rural* non-farm sector in India has been growing in aggregate size and increasingly contributing to *rural* income generation. The growing pace of international trade and globalisation presents both opportunities and challenges for the *Indian* economy, including the small enterprises sector, which consists of small scale, agro & *rural industries* and service/business entities.

Recognising that long-term development of *Indian* economy depends critically on the effective exploitation of the productive potential of the *rural* non-farm sector and development of village *industries*, the Ministry of Agro and *Rural Industries* (MoARI) was set up in September, 2001. This was done with the objectives of facilitating coordinated and focused policy formulation and effective implementation of programmes, projects, schemes, etc., for improving supply chain management, enhancing skills, upgrading technology, expanding markets and capacity building of the entrepreneurs/ artisans and their groups/collectives."

Rural India has a vast potential of biogas generation and application. During the past two decades. biogas has been promoted mostly as a cooking fuel in the rural areas. According to the prevailing practices in these areas, fuel for cooking is not being purchased but collected by the users from the farm fields and surrounding areas. Majority ofrural population feels that biogas generation does not offer them direct/monetary benefits, and therefore many ofthem are reluctant to accept it. However biogas, when used for production activities, say in small scale rural industries, may be able to fill the gap in energy availability and demand in the rural areas. Being a renewable source, biogas, when utilised properly, can replace the commercial and nonrenewable energy sources to a considerable extent in a variety of production activities. Biogas application in the above context has been found to be self sustaining, while fulfilling the rural energy demand. Other important aspects such as employment generation, socio economic and environmental impacts are also examined.stries which cater to the requirements of agriculture may be called as agro-industries. Today agriculture is on a progressive march. For a developed agriculture, different types of tools and implements have become necessary. Agro-industries may produce ploughs, threshers, mowers and other implements. Similarly for irrigated land farmers need tools like bund-formers, buckcrapers, etc., for levelling and reshaping of land. Farmers also need ploughs, picks, wheel barrows, shovels, etc. More and more of seed and fertilizer drills have come to be demanded. Tools and equipments for soil testing, fertilizer mixing and seed processing, etc. have become a part of modern cultivation. Demand for pesticides and insecticides is on the rise. Thus agro-industries have a bright future.

Agro-based industrialization implies growth of industries in rural areas through interdependence of agriculture and industry. It implies a balanced growth of industry and agriculture in which an output of agriculture becomes an input of industry. The agro-processing industries offer a wide and viable field. Processing of rice, cotton ginning, oil extraction, preparation of milk products, dal making, processing of pickles, etc., have a wide prospect. Industries based a agricultural raw materials constitute about 45 per cent of the total industries.

Features of Agro-based Industries

Development of agro-based industries leads to integrated rural industrialization. Agro-based initialisation has certain features:

(1) Agro-based industries foster capital formation.

(2) They provide new avenues of employment with relatively smaller capital investment.

(3) Agro-based industries establish a vital link between agriculture and industry.

(4) These industries serve as an agent for the development of infrastructure which bridges the gap between urban and rural areas.

(5) These industries are labour-intensive.

Agro-based industries would connote the processing of agricultural produce in primary, secondary and tertiary stage. Here, agriculture again is used in a wider sense to include horticulture, animal husbandry etc. as well. Food crops like wheat, rice, etc. have to be processed. Then only they are sold to final consumers. Cash crops such as cotton, tobacco, etc., have to be processed before they could be used as industrial raw materials.

The best examples of agro processing are sugar industry in Maharashtra and dairy processing in Gujarat. Packing, canning and preservation of fruits, processing of fruit, vegetables, potato, onion, oil-seeds, cotton, etc., also are good instances of agro-base industries.

Generally speaking, agro-based industries are those industries "which obtain their major inputs from or which primarily meet the requirements of agricultural sector". Such a broad definition, however, is quite misleading. Because in that case the textile mills located in Mumbay or jute mills located in Kolkatta would be considered as agro-based.

In a broad way, agro-based industries consist of two types of industries. One consists of agricultural processing and allied industries. The other includes industries producing inputs required for agriculture, animal husbandry and fishery, etc. But in practice the former category of industries only are referred to as agro-based industries.

Rural Artisans

A rural artisan is defined as a person having skill and whose financial requirement does not exceed Rs.250,000 and who carries on his industrial activity in an area having a population of less than 50,000 as per census of 1971.

Ancillary Industries

An ancillary industry has been defined as an undertaking having investment in plant and machinery not exceeding Rs.15 laksh and which is engaged in the manufacture of parts, components, sub-assemblies, toolings or intermediates or the rendering of services. Besides, such an undertaking will be considered as ancillary only if it supplies at least 50 per cent of its production or services to other units for the production of other articles. Such an undertaking must not be a subsidiary of or owned or controlled by any other undertaking. Even a small scale industry could function as ancillary to another.

Tiny Industries

The Industries Policy of 1977 evolved another type of industry with in the small scale sector. This was called as "tiny industry". Industries with investments in machinery and equipment up to Rs.1 lakh and situated in towns with a population of less than fifty thousand were called as "tiny industries."

The industrial Policy of 1980 raised the limit of investment in case of tiny industries from Rs. 1 lakh to Rs. 2 lakhs.

Advantage of Agro-based Industries

Ago-based industries play an important role in the planned industrialization of the rural economy. They confer a number of advantages:

1. ***Rural Incomes:*** These industries also lead to an increase in the levels of income of the rural population. The income of the people engaged in agro-based industries increases. The rate of wages in the agricultural sector also goes up. Due to rising income the consumption pattern changes. There is an improvement in the general standard of living of the people.

2. ***Rural Wages:*** Agro-based industries employ a large number of unskilled agricultural labour. There is thus a movement of labour from the farm to the non-farm sector. This raises the productivity and wages in the farm sector. Besides, there is a change in the cropping pattern in favour of the ago-industrial crops. This leads to fuller utilization of existing rural labour. Rural labour gets employment for a larger number of days. This also raises the wage level of the rural workers.

3. ***Rural Employment:*** Agro-based industries provide new avenues of employment. There is the creation of both direct as well as indirect employment. Direct employment is created in the agro-based industries. New indirect employment opportunities are created in agriculture and tertiary sectors. Consequent upon the setting up of agro-based industries, agro-industrial crops are grown in large quantities. Commerce and transport develop. These engage a large number of people. Besides, these industries provide seasonal employment to the agricultural labourers during the non-agricultural season.

Thus, in a way they help in tackling underemployment or disguised unemployment as well.

4. Entrepreneurship: Lack of entrepreneurship is a basic problem of rural industrialisation in our country. Agro-based industries promote rural entrepreneurship.

5. Change in Occupational Structure: The agro-based industries provide employment to the unskilled agricultural laboureres. There in a shift of occupation from agriculture to non-agricultural sector. Besides rural people are able to carry on agro-based industrial activities during the non-agricultural season. During the agricultural season they get engaged in farming. This leads to multiple occupations. There is a decline in dependence on agriculture which is overcrowded.

6. Capital Formation: Usually these industries are capital-light. The majority are started with small savings within the family groups. Normally these savings would have been squandered away. But setting up of agro-based industries leads to a better investment of these small family saving. Thus, industries facilitate the process of capital formation in the rural areas.

7. Industrial Dispersal: The agro-based industries have greater location flexibilities. The urban areas face a number of problems, such as pollution, shortage of power, water, growth of slums, etc. So industrial dispersal has become very urgent. Agro-based industries serve as main instruments for decentralized rural industrialization.

8. Development of Infrastructure: Growth of agro-based industrial complexes in rural area would lead to the development of basic infrastructural facilities such as electricity, water, rural roads, banking, etc.

Development of agro-based industries in the rural areas is expected to lead to an overall economic growth of the area. It has been rightly said "the development of agro-based industries in these areas might arouse the urge to industrialize, earn more, save more and invest in newly established rural industries so as to derive larger share in industrial gains and thereby enjoy a better standard of living. This might make the peasants participate in the national development programme."[5]

Government Measures to Help in Marketing

Marketing was a crucial problem for thousands of cottage and small scale industries. Efficient marketing is a basic element for making an enterprise economically sound. Due to lack of proper marketing, the units fall stick and meet with premature death. According to the All-India Census of Small Scale Industries (1973-74), lack of marketing is a primary problem of these rural industries.

This fact was realized by the Government long ago. So the 1948 as well as 1956 Industrial Policy Resolution considered 'orginsed marketing' of the products of the small scale industries as an important assistance for the promotion of these industries. The International Planning Team (1954) also went into this problem.

Consequent upon its suggestion, two separate central organization came into existence. The Central Small Industries Organisation (CSIO) facilitated the sale of small industrial products by acting as an advisory body.

The National Small Industries Corporation (NSIC) took part in actual marketing of small industry products, under the scheme of Government Stores Purchases.

Handicrafts

Handicrafts are different from other products of cottage industries. They are unique objects of beauty. Besides, the handicrafts are individualistic and local. The handicrafts of different regions vary in design, tradition, and mode of production. They are the products of manual skill, which is the result of long practice and training. "Handicrafts call for great sensitivity, patience and service before results are produced." Indian handicrafts enjoyed an international reputation even in the distant past. However, with the passage of time and under British colonialism the local interest in them gradually declined. As princely States were lost and landed aristocracy lost its importance, the handicrafts were deprived of a rich local market. The interest shifted from the beautiful to the useful. Fashions changed. The artisans also could not rapidly adjust themselves with changing circumstances.

Handicrafts stand for an object produced by hand with great skill. Handicrafts represent our rich cultural heritage and tradition. They reveal the creative urge of the community.

After our independence, again the handicrafts were brought to the limelight. Today, the Government provides all types of encouragement to this sector. This is for several reasons. Our handicrafts are the products of skill and experience of centuries. Handicrafts have a large variety and richness. The amount of capital needed is very negligible. They can provide full-time as well as part–time employment opportunities to the rural folk. Often they use local resources, such as leather, wool, soft wood, stone, horn etc. A sizable section of handicraft artisans belong to the weaker sections. Women and labour also constitute a large part of the work force. They are also decentralized throughout the country. The artisans can work in their own natural setting.

Handicrafts comprise a wide range of artistic products such as carpets, ivory products, metalwares, silver filigree, hand printed textiles, dolls, toys and woodwares, etc.

Orissa is famous for her handicrafts. The State produces different types of handicrafts made of silver, stone, clay, horn, wood and bamboos, etc. There are 48,000 craftsman families in Orissa. By the end of 1982-83 about 7500 families were brought within the co-operative fold, through 221 Handicraft Co-operative Societies. It has been felt that in the co-operative way alone lie the solution of the problems of the State handicrafts. So the approach of the Government has been to strengthen the primary co-operative societies through enlistment of new members, contribution of share capital, training of the handicraft artisans and their rehabilitation through various beneficiary–oriented programmes.

Procurement of raw materials, development of new designs and sale of handicraft items etc. are to be organized through co-operatives. The Orissa Co-operative Handicrafts Corporation promotes the development of handicrafts in the State.

The All–India Handicrafts Board was established in 1952. Since then remarkable progress has taken place in the development of handicrafts. Is main task is to advise the

Central Government on the problem of handicrafts and suggest appropriate measures. Utmost importance is given to improve the quality of the handicrafts and suggest appropriate measures. The craftsmen are provided with technical guidance. Training programmes are conducted for the artisans, jointly by the All-India Handicrafts Board and State Handicrafts Corporations. Efforts are made to improve the designs. To suit modern tastes traditional designs are improved upon. Regional Design and Technical Development Centres have been started at different places to acquaint artisans with modern designs. Research is carried on to introduce improved tools and equipments in the production process. It is proposed to set up two national institutes to introduce improved techniques of production in carpet and hand printed textiles.

The higher cost of production and sub-standard quality of the products were the other problems. Lack of supply of quality raw materials also adds to their problem.

Production must be followed by marketing. Lack of proper marketing has been another problem of the handicrafts. In the past a high proportion of the handicrafts used to be marketed by the private agencies. This also led to exploitation.

Production of handicrafts today exceeds more than Rs.2,800 crores. Handicrafts exports in 1953-54 amounted to Rs.7 crores only. Today it is worth about Rs.1,500 crores. The production of handicrafts exceeded Rs. 5,000 crores. Employment in handicrafts increased to 50 lakh persons.

The handicrafts suffered from the problem of lack of finance. This often drove the artisans to the arms of the middlemen. They provide the needed finance to the artisans. But they take away their products at a nominal rate. In the process the artisans are exploited. The filigree artisans in Orissa have often been the victims of such greedy middleman. Today the State Governments are encouraging the production of handicrafts on co-operative lines.

To provide effective marketing facilities as many as 250 emporia have been opened in different places. A Central Cottage Industries Emporium has been set up at Delhi. There is also a Crafts Museum.

Handicrafts must be protected and promoted at any cost. "The miracle of the magic hands must be realized. We must lift the craftsman from obscurity and give him his rightful place in life... In India too much of industrialization will condemn millions to total unemployment and poverty. We have to preserve our aesthetic and human values and have a living faith in decentralized methods of production."

Handloom Industries

The handloom industry is the largest cottage industry in our country. It thus enjoys a crucial position. Its position comes only next to agriculture in providing livelihood to the masses. Thus, it has a tremendous impact on rural employment and income.

Another problem relates to marketing. The handloom sector has to face stiff competition from the products of well-organised mill-made sector. In recent years the powerlooms have posed a serious problem to the handloom. So it is necessary to reserve certain varieties of cloth for the handloom. The disobedient powerlooms may be punished by the Government.

Lack of modern, up-to-date design is another problem of handlooms.

Through the organization of co operative in handlooms, these problems could be tackled to a large extent. The Karve Committee had suggested that the three major objectives of the development programme for the handloom industry on the production side should be to extend co-operative organization to a large number of handlooms, to raise the technical efficiency and output of the existing handloom and to activise idle looms.

A major problem of handloom industry has been non-availability of raw materials of right quality in time and at reasonable rates. The raw materials which this industry requires are yarn made of cotton, wool, silk or synthetic fibres; and dye stuffs. The shortage of yarn could be over-come by setting up more co-operative spinning mills. Recently the Government have proposed to set up yarn banks in various regions. This also will relieve the problem to some extent.

The handloom industry provides about half of the total cloth requirement. Handloom industry is labour-intensive. Women constitute a large number of handloom weavers. In certain parts of the country, like Manipur, Nagaland, Arunachal, etc., weaving is practiced as a domestic craft. A sizable portion of total silk fabrics is woven on handlooms. India earns valuable foreign exchange by exporting handloom fabrics. Besides, the nature of handloom is based on moral principles and human values.

The importance of the handloom sector in the national economy has been duly recognized by the Government. It has received proper attention in all our plans. The All-India Handloom Board adopted a number of schemes to encourage the handloom sector. Assistance and support for the development of the handloom sector is provided through the Development Commissioner for Handlooms as well. The various measures that have been provided during the Five Year Plans are the following:

(a) The production of certain varieties of cloth, sarees of certain types, dhotis of certain width and borders etc. has been reserved for the handloom sector. The cotton mill industry is prohibited to produce these materials. The share of the handloom sector in the production of controlled cloth also is to go up substantially.

(b) The State Co-operative Banks provide credit for working capital to the handloom co-operatives. Efforts are also being made to ensure a full flow of credit form institutional agencies.

(c) For the Supply of yarn and other essential raw materials at reasonable rates, Co-operative spinning mills have been set up. The National Handloom Development Corporation facilitates the supply of yarn and other essential raw materials. The National Co-operative Development Corporation provides assistance to set up co-operative spinning mills to increase the supply of yarn to the weavers.

(d) Weavers are trained in improved equipment and appliances so as to develop their skill.

(e) Measures have been taken to expand the export of handloom fabrics to the foreign countries. This would brighten the marketing prospect.

(f) The handloom sector has been encouraged to adopt co-operative method of organization. Following the recommendations of Sivaraman Committee on handloom, lakh of weavers have become members of weavers co-operatives. The number of co-operative stood at about 18 lakhs looms in 1996.

In our Five Year Plans the handloom sector has been assigned its rightful place. To coordinate a vast decentralised and dispersed handloom industry is not a very simple task. With the drive towards rural industrialisation it is expected that the handloom sector would enjoy a still vigorous growth. As a result of the various positive measures and support programmes. Production of the handloom industry has increased. Export earning has also increased.

The handloom industry in Orissa has a glorious past. Orissa handloom sarees are famous all over the country for their elegance, exquistite beauty and graceful style. Sambalpuri Sarees particularly have unique design, motif and colour combination. There is a rare combination of finer craftsmanship and artistic design. An artistic Sambalpuri or Cuttaki Saree would evoke admiration anywhere.

In the recent years efforts have been made by the Government to develop and modernize the handloom industry in the State. The major thrust of the development programme was (a) to increase the number of working days in a year, (b) to help handloom weavers o obtain yarn at a reasonable price, (c) improvement and up gradation of their skill and (d) to market their products.

During the Sixth Plan it was proposed to bring one lakh looms into the organized sector and to offer gainful employment to 2 lakh weavers. In the beginning of the Sixth Plan 39,214 looms were there in the organized sector. During 1982-83 the production of handloom cloth in the organized sector was 469 lakh square metres value at Rs. 2616 lakhs. Production of Janata cloth went up to 28 million square metres in 1984-85.

VILLAGE INDUSTRIES

The "Village" industries connote a number of industries which flourish in the rural areas all over the country. These industries may be broadly classified into the following classes, such as : (a) food processing industries like village Ghani oil, processing of cereals and pulses, manufacture of khandsari, gur, palmgur, etc., (b) forest-based industries like cottage and bamboo, (c) textile industries include khadi, lokvastra and polyvastra etc., (d) agricultureal input industries, such as carpentry and blacksmithy, and (e) other consumer goods industries like village leather, lime-stone, gobar gas, village pottery, neo-soap manufacturing hand made paper etc.

These village industries mostly employ family labour. Production is usually carried on at the place of residence. The worker need not migrate to a distant place. Production is mainly organized through manual labour. The market for the products of these industries is usually localized.

Out of the various village industries some, like making of 'gur', khandsari, palm gur, collection of forest seeds for neo-soap making, etc., are seasonal in character. Otherwise most other industries provide full-time employment.

PROBLEMS OF RURAL INDUSTRIES

Introduction

Rural into industries play a vital role in the economy of our country. But they suffer from innumerable problems. The problems of the rural industrial sector are not common. Within the family of rural industrial sector we have modern small scale industries as well as coir, handlooms, handicrafts, khadi and other cottage industries. These differ from each other in their structure, scale of investment, individual characteristics and the role played by them. Often these are not complementary to each other. Sometimes their interests clash. Naturally, their handicaps and problems also are different. A modern small scale unit with an investment of Rs. 35 laksh in plant and machinery cannot have the same problems as that of a cottage unit with an investment of a few thousands. They operate under different sets of conditions. The rural industries consequently suffer from different categories of problems.

We shall discuss below some of the major problems of the rural industries.

The Problem of Location

Rural industries aim at removing regional imbalances. So more and more of rural industries should be started in the industry backward areas. But before starting a rural industry one has to pay due attention to the problem of location. Location is an important factor producing viability of the rural industries.

Before locating a rural industry, one has to find out if the area has certain infrastructural facilities. Facilities such as power, water supply, transport and communication, etc., help a rural industry.

The rural industries are largely based on locally available raw materials in rural areas. Thus, there may be agro-based, forest-based mineral-based or live stock-based industries. These raw materials must be available nearby. There are certain industries based on dispersed raw materials such as saw mills, dairy products, etc., or industries whose products are sold locally and have high costs such as bottled soft-drinks, tiles, paper board boxes, etc., In their case locational factor is important in their profitable operation.

Very often the rural industries have close relationship with agriculture in one from or other. It may be for supply of raw material or for meeting production or consumption requirements of farmers. Thus, the rural industries must have a smooth and proper linkage with agricultural operation of the area. There must be an organic link between agriculture and industry.

Similarly, while deciding upon a location one has to find out if the area has any special advantage from the point of view of availability of skilled labour or nearness to market, etc. The rural industries must cater to the local needs. It must take into account the village society, local skill and unutilized manpower.

The industries must be so located so that the place must serve as a "growth centre". The centre must transmit forces of prosperity to the nearby villages. This should further help in the process of rural industrialization. There must be backward, forward and sectoral linkages.

In the case of a small scale industry one has to pay due attention to the size of the factory area. It should have reasonable space. It should not lead to congestion.

Before establishing an industry it is desirable to have thorugh feasibility study. It should investigate and assess the prospects of the project. Such a feasibility study should take into account the following:

(a) Technical analysis
(b) Economic analysis
(c) Market analysis
(d) Managerial analysis
(e) Financial analysis
(f) Profit analysis
(g) Limiting factor analysis, and
(h) Gap analysis

The overcome the problem of location, the Government has started industrial estates at suitable places. In these estates sheds are provided to the entrepreneurs. These estates provide many facilities which an individual entrepreneur cannot afford independently.

The Problem of Skilled Labour

Many rural industries suffer due to lack of skilled labour. There are certain trades which are family-based in India. Thus skills in pottery, tannery, carpentry, balcksmithy, weaving, etc., are often handed down from generation to generation. But even here, the artisans have failed to move with the changing times. They have failed to update their skills. Consequently, the quality of products is not satisfactory. The designs are outdated. The techniques are old, the cost of production becomes high and the rural industrial products cannot compete with the products produced in the large scale sector.

There are certain industries where the skill has been localized. Thus, match industry in Orissa has not prospered because skilled manpower has to be imported from Tamil Nadu to run the match industry.

The level of literacy in our country is hardly 36 per cent. There is ignorance and supersition. There is lack of formal education. Technical education also is quite inadequate.

Therefore, it is necessary to launch a massive training programme. This training should be given in a number of trades. The training should also cover the various aspects of agro-based, cottage and village industries. Emphasis should also be given to train the local people in the servicing of minor tools and implements.

The present- TRYSEM (Training for Self-Employment) Scheme has already become quite popular. The TRYSEM Scheme provides arrangements for selecting rural youth between the age group of 18 to 35 years hailing from the families below the poverty line. The basic objective of the programme is to impart or upgrade the skills of the trainees, so that they could set up and run industrial units successfully.

The Problem of Capital

No industry can function without capital or capital is necessary to carry on productive activity. Finance is also necessary for development and expansion.

The rural industries require two types of capital –short term and long term. Short term capital is required for the purchase of raw materials, payment of wages and for meeting other day-to-day expenses. Short term capital is also known as "working capital". Long term capital is needed for purchasing land, constructing factory buildings, installing plant and machinery, etc. Such capital is also known as "block capital" or "fixed capital".

Lack of capital is a chronic problem of the rural and small scale industries in India. The rural industries suffer from certain peculiar handicaps. The rural industries lack adequate creditworthiness. They cannot provide necessary security or collateral. They require money in small amounts. So the commercial banks, etc., are reluctant to finance the rural industries although they are eager to finance the large industries.

In the recent years, the rural industries received financial assistance from the Co-operative banks, Commercial banks, State Financial Corporations, Industrial Development Bank of India and the National Small Industries Corporation, etc. But the assistance is never adequate. Before the nationalization of the major commercial banks, their assistance to this sector was negligible. Of late, however, the commercial banks assistance to this sector is constantly rising.

Lack of finance to the small industries is a chronic problem. Even the 1956 Industrial Policy Resolution recognized that lack of financial assistance constitutes one of the serious handicaps of the small scale producer. The Industrial Policy of 1977 also considered that suitable financial assistance by the Government was necessary for the development of the small sector.

In the developed countries also the problem of adequate finance is a crucial problem with the small enterprises. In the U.S., for example, the Government has set up the Federal Small Business Administration to provide financial assistance to the small firms who cannot procure finance. In countries like Australia or Japan, etc., out of the several State measures to help the small enterprises, provision of financial assistance happens to be the crucial one.

The Problem of Raw Materials

According to the All-India census of small scale industries (1973-74) among the major problems faced by the small industries, availability of raw materials is the primary. Some small producers are often hit by shortages of raw materials. There may be a scarcity of indigenous raw materials or imported raw materials. Very often the rural industries suffer from this problem due to their poor financial position. They cannot stock adequate raw materials when available.

At present certain imported raw materials are channeled through the Metals and Minerals Development Corporation or the State Trading Corporation, etc. The Central Government allocates these raw materials to the States. The States then distribute the same to the small scale and cottage industries.

Still the quantity of raw materials available from these sources may not be adequate. Sometimes the supply may not be on time. The artisans may be forced to use inferior or sub-standard raw materials. This would affect their quality. So it is necessary that there should be an organization which would maintain buffer stock of such raw materials. Raw material banks may be set up at central places. This would ensure a fair, regular, and smooth supply of these raw materials to the small scale sector.

Besides, the Central Government should follow a more judicious and rational policy while allocating raw materials to the States. For example, in 1980-81, West Bengal received only 8.5 per cent of its requirements of steel, 9.5 per cent of pig iron requirements, 14.6 per cent of paraffin and 1.9 per cent of the requirement for tallow. Although the State has the maximum number of foundries, yet it received only 7.92 per cent of the total supply of pig iron in the country.

The National Committee on Backward Areas has recommended the establishment of State Rural Industries Development Corporation to ensure a smooth supply of raw materials. Besides, the District Supply and Marketing Society should be given the responsibility for procurement of raw materials.

The Problem of Entrepreneurship

Lack of industrial entrepreneurship is consider to be a serious lacuna in the process of industrialization, in the developing economies. Schumpeter has analysed the role of the entrepreneurs in the process of industrialization of a county. Gunnar Myrdal is of the view that in the developing countries like India there is an sample supply of traders and businessmen. But genuine entrepreneurship is lacking. This also partially explains the higher rate of sickness and mortality of business enterprises.

Progress of entrepreneurship depends not only on the economic factors but also social and cultural factors such as family background, caste, connections, etc. N.A. Leff put that "absence of entrepreneurship in the less developed countries is generally attributed to alleged socio-cultural rigidities".

Several measures have been adopted by the Government to promote entrepreneurship. In 1983, the Central Government decided to establish a National Institute of Entrepreneurship and Small Business Development in Delhi. This institute is to act as an apex body to coordinate the work of all other entrepreneur training and development institutions in the country. It is to devise suitable training programes for various classes of entrepreneurs, particularly the poor. It would conduct research on entrepreneurship development. It would advice the Government on policy to be adopted to promote the rapid growth of entrepreneurship in a short time. It would not replace the existing training centres. It would rather serve as an umbrella organization to fill the gap of training methods, curricula and trained trainers.

The Government have also set up 12 branch small industries service institutes in various parts of the country. They would have workshops equipped with the appropriate machinery and trained staff to train local people, as quickly as possible, in modern techniques of production. This is to improve the quality of products of small units.

The existing specialized centres for technology development like testing centre, tool rooms were being expanded and strengthened.

The Government also introduced an award scheme at the national level for meritorious small entrepreneurs. Weightage would be given to units in backward areas and to poorer persons.

The Problem Marketing

Marketing of rural industrial products is a great abstacle in the success of the rural industries. As the rural industries use borrewed resources, it becomes imperative to improve marketing facilities. Marketing here has a wider connotation. It does not involve only the disposal of final products. Marketing also stands for intensive research to tesus and demand and the factors influencing changes in demand. The village artisans continue their vocations ignoring the consumers taxes. There is a communication gap between product and consumer.

The cities are the trendsetters. With rapid and continuous changes of taste and fashion in the urban areas, the artisans have to adjust with such chances.

The rural industries face certain typical problems in marketing their products. Millions of rural artisans are involved in rural industries. They produce a large variety of goods. These cannot be properly standardized or categorized. sometimes the prices of such products are relativesly higher. They do not get the advertisement in mass media. Nor do they have organized marketing networks spread throughout the country. Organised marketing networks spread throughout the country. Organised marketing needs a thorough study of tastes, nature of demand, quality control, storage, packaging and transportation, etc. The rural industries are at a relative disadvantage when they have to compete with the products of large scale industries.

There are certain special rural industrial products such as silver filigree, handicrafts, handloom, etc., for which there is an assured urban or export market. But for the majority of the rural industries, marketing is a handicap. Besides, the small producers lack resources to adopt sales promotion measures on a wide scale, such as display, discounts, hoarding, advertising, etc.

The rural industries should try to concentrate on the local rural and semi-urban markets. At present trade and commerce are concentrated in the urban areas. Therefore, although 75 per cent of the population lives in villages, urban areas control market and availability of these village industrial products. This is really an ironical matter. Proper care should be taken to develop the marketing of these products in the village areas themselves. Emporia and retail outlets should be opened in large numbers. In fact, after setting up a large number of retail outlets since, 1976, the business of the KVIC village leather industries has gone up satisfactorily.

At present, the major portion of marketing of rural production is carried on by private traders. They control retail as well as wholesale trade. it is necessary to effectively reorganize the marketing pattern. Marketing co-operatives should be encouraged. There should be a planned expansion of co-operative warehousing and trade channels.

The possibilities of expansion of foreign markets were investigated by the Indian Institute of Foreign Trade (I.I.F.T.).

Another organization, the State Trading Corporation of India (STC) also rendered several types of help. it surveyed the export market procured export orders and provided export counseling to the small producers.

In course of time many other organizations were created which provided marketing assistance to the small units. To promote exports of several products, Export Promotion Councils have been set up. Resides Trade Development Authority plays an important role in export marketing. It organizes "buyer-seller meets", among the importers and exporters.

To facilitate the marketing of the products produced in the small scale sector, the Government have reserved more than 837 items to be exclusively produced by the small scale sector. The list of reserved items is being constantly expanded.

Besides, at the State level, there are Small Industries Development Corporation, Agro-Industries Development Corporation, Leather Industries Development Corporation, Electronic Industries Development Corporation, etc., to help in the marketing of products of the small sector.

Marketing assistance rendered by the Government may be of two types. The State may provide direct marketing assistance, whereby a certain organization may buy small industry products to resell them assuming all the risks involved in marketing in the process.

Indirect marketing assistance is provided to supplement the marketing efforts of the small producers. These take the form of market research, publicity, exhibitions, trade fairs, arranging consignment sales, etc.

Suggestions

Marketing of the rural industrial products is a difficult task. Their resources are less. They face severe competition from the large scale sector. The producers are scattered. They are not properly organized. They are usually ignorant of the techniques of sales promotion.

The modern age is the age of advertisement and publicity. The small producers cannot pay for the higher cost of advertisement. The Government may arrange for commercial advertising at concessional rates. Alternatively, a subsidy may be paid for that purpose.

Besides, efforts may be made to organize small industries to form common associations. This will enable them to follow a common programme relating to advertisement.

The Problem of Infrastructure

Any industry, urban or rural, can prosper only when a suitable climate is present. Certain physical facilities must be present. Gone are the days of rural isolation.

The electricity is necessary to run eve the simple tools and machines. But till now electricity has not reached 50 per cent of the villages in the country. Even where power is available, an artisan is too poor to sapre a thousand rupees for electrical installations. In the electrified villages hardly 10 per cent of the households consumed electricity. It is , therefore, not surprising that the adoption of improved technology in the rural industries has been a very slow process.

Roads have been called as the arteries of a nation. But most of the countryside is cut off for a major part of the year, due to lack of all weather roads. Thus raw material cannot reach the rural artisans smoothly throughout the year. As the artisans are poor they have no capacity to store raw materials in advance. In the absence of transport facilities goods produced in the rural centres cannot be marketed properly. Spare parts and service facilities are not available. Even for a minor breakdown tools remain idle for long as these cannot be immediately repaired in the rural areas. Banking and postal facilities are not available in many places.

Therefore, it is essential that proper attention should be given for the development of infrastructure.

The Problem of Competition

The rural industries are supposed to be complementary to the modern small scale as well as large scale industries. But a major threat to the rural industries comes from the large industries. The rural economy no more stands isolated. "Rural India is in "the midst of rapid modernization due to electrification, education, communication, monetization and commercialization". Products produced in the large scale or modern small scale sector are flooding the rural markets. The small units have to compete with the large units for finance, raw materials and markets.

In the earlier times the rural industries formed an integral part of the village community system. The society was based on division of labour. The rural artisans did not face any problem regarding raw materials or markets. It was a static society free from competition and conflict.

The problem of destruction of the traditional rural industries began in the later part of the 18th century, when the British machine-made goods entered the Indian markets. The process continued unchecked till India achieved freedom. During the planned era several measures were adopted for the growth of the small scale sector. But so far as the village and cottage industries are concerned, they continue to face the challenge of competition.

The modern society is a dynamic one. There are constant changes in the pattern of demand, changes in technologies, emergence of substitutes, new materials, new raw designs, etc. The rural industries suffer most in such a dynamic situation. The problem is particularly acute in case of Khadi and village industries. They have to face direct competition form the organized sector, both in respect of quality as well as price.

"If free play of market forces is allowed, the tiny fish would be eaten away by small, small by big and big by bigger and ultimately by the biggest. In free conditions, the small, however beautiful and useful, is always handicapped for getting a place for its very existence, credit to keep its arteries flowing, raw materials to feed and disposal of finished goods".

The problems of the household industries have led to a gradual decline in the number of artisans engaged in the household industries sector. The number of artisans came down from 12.03 million in 1961 to 6.35 million in 1971. The number still further went down in 1981. During the same period, population has gone up by 50 per cent.

The rural industries have to be supported for their social benefit. Government policy support is the key input for the development of the rural industries. The policy support should include a measure of control over the organized industry.

Besides, there should be a differential approach with in-built advantages for the decentralized sector. In other words, both protective as well as positive forms of assistance should be rendered. The protective measures should include reservation of spheres of production, non-expansion of capacity of large scale, medium and modern small scald industries, the imposition of cess on products of these industries, subsidizing the products of the rural industries purchase preference, quota restrictions, etc. There should be well defined earmarking of areas of operation.

The positive forms should include earmarking of financial resources, provision of concessional credit facilities, supply of adequate raw materials at fair prices , fiscal concessions by the Government, provision of adequate facilities for training, research and development.

On the whole, the rural industries should be made complementary rather than competitive with the organized industries. There should be a linkage between the centralized and decentralized industries. The competitive strength of the rural industries should be increased.

The Problem of Technology

In India the rural industries have been often emphasized for the generation of employment opportunities. These have been treated as supplementary sources of income to the artisans. In fact, in 1980, part time employment was 66 per cent of the total employment under the KVIC. In 1955-56, this was as large as 94 per cent. But the problem of rural unemployment is getting more and more acute. There is mass poverty in the countryside. Agriculture alone cannot sustain the rural labour force. So the rural industries must serve as a principal source of income to the artisans. It must provide employment on a full-time basis.

The productivity of the rural industries is low as compared to the large industries. Consequently, the earnings of the artisans are low. The quality of the rural industrial products is not very satisfactory. Their prices are also comparatively higher.

Therefore, it is imperative to improve the technology. The carpenters, blacksmiths, weavers and other rural artisans are still following the age-old techniques of production. They use traditional tools and implements. They have failed to march with the progress of time. So improved tools and implements and upgraded techniques of production must be used. The technology should be labour-intensive. It should also be simple and cheap, so that it can be used by the rural poor.

The introduction of the improved technology would lead to a reduction in the price of the finished products, improve the quality of the products and increase the earnings of the artisans. The Karve Committee had rightly pointed out that the traditional industries could be viable with the adoption of improved technology wherever feasible.

To improve technology, the following measure should be adopted:

(a) Supply of improved tools and equipments and machines on the one hand, and adoption of improved techniques of production on the other.

(b) Provision of technical and consultancy services and help in identification of new raw materials and diversification of production activities.

(c) Provision for setting up research and development organizations in order to improve the techniques of production.

The development of technology should have the following objectives:

(a) Technology should reduce, if not eliminate, drudgery.

(b) Technology should enable the users to earn living wages comparable to ruling agricultural wages in that area.

(c) Technology should improve the scale the scale of productivity and quality.

(d) Technology should use local resources.

(e) Technology should use more and more of non-conventional energy resources .

(f) Technology should not only improve the tools and instruments but should also diversity the products.

The Problem of Organization

So far as the Khadi and village industries are concerned there are two kinds of organizations. The industrial institutions are registered under the Registration of Societies Act. The registered institutions are more or less concerned with the production of Khadi. There are also the co-operative societies. They are generally the producers of other village industries. In 1955-56, there were only 242 registered institutions and 60 co-operatives. In 1983-84, the respective numbers were 1,100 and 30,600. In India, there are more than 5.75 lakh villages. The growth in the number of co-operatives formed is very less. Due to a number of drawbacks such as lack of capital, lack of raw materials, poverty and illiteracy of artisans, etc., the progress of co-operatives has been hampered.

Thus, the absence of organizations at the village level to take up the programme of rural industrialization is a great problem for a rapid extension of rural industries.

The Problem of Sickness

The problem of industrial sickness has become a major issue in the Indian industrial scene. Both large scale and small scale industries suffer from this malady. But the disease is more common with the small scale industries. At present roughly one lakh small units are sick in the country.

Sometimes, some entrepreneurs deliberately make their units sick so as to qualify for the various concessions and facilities offered by the Government. In most of the cases, however, several factors contribute to such sickness. The small units lack resources to modernize. Financial institutions also do not show any interest for the revival of small sick units. Rehabilitation of a sick unit requires proper guidance and consultancy services, which are often lacking. The Government also do not provide any integrated assistance for the rehabilitation of sick units.

To remove this problem managerial efficiency and productivity have got to be improved. The industries have to be modernized. However, mere financial assistance is not enough. There should be a multi-pronged and simultaneous effort by Governmental agencies dealing with other aspects like raw materials supply, marketing and availability of power. Thus a coordinated effort is necessary to overcome the problem of sickness in small industrial units.

Suggestions for the Development of the Rural Industries

Today the Government has put utmost emphasis on the growth of rural industries. In this chapter we have already noted that they suffer from certain limitations. They face certain problems. Therefore, it is essential to remove these problems. Certain suggestions are made below for the rapid growth of rural industries.

1. Raw Materials: With the growth of industrialization, there has occurred a keen competition for raw materials. Consequently the rural industries and individual artisans face great difficulties in procuring these raw materials. The rural industries have been exposed to wide and erratic fluctuations in the prices of raw materials.

Take the case of non-edible oils and soap industry. In addition to oilseeds, it also needs chemicals such as caustic soda, silicate, colours and perfumes. Their supplies are subject to wide variation. Similarly the rural leather industry needs raw hides and skins. It also needs 25 items of tanning materials. One can never be sure of obtaining these at reasonable price.

Consequently the rural industrialists have been exploited by middle-men. The quality of the raw materials also has been often inferior.

The artisans are economically poor. They are dispersed over wide areas. They cannot purchase and store raw materials. So it is necessary to set up raw material banks for various commodities. The banks would procure raw materials and intermediate components of good quality from the open market on behalf of the institution. It would then store them in central places. This would ensure a smooth supply of raw materials to the rural industries.

Once the uncertainty in the supply and pricing of raw material is removed a major problem of the rural industries would be solved.

It is true that there are different types of rural industries. They have multifarious requirements. To solve the problem of raw materials of such a large number of rural industries is not an easy task. However, slowly and steadily steps may be taken in this direction.

2. ***Improvement in Technology:*** The product of the rural industries often cannot withstand the competition from the products of the large industries. They face defeat both on the price front and the quality front. Price depends on the cost of production which again depends on relative efficiency, and productivity. Quality also can be improved only when the technique of production is updated. The technical capabilities and skills of the people at the base level need to be fully developed. The potter, blacksmith, etc., engaged in the cottage industries should be exposed to modern techniques. The technical and technological gaps that are becoming wider every day, ought to be bridged if rural industrialization is to succeed.

3. ***Finance:*** Lack of adequate and timely finance is a problem common to small scale units. A number of financial institutions have been set up to provide finance to the rural industries. Provision of finance, however, involves a lot of bureaucratic and administrative delay. So it is necessary to simplify the lending procedure. A separate special fund, called

the Small Industries Development Fund, is set up in the Industrial Development Bank of India. This Fund will also be charged with the responsibility of providing re-financing assistance for development, expansion and modernization of small scale industry.

4. The Need for Industrial Finance: The small scale industries requires two types of finance, working capital and fixed capital. Working capital is needed to finance purchase and holding of stocks like raw materials, goods in process, finished goods, stores and supplies etc. Such capital is also needed for the payment of wages, rent, electricity charges, etc. It is also needed for sales finance, that is, to provide credit to the unit's customers, etc.

On the other hand, fixed capital is needed for the purchase of immovable assets, such as (a) Land, factory, building or shed etc. (b) plant, machinery and equipment etc.(c) furniture and fixture etc. term loan is provided to supply fixed capital. Such term loan again may be either medium term (3 to 10 years) or long term (10 years and above).

Small scale and cottage industries face different types of problems. But finance is perhaps the biggest problem. If sufficient finance is available all other problems can be more or less solved. The problem of financing small scale units is present in other developed countries as the U.S.A or Japan etc. as well. But the lack of finance for small scale and cottage industries is a more serious drawback in India.

The Administrative Commission Report rightly held that "if the small scale sector is to be developed, the credit requirements of this vital sector are to be fully met,"

5. Marketing: Lack of proper marketing opportunities is a major problem of the rural industries.

6. Development of Rural Infrastructure: Very often rural industries in the past have failed due to lack of developed infrastructure, like transport and communication, banks, educational institutions, etc. Even industrial estates in the semi-urban areas have remained unutilized due to the absence of sufficient infrastructure. Tastes have changed. People in the rural areas have been influenced by the urban life style. Therefore, health, education, entertainment and other facilities should be created in the rural areas.

7. Ancillarisation: Ancillarisation by small and rural industries should be promoted. To promote ancillarisation 16 sub-contracting exchanges have been set up. The Bureau of Public Enterprises has issued guidelines. Several regional and local committees have been set up. Today the purchase of ancillaries is less than one per cent of the total value of the products of large units. With ancillarisation of the problem of marketing of the rural industrial products would be partially solved. There should be an organic link between the large scale and ancillary units.

8. A Clear Definition: There is no clear definition of the rural industrial sector. The absence of a precise definition has adversely affected this sector. The Government have offered several facilities to the people engaged in this sector. But the artisans have not been able to derive full benefit from these facilities and incentives. It is, therefore, absolutely essential that the rural industrial sector be clearly defined. Besides, as the interests of the modern small scale industries and the village industries are not always harmonious, there should be a specific demarcation of activities.

9. People's Participation. The Government have followed several measures for the promotion of rural industries. But successful implementation of any developmental programme needs people's participation. In the rural industrial programmes have not fared satisfactorily, lack of popular participation is an important factor. The various programmes were chalked outside. Very often these did not take into account the needs and problems of the rural people. So it is necessary to motivate the rural people. They should be enthused to involve themselves in the implementation of rural industrial programmes. People's participation cannot be successful if the programmes are imposed from above. People should have a direct role in decision making. It calls for micro level planning. People will develop a sense of involvement only when they are made a party to decision.

10. Simplified Procedure: At present even the smaller units have to maintain registers in the prescribed forms. They have to submit certain returns, under various labour laws, either periodically or under certain special circumstances, like accidents, lockouts, strikes, closures, etc., to various authorities. This puts a lot of hardship on the small establishments. So in the matter of starting a small industry or in the process of its operation complicated procedures should not be followed. A working group set up by the Union Labour Ministry has recently suggested that small establishments employing not more than 19 people be exempted from submitting elaborate forms as is required to be done by larger establishments.

Large-scale *rural* unemployment is one of the major factors that drives most underdeveloped and developing countries to growth. Generally, these economies suffer from the problem of a high *rural* population that is dependent mainly on agriculture for their livelihood. A large part of this population can be substantially utilised in non-farm activities without affecting the agricultural output.

The linking factor between economic development and poverty alleviation in any economy is employment generation. As a greater proportion of the *rural* people in *India* is below the poverty line, any intervention geared towards poverty alleviation must focus on bucolic *India*. The urban areas have better employment opportunities and the poverty in those areas is not as serious as in the *rural* areas. Therefore, effective measures need to be taken to reduce *rural* poverty. In this context, it is important to note that the promotion of the agricultural sector alone will not be enough to achieve the desired results, as it can not absorb the abundant labour force in the *rural* areas and can not attain a high economic growth rate.

Labour being the most abundant resource of the *rural* areas, any programme for *rural* employment generation must maximise its productive use. Also the experiences of many advanced countries demonstrate that industry is an engine of growth. Thus, taking into account the these issues and the extent of poverty prevailing in *rural India,* the creation of employment opportunities through *rural* industrialisation for a faster growth rate of *rural* areas is essential.

The role of industry in *rural* economy is very obvious. The Indian *rural* economy is suffering from mass poverty, which is a consequence of unemployment and the resultant disparities of income and wealth. *Rural industries* are labour-intensive by their very nature. These *industries* provide the maximum employment per unit of capital invested; the labour-capital ratio in these *industries* is higher than that of in large-scale *industries*. A corollary of higher employment potential of *rural industries* is the higher output capacity per unit of capital. Just as a labour-surplus economy tries to maximise the employment potentiality of available capital resources, it also tends to maximise the output potentiality of available capital resources. *Rural industries* with a higher output-generating capacity per unit of capital offer a very useful technique of growth to the developing agrarian economies.

In the past, many government-sponsored schemes have been implemented for the growth of the *rural* economy and to provide employment opportunities

The *Ministry of Agro and Rural Industries* (MoARI), *India* was set up in September, 2001.

OBJECTIVES

This was done with the objectives of facilitating coordinated and focused policy formulation and effective implementation of programmes, projects, schemes, etc., for improving supply chain management, enhancing skills, upgrading technology, expanding markets and capacity building of the entrepreneurs/artisans and their groups/collectives. The Ministry deals with the *khadi* and village and *coir industries* through the Khadi and Village *Industries* Commission (KVIC) and the Coir Board and coordinates implementation of two countrywide employment generation programmes, namely, the *Rural* Employment Generation Programme (REGP) and the Prime Minister's Rozgar Yojana (PMRY) with the cooperation of State Governments, the *Reserve Bank of India* (RBI) and other banks.

Administrative setup

The ministry is headed by the Minister of Agro & *Rural Industries* and is based at Udyog Bhavan, Rafi Marg, *New Delhi*. Shri Mahabir Prasad is the current incumbent.

Recent interest on *rural industries* derives from recognition of thelimits of agriculture and organised manufacturing sector in employment generation especially during the post-liberalisation period in *India*. Historically, industrial development of the West and the East presentcontrasting pictures of *rural industries*. One, the linearity model foundedon the historical experience of the West, holds that development impliesa movement away from traditional subsistence production in *rural* areas to modern industrial production in urban centres. The other, the EastAsian Experience has shown that the growth potential of *rural* industriesis considerable given the under-utilisation of the physical labour and the entrepreneurial ability of *rural* people. A combination of putting out system and subcontracting system-along with modern factory and industrial cooperatives-has persisted in the *rural* manufacturing sector even in the era of economic liberalisation. We find differential capital endowments and socio-economic constraints of *rural* artisans reflecting extensive division of labour, specialisation and fragmentation of the labour process. These do not satisfy the requirements of the linearity model founded in advanced capitalist countries.

7

MICRO FINANCE

Micro-finance refers to small savings; credit and insurance services extended to socially and economically disadvantaged of society. In the Indian context terms like "small and marginal farmers". "rural artisans" and "economically weaker sections" have been used to broadly define micro-finance customers.

"Microfinance" is often defined as financial services for poor and low-income clients. In practice, the term is often used more narrowly to refer to loans and other services from providers that identify themselves as "microfinance institutions" (MFIs). These institutions commonly tend to use new methods developed over the last 30 years to deliver very small loans to unsalaried borrowers, taking little or no collateral. These methods include group lending and liability, pre-loan savings requirements, gradually increasing loan sizes, and an implicit guarantee of ready access to future loans if present loans are repaid fully and promptly.

More broadly, microfinance refers to a movement that envisions a world in which low-income households have permanent access to a range of high quality financial services to finance their income-producing activities, build assets, stabilize consumption, and protect against risks. These services are not limited to credit, but include savings, insurance, and money transfers.

THE DIFFERENCE BETWEEN MICROFINANCE AND MICROCREDIT?

Microcredit refers to very small loans for unsalaried borrowers with little or no collateral, provided by legally registered institutions. Currently, consumer credit provided to salaried workers based on automated credit scoring is usually not included in the definition of microcredit, although this may change.

Microfinance typically refers to microcredit, savings, insurance, money transfers, and other financial products targeted at poor and low-income people.

CLIENTS OF MICROFINANCE

Typical microfinance clients are poor and low-income people that do not have access to other formal financial institutions. Microfinance clients are usually self-employed, household-based entrepreneurs. Their diverse "micro-enterprises" include small retail shops, street vending, artisanal manufacture, and service provision. In rural areas, microentrepreneurs often have small income-generating activities such as food processing and trade; some but far from all are farmers.

Hard data on the poverty status of clients is limited, but tends to suggest that most microfinance clients fall near the poverty line, both above and below. Households in the poorest 10% of the population, including the destitute, are not traditional microcredit clients because they lack stable cash flows to repay loans. Most clients below the poverty line are in the upper half of the poor. It is clear, however, that some MFIs can serve clients at the higher end of the bottom half. Women often comprise the majority of clients.

Over the past decade, a few MFIs have started developing a range of products to meet the needs of other clients, including pensioners and salaried workers. Although little is known about the universe of potential clients, the number of households without effective access to financial services is enormous.

MICROFINANCE AND THE POOR

Experience shows that microfinance can help the poor to increase income, build viable businesses, and reduce their vulnerability to external shocks. It can also be a powerful instrument for self-empowerment by enabling the poor, especially women, to become economic agents of change.

Poverty is multi-dimensional. By providing access to financial services, microfinance plays an important role in the fight against the many aspects of poverty. For instance, income generation from a business helps not only the business activity expand but also contributes to household income and its attendant benefits on food security, children's education, etc. Moreover, for women, who, in many contexts, are secluded from public space, transacting with formal institutions can also build confidence and empowerment.

Recent research has revealed the extent to which individuals around the poverty line are vulnerable to shocks such as illness of a wage earner, weather, theft, or other such events. These shocks produce a huge claim on the limited financial resources of the family unit, and, absent effective financial services, can drive a family so much deeper into poverty that it can take years to recover.

MICROFINANCE, A TOOL TO ADDRESS SOCIO-ECONOMIC PROBLEMS

Financial services, particularly credit, are not appropriate for all people at all times. For loans that will be used for business purposes, microcredit best serves those who have identified an economic opportunity and can capitalize on it if they have access to a small amount of ready cash. Regardless of how loans are used, MFIs can provide long-term, stable credit access only when clients have both the willingness and ability to meet scheduled loan repayments.

Microfinance is particularly inappropriate for the destitute, who may need grants or other public resources to improve their economic situation. Grants are a more efficient way to transfer resources to the destitute than are loans that many will not be unable to repay. Too much risk is placed on the

MFI and client, when the only way a client can repay a loan is by starting a successful business. Basic requirements like food, shelter, and employment are often more urgently needed than financial services and should be appropriately funded by government and donor subsidies.

Governments and development agencies often use microfinance as a tool to address socio-economic problems such as relocation of refugees from civil strife, generating employment among demilitarized soldiers, or assistance following a natural disaster. Microfinance may or may not be able to respond to these situations effectively, and certainly not as a stand-alone intervention. Implementing a successful microfinance program to address these types of situations depends upon a number of factors, the most important of which is a client base capable of making regular repayments.

MFIS AND RATE OF INTEREST

Concerns often arise as to why microcredit interest rates are higher than the bank interest rates that wealthier people pay. The issue is cost: the administrative cost of making tiny loans is much higher in percentage terms than the cost of making a large loan. It takes a lot less staff time to make a single loan of $100,000 than 1,000 loans of $100 each. Besides loan size, other factors can make microcredit more expensive to deliver. Credit decisions for borrowers who have neither collateral nor a salary cannot be based on automated scoring. These decisions require substantial intervention of a loan officer in judging the risk of each loan. MFIs may operate in areas that are remote or have low population density, making lending more expensive. This is often why traditional banks tend to stay away from such areas. If an MFI wants to operate sustainably, it has to price its loans high enough to cover all its costs.

Although microcredit interest rates can be legitimately high, inefficient operations can make them higher than necessary. As the microcredit market matures in a given country, administrative costs usually drop as managers learn from experience and in some cases because competition forces lower pricing and greater efficiency.

THE POOR TOO POOR TO SAVE

The poor already save in ways that we may not consider as "normal" savings— investing in assets, for example, that can be easily exchanged to cash in the future (gold jewelry, domestic animals, building materials, etc.). After all, they face the same series of sudden demands for cash we all face: illness, school fees, need to expand the dwelling, burial, weddings.

These informal ways that people save are not without their problems. It is hard to cut off one leg of a goat that represents a family's savings mechanism when the sudden need for a small amount of cash arises. Or, if a poor woman has loaned her "saved" funds to a family member in order to keep them safe from theft (since the alternative would be to keep the funds stored under her mattress), these may not be readily available when the woman needs them. The poor need savings that are both *safe* and *liquid*. They care less about the interest rates that they can earn on the savings, since they are not used to saving in financial instruments and they place such a high premium on having savings readily available to meet emergency needs and accumulate assets.

These savings services must be adapted to meet the poor's particular demand and their cash flow cycle. Most often, the poor not only have low income, but also irregular income flows. Thus, to maximize the savings propensity of the poor, institutions must provide flexible opportunities— both in terms of amounts deposited and the frequency of pay ins and pay outs. This represents an important challenge for the microfinance industry that has not yet made a concerted attempt to profitably capture tiny deposits.

INSTITUTIONS DELIVERING MICROFINANCE

A microfinance institution is an organization that offers financial services to low income populations. Most MFIs started as not-for-profit organizations like NGOs (non-governmental organizations), credit unions and other financial cooperatives, and state-owned development and postal savings banks. An increasing number of MFIs are now organized as for-profit entities, often because it is a requirement to obtaining a license from banking authorities to offer savings services. For-profit MFIs may be organized as non-bank financial institutions (NBFIs), commercial banks that specialize in microfinance, or microfinance departments of full-service banks.

MICROFINANCE AND PROFITABLE

Yes it can. Data from the Micro Banking Bulletin reports that 63 of the world's top MFIs had an average rate of return, after adjusting for inflation and after taking out subsidies programs might have received, of about 2.5% of total assets. This compares favorably with returns in the commercial banking sector and gives credence to the hope of many that microfinance can be sufficiently attractive to mainstream into the retail banking sector. Many feel that once microfinance becomes mainstreamed, massive growth in the numbers of clients can be achieved.

Others worry that an excessive concern about profit in microfinance will lead MFIs up-market, to serve better off clients who can absorb larger loan amounts. This is the "crowding out" effect. This may happen; after all, there are a great number of very poor, poor, and vulnerable non-poor who are not reached by the banking sector.

It is interesting to note that while the programs that reach out to the poorest clients perform less well as a group than those who reach out to a somewhat better-off client segment, their performance is improving rapidly and at the same pace as the programs serving a broad-based client group did some years ago. More and more MFI managers have come to understand that sustainability is a precursor to reaching exponentially greater numbers of clients. Given this, managers of leading MFIs are seeking ways to dramatically increase operational efficiency. In short, we have every reason to expect that programs that reach out to the very poorest microclients can be sustainable once they have matured, and if they commit to that path. The evidence supports this position.

COMMERCIAL BANKS AND MICROFINANCE

Commercial Banks involve in micro finance increasingly. Formal financial institutions are recognizing the benefits of serving poorer clients.

GOVERNMENT'S ROLE IN SUPPORTING MICROFINANCE?

Governments have a complicated role when it comes to microfinance. Until recently, governments generally felt that it was their responsibility to generate development finance', including credit programs for the disadvantaged. Twenty years of insightful critique of rural credit programs revealed that governments do a very bad job of lending to the poor. Short term political gain is just too tempting for politically controlled lending organizations; they disburse too quickly (and thoughtlessly) and they collect too sporadically (unwillingness to be tough on defaulters). In urban areas, governments never really got into the act, and subsidized microenterprise credit is still relatively rare when compared to its rural counterpart.

Now that microfinance has become quite popular, governments are tempted to use savings banks, development banks, postal savings banks, and agricultural banks to move microcredit. This is not generally a good idea, unless the government has a clear acceptance of the need to avoid the pitfalls of the past and a clear means to do so. Many governments have set up apex facilities that channel funds from multilateral agencies to MFIs. Apex facilities can be quite complicated and there are few successful examples in microfinance. Successful apex organizations in microfinance tend to be built on the backs of successful MFIs, not the other way around. Finally, governments can also get involved in microfinance by concerning themselves with the regulatory framework that impinges on the ability of a wide range of financial actors to offer financial services to the very poor.

THE ROLE OF THE FINANCIAL REGULATOR IN SUPPORTING THE DEVELOPMENT OF MICROFINANCE?

Many feel that the most important role of a financial regulator in supporting the development of microfinance is to create an alternative institutional type that allows sound financial NGOs, credit unions, and other community-based intermediaries to obtain a license to offer deposit services to the general public and obtain funds through apex organizations. In a few countries, this may be an appropriate strategy. In most countries, however, the general level of development of the microfinance industry does not yet warrant the licensing of a separate class of financial institutions to serve the poor. And, in most countries, budgetary restrictions faced by bank regulators make it very unlikely that they will be able to supervise a whole host of small institutions; these institutions' total assets may make up a tiny per cent of the total financial system, but the cost of adequate supervision could eat up between 25 and 50 % of the total budget of the agency.

Rather, regulators can work with the nascent microfinance industries of most countries on issues such as modifying usury limits as stated in the commercial code to allow appropriate levels of interest, generating credit information clearinghouses to share information on defaulting borrowers to limit their ability to go from one MFI to another, working with civil authorities to ensure that private loan contracts can be recognized by courts in those transition economies that lack even basic legislative infrastructure, and reporting requirements that will prepare MFIs to eventually become regulated.

Regulators can also examine the laws, executive decrees, and internal regulations that limit the ability of traditional banking institutions to do microfinance. These regulations include limits on the per cent of a loan portfolio that can be lent on an unsecured basis, limits on group guarantee mechanisms, reporting requirements, limits on branch office operations (scheduling and security), and requirements for the contents of loan files. Not least, banking regulators may need to look at the way in which they would evaluate microloan portfolios within large banks.

TRAINING COURSES ON MICROFINANCE

A number of institutions provide workshops and trainings on microfinance topics from product costing to accounting to MFI management to reaching the poor, and much more. Trainings vary in length, location, and cost...please consider the institutions listed below as a starting point in learning more about microfinance training.

The recent Task Force on Micro Finance has defined it as "provision of thrift, credit and other financial services and products of very small amounts to the poor in rural, semi-urban or urban areas, for enabling them to raise their income levels and improve living standards". At present, a large part of micro finance activity is confined to credit only. Women constitute a vast majority of users.

The micro finance is recognized as a key strategy for addressing issues of poverty alleviation and women of empowerment. The women become economically self reliant, contribute directly to the well-being of their families; play a more active role in decision-making and are able to control systematic gender inequalities. Self-Help is micro credit groups and recognized as useful tool to help the poor, access financial resources which is not available to the their previously and help them from the clutches of exploitative money lenders.

Micro Finance is recognized as a key strategy for addressing issues of poverty alleviation and women empowerment. Access to financial service and the subsequent transfer of financial resources to poor women enables them to become economic agencies of change. The women become economically self-reliant, contribute directly to the well being of their families, play a more active role in making and are able to control systematic gender inequalities.

India is primarily an agricultural country with its economic and social life is based on villages. The agricultural activities are the major occupation of the rural households. The agricultural sector is playing a vital place in the economic development of the country as it contributes 8 per cent GDP to the national economy and employs 70 per cent of work force. A large number of land holdings are owned by small farmers and are scattered. The agriculture has strong weather related problems and the first major areas is to concentrate on sustainable growth. To reduce such vulnerability the Government is initiating sword measures under Five Years Plans to accelerate the credit availability thereby to increase agricultural production and rural income for reducing such vulnerability.

The financial services, mainly savings and credit to the poor in agricultural rural India are provided by both public and private financial systems. The public systems is primarily owned and controlled by the Government. These public institutions are Co-operative Credit Societies, Commerical Banks, Regional Rural Banks, National Bank for Agriculture and Rural Development (NABARD), and Government supported financial institutions.

The rural poor in the informal market think that the existing credit behaviour is highly credit worthy and reliable, paying market rate of interest, and savings and repaying regularly. Their on the agricultural cycle. But they are having multiple credit requirements. They do not have any collateral assets to avail loans from the formal credit systems. Moreover they high financial dependency on informal sources like moneylenders, traders, merchants and rich farmers.

Grameen Foundation has been working for over six years to support the microfinance sector in India. Generally, we enter into partnerships with MFIs that have strong business plans and outreach potential in order to help them become sustainable and achieve significant growth. Since 2000, we have entered into partnerships with five microfinance institutions and supported their growth from 49,000 to more than one million clients. We have also supported several MFIs in relief and recovery efforts related to the tsunami of December 2004.

MFIs will also be able to access *Mifos,* Grameen Foundation's innovative, open-source platform for information management. Details of our technical assistance to MFIs can be found in our *Toolbox.*

Our partner microfinance institutions in India collectively serve well over one million poor clients:

- Activists for Social Alternatives (ASA)
- CASHPOR Financial and Technical Services (CFTS)
- Covenant Centre for Development (CCD)
- Evangelical Social Action Forum (ESAF)

- Grameen Koota
- SHARE Microfinance Limited
- SKS Microfinance
- Sonata Microfinance Private, Ltd.

DEMAND FOR CREDIT

In terms of demand for micro-credit, there are four segments:

Landless Farmers

At the very bottom in terms of income and assets, and most numerous, are those who are landless and are engaged in agricultural work on a seasonal basis, and manual labourers in forestry, mining, household industries, construction and transport. This segment requires first and foremost consumption credit during those months when they do not get labour work, and for contingencies such as illness. They also need credit for acquiring small productive assets, such as livestock, using which they can generate additional income.

Small and Marginal Farmers

The next market segment is small and marginal farmers and rural artisans, weavers and those self-employed in the urban informal sector as hawkers, vendors, and workers in household micro-enterprises. This segment mainly rural areas, one of the main uses of working capital, a small part of which also serves consumption needs. In also needs term credit for acquiring additional productive assets, such as irrigation pumpsets. borewells and livestock in case of farmers, and equipments (looms, machinery) and work sheds in case of non-farm workers. This market segment also largely comprises the poor but not the poorest.

Commercial Croppers

The third market segment is of small and medium farmers who have gone in for commercial crops such as surplus paddy and wheat, cotton, groundnut, and others engaged in dairying, poultry, fishery, etc. Among non-farm activities, this segment includes those in villages and slums; engaged in processing of manufacturing activity, running provision stores, repair workshops, teashops, and various service enterprises. These persons are not always poor, through they live barely above the poverty line and also suffer from inadequate access to formal credit.

Women

One market segment, which is of great importance to micro-credit, is women. The 2001 census figures reveal that out of total 2.81 million marginal workers. 2.54 million were women and their further break-up shows that out of a total of 2.67 million rural marginal workers, 2.44 million were females. Further, many more women were willing to work. This has been corroborated by the results of survey done by the National Sample Survey Organization (NSSO), 43rd round, which has revealed that there is a vide variety of work which rural women combine with household work.

Table 1
Assistant Required by Women

Assistant Required (By Women Marginal Workers Seeking or Available for Work at their Household Premises)	*Per cent of Women Seeking Assistant*
No assistance	2.1
Initial finance on easy terms	53.6
Working capital facilities	22.2
Raw materials availability	4.6
Marketing	1.7
Training	10.5
Accommodation	0.4
Other assistance	4.9
Total	*100*

In the NSSO survey it has also been estimated that a large percentage of rural women in the age group of 15 years and above, who are usually engaged in household work, are willing to accept work at household premises (29.4 per cent), in activities such as dairy (9. 5 per cent), poultry (3 per cent), cattle rearing, spinning and weaving(3.4 per cent), tailoring (6.1 per cent) and manufacturing of wood and cane products ect. Amongst the women surveyed, 27.5 per cent rural women were seeking regular full-time work and 65.3 per cent were seeking part-time work. To start or to carry on such work, 53.6 per cent women wanted initial finance on easy terms, and 22.2 per cent wanted working capital facilities, as can be seen from the table below.

SUPPLY OF MICRO-FINANCE SERVICES

RBI data show that informal sources provide a significant part of the total credit needs of the rural population. The magnitude of the dependence of the rural poor on informal sources of credit can be observed from the findings of the All India Debt and Investment Survey, 1992, which shows that the share of the non-institutional agencies (informal sector) in the outstanding cash dues of the rural households was 36 per cent. However, the dependence of rural household, on such informal sources had reduced of their total outstanding dues steadily from 83.7 per cent in 1961 to 36 per cent in1991. This is shown in the table below:

Table 2
Outstanding from Informal Sources as a Percentage of Total Dues, for Various Occupational Categories of Rural Households

Year	*Cultivators*	*Non-Cultivator*	*All*
1961	81.6	89.5	83.7
1971	60.3	89.2	70.8
1981	36.8	63.3	38.8
1991	33.7	44.7	36.0

Among formal institutional sources banks and co-operatives provided credit support to almost 56 per cent of the rural households, while professional and agricultural moneylenders were providing credit to almost one-sixth of the rural households. The details by source are given below:

Though the overall share of institutional credit for rural households has gone u Steadily households in the lower asset groups were more deperment on the non-institutional credit agencies. The share of debt from the non-institutional credit agencies was 58 per cent in the case of lowest asset group of "less than Rs. 5,000" as against a low of 19 per cent in the highest asset group of Rs. 2.5 lakh and above.

Table 3
Sources of Credit for Rural Households

Credit Agency	*No. of Rural Households, 1991*
Government etc.	6.1
Cooperative Societies	21.6
Commercial banks and RRBs	33.7
Insurance	0.3
Provident Fund	0.7
Other institutional Sources	1.6
All Institutional Agencies	64.0
Landlords	4.0
Agricultural Money-lenders	7.0
Professional Money-lenders	10.5
Relative and Friends	5.5
Others	9.0
All Non-institutional Agencies	36.0
All Agencies	100.0

Over the decades following India's independence in 1947, Government of India (GOI) has made concerted efforts to provide micro-finance to the rural poor through the formal financial sector namely the co-operatives. However, the limited success of the co-operatives in the mid-fifties to the sixties forged the need for natioanlisation of commercial banks (CB) in 1971 and 1980 and the establishment large network to reach every village, and every segment of the population. In the mid-1970s, Regional Rural Banks (RRB) were also established to continue further the outreach of the banking sector in reaching the rural poor. All these programs were supported by a policy of mandated credit programs for the low-income households that were supported by the Integrated Rural Development Programme (IRDP), launched in 1980. The IRDP was designed to provide a mix of subsidy form the government and credit from the banking system to enable the asset acquisition of the poor.

MICRO CREDIT

As a result of these programmes, India has one of the largest banking networks in the world with close to 50,000 CB outlets; 14,420 RRBs; and 90,000 primary agricultural cooperative societies. Close to 43 per cent of the CB, and RRB branches are located in the rural areas. Even more impressive is the fact that, there is a financial intermediary branch for every 15,000 households, and a co-operative in every village.

Table 4
Share of Debt from Institutional and Non-institutional Sources, by Asset Holdings of Households

Household Assets (Rs. '000)	*Institutional Agency's Share as %*	*Non-Institutional Agency's Share as %*	*All*
Less than 5	42	58	100
5-10	47	53	100
10-20	44	56	100
20-30	68	32	100
30-50	55	45	100
50-70	53	47	100
70-100	61	39	100
100-150	61	39	100
150-250	68	32	100
250 and above	81	19	100
All Classes	64	36	100

Due to the extensive expansion of the banking network and emphasis on lending to small borrowers, there have been a lot of small loans by banks. In terms of amount, this was 13.2 per cent of the total credit outstanding from commercial banks and RRBs. As per RBI data for March 1994, the number of accounts below Rs. 25,000 was 5.6 million, or 93.6 per cent of total loan accounts, with 18.6 per cent of the outstanding amount. Of these, accounts with outstanding below Rs. 7500 comprised 80.5 per cent of the number of accounts and 49.5 per cent of amount outstanding. In terms of purpose, 45.8 per cent of amount was for small agricultural loans, 20.2 per cent for industry and 18.8 per cent of trade and services.

By March 1997, the number of small borrower accounts with a credit limit below Rs. 25,000, had come down by as many 0.6 million accounts to 5.0 million, or 90.1 per cent of the outstanding loan accounts. This decline in number of accounts clearly shows the post-liberalisation trend, with banks concentrating their efforts on larger loans and becoming ever more reluctant to extend credit to small borrowers.

While banks have been engaged in financing small borrowers, the manner in which this being done can hardly be called micro-finance. The procedure are cumbersome, the staff unfriendly and the transaction costs high. Repeat loans, except fro crop production, are rare, even fro borrowers who have repaid fully. Furthermore, even though the many of the loans extended to the poor by the public sector financial institutions are subsidized, their ultimate cost to the borrowers is high: factoring in out-of-pocket costs, payments to middle men, wage and business loss due to time spent in getting the loan approved. Effectively, the total cost of funds to the borrower ranges between 22-30 per cent as against the 12-14 per cent nominal lending rates specified for commercial bank loans below Rs. 2,00,000. All this results in low repayment rates, leading to a vicious cycle of non-availability and non-repayment.

Microfinance typically refers to microcredit, savings, insurance, money transfers, and other financial products targeted at poor and low-income people.

CLIENTS OF MICROFINANCE

Typical microfinance clients are poor and low-income people that do not have access to other formal financial institutions. Microfinance clients are usually self-employed, household-based entrepreneurs. Their diverse "micro-enterprises" include small retail shops, street vending, artisanal manufacture, and service provision. In rural areas, microentrepreneurs often have small income-generating activities such as food processing and trade; some but far from all are farmers.

Hard data on the poverty status of clients is limited, but tends to suggest that most microfinance clients fall near the poverty line, both above and below. Households in the poorest 10% of the population, including the destitute, are not traditional microcredit clients because they lack stable cash flows to repay loans. Most clients below the poverty line are in the upper half of the poor. It is clear, however, that some MFIs can serve clients at the higher end of the bottom half. Women often comprise the majority of clients.

Over the past decade, a few MFIs have started developing a range of products to meet the needs of other clients, including pensioners and salaried workers. Although little is known about the universe of potential clients, the number of households without effective access to financial services is enormous.

MICROFINANCE AND THE POOR

Experience shows that microfinance can help the poor to increase income, build viable businesses, and reduce their vulnerability to external shocks. It can also be a powerful instrument for self-empowerment by enabling the poor, especially women, to become economic agents of change.

Poverty is multi-dimensional. By providing access to financial services, microfinance plays an important role in the fight against the many aspects of poverty. For instance, income generation from a business helps not only the business activity expand but also contributes to household income and its attendant benefits on food security, children's education, etc. Moreover, for women, who, in many contexts, are secluded from public space, transacting with formal institutions can also build confidence and empowerment.

Recent research has revealed the extent to which individuals around the poverty line are vulnerable to shocks such as illness of a wage earner, weather, theft, or other such events. These shocks produce a huge claim on the limited financial resources of the family unit, and, absent effective financial services, can drive a family so much deeper into poverty that it can take years to recover.

MICRO-FINANCE INSTITUTIONAL STRUCTURE

The different organizations in this field can be classified as "Mainstream" and "Alternative" Micro Finance Institutions (MFI).

Mainstream Micro Finance Institutions

National Agricultural Bank for Rural Development (NABARD), Small Industries Development Bank of India (SIDBI), Housing Development Finance Corporation (HDFC), Commercial Banks, Regional Rural Banks (RRBs), the credit co-operative societies etc. are some of the mainstream financial institutions involved in extending micro finance.

Alternative Micro Finance Institutions

These are the institutions, which have come up to fill the gap between the demand and supply for micro finance. MFIs were recently defined by the Task Force as those, which provide thrift, credit and other financial services and products of very small amounts, mainly to the poor in rural semi-urban or urban areas for enabling them to raise their income level and improve living standards. The MFIs can broadly the classified as:

- NGOs, which are mainly engaged in promoting self-help groups (SHFs) and their federations at a cluster level, and linking SHGs with banks, under the NABARD scheme.
- NGOs directly lending to borrowers, who are either organized into SHGs or into Grameen Bank style groups and centres. These NGOs borrow bulk funds from RMK, SIDBI,FWWB and various donors.
- MFIs, which are specifically organized as cooperatives, such as the SEWA Bank and various Mutually Aided Cooperative Thrift and Credit Societies (MACTS) in AP.
- MFIs, which are organized as non-banking finance companies, such as BASIX, CFTS, Mirzapur and SHARE Microfin Ltd.

PROBLEMS FOR ALTERNATIVE MICRO-FINANCE INSTITUTIONS

Microcredit and microfinance is not the answer to all the problems of poverty in developing countries, but it is indeed an 'inducer' to a great many actions that can lead to a better quality of life for the low-income groups. The Virtual Library on Microcredit is a repository of information on alternative, non-conventional financial systems and microfinance/ microcredit issues.

The main aim with which the alternative MFIs have come up is to bridge the increasing gap between the demand and supply. A vast majority of them set up as NGOs for getting access to funds as, the existing practices of mainstream financing institutions such as SIDBI and NABARD and even of the institutions specially funding alternatives, such RMK and FWWB, is to fund only NGOs, or NGO promoted SHGs. As a result, the largest incentive to enter such services remains through the non-profit route. The alternative finance institutions also have not been fully successful in reaching the needy. There are many reasons for this:

- Financial problems leading to setting up of inappropriate legal structures.
- Lack of commercial orientation.
- Lack of proper governance and accountability.
- Isolated and scattered.

Inappropriate Legal Forms

NGOs invented micro-finance but NGOs are not the best type of agencies to carry out micro-finance on a long-term sustainable basis. If an MFI opts to become an NGO, it has the following problems:

- The major sources of funds of NGOs are grants, which are very limited.
- If the NGOs earn a substantial part of their income from lending activity, they violate Section 11(4) of the Income Tax Act and can lose their charitable status under Section 12.

- Moreover, NGOs do not have the appropriate financial structure for carrying out micro finance activities. NGOs being registered as societies or trusts do not have any equity capital and can never be "capital adequate".

The other alternative for an MFI is to become a cooperative or a company. As in the long run, the primary source of lending funds for MFIs is deposits, till that stage, the MFI has to rely on borrowings. To be able to attract borrowings, the MFI has to have equity capital. Thus, it is only possible to establish to establish a financially sustainable MFI either as a cooperative or as a company.

In most states, with exception of Andhra Pradesh, Maharashtra, and Gujarat, cooperatives are politized and state controlled and thus not an appropriate form of incorporation for an MFI. That leaves and MFI with the choice to be incorporated as a company and then become an NBFC or a Bank. The latter requires a licence and a minimum start up capital of Rs 5 crores, has only yet been operationalised by the government. If an MFI opts to become an NBFC, it has the following problems:

- The minimum entry-level capital requirements are Rs. 2 Crores w.e.f. April 1999.
- It is difficult to mobilize any borrowings from Indian financial Institutions due to the negative image of NBFCs in general. Further, even deposit mobilization is not possible at least for the first three years, till a satisfactory credit rating is obtained.
- That leaves the option of borrowing from foreign institutions, which is difficult in the first place, due to RBI's requirement of at least two credit rating. Further, very few foreign institutions are willing to give rupee denominated loans. Thus

THE PROBLEMS ASSOCIATED WITH MAINSTREAM MFIS

To enable the reach of micro finance services to the needy, the problems associated with the legal, regulatory, organizational systems and the attitudes should be addressed to and the desired changes brought in these, to make them more effective.

The mainstream financial institutions are flush with funds and have access to enormous amounts of low cost savings deposits. Indeed, the poorer the region, the lower the credit deposit radio–most of the eastern UP, Bihar, Orissa and the North-East have Credit Deposit rations of 20-30 per cent. Thus while banks are physically present in rural areas and offer concessional interest rates, rural producers are not able to access, with the result that the rest of the deposits are finding their way into the financial sector. Some of the main reasons for the above are:

Borrower Unfriendly Products and Procedures

With a majority of the customers being illiterate, and a majority of them needing consumption loans and a majority of them requiring high documentation and collateral security, the products are not reaching the rural poor.

Inflexibility and Delay

The rigid systems and procedures result in lot of time delay for the borrowers and de-motivate them to take further loans.

High Transaction Costs, both Legitimate and Illegal

Although the interest rate offered to the borrowers is regulated, the transaction costs in terms of the number of trips to be made, the documents to be furnished etc, plus the illegal charges to be paid, result in increasing the cost of borrowing. Thus, making it less attractive to the borrowers.

Social Obligation and not a Business Opportunity

Micro-finance has historically been seen as a social obligation rather than a potential business opportunity.

Finance to Alternative MFIs

NABARD Act does not permit them to refinance any private sector FI and do any direct financing (NABARD's direct lending to micro-finance NGOs so far has been out of donor funds), similarly SIDBI Act restricts it from extending loans to the agricultural and allied sectors, whereas many of the members of the self help groups are engaged in such activities.

Legal and Regulatory Framework

- The policymakers feel that farmers and poor people need low interest and subsidized credit. Thereby we have regulated interest regime for the loans up to Rs. 25,000 and Rs. 2,00,000/- with an interest cap of 12 per cent and 13.5 per cent respectively. They believe that poor cannot save, they are unwilling to repay the loans, and the administrative costs of servicing them are high.
- Also small loans have been used as a tool for disbursing political patronage, undermining the norm that loans must be repaid. Thus the mainstream institutions feel that these loans are risky, difficult to serve and have a low or negative net spread.

NOTE ON KALANJIAM

Creation of local financial institutions: The focus of the initiative is to create sound local financial institutions managed by women at hamlet, cluster and block level which will link with mainstream financial institutions. Primary purposes of these local financial institutions are:

- To provide a separate line of credit for consumption and emergencies, though their own savings to prevent investment credit from liquidation.
- To move out of exploitative informal financial system primarily from moneylenders.
- To establish a sound mechanism to regulated the household cash flow for managing the seasonality of income.
- To internalize the practice of treating external loan as their own fund. (Not being part of loan mela and loan waiver syndrome).
- To formalize the indigenous savings and credit system to provide continuity to people's initiative and to recognize the potential of the local system and

- To localize the financial institution, managed by people, to ensure 100 per cent repayment and to reduce the lending and borrowing cost by linking with mainstream financial institution.

KALANJIAM-HAMLET LEVEL FINANCIAL INSTITUTION

The primary focus of the programme is to create access and control over credit to poor women living in rural areas. The first step in this directionis formation of 'Kalanjiams' of poor women at hamlet level.

Insurance Corporation of India had adopted the Bima Grama Scheme a couple of decades ago. Under this scheme, a village would be considered as fairly well covered by insurance, if 75 per cent of the eligible persons of the eligible persons in the village are insured. The modus operandi adopted by banks for 100 per cent coverage is usually not made known to the public. What is intriguing is the fact that one of the micro credit schemes, which is in operation for 35 years, has not been successful in reaching its modest target of extending one per cent of the total bank credit to the poor at concessional rate of interest.

Differential rate of interest scheme

The Differential Rate of Interest scheme introduced in 1972 was one of the earliest experiments in micro credit. Banks were directed to lend at least 0.5 per cent of their total advances to the poor at the interest rate of 4 per cent. Later in 1978, this target was raised to one per cent. The interest rate was fixed 2 per cent lower than the then prevailing Bank Rate of 6 per cent. While initially only the public sector banks were directed to implement this scheme, from 1978, private sector banks also agreed to lend under this scheme.

The ceiling on advances was fixed at Rs. 6500 per borrower. The beneficiaries were the poor from both rural and urban areas. Income criteria adopted for fixing the eligibility in urban areas was that the family's annual income should be less than Rs. 7200 and in rural areas it was to be less than Rs. 6400. It was stipulated that 33 per cent (later raised to 40 per cent) of the DRI advances should be made to the borrowers belonging to scheduled classes and scheduled tribes in the villages. To ensure that the benefits of the scheme are made available to the rural borrowers, it was directed that 66 per cent of the advances should be made in rural and semi-urban branches. The progress made was however very poor. In most of the regional consultative committee meetings held periodically in different states under the chairmanship of the Union finance minister, banks were cajoled for their failure, if not indifference, to this scheme.

Poor Record...

Though this scheme has been in operation for over three decades, the flow of credit under it is unbelievably low. According to the latest data, there are 2.60 lakh borrowing accounts the amount lent as on March 2007 is Rs 634.46 core accounting for 0.06 per cent of the total credit. The number of accounts has been consistently declining from 1991, incidentally after the Financial sector reforms were introduced, from 34.49 lakh to less than 3 lakh at present. The amount involved was varying, though the percentage share of the advances under the scheme was consistently moving south.

In the Union Budget of 2007-08, the scope of the scheme was widened raising the ceiling on loan from Rs. 6500 to Rs 15,000 and for housing from Rs 5000 to Rs 20,000. The interest rate however remains unchanged at 4 per cent. Some increase in the disbursement is likely to take place as a result. The latest data published in the Statistical Tables Relating to Banks in India 2007 are provisional and there appears to be some discordant movements in the number of accounts and the amount outstanding.

Advances Under Differential Rate of Interest Scheme

DRI scheme has been a failure despite the fact that there was neither the funds constraint for lending nor the dearth of the eligible poor. During the last financial year FY 2007, the number of DRI borrowing accounts has come down from 3.88 lakh to 2.60 lakh, closing 1.28 lakh accounts, though the amount outstanding has gone up by Rs 144 crore. While the increase may be attributed to the enhancement of housing loan limits, the inference is that the DRI scheme has not made any contribution to enhancing financial inclusion.

Table 5

Year	*Number of Accounts*	*Advances Outstanding (Rs crore)*	*Share in Total (Percentage)*
1990	37.35	607.24	0.74
1991	34.49	618.82	0.67
1992	31.94	716.25	0.67
1993	29.05	705.33	0.62
1994	24.25	694.18	0.51
1995	19.46	683.03	0.49
1996	15.52	677.66	0.41
1997	14.29	654.76	0.34
1998	9.05	543.65	0.28
1999	7.29	485.00	0.21
2000	5.89	422.00	0.31
2001	5.14	358.00	0.10
2002	na	na	Na
2003	3.70	300.00	0.08
2004	3.68	315.00	0.07
2005	3.33	385.27	0.07
2006	3.88	490.22	0.07
2007	2.60	634.46	0.06

Financial Inclusion, Partial?

Migrant agricultural labourers are a class, likely to remain beyond the reach of bank's efforts towards financial inclusion. As they migrate from villages to cities, the percentage of rural population un-reached by banks comes down by default. In the cities, where they join the slum-dwellers, in all probability, they remain beyond the reach of banks, may be with some exceptions. Though there are some instars ces of the initiative taken by banks to open branches and also installing AFMs in some slums. If may be difficult for banks to achieve 100 per cent coverage of these families. Construction workers and the casual industrial workers, whose number is ever increasing in most of our cities, are the people, who are bankable. But since they do not have a permanent residential address, banks have difficulties in enlisting them as bank customers. Two fathers and two sons entering the bank may, therefore, result in the number of customers going up by only three and not four.

8

RURAL CREDIT INSTITUTIONS

ORGANISED BANKING SECTOR IN INDIA

The *Indian money market* is classified into: the organised sector (comprising private, public and foreign owned *commercial banks* and *cooperative* banks, together known as *scheduled banks*); and the unorganised sector (comprising individual or family owned indigenous bankers or *money lenders* and *non-banking financial companies* (NBFCs)). The unorganised sector and *microcredit* are still preferred over traditional banks in *rural* and sub-urban areas, especially for non-productive purposes, like ceremonies and short duration loans.

Prime Minister *Indira Gandhi nationalised* 14 banks in 1969, followed by six others in 1980, and made it mandatory for banks to provide 40% of their net credit to priority sectors like agriculture, small-scale industry, retail trade, small businesses, etc. to ensure that the banks fulfill their social and developmental goals. Since then, the number of bank branches has increased from 10,120 in 1969 to 98,910 in 2003 and the population covered by a branch decreased from 63,800 to 15,000 during the same period. The total *deposits* increased 32.6 times between 1971 to 1991 compared to 7 times between 1951 to 1971. Despite an increase of *rural* branches, from 1,860 or 22% of the total number of branches in 1969 to 32,270 or 48%, only 32,270 out of 5 *lakh* (500,000) villages are covered by a scheduled bank.

Since liberalisation, the government has approved significant banking reforms. While some of these relate to nationalised banks (like encouraging mergers, reducing government interference and increasing profitability and competitiveness), other reforms have opened up the banking and insurance sectors to private and foreign players 87% of marginal farmers and 70% of small farmers in India had no access to credit from a formal financial body, often relying on local money lenders who charge heavy rate of interest.

Agriculture is a seasonal activity and not an organized one. The farming size and finance requirements vary from place. Without employing cash. The agricultural activity cannot progress. The requirement at times become urgent. Timely availability of credit facilities to the farmer becomes essential. The cost of cultivation of varied crops is different that is one farmer's credit requirement is not same as another. Because of specialities in agriculture produce, the credit requirements of an industry are different from that of agriculture.

The rural credit institutions are listed here under

(i) Nationalised Bank or Public Sector Commercial Banks

(ii) Private Commercial Banks

(iii) National Bank for Agriculture and Rural Development (NABARD)

(iv) Cooperatives

(v) Regional Rural Banks

(vi) District Central Co-operatives Bank

(vii) Farmer's Service Societies

(viii) Agricultural Credit Societies.

(ix) Traders

(x) Land Lords

(xi) General Money Lenders

(xii) Agriculture Money Lenders

(xiii) Commission Agents and

(xiv) Friends

(xv) The Task Force on *Rural Credit* for the Tenth Plan projected the institutional *credit* flow to agriculture and allied activities to be Rs 7,36,570 crore during the period 2002-2007, which is more than three times (320 per cent) the *credit* flow (Rs 2,29,853 crore) during the Ninth Plan (1997-2002).

(xvi) The farm sector is emerging as a part of the new economic order arising out of globalisation and implementation of Agreement on Agriculture (AoA) under the World Trade Organisation. At the Cancun round, the negotiations on agriculture may not have arrived at the final stages of consensus between developed and developing countries. If some agreement is reached at the WTO negotiations sooner than later, the agriculture sector is poised for a radical transformation. To withstand the global competition, enhanced productivity and sustainability of the sector has become imperative.

(xvii) The *Rural* Non-Farm Sector (RNFS) has emerged an area of focus for creating employment in the *rural* sector and to enable migration from the over-stretched farm sector. The future strategy of *rural credit* institutions would have to include strengthening the *credit* delivery system for increasing RNFS employment. Development of entrepreneurs' skills, enhanced *credit* flow to women and other weaker sections, supporting tiny, cottage and village industries, and coverage of wide variety of service sector activities would require larger and wider role of *rural* financial institutions in RNFS sector.

(xviii) The growing role of microfinance through self-help groups (SHGs), especially of women, in the unique process of socio-economic engineering has assumed a critical challenge. The SHG movement has so far been mostly South-centric (constituting 64 per cent share) but is yet to take off in other regions. Nabard's goal of reaching microfinance services to one-third of the *rural* poor—about 100 million—through one million SHGs by 2006-2007 poses many challenges for *rural* financial institutions.

(xix) The socio-economic conditions of a majority of the *rural* population continues to be the cause of concern for policy-makers in this era of reforms and the WTO.

(xx) There are still more than 200 million people in *rural* areas who live below the poverty line and for whom banking access is still not a reality and, despite a large bank network, the critical gap in *rural credit* still exists.

(xxi) Therefore, the requirement for strong and flexible structure of *rural* financial institutions in *rural* and semi-urban segment need not be overemphasised.

(xxii) The financial sector reforms without social and *rural* sensitivity would only aggravate the complexities of agrarian sector reforms, which are yet to take shape. Therefore, it is hoped that the Advisory Committee, being constituted by the *RBI*, will be a High-Powered one (on the lines of the All India *Rural Credit* Survey Committee of 1954) and take a comprehensive review of the current *rural credit* structure and suggest innovative measures with a definite roadmap to meet the emerging needs/challenges in *rural*

Suggestions for evolving a policy that would make rural financial intermediaries operationally sustainable and reduce their transaction costs:

- Diversification of farming activity to make it bankable;
- Focus on the provision of credit to all sectors of the rural economy;
- Establishment of credit societies and *farmers'* societies by banks;
- Reduction of transaction costs;
- Employment of experienced, trained loan officers.

Table 1
Sources of Agriculture Credit

(Percentage Share)

Source	*1951-52*	*1961-62*	*1970-71*	*1981-82*	*1991-92*	*2002-03*
Government	3.3	2.6	3.6	4.0	6.1	3.0
Co-operative Societies	3.1	15.5	22.7	28.6	21.6	26.0
Commercial Banks	0.9	0.6	4.0	28.0	33.7	27.0

SPECIAL DRAWBACKS OF SMALL SCALE AND COTTAGE INDUSTRIES

Industrial finance is more complex than either commercial or agricultural finance. These industries require adequate and need-based finance at reasonable rates of interest and without much delay.

PROVIDING INDUSTRIAL CAPITAL TO THIS SECTOR IS BESET WITH CERTAIN DIFFICULTIES.

(1) Loans are given on the basis of some collateral or security. The rural industrialists usually lack resources that can serve as security. Their creditworthiness is very poor. So credit institutions usually do not prefer to provide financial assistance to these industries. due to this reason the rates of interest charged are usually higher.

(2) Many small units do not have proper books of account to reveal their sakes, assets and liabilities, etc. This may happen out of ignorance or lack of sufficient resources. This also proves to be a serious obstacle.

(3) In some cases small units do not have a clear idea about the amount of finance needed by them. they also seem to be ignorant of utilizing the loan asked for in an effective manner.

(4) The nature of small and rural industries thus imposes an extra burden on the banker in granting loans to them. To know and understand the technical, physical, financial and marketing problems, so as to assist them in financial planning and to subject themselves to financial discipline, an industrial banker has to keep in constant touch not only with the borrower, but with the progress of his project also.

CURRENT SCENARIO OF RUAL CREDIT

The small units are engaged in a wide range of productive activities. The financial institutions do not want to assume botheration by financing such diverse area:

- The share of formal credit to rural households–particularly to the poor and *marginal* is declining. This is evidenced by the All *India* Debt and Investment Survey reports.
- From statistics, it is also clear that there is a decline in the credit-deposit ratio of RRBs, thus increasing skimming of rural savings, and reducing relative flow of credit.
- There is a fall in the *small* borrower accounts of commercial banks. The bottom-line orientation of the commercial banks has led them to ignore the smaller borrowers, particularly in the rural areas.
- Inadequate attention being paid to the co-operative credit structure–an overwhelming amount of policy attention is on microcredit.
- In the past few years, the banking system has been unable to meet the priority sector lending obligations, particularly to agriculture.
- There still is a need to recognise that there is a hierarchy of credit needs of the *marginal* and *small farmers*–the entire spectrum of needs is to be addressed with multiple products keeping in view that money is fungible and therefore there could be adverse usage.
- There are not adequate instruments to address the two major risks faced by the farming community–the yield risk and the price risk. This affects the credit cycle and leads to accumulation of debts. This results in inability to service accumulated debts calling for two extreme fall outs–write off of loans so that the cycle could be started afresh or suicide deaths by *farmers* as evidenced by the *farmers* of Andhra Pradesh.

SOURCES OF FINANCE FOR RURAL INDUSTRIES

What is Industrial Finance?

No firm can come into existence without finance. Productive resources such as Land, Labour, Capital etc. are scarce. They have to be paid for. Thus bringing together different factors of production and to start production money expenditure is necessary. Once production starts, the firm has to continue production. Productive factors must be continually available to it. Thus requires recurring expenditure.

Thus to start production as well as maintain the production process in a continuous manner finance is required. The finance that a firm requires for the starting of production or maintenance of production is called as industrial finance. Industrial finance plays a crucial role in the establishment of industries as well as their successful operation.

Sources of Industrial Finance

The sources of finance for rural industries are of two types – internal and external. Internal source consists of initial capital and profits reinvested. External source consists of loans and other assistance from the non-institutional and institutional sources.

Non-institutional Agencies

Even today non-institutional agencies constitute a dominant source of working capital for the rural industrialists. As finance from other institutional source is scarce naturally the rural industrialists have to depend on the non-institutional sources for relief.

1. Moneylenders: 'Among the non-institutional sources, the most important, of course, is the village moneylender. The moneylenders constitute the traditional sources of finance for rural and cottage industries. There are several reasons behind the popularity of the moneylenders in our rural areas. Until very recently they enjoyed a monopolistic position. There were few financial institutions in the rural areas. The moneylenders have an intimate knowledge of their borrowers. They are familiar with the nature and economic position of the borrowers. They operate in a very simple manner. No forms need be filled up. There is no bureaucratic formality. Sometimes even the written records are absent. The moneylenders lend money for all purposes-productive as well as unproductive. An artisan sometimes has to borrow not only for his trade but also consumption purposes. The loans are provided promptly at the nick of time, when it is most urgently needed. Most important of all, they often lend without any security.

The moneylenders played an active and useful role in the rural setup. But their activities have been highly criticized.

They often charge very high rages of interest. The loan supplied by the moneylenders thus is expensive. They adopt a number of malpractices to exploit the borrowers. They often manipulate the accounts and cheat the illiterate artisans. Sometimes the artisans engaged in various rural industries are simply ruined by these moneylenders.

In the recent years several laws have been passed to control the activities of the moneylenders. They have to obtain licence. The lending and borrowing operations are duly rewarded. The rate of interest also has to be mentioned. In spite of all these restrictions, the moneylenders thrive.

2. ***Traders:*** Another important source of non-institutional credit is the traders. In many village industries, notably handicrafts, handloom, etc., the traders advance loans to the artisans. They also supply raw materials on credit. The conditions is that the produced goods are to be sold to the traders. For example, the traders provide loans to the filigree workers at Cuttack. Later on the highly artistic and valuable filigree objects are handed over to the greedy traders against normal prices. In the process the artisans are exploited. Sambalpuri handloom weavers also have often been victims of such exploitation by traders.

3. ***Relatives:*** Sometimes capital is also provided to the rural industrialists by the relatives. They, however, constitute a minor sources. Over the year their importance has been falling. In 1951, they provided 14 per cent of the rural credit. In 1961, they provided hardly 9 per cent of the rural credit requirements.

As the relatives themselves are poor they can hardly meet the capital requirements of the rural industrialists on a large scale.

Institutional Agencies

The institutional agencies constitute the most important source for the provision of capital to rural industrialists. Among the institutional sources are the State Government, Industrial Co-operatives, Commercial Banks, National Bank for Reconstruction and Development and other specialized institutions. We shall discuss about some of them.

1. State Government: The State Government provide finance in the form of loans raised from sales, subscription to shares and debentures etc. These loans are repayable in easy instalments. They are advanced on soft terms. The rates of interest are not uniform. The rates vary from Sate to State. Similarly the amount of loan offered also varies from State to State.

2. State Financial Corporation: To provide financial assistance to the small and medium industries, the State Financial Corporations were set up in 1951.

At present there are 18 SFCs. The authorized capital of a State Financial Corporation varies between Rs. 50 lakhs and Rs. 5 crores. It can raise additional resources through the sale of bonds and debentures, receiving public deposits and by borrowing from the Industrial Development Bank of India, and the Reserve Bank of India. In fact, refinancing by the I.D.B.I. to SFCs has proved to be a major source of funds to them.

These corporations grant loans to all types of Industrial concerns. Loans are repayable within a period of 20 years. They guarantee loans raised by the industrial concerns from the banks. They underwrite the issue of shares, bonds and debentures of these concerns. They can themselves subscribe to the debentures of industrial concerns. They also provide guarantee in respect of deferred payments, for purchase of plant and machinery, etc.

The aggregate assistance sanctioned by 18 SFCs was Rs. 637 crores in 1982-83. Total assistance outstanding at the end of March 1983 was Rs. 1,503 crores.

The State Financial Corporation have been playing a creditable role. Their assistance to the small industries has vastly gone up. They are paying special attention for the development of industries in the backward areas.

The SFCs also suffer from certain limitations. In the recent years the demand for financial assistance by the small industries has vastly gone u. But the resources of these corporations are inadequate. The performance of the various corporations are inadequate. The performance of the various corporations is uneven, very often a lot of delay is involved in sanctioning loan. The percentage of over dues is on the rise. They often lack a self-sufficient organizational setup. They lack competent and trained staff.

1. State Industrial Development Corporation: Today all the State Governments are keenly interested to promote industrial development in their respective States. Hence, in addition to the State Financial Corporations, Industrial Development Corporations have been set up in different States. Such corporations were first set up in Bihar and Andhra Pradesh in 1960. These are wholly owned by the State Governments.

These corporations particularly cater to the needs of small enterprises. These corporations provide loans. They also subscribe to the shares and debentures of industrial concerns. They also provide many other facilities to promote industrial development. They provide industrial sheds. They may also provide project ideas and technical assistance, etc. They also pay special attention to develop the backward areas. Sometimes, they may mange industrial projects themselves.

2. Orissa State Khadi and Village Industries Board: In every State there is a statutory Khadi and Village Industries Board. Such a Board functions in the States of Orissa and Tamil Nadu as well. The State Board obtains loan and grants from the Khadi and Village Industries Commission, for the development of Khadi and village industries in the States. The Board performs certain functions directly. For the implementation of certain other programmes, it disburses loans and grants to co-operative societies and other registered institutions.

3. Industrial Co-operatives and Urban Co-operative Banks: Urban co-operative banks also can play an effective role in the financing of small scale industries. The cater to the needs of individual living in urban areas who are engaged in a variety of industrial activities. Recognising this, the sub-committee of the Small Scale Industries Board set up in 1956 made detailed recommendations for using the medium of urban banks for providing finance to small scale industries.

Industrial co-operatives constitute an important source of finance to the rural industries. Besides, they also render a variety of assistance to the rural industrialists. Elsewhere we have discussed in detail about the forms, constitution and problems of these industrial co-operatives. The Government have always encouraged the organization of industrial co-operatives to solve the problems of rural industries.

Commercial Banks

When 14 *banks* were nationalised in 1969 and earlier social control of *banks* was promulgated in 1967 with the objective of providing a thrust to *rural* banking, the *banks* were not geared for discharging the new responsibilities. These *banks* so far were urban oriented. The employees were graduates and post graduates selected from the cities. Lending to agriculture is a task about which they had no prior experience or awareness. *Banks* had therefore to be geared for the task through extensive preparation straight from the scratch.

This was also the early phase of the green revolution in India, a new found prosperity entering the Indian villagesa. This was the ideal period for nationalized *banks* to mop up new untapped *rural* liquidity. The declared objectives of the new policy, known as "social and development banking", were the following

- to provide banking services in previously unbanked or under-banked *rural* areas;
- to provide substantial *credit* to specific activities including agriculture and cottage industries; and
- to provide *credit* to certain disadvantaged groups such as, for example, Dalit households.

The Government of India and the Reserve Bank of India (RBI) issued, from time to time, specific directives regarding "social and development banking". These included setting targets for the expansion of *rural* branches, imposing ceilings on interest rates, and setting guidelines for the sectoral allocation of *credit*.

LEAD BANK SCHME & DISTRICT LEVEL CONSULTATIVE COMMITTEE

To support the public sector *banks* and other institutions in *rural* banking the Government of India and RBI evolved these two Institutions of Lead Bank and District Consultative Committee. The Lead Bank Scheme was evolved and introduce by the Reserve Bank of India towards the end of 1969 to provide an appropriate organization framework for ensuring co-operation and co-ordination by various financial institutions with the concerned Governmental agencies in assisting developmental efforts. These efforts were to be undertaken on an area basis, with the district as the unit to ensure that the *credit* requirement of the *rural* economy were addressed adequately. The Lead Bank Scheme envisages assignment of lead roles to individual *banks* (both in public sector and private sector) for the districts allotted to them. A bank having a relatively large network of branches in the *rural* areas of the given district and endowed with adequate financial and manpower resources has generally been entrusted with the lead responsibility for the district. Accordingly, all the districts in the country (excepting the metropolitan cities) have been allotted to various *banks*. The lead bank acts as a consortium leader for coordinating the efforts of all *credit* institutions in the allotted districts to increase the flow of *credit* to agriculture, small scale industries and other economic activities included in the priority sector in the *rural* and semi-urban areas, with the district being basic areal unit. This scheme gave a tremendous boost to *rural* branches and government-sponsored programmes such as poverty-alleviation, self-employment, and crop-production.

Under this Lead Bank Scheme, the lead bank have been preparing District *Credit* Plans since 1973. The Reserve Bank of India gave these *Credit* Plans a uniform and systematic shape in 1980-82. These District *Credit* Plans take stock of the followings:

- Government's various programmes on poverty alleviation;
- Long-term/short-term trend in *credit* disbursements by financial institutions for each of the farm and non-farm sector programmes on poverty alleviation;
- *Credit*-based/non-*credit*-based promotional programmes for *rural* industrie and service sector on a district location basis;

The lead bank is the convener of the District Consultative Committee meetings to be presided over by the District Collector, and participated by all officials representing the development wing of the Collectorate, along with representatives of each bank in the area (designated as district coordinators by the non-lead *banks* in the district). Common problems faced by *Banks* in funancing developmental projects were discussed and sorted out in these meetings. This focussed better liaison between the local government machinery and the *banks* operating in the district. Targets under District *Credit* Plan were allocated to individual *banks* according to their representation in the district. The Lead Bank also compiled the District Survey Report giving all information about the district, which were relevant and useful for the *banks* operating there. It surveyed unbanked centres in the district and identified centres with potential for opening new branches. These centres were allotted to the *Banks* in the district, priority being given to the Lead Bank and the all India/regional *banks* having sizeable representation in the District.

The *banks* as an initial venture recruited agricultural graduates and designated them as Technical Officers (Agriculture). Head office of the *banks* issued Manuals explaining operational guidelines and procedures for *rural* advances. *Credit* Schmes were drafted and circulated. Training programmes were conducted and Field level programmes (Agricultural Workshops) were initiated. Officers were given categorical assurances that if they acted bonafide they will not be held responsible even if there were to be unexpected losses occuring or things going wrong otherwise, on account of factors beyond their realm.

OPENING RURAL BRANCHES BY BANKS

RBI controlled branch licensing. It settled every year with each bank its branch expansion plan and decided the number of new branches to be opened by the bank and its composition (*rural*, semi-urban, urban and metropolitan). Initially the *banks* were to complete their quota of opening *rural* and semi-urban branchs and only thereafter this the licences for Urban and Metropolitan Centers were normally issued to them. As the centres for opening *rural* branches are identified by the Task Force of the Lead Bank and allotted to different *banks*, the process of opening a large number of *rural* branches in quick succession became smooth and easier. Thus while in 1969 there were 1443 *rural* branches representing 17.6% of the total bank branches in the country, the number of *rural* branches in 1995 increased to 35008 forming 56.2% of the branch network of all *banks*. After the onset of the banking reforms uneconomic/non-viable *rural* branches were merged with other bigger units, complying ceretain norms as per guidelines issued bt thr RBI. Consequently the number of *rural* branchs as at the year 2000 decreaed to 32673 covering 48.7% of the total branches.

PERFORMANCE UNDER RURAL BANKING OF COMMERCIAL BANKS

Aggregate deposits of *rural* branches of all *commercial banks*, which was a meagre Rs.306 Crores (6.3%) in 1969 (brfore nationalisation) swelled to Rs.120,539 Crores (14.7%) in the year 2000. In terms of *rural credit* the comparative figures as at 1969, and 2000 are Rs. 115 Crores (3.3%) and Rs. 48753 Crores (10.6%) respectively.

Banks were under obligation to extend *credit* to priority sectors to an extent of 40% of their aggregate outstanding *credit*. As part of the overall PS-*Credit*, they are also to extend 18% of their aggregate *credit* to direct agriculture & indirect agricutlure category of borrowers. Performance of individual *banks* in achieving priority sector targets were reviewed regularly at quarterly intervals by the Finance Ministry & RBI. In the intial years of nationalisation the thrust was on "social & Developmental banking", the objectiveds of which are-

- to provide banking services in previously unbanked or under-banked *rural* areas;
- to provide substantial *credit* to specific activities including agriculture and cottage industries; and
- to provide *credit* to certain disadvantaged groups such as, for example, scheduled caste/scheduled tribe beneficiaries.
- *Rural* presence of *commercial banks* has come to stay. These *rural* branchs have proved to be viable and stable growth centres. In fact these branches have a role in ushering the green revolution and later the white revolution in the country. Precisely the "every-where presence" is one of the unique strengths of the state-owned and the old private sector *banks,* as against the new private and foreign *banks.* More appropraitely it is also a distinguishing factor that makes the banking network of our country as one of the widest in its spread globally. As agriculture becomes more and more of a *commercial* venture in contrast to being a mere "way of life" as it turned out to be earlier, as infrastructure development, social, educational and economic resurgence reaches the villages, as villages boom with all diverse economic enterprises, and not merely being confined predominantly to agriculture and animal husbandry, these branches are sure to turn into robust and thriving business centres providing multiple service facilities to pose as an equal rival to the overcrowded branches of the urban centres. This process has started already.
- ICICI Bank
- Nachiket Mor is the deputy managing director of ICICI Bank, which is currently the second-largest bank in

India with total asset of US$ 56 billion. The bank is among the leading investors in the agriculture, food and health care sector in India. Dr. Mor also is the chairman of the Managing Committee of the Institute of Financial Management and Research, which has recently established the Centre for Micro-Finance Research in Chennai. In these capacities Dr. Mor has been actively involved in development initiatives at the micro-level. Mor has a Ph.D. from the University of Pennsylvania's Wharton School of Business. In 2004 he was a Yale World Fellow. He is on the Board of International Food Policy Research Institute. Dr.Mor leads several initiatives of ICICI in India that are focused on improving public health and agriculture sector in India; ICICI Agri-Knowledge Forum is an initiative that aims at enhancing the income of small farmers in India; and ICICI Knowledge Park is one of the largest incubators supporting several life science enterprises. We will also be organizing a lunch for interested students and faculty with Mor on Oct 2. Email mt22@cornell.edu to include your name so that we can confirm the location and time.

- In most countries, commercial banks constitute the largest sources of institutional finance to the small scale industries. In Japan, for instance, about 80 per cent of the small units use bank finance. Banks contributes about 25 per cent of their total resources.

In India, however, in the beginning, the commercial banks used to ignore the small industries. These banks were under the control of large business houses. Beside, these banks used to avoid the huge risks involved in lending to small units. A modest beginning was, therefore, made by the State Bank of India in this respect which was established in 1955. But the real progress was made only after the nationalization of 14 major commercial banks in 1969. Six more banks were nationlised in1980.

Since then the commercial banks have come to the aid of the small scale and cottage industries in a big way. This may be seen from the fact that in June 1969, the total credit to the small scale industries amounted Rs. 251 crores. This was hardly 69 per cent of the total bank credit in 1985, the total credit to these units stood at R. 3,710 crores forming more than 15 per cent of the total bank credit.

Today, greater emphasis put on priority sector lending. It 1980 the public sector banks were directed to ensure that by March 1985, at least 40 per cent of the total credit should go to the priority sector, which includes small scale and cottage industries. This has already been achieved. Still the banks mostly provide working capital to the small units. So far as term loan is concerned, the banks meet the requirements for medium term loans is concerned, the banks meeting the long term capital requirements the small units have to look forward to other term lending institutions.

The banks today provide credit facilities such as working capital and term loan and deferred payment guarantee. Credit facilities are provided to both the newly established small units, for expansion and modernization. Term loans again may be either for a medium, term (3 to 10 years), or long term (11 to 25 years).

Credit facilities granted by the commercial to the small scale sector may assume several forms:

(a) cash credit facilities against hypothecation or pledge of goods,
(b) discounting facilities against bills,
(c) overdraft facilities against book depts. and bills drawn against supplies made to government, etc.,
(d) letter of credit for supply of raw materials or machinery,
(e) financing of export,
(f) clean limits granted for short period to get rid of financial problem due to payment for raw materials, etc.,
(g) financing guarantee, and
(h) deferred payment guarantee for purchase of capital goods.

Credit facilities again may be either secured or unsecured. Since 1977, the commercial banks are adopting a need-based approach while extending credit to the small scale sector, Previously, the approach was more security-based. At least the supple of working capital should be based on a need-based approach.

The rate of interest varies with purpose, amount and the length of the period. The working capital loan is repayable annually. Term loan is repayable in 2-7 years, depending upon cash generation.

All loans advanced by the commercial banks to small scale industrial units are protected by the Credit Guarantee Scheme of the Reserve Bank of India. There is a guarantee fee, at the rate of ¾ of one per cent for amounts exceeding Rs, 25,000, to be borne by the borrower. The fee up to the limit of R. 25,000 is borne by the bank.

Total number of Operational Holdings in the category of *small* and *marginal farmers*(SF,MF) i.e., those owning less than 2hectares or 5 acres: 537.21lacs as per the statistical Hand Book of Directorate of Economics and Statistics of the Ministry of Agriculture, Government of *India.* Total number of members having accounts with Primary Agricultural Cooperative Credit Societies that dispense short term agriculture credit to *farmers:* 127.41mn (Hand Book of Statistics on Indian Economy, 2006-07, RBI) Even if 80 per cent of the members are *small* and *marginal farmers* then they should be around 102mn accounts.

Total number of Direct Agriculture Accounts of SF&MF category: 131.72mn (Trend and Progress of Banking in *India,* RBI)

Therefore, Banks and cooperatives together hold accounts fifty times the owners of the *small* and *marginal* farmer holdings. Multiple accounts to a single farmer and the Kisan Credit Card figures could account for such huge figures in the Banks' portfolio. Another r reason for such large number of *small* and *marginal farmers'* accounts is because of the way the Banks classify the accounts while originating credit.

Acreage shown in the application of the farmer and not the acreage owned as per revenue record, is the basis for classifying a farm account as SF or MF. Since the loans below Rs. 2 lacs per farmer and *farmers* cultivating crops in areas less than 5 acres qualify for concessionary rate of interest as well, Banks accommodate even large *farmers* under this category.

Second, several Banks issued Kisan Credit Cards and those dues under the credit cards does not really become overdue and therefore do not qualify for the write-off.

Total amount of outstanding short term loans direct to agriculture as on 31st March 2007 as per the RBI statistics is Rs.1,46,941cr of which Rs.41,258cr is reported as lent for the *small* and *marginal farmers.*

Under the specific directives of the Union Government, public sector banks have doubled up credit to somehow.

There are a number of schemes with the commercial banks, to help the entrepreneurs to establish small scale units. Some of these schemes are described below:

Financing Qualified Entrepreneurs/Technocrats

Sometimes there are qualified entrepreneurs who possess technical competence, organizing skill and managerial aptitude, to set up small industries. The banks have a scheme to assist this class of people in setting up different types of small scale industries. The maximum limit allowed under this scheme is Rs. 5 lakhs.

Rural Workshop Scheme

Some industrial development corporations formulated a scheme to provide assistance to construct workshops. Such workshops provide employment. At the same time they provide repair facilities for agricultural implements, etc. Credit to the tune of Rs. 2 lakhs is available from the commercial banks, which is repayable in 10 years.

Financing Hire-Purchase Scheme

The commercial banks also provide financial assistance for supplying machines on hire-purchase scheme to the small scale units.

Self-employment Scheme

In October 1969, the Government introduced a scheme known as self-employment scheme. The commercial banks were advised to finances under the scheme.

Half-a-million Job Programme

Educated or uneducated, both categories of people derive benefit from this scheme. Priority is given to small scale industries. A branch of a bank normally provides credit under this scheme to persons living within a radius of 15 kms. Technically qualified people such as engineers, technicians or war widows, etc., are given preference in obtaining financial assistance under this scheme.

Different Rate of Interest Scheme (DRI)

The Government introduced a scheme in 1972 to help socially desirable and economically weaker sections of the society. This led to a shift from class banking to man banking. Distribution of credit was based on equity and social justice. According to this schema, the public sector banks were to advance loans to the weaker sections and depressed classes undertaking productive activities at a concessional rate of 4 per cent per annum.

The maximum amount of loan granted is Rs. 6,500 working capital is to be rapid within one year. Repayment for term loan should be over in 5 years. One per cent of the total loan sanctioned by a bank should be under the DRI scheme. In 1985, this percentage was 1'2.

Another stipulation is that of the total DRI advances, 40 per cent should be given to the weaker sections, such as S.C./ S.T., etc. In the year of introduction of this scheme a sum of Rs. 88 lakhs was advanced to 26,000 account. In 1985, there were 42.98 lakh accounts. The total credit advanced under this scheme was Rs. 443.60 crores.

Scheme for Providing Employment to Educated Unemployed Youth

To provide employment to educated unemployed youth a scheme was introduced on 15th August 1980. The objective of the scheme is to encourage the educated unemployed youth to undertake self-employment activities in agriculture, industry, service and business, etc. The selection of the applicants is done by the representatives of the Lead Bank of the district and the District Industries Centre. The applicant should be at least a matriculate and within the age group of 18 to 35 years. The eligible entrepreneur is given a composite loan of Rs.25,000. No collateral security or third party guarantee is necessary under the scheme. The loans are covered by the credit guarantee scheme, and eligible for refinance under NABARD.

Financing Rural Artisans

Rural artisans have skill in certain activities, such as smithy, carpentry, repair work, etc. Credit requirements of rural artisans from the area having population less than 50,000 and where credit requirements for their activities do not exceed Rs.25,000 are to be considered under the scheme.

Central Grant or Subsidy Scheme

This scheme was introduced in 1971. According to this scheme, the individual units to be set up in selected backward district areas would be give 10 per cent outright grant or subsidy. This subsidy is granted to the new as well as existing industrial units for substantial expansion.

Entrepreneurship Development Programme

A Rural Development Committee was set up in July 1978. It formulated a scheme called "Entrepreneurial Development Scheme", to promote industrial development. The scheme intends to provide training to the educated youths, properly motivate them and develop technical skill. Project reports are prepared. Then financial assistance is provided by the banks. Various other incentives are secured from the concerned organizations. The programme is for a maximum period of 3 months. District Industries Centres us for a maximum period of 3 months. District Industries Centres as well as the District Rural Development Agency organize similar training programmes.

Village Adoption Scheme

The village adoption scheme is based on an "area approach" to economic development. Its objective is to bring about an all-round development of village. It thus aims at developing and promoting village and small industries. The scheme involves the adoption of a village by a bank. The bank would then carry out a survey to assess the economic resources of the village. Developmental programmes would be chalked out. Eligible businessmen would be identified. Credit would be provided to them to implement these programmes.

Cottage and Village Industries

Banks provide financial assistance to the cottage industries on a large scale. Composite loan of 25,000 is sanctioned for the cottage industries. Consumption finance up to Rs. 500 is given in genuine castes. The branch managers use their discretionary powers in sanctioning the loans. The security is based on purpose of loan or type of activity, etc. Borrowers under the D.R.I. scheme are charged at the rate of 4 per cent. In backward areas the rate is 9'5 per cent. In other areas it is 11 per cent per annum. The loan is repayable within 3 to 7 years.

Credit Guarantee Scheme for Small Industries

In the beginning, the commercial banks were reluctant to provide liberal financial assistance to small scale industries. Without cheap and adequate financial assistance the small scale sector could not play an effective role in the industrialization of the country. Realising this problem the Government of India introduced the Credit Guarantee Scheme for small scale industries in 1960. The scheme was administered by the Credit Guarantee Organisation (CGO) of the Reserve Bank of India.

The purpose of this scheme is to provide a high degree of protection to the lending institutions against possible losses on credit facilities granted by them to small scale industries. From February 1970 a modified Credit Guarantee Scheme came into operation. According to this modified scheme, the R.B.I has agreed to cover all the eligible advances of the banks made to the small scale units. From 1st April, 1976, the small scale ancillary units also are covered by this scheme. The R.B.I. charges one per cent as the guarantee fee. About 300 financial institutions such as commercial banks, State financial corporations and several cooperative banks are covered by this scheme.

The total amount of outstanding guarantees in 1985 was more than Rs. 5,000 crores, as against Rs. 662 crores at the end of June 1970. In 1971, another scheme called as 'Small Loan Guarantee Scheme' was introduced to cover the risks of loans to small borrowers. Accordingly, the Deposit Insurance and Credit Guarantee Corporation (DICGC) was founded which covered both the schemes. A new scheme for assisting small scale units has been formulated and introduced in April 1981. This is known as "Credit Guarantee organization Scheme". This scheme in merged with the Deposit Insurance and Credit Guarantee Organisation from April 1981 and the former credit guarantee scheme has been closed. The credit guarantee organization automatically covers the liability of principal amount interest overdue and other recoverable charges of the financial institutions. All Cornmercial Banks. Regional Rural Banks, Co-operative Banks. State Financial Corporation are eligible for guarantee cover. For availing the guarantee facility financial institutions have to execute an agreement with the D.I.G.C. The risk coverage is 75 per cent of the amount in default.

Co-operative Banks: In 2007, the Government of India approved measures worth more than $3 bn to refinance the country's ailing co-operative banks so that they could offer cheaper loans to farmers. The World Bank has approved a $ 600 mn loan aimed at helping millions of poor farmers across India. Because thousands of farmers have committed suicide in the recent years saddled by debts they could not repay. The worst hit states for farmers' suicide are Andhra Pradesh, Karnataka, Kerala and Maharashtra. Since 2001, the number of deaths in these four states alone ranges from 3600 to 18,000.

State Bank of India: The State Bank of India came into existence in 1955 when the Imperial Bank of India was nationalized. Since its very inception the State Bank of India has paid attention to provide financial assistance to the small scale units.

In 1956 it introduced a pilot scheme of coordinate finance, popularly known as "Liberalised Scheme of Financing Small Scale Units", at nine selected centres. Only working capital was provided in the beginning. By 1960 the scheme was extended to all branches of the State Bank and its subsidiaries. Up to 1968, the State Bank and its subsidiaries were the only public sector banks. The number of units assisted and the outstanding amount to these units had a rapid increase. The result, however, was not very encouraging.

After the nationalization of the commercial banks in 1969, great emphasis was put on financing of small scale industries. The outlook of the banks changed. New schemes were introduced. Rules were liberalized. Procedures were simplified. The State Bank Group was in a better position via-a-vis other public sector banks, so far as the provision of finance to small scale industries was concerned. The State Bank Group had a number of branches. In February 1985 the State Bank and its subsidiaries had a total number of 10,184 branches. This was about 20 per cent of the total public sector commercial banks. The State Bank group had a well-experienced personnel. Most important of all, it had a well-established organization.

Consequently, the State Bank of India made a notable contribution in financing small scale industries, both from the point of view of the number of units financed, as well as the amount of outstanding credit to the small units.

As a result of working capital advances by the SBI, a variety of small scale industries were benefited. However, usually these industries were based on modern techniques and were located at urban centres. Small industries located in the rural or semi-urban areas were more or less neglected.

STATE BANK INSTITUTE OF RURAL DEVELOPMENT, HYDERABAD IS STATE BANK'S APEX TRAINING INSTITUTE FOR TRAINING BANK OFFICIALS IN RURAL BANKING

Background

State Bank of India (SBI), the largest commercial bank in the country, along with its seven Associate banks has a major responsibility in the process of rural development. Out of about 14,000 branches of SBI and its Associates, 74 % are located in rural and semi-urban areas. Their main focus is financing agriculture and allied activities, agro-processing, small & medium enterprises, rural crafts, and personal needs, besides accepting deposits and providing other banking services to the clientele.

To meet the need to train the executives working in large network of branches dealing with rural credit, the State Bank Institute of Rural Development (SBIRD) was established in 1981; its mission is to enhance the sensitivity of the Bank officers to rural environment, to equip them with the skills and knowledge and to provide the required orientation for rural banking. The objective is to enable them to creatively convert the scope into innovative schemes through extension, co-ordination and consultancy, and contribute to the process of rural development.

State Bank of India Caters to the needs of agriculturists and landless agricultural labourers through a network of 6600 rural and semi-urban branches.There are 972 specialized branches which have been set up in different parts of the country exclusively for the development of agriculture through credit deployment.These branches include 427 Agricultural Development Branches (ADBs) and 547 branches with Development Banking Department (DBDs) which cater to agriculturists and 2 Agricultural Business Branches at Chennai and Hyderabad catering to the needs of hitech commercial agricultural projects.

Our branches have covered a whole gamut of agricultural activities like crop production, horticulture, plantation crops, farm mechanization, land development and reclamation, digging of wells, tube wells and irrigation projects, forestry, construction of cold storages and godowns, processing of agri-products, finance to agri-input dealers, allied activities like dairy , fisheries, poultry, sheep-goat, piggery and rearing of silk worms.

The branch also has farmer's meet in villages to explain to farmers about various schemes offered by the bank.

To give special focus to agriculture lending Bank has set up agri business unit. Bank has also agri specialists in various disciplines to handle projects/guide farmers in their agri ventures. Advances are given for very small activity covering poorest of the poor to hitech activities involving large fund outlays.

We are the leaders in agri finance in the country with a portfolio of Rs. 18,000 crs in agri advances to around 50 lac farmers.

"For all your product and service related queries, you can call our helpline number 1800112211 (TollFree from BSNL/ MTNL landlines) or 080-26599990 which is open 24 hours on all 365 days."

THE NEW RESPONSIBILITY SUDDENLY UNFOLDING

When 14 *banks* were nationalised in 1969 and earlier social control of *banks* was promulgated in 1967 with the objective of providing a thrust to *rural* banking, the *banks* were not geared for discharging the new responsibilities. These *banks* so far were urban oriented. The employees were graduates and post graduates selected from the cities. Lending to agriculture is a task about which they had no prior experience or awareness. *Banks* had therefore to be geared for the task through extensive preparation straight from the scratch.This was also the early phase of the green revolution in India, a new found prosperity entering the Indian villagesa. This was the ideal period for nationalized *banks* to mop up new untapped *rural* liquidity. The declared objectives of the new policy, known as "social and development banking", were the following

- to provide banking services in previously unbanked or under-banked *rural* areas;
- to provide substantial *credit* to specific activities including agriculture and cottage industries; and
- to provide *credit* to certain disadvantaged groups such as, for example, Dalit households.The Government of India and the Reserve Bank of India (RBI) issued, from time to time, specific directives regarding "social and development banking". These included setting targets

for the expansion of *rural* branches, imposing ceilings on interest rates, and setting guidelines for the sectoral allocation of *credit*.

LEAD BANK SCHME AND DISTRICT LEVEL CONSULTATIVE COMMITTEE

To support the public sector *banks* and other institutions in *rural* banking the Government of India and RBI evolved these two Institutions of Lead Bank and District Consultative Committee. The Lead Bank Scheme was evolved and introduce by the Reserve Bank of India towards the end of 1969 to provide an appropriate organization framework for ensuring co-operation and co-ordination by various financial institutions with the concerned Governmental agencies in assisting developmental efforts. These efforts were to be undertaken on an area basis, with the district as the unit to ensure that the *credit* requirement of the *rural* economy were addressed adequately. The Lead Bank Scheme envisages assignment of lead roles to individual *banks* (both in public sector and private sector) for the districts allotted to them. A bank having a relatively large network of branches in the *rural* areas of the given district and endowed with adequate financial and manpower resources has generally been entrusted with the lead responsibility for the district. Accordingly, all the districts in the country (excepting the metropolitan cities) have been allotted to various *banks*. The lead bank acts as a consortium leader for coordinating the efforts of all *credit* institutions in the allotted districts to increase the flow of *credit* to agriculture, small scale industries and other economic activities included in the priority sector in the *rural* and semi-urban areas, with the district being basic areal unit. This scheme gave a tremendous boost to *rural* branches and government-sponsored programmes such as poverty-alleviation, self-employment, and crop-production. Under this Lead Bank Scheme, the lead bank have been preparing District *Credit* Plans since 1973. The Reserve Bank of India gave these *Credit* Plans a uniform and systematic shape in 1980-82. These District *Credit* Plans take stock of the followings:

- Government's various programmes on poverty alleviation;
- Long-term/short-term trend in *credit* disbursements by financial institutions for each of the farm and non-farm sector programmes on poverty alleviation;
- *Credit*-based/non-*credit*-based promotional programmes for *rural* industrie and service sector on a district location basis;

The lead bank is the convener of the District Consultative Committee meetings to be presided over by the District Collector, and participated by all officials representing the development wing of the Collectorate, along with representatives of each bank in the area (designated as district coordinators by the non-lead *banks* in the district). Common problems faced by *Banks* in funancing developmental projects were discussed and sorted out in these meetings. This focussed better liaison between the local government machinery and the *banks* operating in the district. Targets under District *Credit* Plan were allocated to individual *banks* according to their representation in the district. The Lead Bank also compiled the District Survey Report giving all information about the district, which were relevant and useful for the *banks* operating there. It surveyed unbanked centres in the district and identified centres with potential for opening new branches. These centres were allotted to the *Banks* in the district, priority being given to the Lead Bank and the all India/regional *banks* having sizeable representation in the District.The *banks* as an initial venture recruited agricultural graduates and designated them as Technical Officers (Agriculture). Head office of the *banks* issued Manuals explaining operational guidelines and procedures for *rural* advances. *Credit* Schmes were drafted and circulated. Training programmes were conducted and Field level programmes (Agricultural Workshops) were initiated. Officers were given categorical assurances that if they acted bonafide they will not be held responsible even if there were to be unexpected losses occuring or things going wrong otherwise, on account of factors beyond their realm.

OPENING RURAL BRANCHES BY BANKS

RBI controlled branch licensing. It settled every year with each bank its branch expansion plan and decided the number of new branches to be opened by the bank and its composition (*rural*, semi-urban, urban and metropolitan). Initially the *banks* were to complete their quota of opening *rural* and semi-urban branchs and only thereafter this the licences for Urban and Metropolitan Centers were normally issued to them. As the centres for opening *rural* branches are identified by the Task Force of the Lead Bank and allotted to different *banks*, the process of opening a large number of *rural* branches in quick succession became smooth and easier. Thus while in 1969 there were 1443 *rural* branches representing 17.6% of the total bank branches in the country, the number of *rural* branches in 1995 increased to 35008 forming 56.2% of the branch network of all *banks*. After the onset of the banking reforms uneconomic/non-viable *rural* branches were merged with other bigger units, complying ceretain norms as per guidelines issued bt thr RBI. Consequently the number of *rural* branchs as at the year 2000 decreaed to 32673 covering 48.7% of the total branches.

PERFORMANCE UNDER RURAL BANKING OF COMMERCIAL BANKS

Aggregate deposits of *rural* branches of all *commercial banks*, which was a meagre Rs.306 Crores (6.3%) in 1969 (brfore nationalisation) swelled to Rs.120,539 Crores (14.7%) in the year 2000. In terms of *rural credit* the comparative figures as at 1969, and 2000 are Rs.115 Crores (3.3%) and Rs.48753 Crores (10.6%) respectively.*Banks* were under obligation to extend *credit* to priority sectors to an extent of 40% of their aggregate outstanding *credit*. As part of the overall PS-*Credit*, they are also to extend 18% of their aggregate *credit* to direct agriculture & indirect agricutlure category of borrowers. Performance of individual *banks* in achieving priority sector targets were reviewed regularly at quarterly intervals by the Finance Ministry & RBI. In the intial years of nationalisation the thrust was on "social & Developmental banking", the objectiveds of which are-

- to provide banking services in previously unbanked or under-banked *rural* areas;
- to provide substantial *credit* to specific activities including agriculture and cottage industries; and
- to provide *credit* to certain disadvantaged groups such as, for example, scheduled caste/scheduled tribe beneficiaries.

20-POINT ECONOMIC PROGRAMME

The programme was initiated by the Prime Minister Mrs.Indira Gandhi during July 1975 after decalring emergency in the country. It is a package of twenty measures for the quick social and economic upliftment of the poor. The programme was popular and brought about good results in realms of releasing bonded labours, steps against *rural*-indebtedness, providing subsidised foodgrains through fair price shops etc. However after the emergency, the new Government did not pursue it further.A recent innovation is the institution of Micro-*credit* and SHGs. The subject has been dealt with elaborately in separate pages. These Institutions bears the potential for bringing productive *credit* within the easy reach ofthe poorestof the poor & transforming our villages into vibrant and self-reliant activity & growth centres. *Rural* presence of *commercial banks* has come to stay. These *rural* branchs have proved to be viable and stable growth centres. In fact these branches have a role in ushering the green revolution and later the white revolution in the country. Precisely the "every-where presence" is one of the unique strengths of the state-owned and the old private sector *banks,* as against the new private and foreign *banks.* More appropraitely it is also a distinguishing factor that makes the banking network of our country as one of the widest in its spread globally. As agriculture becomes more and more of a *commercial* venture in contrast to being a mere "way of life" as it turned out to be earlier, as infrastructure development, social, educational and economic resurgence reaches the villages, as villages boom with all diverse economic enterprises, and not merely being confined predominantly to agriculture and animal husbandry, these branches are sure to turn into robust and thriving business centres providing multiple service facilities to pose as an equal rival to the overcrowded branches of the urban centres. This process has started already.

RURAL MARKET BOOMING WITH BUSINESS PROSPECTS

Indian *rural* markets are expanding faster than urban ones. Interestingly, *rural India* accounts for 60 per cent of the total national demand. This segment is no more an inferior option of investment for big brands like ITC, Reliance, HLL, Godrej etc. CJ: Mandeep Singh Nayyar, 4 Sep. 2008 Views:1391 Comments:0

RURAL INDIA with its traditional perceptions has grown up over the years, not only in terms of income, but also in terms of thinking. The *rural* markets are growing at about two time faster pace than urban markets, not surprisingly, *rural India* accounts for 60 per cent of the total national demand.

According to a survey conducted by Mckinsey in 2007, *rural India* with a population of 630 million (approximately) would become bigger than total consumer *market* in countries such as South Korea or Canada in another 20 years and it will grow at least four times from its existing size.

Gone are the days when *rural* consumer went to nearby city to buy 'branded products and services'. The *rural* consumer is growing and this is an opportunity to grab the *market* share for all the global players in the *market* — whether it is into Fast Moving Consumer Goods (FMCG) sector or retail sector (either insurance or banking or for that sake any other sector).

The FMCG sector includes companies like Indian Tobacco Corporation (ITC), Godrej, Hindustan Lever Limited (HLL), Gujarat Cooperative Milk Marketing Federation (GCMMF-Amul) and Dabur *India* Limited. All these have shown a strong global presence in the *rural* sector and it can be said that all the FMCG companies should target the *rural* sector.

Some FMCGs products like toothpaste, hair oil and other like shampoos have done much better in the *rural* areas than the urban and the semi urban areas. It has been a phenomenon that the sales of many companies have gone up; Coca-Cola,

Nestle and Godrej too have also reported better sales in *rural* areas.

The retail sector has a huge potential for growth as a study shows that opportunities in *rural* retail sector were estimated to be over $34 billion in the year 2007, which is expected to touch $43 billion by the year 2010. It can be seen from the *market* that companies like Reliance, Subhiksha are expanding in the *rural market.* ITC has launched its first *rural* mall 'Chaupal Sagar', which offers products ranging from FMCG to electronic appliance to automobiles. Indian Oil is planning to invest $ 189.10 in the *rural* areas during the financial year 2009.

Insurance sector has one of the biggest potential in the upcoming scenario and the fact lies in the statement that only eight to 10 per cent of the *rural* households are covered by life insurance. *Rural* investments are limited to their available option—post offices and a few limited *commercial banks rural* extension counters. The remaining 90 per cent offer a huge potential as such for the insurance companies. The *rural market* is vibrant and holds tremendous potential for growth of insurance business, particularly because of the strong saving habits. LIC has a target of selling four million policies in the current financial year.

Telecom sector is one of the booming sectors of the economy. There are a large number of mobile subscribers in *India* and with the next 100 million to come from non-urban areas, many Indian mobile service providers are targetting the *rural market* with aggressive tariffs and low cost hand sets. In this regard Reliance Communication has targetted the *rural* segment by its 'Grameen programme' for *rural* subscribers. Spice Telecom is into the process of launching local *market* rates for the commodities across Karnataka to connect with *rural* customers. BSNL plans a $ 125.38 million to be spent on its *rural* infrastructure.

Consumer durable industry is also on the verge of making a foray into the *rural India* as it is all set to witness 12 per cent growth in the year 2008. Many companies like LG, Samsung are all set to put themselves into *rural* sector.

With *India* entering the globalisation mode and the *rural* revolution being governed by rising purchasing power, increased savings, changing consumer habits, there are sure and positive signs that a new dawn of *rural India* is going to come.

Union Finance Minister P.Chidambaram on 2nd November 2008 launched IFFCOTOKIO's Janata Bima Yojna, a micro insurance product in Tamil Nadu State. According to the scheme, Rs. 20,000 is assured to the policyholders a year by paying a premimum of just Rs.100. It (preminum) is just 25 paise a day. It would suit all, including the poor. Members of self-help groups had been selected to to agents. IFFCO has come forward to contribute 50% of the cost. The State Govermnents would contribute the remaining fund.

K.Srinivas Gowda, Chairman, IFFCO-TOKIO General Insurance said that Janata Bima Yojna is aimed at empowering the masses to protect themselves financially. It would cover property and critical illness cover. The policy has already been launched in Karnataka, Uttar Pradesh, Gujarat and other States.

REVITALISE RURAL CREDIT THROUGH 'NABARD'

The huge gap in rural credit still exists in spite of a wide rural credit structure. Therefore, the time has come to leverage Nabard's formidable financial strength to revitalise the rural credit structure.

THE National Bank for Agricultural and *Rural* Development (Nabard) was set up on July 12, 1982, as a development bank under an Act of Parliament. The bank began its journey by taking over the agriculture *credit* functions of the Reserve Bank of India and the refinance functions of the then Agricultural Refinance and Development Corporation (ARDC).

Nabard's mission is to "promote sustainable and equitable prosperity in *rural* India through effective *credit* support, related services, institution development and other innovative initiatives." Its prime function continues to be that of refinancing, supplementing the resources of co-operative *banks*, regional *rural banks* (RRBs) and *commercial banks* against the amounts lent at the grassroots level for agriculture and *rural* development.

Apart from its developmental role, Nabard has also been entrusted with certain supervisory functions in respect of co-operative *banks* and RRBs under the Banking Regulation Act, 1949. It may be noted that co-operative *banks* and RRBs have been in existence much before Nabard.

In the 1990s, gross capital formation (GCF) in agriculture witnessed a declining trend. This apart, *commercial banks*, which were assigned the task of channelling at least 18 per cent of their total lending to agriculture, were not able to fulfil their commitment.

It was, therefore, considered desirable to create the *Rural* Infrastructure Development Fund (RIDF) out of the shortfall in *commercial banks'* lending to agriculture, to be managed and operated by Nabard.

The fund was set up in 1995-96 with an initial corpus of Rs 2,000 crore for providing loans to State governments and state-owned corporations for projects relating to minor and medium irrigation, soil conservation, watershed management and *rural* infrastructure (such as roads, bridges and market yards).

Investment projects under social infrastructure, such as construction of primary health centres/schools, providing drinking water, and so on, were also supported under the RIDF.

Financial Scorecard

Through its main refinance portfolio to *rural* financial institutions (RFIs) and mobilisation and disbursements under the RIDF, Nabard has over the past two decades built up a strong financial base. Its working capital and income showed marked improvement after the management of the RIDF was taken over in 1995-96.

Rural Financial Institutions

Grassroots level RFIs comprise cooperative *banks* and RRBs.

Co-operative Credit Structure: Co-operative *credit* institutions, in existence since Independence, continue to play a crucial role in dispensation of *credit* for agriculture and *rural* development.

They are run by the respective State governments, and the short-term *credit* structure is managed by State co-operative *banks* (SCBs) and district central co-operative *banks* (DCCBs). Primary agricultural *credit* societies (PACSs) are short-term co-operative *credit* institutions dealing directly with individual borrowers.

The long-term co-operative *credit* structure is managed by State co-operative and agriculture *rural* development *banks* (SCARDBs) and primary co-operative agriculture and *rural* development *banks* (PCARDBs).

RRBs: These were set up in 1975 under an Act of Parliament to exclusively cater to the *credit* needs of the *rural* population, especially small and marginal farmers. The ownership structure of RRBs is, the Central Government (50 per cent), the State government concerned (15 per cent) and the sponsor *commercial* bank (35 per cent). The sponsor bank manages the RRB concerned. There are 196 RRBs spread over 516 districts with a branch network of 14,433. At the grassroots level, RFIs are under financial stress because of the prevailing agrarian crisis coupled with frequent droughts in the hinterland.

As on March 31, 2003, 43,511 of the 98,247 PACSs incurred losses. Under the co-operative *credit* structure, 527 of the 1,185 elected bank boards have been superseded by Nabard owing to weak financials. And the RBI has classified 97 of the 196 RRBs as weak.

Nabard, on the other hand, has built an enviable balance-sheet *vis-à-vis* other developmental *banks* on crucial indicators. As on March 31, 2004, Nabard's net worth (capital plus reserves) was Rs 7,291 crore and the capital-to-risk-weighted assets ratio (CRAR), 39.41 per cent. The NPAs were 0.0035 per cent and standard assets, 99.996 per cent.

There are 11.55 crore farmer households in the country, of which, 9.27 crore belong to small and marginal farmers. Institutional *rural credit* is accessible to only around 50 per cent of these farmers.

At the same time, as on March 31, 2003, 42 per cent (Rs. 29,706 crore) of aggregate institutional *credit* flow to agriculture and allied activities (Rs. 69,560 crore) was contributed by RFIs alone.

Only five of the 27 public sector *banks* (PSBs) and two among the 27 private sector *banks* are meeting the target of 18 per cent under agricultural *credit.*

The huge gap in *rural credit* still exists in spite of a wide *rural credit* structure. Therefore, the time has come to leverage Nabard's formidable financial strength to revitalise the *rural credit* structure.

Recommendation

Over the past two decades, Nabard has evolved into a strong and *rural*-sensitive apex developmental institution with a complete grassroots level understanding of the complexities of the agricultural and *rural* sectors.

Nabard is now a major shareholder in the Agricultural Insurance Corporation of India. It also has equity stake in NCDX (National Commodity and Derivatives Exchange) in association with other national-level institutions such as ICICI Bank, the LIC and the NSE (National Stock Exchange).

Nabard needs to acquire from the Central and State governments, equity stake in grassroots RFIs to play a more direct and proactive role in *rural credit.* The bank is fully equipped organisationally, financially and domain knowledge-wise to emerge as a strong player in the *rural credit* system. Promoting self-help groups reflects Nabard's capabilities in capacity-building and nurturing the *rural credit* delivery system.

Thus, Nabard needs to be fully vested with ownership role and proactive operational responsibility of administering and managing the *rural credit* structure and divested of its supervisory role in favour of the RBI. Only such a bold and innovative measure would pave the way for doubling of *rural credit* in the next three years in a sustainable manner. Many Indian *farmers* have been hit hard by debt

The World Bank has Approved a $600m (£300m) Loan Aimed at Helping millions of Poor Farmers Across India

Better access to finance for India's rural poor was "absolutely critical", the bank said in a statement.

The money would boost a programme to make thousands of rural co-operative banks responsive to the needs of poor Indian *farmers* seeking loans, it said.

Thousands of the *farmers* have committed suicide in recent years, saddled by debts they could not repay.

'Extortionate lenders'

Last year, India's government approved measures worth more than $3bn to refinance the country's ailing co-operative banks so that they could offer cheaper loans to *farmers.*

The World Bank said its offer of loan and credit was aimed at transforming *farmers'* access to financial services.

It said estimates suggested that 87% of *marginal farmers* and 70% of small *farmers* in *India* had no access to credit from a formal financial body, often relying instead on "extortionate money lenders".

"By providing small *farmers* with improved financial services, such as credit, savings, remittances and insurance, this project will play a significant role in helping India's rural poor benefit from growth opportunities," the bank's country director for *India,* Isabel Guerrero, said.

Although agriculture makes up just a fifth of India's economy, two-thirds of the population make a living from the land.

The worst-hit states for farmer suicides are Andhra Pradesh, Karnataka, Kerala and Maharashtra.

Estimates for the overall number of deaths among *farmers* in the four states since 2001 range from 3,600 to 18,000.

ICICI Bank

Nachiket Mor is the deputy managing director of ICICI Bank, which is currently the second-largest bank in India with total asset of US$ 56 billion. The bank is among the leading investors in the agriculture, food and health care sector in India. Dr. Mor also is the chairman of the Managing Committee of the Institute of Financial Management and Research, which has recently established the Centre for Micro-Finance Research in Chennai. In these capacities Dr. Mor has been actively involved in development initiatives at the micro-level. Mor has a Ph.D.

from the University of Pennsylvania's Wharton School of Business. In 2004 he was a Yale World Fellow. He is on the Board of International Food Policy Research Institute. Dr.Mor leads several initiatives of ICICI in India that are focused on improving public health and agriculture sector in India; ICICI Agri-Knowledge Forum is an initiative that aims at enhancing the income of small farmers in India; and ICICI Knowledge Park is one of the largest incubators supporting several life science enterprises.

RBI-RURAL PLANNING AND CREDIT DEPARTMENT

The Rural Planning and Credit Department formulates policies relating to rural credit and monitors timely and adequate flow of credit to the rural population for agricultural activities and rural employment programmes. It also formulates policies relating to the priority sector which includes agriculture, small-scale industries, tiny and village industries, artisans and retail traders, professional and self-employed persons, state sponsored organisations for Scheduled Castes and Scheduled Tribes and Government Sponsored credit-linked programmes like Swarnjayanti Gram Swarojgar Yojana (SGSY), Prime Ministers Rojgar Yojana (PMRY) etc. It implements and monitors the Lead Bank Scheme which is aimed at forging a coordinated approach for providing bank credit to achieve overall development of rural areas in the country. The department also oversees implementation of the Banking Ombudsman Scheme and setting up of Local Area Banks (LABs).

Priority Sector Lending by Commercial Banks

Targets/Sub-Targets

The targets and sub-targets set under priority sector lending for domestic and foreign banks operating in India are:

Challenges in Rural Credit—RBI Advisory Committee Must Sow the Right Seeds

The financial sector reforms without social and rural sensitivity would only aggravate the complexities of agrarian sector reforms, which

Table 1

Category of Advances	*Domestic Banks*	*Foreign Banks in India*
Aggregate advances to priority sector	40 per cent of net bank credit	32 per cent of net bank credit
Advances to agriculture	18 per cent of net bank credit	No target
Advances to weaker sections	10 per cent of net bank credit	No target
Advances to SSI	No target	10 per cent of net bank credit
Export Finance	Export finance does not form part of priority sector for domestic banks	12 per cent of net bank credit

are yet to take shape. It is thus hoped that the Advisory Committee, being constituted by the RBI, will be a High-Powered one suggest innovative measures with a definite roadmap to meet the emerging challenges in rural credit.

THE Reserve Bank of India has indeed made a categorical move in the matter of *rural credit.* Its initiative in this respect has been outlined in its recent Monetary and *Credit* Policy as under:

Table 2
Trends in Rural Lending: Post-reforms

Loans and Advances	*1984*	*2002*
Priority sector accounts of scheduled commercial banks (No. of accounts)	34.6 million	26.16 million
Rural advances of schedules commercial banks	13.90%	13.37%
Agricultural advances of schedules commercial banks	15.30% – 1991	9.79%
No. of agricultural accounts of schedules commercial banks	25 million	20.35 million
Loans accounts <Rs. 25,000 of schedules commercial banks (No. of accounts)	55.8 million	37.32 million
Small loans <Rs. 25,000 to total loan amounts	18.30%	5.90%

Per cent are to total bank credit
Source: RBI's handbook on bankers statistics

"In order to progress further in meeting the *credit* needs of the agriculture sector, it is proposed to constitute an Advisory Committee to suggest short & medium term measures Table to enhance *credit* flow to this sector. The Committee would, *inter alia*, look into Nabard's role in the development of the sector; the present structure and deployment.

The growth of commercial banks' lending to agriculture and allied activities saw a substantial decline in the 1990s compared to the 1980s. Agriculture's share in scheduled commercial banks' total outstanding *credit* as on March 31, 2002, was only Rs 64,008 crore (9.8 per cent). The declining penetration in *rural* banking during post-reforms is given in Table 2.

Apart from lending less than the stipulated 18 per cent target, many scheduled commercial banks are shying away from agriculture and priority sector lending by resorting to the soft option of investing in the RIDF window of Nabard. As contributions to the corpus of RIDF, Rs 16,145 crore was received by Nabard since 1995-96 from scheduled commercial banks against their shortfall in priority sector/agricultural lending during the preceding year. The outstandings of RIDF deposits at end-March 2003 stood at Rs 12,159.23 crore.

Table 3
Usage of Banking Services by Indian Households

	Total No.	*% of HHs*	*Rural*	*% of Total HHs*	*Urban*	*% of Total HHs*
HHs	19.19		13.83	72	5.36	28
No. of HHs which use banking services	6.8	35.5	4.16	30.1	2.55	49.5

Sources: Census of India 2001.

Apart from the above, the 2001 Census figures give an alarming picture about the usage of banking services among the Indian households in urban and *rural* areas despite wide banking network in the country. Table 3 reinforces the conclusions about the low level of banking usage among Indian households, in general (35.5 per cent), and *rural* households, in particular (30.1 per cent), and also reflects the latent potential demand for *credit* in *rural* segment.

RBI RELEASES DRAFT REPORT OF THE INTERNAL GROUP ON RURAL CREDIT AND MICRO FINANCE

The Reserve Bank of India *(RBI)* today released the *Report of the Internal Group on Rural Credit and Micro Finance.* The Group was set up to examine the issue of allowing banks to adopt the 'agency' model by using the Civil Society Organisations (CSOs) and other external entities for providing *credit* support to the *rural* and farm sectors, study the feasibility and modalities of appointment of 'Banking Correspondents' to function as intermediaries between the lending banks and the beneficiaries, suggest steps to promote Micro Finance Institutions (MFIs) and examine the extent of regulation, if need be, of MFIs.

It may be recalled that the Hon'ble Finance Minister in his statement on Union Budget - 2005-06 had suggested that the *RBI* should examine the above issues so that the banks would give more focus to provide *credit* to the *rural* and farm households through innovative measures and promote and empower MFIs so that they can intermediate between the lending banks and the beneficiaries. Dr.Y.V.Reddy, Governor, *RBI,* in his *Annual Policy Statement-2005-06* had also stressed the need for the banks to review their existing practices so as to align them with the objectives of financial inclusion.

The Group examined various policy options and strategies for enlarging the outreach of the banks through wide consultations with various stake holders and also reviewed the recommendations made by various committees on regulation of the micro finance sector. To deepen and widen the financial services provided by banks particularly to the under-serviced areas and the *rural* poor, the Group has suggested two Models, viz. the Business Facilitator Model and the Business Correspondent Model for providing non-financial support services and financial services as 'pass through' agents respectively by leveraging MFIs/NGOs, Civil Society Organisations and other external entities. The Group has also made recommendations relating to promotion, development and rating of MFIs and other outreach entities and mechanisms including widespread use of Information and Communication Technology (ICT) for expansion of banking outreach in a convenient, secured and cost effective manner. In relation to the regulation of MFIs, the Group has noted that the major players undertaking micro finance activities are well regulated entities like banks and NBFCs and the models of Business Facilitators/Correspondents suggested by the Group would forge stronger linkage between the NGOs-MFIs and the banks under a framework of due diligence and rating. As such, most part of micro finance port-folio will remain under the banks and the NBFCs, which come under the regulatory framework of *RBI.* Hence, a separate and exclusive regulatory framework for MFIs may not be required for the present.

The draft report of the Group is available on the RBI's website (*www.rbi.org.in*). Views/comments may be faxed to 022-2265 8276/022-2265 8273 by July 02, 2005.

The National Bank for Agriculture and Rural Development (NABARD)

NABARD's credit functions cover planning, dispensation and monitoring of credit. This activity involves:

- Framing policy and guidelines for rural financial institutions
- Providing credit facilities to issuing organizations
- Preparation of potential-linked credit plans annually for all districts for identification of credit potential
- Monitoring the flow of ground level rural credit

DEVELOPMENT AND PROMOTIONAL FUNCTIONS

Credit is a critical factor in development of agriculture and rural sector as it enables investment in capital formation and technological upgradation. Hence strengthening of rural financial institutions, which deliver credit to the sector, has been identified by NABARD as a thrust area. Various initiatives have been taken to strengthen the cooperative credit structure and the regional rural banks, so that adequate and timely credit is made available to the needy. In order to reinforce the credit functions and to make credit more productive, NABARD has been undertaking a number of developmental and promotional activities such as:

- Help cooperative banks and Regional Rural Banks to prepare development actionsplans for themselves
- Enter into MoU with state governments and cooperative banks specifying their respective obligations to improve the affairs of the banks in a stipulated timeframe
- Help Regional Rural Banks and the sponsor banks to enter into MoUs specifying their respective obligations to improve the affairs of the Regional Rural Banks in a stipulated timeframe
- Monitor implementation of development action plans of banks and fulfillment of obligations under MoUs
- Provide financial assistance to cooperatives and Regional Rural Banks for establishment of technical, monitoring and evaluations cells
- Provide organisation development intervention (ODI) through reputed training institutes like Bankers Institute of Rural Development (BIRD), Lucknow, National Bank Staff College, Lucknow and College of Agriculture Banking, Pune, etc.
- Provide financial support for the training institutes of cooperative banks
- Provide training for senior and middle level executives of commercial banks, Regional Rural Banks and cooperative banks
- Create awareness among the borrowers on ethics of repayment through Vikas Volunteer Vahini and Farmer's clubs
- Provide financial assistance to cooperative banks for building improved management information system, computerisation of operations and development of human resources.

SUPERVISORY FUNCTIONS

Overview

As an apex bank involved in refinancing credit needs of major financial institutions in the country engaged in offering financial assistance to agriculture and rural development operations and programmes, NABARD has been sharing with the Reserve Bank of India certain supervisory functions in respect of cooperative banks and Regional Rural Banks (RRBs).

As part of these functions, it

- Undertakes inspection of Regional Rural Banks (RRBs) and cooperative banks (other than urban/primary cooperative banks) under the provisions of Banking Regulation Act, 1949.
- Undertakes inspection of State Cooperative Agriculture and Rural Development Banks (SCARDBs) and apex non-credit cooperative societies on a voluntary basis
- Undertakes portfolio inspections, systems study, besides off-site surveillance of cooperative banks and Regional Rural Banks (RRBs)
- Provides recommendations to Reserve Bank of India on opening of new branches by State Cooperative Banks and Regional Rural Banks (RRBs)
- Administering the Credit Monitoring Arrangements in SCBs and CCBs.

Core Functions

NABARD has been entrusted with the statutory responsibility of conducting inspections of State Cooperative Banks (SCBs), District Central Cooperative Banks (DCCBs) and Regional Rural Banks (RRBs) under the provision of the Banking Regulation Act, 1949. In addition, NABARD has also been conducting periodic inspections of state level cooperative institutions such as State Cooperative Agriculture and Rural Development Banks (SCARDBs), Apex Weavers Societies, Marketing Federations, etc. on a voluntary basis.

Objectives of Inspection

- To protect the interest of the present and future depositors.
- To ensure that the business conducted by these banks is in conformity with the provisions of the relevant Acts/Rules, regulations/Bye-Laws, etc.
- To ensure observance of rules, guidelines, etc. formulated and issued by NABARD/RBI/Government.
- To examine the financial soundness of the banks.
- To suggest ways and means for strengthening the institutions so as to enable them to play more efficient role in rural credit.

Instruments of Supervision

- Periodic on-site inspection of 31 SCBs, 366 DCCBs, 20 SCARDBs and 102 RRBs and other Apex level Cooperative institutions.
- Supplementary Appraisal.
- Off-site Surveillance System (OSS).
- Portfolio inspection/System study.
- CMA returns.

Supervisory Strategy

In the wake of the banking sector reforms, new set of international norms/practices were made applicable to Commercial Banks (CBs) to make them more competitive and sustainable in the changing scenario. The co-operative banks and RRBs were also to function in the general banking environment, emerging out of the financial sector reforms, introduced by the GOI/RBI. Accordingly, the prudential norms were extended to them in phases. While the capital adequacy norm has not yet been made applicable to these banks, the other prudential norms viz. income recognition, asset classification and provisioning, which were made applicable by RBI to the commercial banking sector had been extended to cover RRBs in 1995-96, SCBs and DCCBs in 1996-97 and to SCARDBs in

1997-98. NABARD, through a concrete and time-bound supervision strategy, facilities these banks to adjust to the new financial discipline so as to internalize prudential norms stipulated.

Current Focus

Under the revised strategy, a sharper focus of the NABARD's inspection was given on the core areas of the functioning of banks pertaining to Capital Adequacy, Asset Quality, Management Earnings, Liquidity and Systems Compliance (CAMELSC). Thus, NABARD's focus in its statutory 'on-site' inspections is on core assessments leaving the collateral appraisals to supplementary inspections. The micro level aspects are to be taken care of by the banks themselves by way of internal inspections or by other agencies such as auditors. In this direction, through a series of workshops and meetings held with the Chief Executives and the Chief Auditors of cooperative banks, NABARD attempted to ensure that the other areas, particularly relating to the internal checks and controls, revenue and income realization by way of interest on loans and deposits and other routine features of carrying out general banking transactions were suitably taken care of by the respective banks and their concurrent/statutory audit systems.

Off-site Surveillance

As a part of the new strategy of supervision, a system of `Off-site Surveillance' has been introduced as a supplementary tool to the on-site inspection. Its objectives are to obtain and analyse critical data on a continuous basis, to identify areas of supervisory concern and to identify early warning signals and risky areas requiring further probe. The system basically envisages desk scrutiny of operations of cooperative banks and RRBs through a set of statutory and non-statutory returns. While the periodical statutory on-site inspections attempt an overall evaluation of the performance of the banks with a stipulated period, off-site surveillance envisages continuous supervision supplementing the on-site inspections with additional instruments of supervision.

Board of Supervision (for SCBs, DCCBs and RRBs)

Board of Supervision (for SCBs, DCCBs and RRBs) has been constituted by NABARD under Section 13(3) of NABARD Act, 1981 as an Internal Committee to the Board of Directors of NABARD.

The broad powers and functions of the Board of Supervision are:

- Giving directions and guidance in respect of policies and on matters relating to supervision and inspection, reviewing the inspection findings, suggesting appropriate measures
- Reviewing the follow-up action taken by Department of Supervision (DoS) on matters of frauds and internal checks and control
- Identifying the emerging supervisory issues in the functioning of cooperative banks/RRBs such as NPAs recovery, investment portfolio, credit monitoring system, management practices, frauds, etc.
- Suggesting necessary follow-up measures
- Recommending appropriate training for Inspecting Officers of NABARD for imparting necessary skills and knowledge
- Suggest measures for strengthening of DoS
- Recommend issue of directions by RBI
- Oversee the quality of inspections carried out and the reports issued
- Review the information generated through off-site surveillance and other supplementary vehicles, action taken thereon
- Undertake any other functions entrusted from time to time by the Board of Directors of NABARD The Board of Supervision, since its formation on 20 November 1999 , has held 31 meetings till 10 January 2007 and reviewed the financial position of Cooperative Banks and RRBs. Based on the observations of BoS, authorities concerned have been apprised of the weaknesses.

Other Initiatives

- The day-to-day functioning of the supervised banks is being monitored through various statutory returns prescribed by the RBI/NABARD including OSS returns
- Periodic coordination Meets are conducted with RPCD, RBI to discuss the policy and operational matters relating to supervision
- State level groups comprising RCS, Apex bank, Cooperation and Finance Department, State Government, Director of Audit and non-compliant banks have been constituted/ convened for preparing/discussing suitable strategy for Section 11 non-compliant banks and monitoring the progress of Action Plan prepared by them to facilitate them recompliance with the provision.
- Periodic discussions are held with the MD, Apex Banks, RCS, State Government etc. to discuss the supervisory concerns.

RO Set up

Suitable and adequate officers are placed in DoS units at RO level to undertake inspection of banks, issue inspection reports and take other follow up measures including review, monitoring compliance and OSS, etc. in conformity with DoS, HO guidelines.

HISTORY

NABARD was established by an act of Parliament on 12th July *1982* to implement the *National Bank for Agriculture and Rural Development Act 1981*. It replaced the Agricultural Credit Department (ACD) and Rural Planning and Credit Cell (RPCC) of *Reserve Bank of India,* and Agricultural Refinance and Development Corporation (ARDC).

NABARD

(1) serves as an apex financing agency for the institutions providing investment and production credit for promoting the various developmental activities in rural areas.

(2) takes measures towards institution building for improving absorptive capacity of the credit delivery system, including monitoring, formulation of rehabilitation schemes, restructuring of credit institutions, training of personnel, etc.

(3) co-ordinates the rural financing activities of all institutions engaged in developmental work at the field level and maintains liaison with *Government of India*, State Governments, *Reserve Bank of India* (RBI) and other national level institutions concerned with policy formulation.

(4) undertakes monitoring and evaluation of projects refinanced by it.

NABARD's refinance is available to State Co-operative Agriculture and Rural Development Banks (SCARDBs), State Co-operative Banks (SCBs), Regional Rural Banks (RRBs), Commercial Banks (CBs) and other financial institutions approved by RBI. While the ultimate beneficiaries of investment credit can be individuals, partnership concerns, companies, State-owned corporations or co-operative societies, production credit is generally given to individuals.

NABARD has Its Head Office at Mumbai, India

NABARD operates throughout the country through its 28 Regional Offices and one Sub-office, located in the capitals of all the states/union territories.Each Regional Office[RO] has a Chief General Manager [CGMs]as it's head, and the Head office has several Top executives like the Executive Directors[ED], Managing Directors[MD], and the Chairperson.It has 336 District Offices across the country, one Sub-office at *Port Blair* and one special cell at *Srinagar*. It also has 6 training establishments.

NABARD is also known for its 'SHG Bank Linkage Programme' which encourages India's banks to lend to *self-help groups* (SHGs). Because SHGs are composed mainly of poor women, this has evolved into an important Indian tool for *microfinance*. As of March 2006 2.2 million SHGs representing 33 million members had to been linked to credit through this programme.

In March 1979, a high level committee was setup by the Reserve Bank of India. It is known as the Sivaraman Committee or the Committee to Review the Arrangements for the Institutional Credit for Rural Development (Craficard). Its main job was to examine the need for integrating short and medium term credit with long term credit structures at all short and medium term credit with long term credit structures at all levels for the purpose of rural development. This committee recommended the establishment of a national level institution for providing refinancing facilities to the institutions engaged in rural and agricultural development. Accordingly, the National Bank for Agriculture and Rural Development (NABARD) was established, under an Act of Parliament, with effect from July 12, 1982.

The management of NABARD is entrusted with one Chairman, one Chief Executive and a team of executive directors who will be incharge of major development. The Board of Directors will consist of 15 members. Besides, there are Advisory Council, Executive Council and Management Committee, etc., for the smooth functioning of the organization.

The main objectives of the Bank are the following:

(1) It will be an apex organization for agriculture and rural development in the country.

(2) It will be providing credit for the promoting of agriculture, small scale industries, cottage and village industries, handicrafts and other rural crafts and other allied economic activities in rural areas for promoting integrated rural development.

(3) It will also provide direct lending facilities to any institution as may be approved by the Central Government for the purpose.

(4) It will be maintaining a close link with the R.B.I in these matters.

The NABARD pays due attention to extra agricultural as well as tertiary activities along with the land-based activities. Balanced growth of the rural India can be achieved only through the development of agricultural and non-agricultural sectors.

Activities

Broadly, the activities/purposes financed by banks included in priority sector are:

(a) Agriculture,

(b) Small scale industry,

(c) Small road and water transport operators,

(d) Retail traders and small business operators,

(e) Professional and self-employed persons,

(f) State-sponsored organisations for Scheduled Caste/ Scheduled Tribe,

(g) Educational loans,

(h) Housing (up to Rs 0.5 million in rural/semiurban areas and Rs 1 million in urban/metropolitan areas),

(i) Consumption loans for weaker sections,

(j) Self Help Groups/ Non Governmental Organisations,

(k) Software industry (having credit limits up to Rs. 10 million from the banking system),

(l) Food and agro based processing sector,

(m) Investment in venture capital.

Weaker Sections

The categories of borrowers included under weaker sections are:

(i) Small and marginal farmers with land holdings of five acres and less, landless labourers, tenant farmers and sharecroppers;

(ii) Artisans, village and cottage industries where individual credit requirements do not exceed Rs. 25,000 ;

(iii) Beneficiaries of Integrated Rural Development Programme (IRDP), Scheme for Urban Micro Enterprises (SUME) and Scheme for Liberation and Rehabilitation of Scavangers (SLRS);

(iv) Scheduled castes and scheduled tribes;

(v) Beneficiaries under the Differential Rate of Interest (DRI) scheme;

(vi) Self Help Groups.

Performance of Banks

Table 4 Domestic & Foreign Banks

Table 4

Domestic Banks	*March 1997*		*March 1998*		*March 1999**	
	Public Sector Banks	*Private Sector Banks*	*Public Sector Banks*	*Private Sector Banks*	*Public Sector Banks*	*Private Sector Banks*
Percentage of Priority sector advances to NBC	41.72	41.13	41.85	40.89	43.54	41.37
Percentage of Adv. to agriculture to NBC	16.35	9.02	15.72	9.57	16.28	9.52
Percentage of advances to weaker sections to NBC	8.69	2.33	8.31	2.21	7.64	2.20

Foreign Banks	*March 1997*	*March 1998*	*March 1999**
Percentage of priority sector Advances to net bank credit	37	34	37
Percentage of export credit to Net bank credit (12)	27	24	25
Percentage of SSI advances to Net bank credit (10)	11	10	11

* Data provisionals

Some of the NABARD schemes for the assistance of the rural industries are described below:

Refinance to Coir Industry

NABARD has decided to extend refinance facilities to the State Co-operative Banks (SCBs) on behalf of the Central Co-operative Banks (CCBs) by way of term loans for financing primary coir co-operative societies for installation of defibering units. Similar facilities were extended to all scheduled commercial banks (other than Regional Rural Banks) in respect of their loans to individual entrepreneurs who have arrangements beneficiaries should at least be to the extent of

20 per cent of the cost of investment or the cost of land whichever is more. NABARS's refinance would be limited to 90 per cent of the loans given by the banks. The rate of interest charged to SCBs would be 6'5 per cent. The primary co-operative societies, however, would get the loan at 9 per cent per annum. The commercial banks would be provided refinance at 8 per cent per annum and the bank lending rates should not exceed 12'5 per cent. The loan would be repayable within a period of 10 years.

Refinance to Handloom Weavers

During 1984-85, NABARD's Policy with regard to the short term financial accommodation available to the SCBs on behalf of the CCBs for financing the productive and marketing activities of the Primary Weaver's Co-operative Societies and for financing the Apex/Regional Weavers' Societies for their procurement and marketing of clothe remained unchanged.

NABARD had decided to extend refinance facilities for term loans advance for setting up of new emporia and renovation of existing ones by Apex Weaver's Societies. It has approved setting up of 5 new emporia and renovation of 30 existing ones. Post amalgamation Bank has got 16 RRBs with a network of 2,351 branches spread over 115 districts and 16 states in the Country. The aggregate deposits and advances of the sponsored RRBs stood at Rs.13,573 crore and Rs.7,856 crore respectively as on 31st March 2008. The profits have jumped from Rs.32.77 crore as on March 2007 to Rs.115.68 as on March 2008. During the year, a remittance product – Grameen Pay Order (GPO) was introduced for facilitating remittances from remote areas to increase fee income in RRBs. Post amalgamation; RRBs have broadbased their product profile by introducing Debt Swap Scheme, Warehouse Receipt Financing.

Refinance Facilities for Sericulture Development

NABARD extended term loan refinance facilities with effect from Dec. 21,1984 for reeling and twisting activities, irrespective of whether these activities are carried on by sericulturists along with the rearing activity or independently, so that the entire range of sericulture activities from mulberry plantation and reeling to the production of raw silk is covered. Repayment period is 3 years for Chakhas and 7 years for cottage basins and twisting units.

To enable silk reelers' co-operative societies to avail refinance assistance NABARD extended refinance facility with effect from Dec. 21, 1984 to such societies for their working capital requirements.

National Small Industries Corporation (NSIC)

In 1953, the Ford Foundation Team made a survey of the small scale industries in India. it recommended the establishment of a national corporation to assist actively in the growth and modernization of such industries. Accordingly, the NSIC was set up in 1955.

The most important function of the NSIC originally has been to provide the facility of supplying plant and machinery, indigenous and foreign, on hire-purchase basis, on easy terms to the small units. It also provides financial assistance by underwriting and guaranteeing loans provided to the small industries by specified banks and other financial institutions. The NSIC has also been distributing raw materials and components to small industries. The raw materials allocated are zinc, copper, lead, aluminium sheets, etc.

Another area in which "the NSIC has made significant impact is in providing direct marketing assistance to small industries through wholesale depots, mobile vans, intensive marketing campaigns, exports particularly of leather footwear. The Contract Division of the NSIC establishes contract with Government purchase departments. It arranges for giving contracts to small units.

It sponsored a credit guarantee scheme, according to which financial assistance would be rendered to the small units that secure government contracts, to enable them to carry on production and sale. It also helps them to secure a reasonable share of Government orders. It also provides technical assistance. The NSIC has succeeded in creating a significant class of small entrepreneurs. It has been suggested teat the NSIC should hand over its hire-purchase business to State Financial Corporations and restrict itself to the position of being a clearing house for technical and market information. In that case the strain on the resources of the NSCI would be lessened.

The Industrial Development Bank of India (IDBI)

The IDBI was set up in July 1964. It functioned as a subsidiary of the Reserve Bank of India. In February 1976, it was separated from the RBI and made an autonomous institution. The authorized capital of IDBI is Rs. 200 crores and paid-up capital is Rs. 145 crores. It performs a special function for planning, promoting and developing industries. It provides finance to all types of large, medium and small scale industries. It is a primary lending institution. It also serves as an apex institution for other primary lending institutions.

The IDBI follows different schemes of assistance:

1. ***Project Finance Scheme:*** This constitutes direct financial assistance to industries. Such assistance is provided in the form of advancing loans to the concerned units underwriting their shares and debentures, direct subscription to the shares and debentures and providing guarantees. Such help is rendered both for setting up of new units, as well as for expansion of existing units.

2. ***Refinance of Industrial Loan Scheme:*** The IDBI also undertakes refinancing. This is a type of indirect financing. It refinances long term loans which might have been given by other financial institutions, such as the IFC or the SFCs. Such a loan is for a period ranging from 3 years to 25 years. It also refinance medium term loans, repayable between 3 and 10 years, granted by the commercial banks, or the State co-operative banks.

3. ***Export Finance:*** The IDBI provides financial assistance for export promotion.

4. ***Promotional Functions:*** The IDBI also provides assistance to perform certain promotional functions. These promotional functions include (a) assistance to backward areas, (b) assistance to small scale industrial sector, (c) assistance to technical entrepreneurs (d) soft loan scheme for modernization,

and (e) conducting feasibility studies tendering technical assistance, etc.

For encouraging industrialisation of backward areas the IDBI provides the following assistance, direct financial assistance at a lower rate of interest, longer initial grace period for repayment of advances, concessional refinance assistance to projects in backward areas and special concessions to projects in North Eastern area.

The IDBI also operates schemes under which the small scale industries are provided with financial assistance at concessional rates. The IDBI also provides indirect assistance to entrepreneurs who possess technical skill and have viable projects in hand but lack sufficient capital to go ahead with their projects.

Up to June 1982, the IDBI has sanctioned financial assistance totaling Rs. 8,811.30 crores, out of which Rs. 6,087 crores has been disbursed. More than 45 per cent of the assistance sanctioned by the IDBI has gone to the backward areas. About 30 per cent of the assistance sanctioned has gone to the small scale sector.

The volume of financial assistance rendered by the IDBI has gone up quite fast during the past several years. The Bank has contributed much towards industrial development. But the benefits of the IDBI have not been equally shared by all the States. This may be known if either we compare the total assistance given to the various States or compare the per capital assistance. About 18 per cent of the total assistance has gone to Maharashra. Gujarat occupied the highest position in per capital disbursal, with Rs. 235'70. Thus, States like Gujarat, Haryana, Karnataka, Maharashtra, Punjab and Tamil Nadu, etc., have benefited most from IDBI loans. States like Bihar, Assam, Orissa, etc., have not fared well.

Small Industries Development Fund

In order to provide a focal point for coordinating financial assistance to the small scale sector at the apex level in the 1986-87 budget it has been proposed to set up a separate special fund called the Small Industries Development Fund in the

Industrial Development Bank of India. The Bank will also be charged with the responsibility of providing refinancing assistance for development expansion and modernisation of small scale industry.

REGIONAL RURAL BANKS

The Narsimham Committee conceptuated the creation of RRBs in 1975. The RRBs were set up through the promulgation of RRB Act of 1976. RRBs are "the small man's bank". They play a key role in rural institutional financing. In December 1975, there were 6 RRBs with 17 branches covering 12 districts. Now, there are 196 RRBs with 14,446 branches working in 518 districts across the country.

Table 5
No. of RRBs-State-wise

Name of the State	*No. of RRBs*
Andhra Pradesh	16
Arunachala Pradesh	1
Assam	5
Bihar	16
Chattisgarh	5
Gujarat	9
Haryana	4
Himachala Pradesh	2
J & K	3
Jharkhand	6
Karnataka	13
Kerala	2
Madhya Pradesh	19
Maharashtra	10
Manipuri	1
Meghalaya	1
Mizoram	1
Nagaland	1
Orissa	9
Punjab	5
Rajasthan	14
Tamil Nadu	3
Tripura	1
U.P.	36
Uttaranchal	4
West Bengal	9
Total	196

Though the RRBs have only 3% of total assets of Indian Banking Sector and of *rural* infrastructure development fund (RIDF); the role of RRBs; and the incentive and attitudinal aspects of *credit* delivery. It would suggest appropriate changes in the institutional and procedural arrangements for the smooth flow of *credit* to agriculture. The committee is expected to help in capturing technological developments in the cause of improving *credit* delivery."

For the task of the proposed committee, a look at the current trends and challenges in *rural credit*:

Table 6
Banking Profile at Metro/Urban/Semi-Urban/Rural Centres and RRBs (As on March 31, 2003)

	No. of Bank Branches	*Deposits (Rs. crore)*	*Credit (Rs. crore)*	*Credit (Deposit Ratio)*
All India	66,435	1,278,667	7,59,210	59,30%
Metro centres	8,664 (13%)	571,852 (44.9%)	474,461 (62%)	83%
Top 1011 centres (inclusive of metro centres)	15,066 (22.6%)	780,291 (61%)	575,945 (76%)	74.30%
Urban centres inclusive of metro & other centres	19,379 (29%)	861,875 (67%)	599,751 (79%)	69.50%
Semi-urban centres	14,813 (22%)	240,523 (19%)	84,683 (11%)	35%
Rural centres	22,244 (49%)	170,258 (14%)	74,775 (10%)	42%
Regional rural banks	14,452	49,776 (21%)	22,058 (4%)	44% (3%)
Combined CD ratio of banks at semi-urban & rural centres.				36%

Source: RBI's quarterly handbook on banking statistics.

CURRENT TRENDS IN RURAL CREDIT

The current banking profile (as on March 31) reflects the low *credit*-deposit (CD) ratio of 42 per cent and 35 per cent at the *rural* and semi-urban centres respectively compared with 69.5 per cent in the urban centres (inclusive of metro centres) and 59.3 per cent at the national level. The CD ratios at the metro and the top 100 urban centres are as high as 83 per cent and 74 per cent respectively. The exclusive CD ratios of banks' *rural* and semi-urban branches were 37.2 per cent and 39.7 per cent respectively at end-June 1969 (the time of nationalisation) and rose to 57.7 per cent and 49.1 per cent at end-June 1981. Post-reforms, the exclusive CD ratios at the *rural* and semi-urban branches almost plummeted to the levels prevalent during the period of nationalisation of banks. Despite the widespread banking network now, these trends indicate the continued migration of *rural*/semi-urban savings to urban/metro centres.

Though they operate with a rural focus, they are primarily scheduled commercial banks with a commercial orientation. They have a network of 43% of total rural banks of commercial banks. Between 1990 and 2004, the deposits and advances of RRBs grew by 14 times and 7 times respectively. Their main objective is to develop rural economy. They have organized 12 lakh Self Help Groups (i.e. about 45% of SHGs in the country). They have issued 40 lakh Kisan Credit Cards and organized 5000 Farmer's Clubs. The Government of India (Ministry of Finance) issued 9 notifications on September 12, 2005 for amalgamation of 28 RRBs into 9 new RRBs sponsored by 9 banks in 6 states. These amalgamated banks have become effective from September 12, 2005.

Post amalgamation Bank has got 16 RRBs with a network of 2,351 branches spread over 115 districts and 16 states in the Country. The aggregate deposits and advances of the sponsored RRBs stood at Rs.13,573 crore and Rs.7,856 crore respectively as on 31st March 2008. The profits have jumped from Rs.32.77 crore as on March 2007 to Rs.115.68 as on March 2008. During the year, a remittance product – Grameen Pay Order (GPO) was introduced for facilitating remittances from remote areas to increase fee income in RRBs. Post amalgamation; RRBs have broadbased their product profile by introducing Debt Swap Scheme, Warehouse Receipt Financing.

3 CRORE SMALL AND MARGINAL FARMERS TO BENEFIT FROM CHIDAMBARAM'S LARGESSE

To give a boost to the agricultural sector, the scheme of Debt Waiver and Debt Relief for *farmers* has been announced by the

Finance Minister, Shri P Chidambaram.All agricultural loans distributed by scheduled commercial banks, regional rural banks and cooperative credit institutions upto March 31, 2007 and overdue as on December 31, 2007 will be covered under Debt Waiver and Debt Relief scheme.For *marginal farmers* and *small farmers* there will be a complete waiver of all loans that were overdue on December 31,2007 and which remained unpaid until February 29,2008. In respect of other *farmers*, there will be a One Time Settlement (OTS) scheme for all loans that were overdue for the above period. Under the OTS, a rebate of 25% will be given against payment of the balance of 75%.Agricultural loans which were rescheduled and are restructured during 2004-06 as per the RBI guidelines will also be eligible for a waiver or an OTS on the same pattern.The implementation of the Debt Waiver and Debt Relief scheme will be completed by June 30, 2008. Upon being granted debt waiver or signing an agreement for debt relief under the OTS, the farmer would be entitled to fresh agricultural loans from the banks.Three crore *small* and *marginal farmers* and one crore other *farmers* will benefit from the scheme. The total value of overdue loans being waived is estimated at Rs.50,000 crores and the OTS relief on the overdue loans is estimated at Rs. 10,000 crores.s

Source: Press Information Bureau.

9

TECHNICAL SKILLS DEVELOPMENT AND UPGRADATION

Any worthwhile programme of rural industrialisation especially of the non-traditional variety presupposes ready availability of skills, such as factory operatives, machine tenders, skilled mechanics, and industrial craftsmen. In Technical training institutes were opened in India to fulfil the need of the local industry. However, the experience in this regard has not been happy so far. These training centres were established without much understanding of the actual need for trained people in the local industry. With the result, a large number trained man-power remained either unemployed or were forced to seek employment outside the district. Further, even the quality of training imparted was found to be wanting in more than one way.

Due to these considerations we have to take adequate steps promote to industrial talent backed by suitable training programmes. However, in view of rather poor educational levels, we had to limit the range of vocational training courses to a very elementary level.

The list of various training programmes offered to the village youth and the corresponding minimum educational levels required for enrolment in each case is given as follows:

As can be seen above, even though the minimum educational qualifications prescribed to be eligible for enrolment were rather low, the response was far from

Table 1

Trade	*Minimum Educational Level*
Tractor mechanics	Matriculation
Motor winding	Matriculation
Pumpset repairs	Eighth standard
Auto mechanic	Eighth standard
House-wiring	Eighth standard
Lathe mechanic	Literacy
Tailoring	Literacy
Carpet weaving	Literacy
Blanket weaving	Literacy
Leather goods and shoes	Literacy

encouraging. Even these eligibility conditions had to be waived in certain cases where the motivational level was found to be exceptionally high, even through not suitably qualified.

In view of a near absence of entrepreneurial and technical skills in the villages, we have to start a parallel programme of technical skills development along with industries development. As such, along with enlisting the villagers to take up industrial ventures, the expert team must encourage and motivate literate and semi-literate unemployed young boys and girls to learn some technical skill so as to become bread earners in due course.

But the task of enlisting the village youth for various training programmes proved to most hazardous and the team had to use all its persuasive power to motivate them. In each of the villages the young boys wanted an assurance that the team would get them some employment after the training was over. The reason for such an attitude was found to be prevalent among the youth as also their elders because of the presence of unemployed ITI-trained boys in most of the larger villages.

These villagers had, over the years, come to firmly believe that mere training was of no use, if it did not carry with it a guarantee of immediate absorption into a job. Finally, when the team did succeed in persuading some boys to get enlisted for certain training programmes like motor winding, pumpset repairs and house wiring, the villagers came up with another objection when told that the team had made arrangements with the ITI for conducting these programmes. They would have nothing to do with any training programme conducted by the local ITI.

Inquiries from the ITI-trained boys and others in the villages revealed that the training had proved to be of no practical use in most cases. The boys had been lured by the stipend of Rs.80 per month offered by the ITI, but the training was never conducted seriously. As a result the boys had not learnt anything, and simply wasted their time, which could have been more fruitfully utilized in the fields or on any other family vocation.

Under the circumstances, we had to give an assurance to the boys as also to their parents that through we could not give any guarantee we would try to arrange to conduct the training programme outside the local ITI. Besides the literate and semi-literate youth, the project team also sought the participation of such persons in the rural areas. who had neither any technical skill nor any practical experience of running a particular industry, but were otherwise desirous of setting up a new industrial venture after taking the required training. But in both the cases only a limited range of specific technical skills was offered, which if learnt, could help the individual become a bread-earner in due course.

However, on account of the pathetically low levels of education throughout the rural areas, the range of technical courses which could be offered to the rural aspirants, had to be restricted to a rather rudimentary level. The following is the list of various vocational training/skill upgradation courses offered under the project:

(a) Tailoring
(b) House wiring
(c) Pump-set repairs
(d) Tractor mechanics
(e) Blanket weaving
(f) Motor winding
(g) Auto mechanic

(h) Leather goods and shore making
(i) Pottery glazing
(j) Carpet weaving
(k) Lathe machine

REGULATED MARKETS

Introduction

The present system of agricultural marketing is highly deplorable. All the possible malpractices such as adulteration, short weighing, charging excessive commission, collection of unnecessary charges etc., are quite common amongst the traders. To remove these defects, the Royal Commission on Agriculture (1928) suggested the establishment of regulated markets on sound lines so as to remove the malpractices in the existing system and to ensure a fair deal to the cultivators. Thus, regulated markets is the only medicine to cure the several ills of the agricultural marketing system. Before proceeding further, we shall study the historical development of the regulated markets in India briefly.

History of Regulated Markets in India:

Efforts for some kind of regulation of the market were made as early as in 19th century. The first of such attempts was the passing of the Berer Cotton and Grain Marketing Law in 1897. But it did not serve any useful purpose due to certain inherent defects in it. Later, the Bombay Cotton Market Act was enacted in 1927. This became a model for all the future legislations on regulated markets. The main object of this Act was to secure to the cultivator better prices, fair weighing and freedom from illegal deductions.

Subsequently in 1926 the Royal Commission on Agriculture was set up to make an overall survey of the India Agriculture. The report was submitted by the commission in 1928. The Royal Commission in its Report vehemently criticized the existing conditions of agricultural marketing and described the agricultural marketing practices as "nothing less than theft".

The commission recommended the establishment of regulated markets to cure the serious defects of the marketing system. Following the recommendations of the Commission, various provincial governments introduced market legislation. the Madras Commercial Crops Market Act 1933 was the first legislation passed in India towards this direction. These acts in general are described as Agricultural Produce Markets Acts. These initial efforts gave great impetus to market legislation in India. Subsequently various Regulated Markets were established all over the country. At the outset of the Second World War, there were in all 122 regulated markets. The total number of such markets increased to 283 in 1949-52 and 450 in 1955-56. After independence, the Fiver Year Plans visualized the regulation of new markets throughout the country.

In October 1955, an All India Conference on Marketing and Co-operation was held at Hydrabad. It made may recommendations for accelerating the progress of regulated markets during of the Second Five Year Plan and to effect improvement in the working of the existing markets.

The Third Plan contemplated the regulation of markets in different parts of the country and the consolidation of the working of the markets already established by the end of the Second Five Year Plan. At the beginning of the third Plan legislation for establishment of such markets was in force in 9 states. Later on 4 other states have also enacted the Agricultural Produce Market Act. In the Fourth Plan, it was envisaged that the remaining states will also enact legislation for regulated markets. Among the union territories, Andaman and Nicobar, Manipur, Lakshdeep, Dadra and Nagar Haveli, Arunachala Pradesh are yet to make necessary legislation of markets. The number of regulated markets was only 450 in 1955 but their number has increased to 2803 by the end of 1972.

What is a Regulated Market?

Regulated market is a wholesale market where dealing of buying and selling are regulated or controlled by the state government through a market committee. The market committee consists representatives of the traders, agents, local bodies, co-operative societies and the government. In the regulated markets the activities are to take place under the set rules and regulations and malpractices like incorrect weighment, unnecessary deduction are curbed. Moreover, the regulated markets provide machinery for settlement of disputes, if any, amongst the sellers and buyers.

Objectives of Regulated Markets

The regulated are established to fulfill the following objectives.

(1) To enable the producers to get the best possible prices for their produce.

(2) To safeguard the interest of the producers who are unorganized

(3) To reduce the gap between the price received by the producer and price paid by the final consumer.

(4) To facilitate smooth transfer of goods and orderly transactions by making provisions for settlement of disputes.

(5) To provide facilities for transportation, communication, storage and all other facilities.

(6) To facilitate immediate sale of the surplus produce for cash.

(7) To create conditions for fair competition amongst the producers and sellers.

Special Features of the Regulated Markets

The regulated markets have certain special characteristics of their own. They are :

1. ***Market Committee:*** In accordance with the requirements of the Act, a market committee is to be constituted. The market committee should consist of the representatives of the farmers, traders, agents, Government, social bodies and in some cases co-operative societies. The members may be either elected or nominated by the state government. The market committee has certain rights and powers. It has also the power to penalize those, who contravene or break the rules and regulations.

2. ***Area of Operation :*** The area of operation of regulated market may be confined to the municipal limits of a revenue district or even larger. The area covered by the market is generally notified by the government in the official gazette.

3. ***Method of Sale:*** In order to avoid all the ills of the existing marketing system, the regulated markets provide for open auction sales method. Private negotiations are thus discouraged and underhand dealings are totally prohibited.

4. ***Licensing of the Functionaries:*** All the functionaries like the commission agents, brokers, traders, weighmen must obtain a licence from the market committee. Separate licences are issued to deal with different commodities. A certain amount of fee should be paid to obtain a licence. The rate of commission, allowance and other charges payable to the functionaries are also fixed.

5. ***Market Levies:*** A small amount is to be paid by the grower seller as well as by the buyer as the market fee or cess. This levy is usually calculated on the basis of the value or volume of the goods bought or sold or it may be on the basis of cart load or truck load. The licence fees, fines and market cess are the only source of income to the market committee to meet the expenses for managing the affairs.

6. ***Settlement of Disputes:*** The regulated markets provide a separate machinery for setting the disputes. The usual disputes that may arise in the course of the transactions are prices to be paid, allowances to be given to the middlemen etc. A separate committee called "Arbitration Committee" is also, formed to settle the difference and disputes. Its decision is final and binding on both the parties.

In Bihar and West Bengal sub yards include cold storages and hence figures of total regulated markets and wholesale markets are not comparable.

All principal regulated markets are wholesale markets, whereas sub market yards may/may not be a wholesale market as it also includes some of Rural Primary Markets notified for regulation.

Table 2
Number of Whole Sale, Rural Primary & Regulated Markets in India

As on 31. 03. 2008

State/u.ts Sale	*Whole - Primary*	*Rural*	*Total*	*Principal*	*Submarket Yards*	*Total*
	Number of Markets			*Regulated Markets*		
Andhra Pradesh	314	577	891	314	577	891
Arunachal Pradesh	6	56	62	14	48	62
Assam	405	735	1140	20	204	224
Bihar*	325	1469	1794	95	431	526
Jharkhand	205	603	808	28	173	201
Goa	4	24	28	1	7	8
Gujarat	207	129	336	196	218	414
Haryana	284	187	471	106	178	284
Himachal Pradesh	42	35	77	10	32	42
Jammu & Kashmir	26	834	APMR Act not yet implemented			
Karnataka	498	730	1228	146	352	498
Kerala	348	1014	1362	APMR Act not enacted		
Madhya Pradesh	237	1321	1558	237	264	501
Chhattisgarh	2	1132	1134	73	108	181
Maharashtra	880	3500	4380	295	585	880
Manipur	20	98	118	APMR Act not enacted		
Meghalaya	101	112	213	2	–	2
Mizoram	10	105	115	APMR Act not implemented		
Nagaland	8	144	152	–	Nil	–
Orissa	398	1150	1548	45	269	314
Punjab	437	0	437	145	292	437
Rajasthan	428	312	740	125	303	428
Sikkim	7	12	19	1	–	1
Tamil Nadu	300	677	977	277	15	292
Tripura	89	559	648	21	–	21
Uttar Pradesh	584	3244	3828	245	342	587
Uttarakhand	20	29	49	25	31	56
West Bengal	279	2925	3204	43	641	684
A & N Island	0	0	0	APMR Act not enacted		
Chandigarh	1	0	1	1	–	1
D & N Haveli	0	0	0	APMR Act not enacted		
Daman & Diu	0	0	0	Reported	Nil	
Delhi	30	0	30	9	14	23
Lakshdweep	0	0	0	APMR Act not enacted		
Puducherry	8	0	8	4	4	8
Total	6503	20887	27390	2478	5088	7566

Note: * Bihar Agril.Produce Marketing (Regulation) Act Repealed From 1st September, 2006.

BENEFITS OF REGULATED MARKETS

As we have observed and noted that the regulated markets are helpful to many ways to the farmers, traders, middlemen etc., to avoid, eliminate and to reduce the adverse effects of the defects, which were prevalent in the marketing of rural goods in our country; so also number of benefits are derived from them. Now, let us examine the advantage:

Correct Weighment

There was manipulation in weighing, prior to the establishment of regulated markets. But now, they have introduced correct weights and measures in the markets; weighing is done by licensed weighment. Hand balances are replaced by beam balances and weighbridges. Metric system of weighment is adopted. The weights are also standardized now. This assures correct weighment to the producers and thus, eliminates manipulation in weights.

Marketing Services: Grading of agricultural goods has been accepted as one of the important functions of the regulated markets. It solves may problems like better prices, continued markets etc. Certain market committees provide godown and packing facilities. A few committees are also publishing weekly reports showing the market conditions and quantities marketed in each regulated market.

Reduction in Market Charges

Payment of commission, weighing charges, brokerage, hamali, charity etc., are prescribed by the Market Committee. Thus, all the unauthorized deduction are prohibited. Thus, the producer's share in the actual price has increased. Prior to regulation, these marketing charges varied from market to market, with an average of 3.41% now have come down to 1.79% resulting a saving of 1.62%.

Reduction in Village Sales

The establishment of regulated market has led to the decrease in villages sales. The grower-sellers are made aware of the fair practices in the regulated markets. Now, they bring the saleable produce to these markets. The rural goods brought to the markets have risen from 20% in 95%.

Marketing Facilities

Number of facilities are being provided by the regulated markets like drinking water facilities for both men and animals, parking arrangement , storage, cold storage, auction sheds etc. All these amenities are available only in the regulated markets.

The regulated market play a vital role in removing majority of the defects and malpractices and, therefore, more and more regulated markets are to be established and operated on proper lines, in those areas where they are present by their absence.

Marketing Service

Grading of rural goods has been accepted as one of the important functions of regulated markets. It solves many problems like better prices, continued market etc. 'Agmark' standards have been accepted by all. That is why, today we find this mark on packages of many products like, grains, honey, ghee, vanspati etc., which speaks of the quality. It becomes easy to determine the pice.

Fair Prices

The prices determined in the regulated markets are fair and reasonable to both the producers as well as dealers and not one sided. Thus, the producers are assured of getting higher share in the price. The producers are having kindling of the candle of incentive to grow more and earn more.

DEFECTS IN THE EXISTING REGULATED MARKETS

In spite of the sincere efforts taken by the various state governments the present system is subject to various defects. The various defects of the regulated markets are summarized as follows.

Lack of Uniformity

The regulations are not uniform throughout the country. The various Acts in different states prescribe different methods and procedures and so there are apparent differences in their functioning. They vary not only from state to state but also from region to region within the same state. Variations are generally-found in definitions of agricultural produce, the by-laws of the constitution, composition of market committees, levy of cess and licence fees , market rates etc. For instance in our state cess is payable by the farmer who sells his produce.

Constitution of Market Committees

The pattern of constitution of the market committees also vary widely from state to state. Their maximum and minimum number of members also vary widely. Representatives of growers, traders, local bodies and government are generally included in the market committees. But their proportion widely differs. For instance, in Punjab the growers are in majority while other states they are minority. Mumbai has given representation to co-operative also.

Absence of Suitable Market Yard

Spacious market yards are a must for the development and progress of regulated markets. But most of the regulated markets have no such market yards to transport their business. According to a recent data only 170 markets have suitable market yards.

Defects of a Auction System

Most of the regulated markets follow auction sale system which, in fact, is not an unmixed blessing. According to an enquiry conducted by Dr. Dan Wale, fictitous sales and mock auctions take place in the regulated markets after the deal has been mutually settled.

Difference in the Administration of the Act

The organization and supervision of the regulated markets lies in the hands of different department in different states. For instance, in our state the Act is administered by the Department of Agriculture, while in Karnataka, the control and supervision of the Act lies with the Co-operative Departments.

Sellers and Buyers Resistence

Many sellers as well as buyers are hesitating to transact through the medium of regulated markets. Though the number of sellers who bring their produce to the regulated markets has increased sufficiently, the traders are still reluctant to bid on the strength of the official grading. In most cases the sellers bring small lots and the buyers are not willing to buy such small lots.

Insufficiency of Funds

Most of the regulated markets are functioning without enough funds. Therefore, they are not in a position to supply enough facilities to the farmers and traders to transact their business.

Undue Delay in Payment of the Price

Most of the farmers have a grievance over the undue delay in payment of the price for their produce. the farmers who come from distant places in the previous night itself are forced to wait till very late in the next evening to receive payment. As a result most of them are afraid to return home in the late nights and so stay in the town with the money in their possession.

However the drawbacks cited above are not uncurable defects but can be cures by suitable measures. As such it is no exaggeration to say that regulated market is really a boom to the poor Indian farmer.

CONCLUSIONS

To conclude, the principal aim in regulating the markets viz., removing the malpractices and ensuring a fair deal to the farmers has been achieved in a good measure, But regulation of markets alone does not bring the desired results. What the legislation can do under normal circumstances is to create conditions conductive to more perfect competition, to make the cultivators market conscious, to eliminate malpractices and to enable the producers to have control over the marketing machinery. To achieve all these, full co-operation between produces and the buyers is necessary.

MEANING OF CO-OPERATIVE MARKETING

A co-operative sales association is a voluntary business organization established by its member patrons to market farm products collectively for their direct benefit. It is governed by democratic principles, and savings are apportioned to the members on the basis of their patronage. The members are the owners, operators and contributors of the commodities and are the direct beneficiaries of the savings that accrue to the society. No intermediary stands to profit or loss at the expenses of the other members. Co-operative marketing organizations are association of producers for the collective marketing of their produce and of securing for the members the advantages that result from large-scale business which an individual cultivator cannot secure because of his small marketable surplus. In a co-operative marketing society, the control of the organization in the hands of the producers, and each member has one vote irrespective of the number of shares purchased by him. The profit earned by the society is distributed among the members on the basis of the quantity of the produce marketed by him. In other words, co-operative marketing societies are established for the purpose of collectively marketing the products of the member producers. It emphasizes the concept of commercialization. Its economic motives and character distinguish it from other associations. These societies ressemble private business orgənization in the method of their operations; but they differ from the capitablistic system chiefly in their motives and organizations.

HISTORY OF THE CO-OPERATIVE MARKETING

The Royal Communication of Agriculture (1928) stressed the need for group marketing instead of individual marketing. The Central Banking Enquiry Committee (1931) also underlined the need for organized marketing. The XI Conference of Registrars of Cooperative Societies (1934) emphasised the importance of Cooperative marketing. In 1945, the cooperative Planning Committee recommended that atleast 25 per cent of the marketable surplus should be channellised through Cooperative Societies within the next 10 years by forming one society for a group of 200 villages. The All India Rural Credit Survey Committee (1954) brought to light the dismal performance of the existing ,marketing cooperative. In a sample of 75 district surveyed, there was no cooperative marketing society in 63 district. In remaining district only around one per cent of the total sale of rural produce was done through the societies. The committee suggested the establishment of primary cooperative marketing societies and linking of credit with marketing. The First Five Year Plan (1951-56) laid stress on the establishment of rural marketing and processing cooperative societies. In 1958, the National Agricultural Cooperative Marketing Federation (NAFED) was established as the apex body of cooperative marketing. In 1963, the National Cooperative Development Corporation (NDC) was set up for promoting programmes relating to processing storage and marketing of rural produce through cooperative markets.

The Mirdha Committee (1965) recommended that the membership of Agriculture Marketing Societies should be restricted to the agriculturists and traders should not be allowed to join agricultural marketing societies. The Dantwala Committee (1966) stressed the need for cooperation and integration among the various cooperative organizations after reviewing the pattern of cooperative marketing, distribution of inputs to producers and supply of consumer products. Based on the survey of the cooperative marketing societies in 1968, the Reserve Bank of India recognized that effective linking of credit with marketing was necessary. The All India Rural Credit Review Committee, 1969 also recommended the strengthening of cooperative marketing with a view to helping the government agencies in the execution of price support programmes and thus fulfilling the interests of the producers. India created a system of *rural* cooperatives in the 1950s and expanded branch banking into *rural* areas in the 1970s.

FUNCTIONS OF CO-OPERATIVE MARKETING

The main functions of co-operative marketing societies are:

(1) To arrange for the export of the produce of the member so that they may get better returns;

(2) To make arrangements for the transport of the produce of the members from the villages to the market on collective basis and bring about a reduction in the cost of transportation;

(3) To arrange for the supply of the inputs required by the producers, such as improved seeds, fertilizers, insecticides and pesticides.

(4) To market the produce of the members of the society at fair prices;

(5) To safeguard the members from excessive marketing costs and malpractices;

(6) To make credit facilities available to the members against the security of the produce brought for sale;

TYPES OF CO-OPERATIVE MARKETING SOCIETIES

On the basis of the commodities dealt in by them, the cooperative marketing societies may be grouped into the following types:

Single Commodity Co-operative Marketing Societies

They deal in the marketing of only one rural commodity. They get sufficient business from the farmers producing that single commodity. The examples are Sugarcane Co-operative Marketing Society and the Cotton Co-operative Marketing Society.

Multi-commodity Co-operative Marketing Societies

They market a large number of commodities produced by the members, such as foodgrains, oilseeds and cotton.

Multi-purpose, Multi-commodity Co-operative Marketing Societies

These societies market a large number of commodities and perform such other functions as providing credit to members, arranging for the supply of the inputs required by them, and meeting their requirements of essential domestic consumptions goods.

Our rural marketing system has been suffering from a number of problems for which suitable steps and constrictive suggestions can be implemented. Commercialisation of agriculture warrants guranteed marketing system to push the enhanced production quickly, easily and at fair prices. To give increased share in the price of the products, the cultivations must be capable of selling their produce at fair prices. This is possible only when, the producer can get the benefits of improved and better methods of marketing his produce. The establishment of cooperative marketing societies is another step which has been taken to overcome the problems arising out of the present system of marketing rural produce. The objectives of economic development and social justice can be furthered by channellising rural produce through co-operative institutions.

Private agencies dominate the India foodgrains trade. Farmers complain of the marketing system because they get lower prices, due mainly to high marketing charges and the prevalence of malpractices. The efforts of the government to improve the marketing system of rural commodities have been only partially successful in creating healthy conditions for scientific and efficient marketing. Moreover, the progress of regulated markets is not uniform in all areas. The need for strengthening co-operative organization has, therefore, been recognized for the marketing of the produce of producers and for marking inputs available for them at the right price and time. The co-operative institutions are expected to function as competition of private traders in the markets. These organizations pool the produce of the small producers having a small surplus to market and improve their bargaining power. They have also helped government agencies in the execution of the policy decisions bearing on the procurement and distribution of food grains and other essential commodities.

NEED OR OBJECTIVES OF CO-OPERATIVE MARKETING

To Stabilise the Agricultural Prices

If the market mechanism is completely left to the sweet will and caprice of the private intermediaries, one can hardly expect price stabilization, which is essential ingredients of a balanced economic development. So long as private sector dominates; "profit motive" will have upper hand, where normal market conditions deviate from healthy practices to the unwanted practices of speculation; hoarding will be resorted to resulting in price manipulation and reflection of undesirable price fluctuations.

To Eliminate Malpractices

Different malpractices prevailing in the system of Rural marketing, and such as arbitrary deductions from the price, manipulation of weights and measures, collusion between brokers and the business buyers, are of special mention. These malpractices were regarded as "nothing less than scientific theft" by Royal Commission. The impact of these was further aggravation by critical financial position where producers are indebted to traders or money-lenders. In such a situation, co-operative marketing can help the producers to reduce, if not to eradicate malpractices, to a greater extent.

Concomitant of Integrated Programme

Co-operative marketing has developed as concomitant of large scale expansion of co-operative credit. Co-operative marketing societies will be acting as the agents to collect or to recover the loans advanced by co-operative credit societies. Therefore, the successful working of credit co-operatives, depends largely, on the development of marketing societies. that is, only co-operative marketing societies constitute a vital feature for integrated programme of co-operative development, envisaged in the country.

To Establish Appropriate Reward for the Efforts

There exists a large army of middlemen participating, with deep interest in collection, storage, financing, insuring, grading, scale and transportation of rural produce. One must appreciate their services that are vital for victorious marketing. However, their charges for such services are not proportionate and hence not appropriate. In some cases, such charges are not only prohibitive but exorbitation. As a result, poor producers do not get their due share in the price paid by the ultimate users. Co-operative marketing, if efficiently and honestly organized, will be able to reduce the 'price spread' between the producer and the consumer, thereby giving fair return to the producers, without affecting the interests of the consumers.

METHODS OF BUSINESS ADOPTED BY MARKETING CO-OPERATIVES

Agency Method

The relationship of members and society is that agency, wherein the society buys and sells the produce of its members as an agent. That, is it does not take title to the goods nor pays cash immediately. For performing the services of an agent, these Agencies charge certain commission; thus it collects the produce of the member-farmers and remits the amount to the members, just after the sale by subtracting some commission and other incidental charges. This method has its own advantages and disadvantages.

Merits

It has three merits:

(a) The producers obtain the prices which the quality of their products can fetch in the open market. The marketing co-operative, however, help the members to obtain higher prices with wider contact working with the least developments in the markets;

(b) As the co-operatives are acting only as the agents of the members, they are not to make the payment for the price immediately; they pay only when they sell and collect the bill from the buyers;

(c) As they are acting as only intermediacies they are not to assume the risks which are the botheration of the farmers themselves; thus the risks associated with the price fluctuations of even stock pilling are avoided.

Demerits

The disadvantages are two, in number:

(a) the marketing co-operatives are compelled to charge, higher rate of commission, since the cost of maintaining records and keeping of accounts and conducting actual business is more

(b) As the societies are interested only in getting commission, they may fail in obtaining higher prices for the member's produce.

Outright Purchase and Sale

Outright purchase and sale implies the actual buying of commodities by paying cash at the ruling prices in the market and then reselling to others. Here, the Marketing co-operatives buy the produce of their members, at the price prevailing in the marketing and make them payment of cash immediately; hence the section afford all the risks of storing the goods and fluctuations of prices. The society deducts all the expenses involved in buying and selling and the specified dividend to be declared amongst the members, on the basis of the amount of business done with the society or through the society. Mass marketing co-operatives handle the produce of their members by this methods. This method has the following merits:

Merits

There are advantages that are enjoyed by the producers through this method.

Immediate requirements of cash in assured. The immediate payment made by the marketing co-operative, helps the farmer-members, to tide over their financial difficulties and other obligations with social and psychological stings. Therefore, the producers can sell their produce only to the society and thus secure better prices because of co-operatives; moreover there is no cheating as it is their own organization. Further co-operatives are following the usual practices prevalent in the market and therefore, the producers are conversant with them.

Demerits

As per the opinions of experts, this method has three defects too.

(a) The co-operatives have to take for granted the risks along with the purchase; that is to say, the market risk of price fluctuation is to be shouldered by the society itself, which sometimes proves to be costlier. At times, they have assume the risk of piling up of stocks, as the demand pattern is not encouraging.

(b) Moreover working capital is warranted to make the purchases as immediate cash is to be paid. This brings pressure on the working capital position, and more in the off seasons

(c) Co-operatives have to appointed skilled managerial personnel for carrying on such a business acumen will be available only at higher salaries. This increases the overall cost of management.

Sales Polices of Marketing Co-operatives

In order that the marketing co-operative become real success, they have to follow, design and develop sound sales policies. The aim of obtaining higher prices for members produce can be achieved by pursuing sound sales policies. The co-operatives sell the produce to the wholesalers in central markets or through the brokers or commission agents or auction companies, that are working in central markets. Majority of societies, sell directly to the manufactures or the buyers who are desirous of purchasing in larger quantities. Such as large scale retail organizations and public institutions.

Pooling

The third method of handling members, produced by the marketing co-operatives is pooling. Pooling is defined by Bakken and Sachaars as "the Commingle of products of many producers and after deducting average expenses, paying the average price received for the same, usually on the basis of established grades. "From this definition, it is clear, pooling may (a) involve the physical mixing of the products of different members, however, in actual practice, it does not imply only the mingling of the produce but the delivery of the produce of products by the members and the sale of the same by the co-operatives separately also. Of the products, that are delivered to co-operatives, are in small lots. The societies may commingle the products so as to make it convement to sell, on the basis of the grades already established. On the contrary, if they are in sufficiently larger quantities, they need not be mixed and therefore may be sold distinctly.

The payment to the members, under the method is made in three distinct ways. If the product pooled by the members are sold without grading, the societies realize the sale proceeds and distribute the same amongst the members as per the quantity delivered by each member, after deducting the expenses thereto (b) If products are graded and pooled in a single pool, payment is made on the basis of quality of the products or on the bais of quantity, if they are put in a separate pool after grading (c) If the products are sold separately without mixing, the co-operative collect the sale proceeds and deduct the proportionate share in the common expenses and pay the remaining to the individual members. The method has the following merits and demerits.

Merits

The merits accruing to the members are :

(a) it helps in minimizing the risk to loss due to fire, theft, damage etc. The pooling method, provides for the loss arising out of price fluctuation.

(b) Orderly marketing of products is facilitated by this method. The surplus quantities are stocked and the quantity demanded in the market is released, thus encouraging the better prices.

(c) On account of orderly marketing, the bargaining capacity of producers also increases via co-operatives, as the pooling facilities standardization, and grading

(d) Pooling also results in reduced cost of transportation, grading and storage, as they are in larger quantities. It assists in finding out new markets for the members produce and expanding the operations of existing markets.

Demerits

That way, every method has its own laxities, which cannot be plugged completely. The demerits of pooling system are not very severe and therefore, we have conveniently left. It can be said that the merits outweigh the demerits and, therefore, the defects are not being given hair splitting importance.

Advancement of Credit and Procurement of Foodgrains

Co-operative marketing societies advance finance to producers against their stock of foodgrains in the godowns of the societies. This increase the holding power of the producers and prevents distress sales. Generally, societies advance credit to the extent of 60 to 75 per cent of the value of the produce stored with them. The recoveries are effected from the sale proceeds of .the produce of the producer. This function involves no risk to the society. Moreover, it increases the business. Co-operative marketing societies act as agents of the government in the procurement of foodgrains at the announced procurement prices.

Members Contract with Co-operative

The success of marketing co-operatives lies in the regular and continuous business that it transacts. Regular supply of products can be assured by the members to the society, through the execution of a contact. In this contract, the member assures and gives guarantee of the delivery of produce to the co-operative only. Further, the contract specifies are to be paid by the members if the contract is broken. Thus, members contract ensures steady, regular and continuous business to the marketing co-operatives.

ADVANTAGES OF CO-OPERATIVE MARKETING

Co-operative venture has its own set of merits to its credit and a few limitations on the counterpart.

Merits

Instruments of Education

Producers can better appreciate their problems and difficulties as they are made to govern themselves. They learn as to what problems are practically faced, and how to solve them. Thus, this society becomes a training ground. They are bound to get enlightened on the importance of co-operation that is based on "one for all" and "all for one" "self help through mutual help".

Development of Orderly Marketing

Development of orderly marketing implies, establishing balance between the demand and supply forces, to better the position of the producers, which is the need of the hour. Our producers, do sell, in villages especially at the time of harvest, that results into dumping and creating glut in the markets, whereby, the price level swings down to the bottom, thus leaving nothing but pessimism. Co-operatives by buying or collecting produce, from producers would be able to regulate the demand and supply position. The supply is made as per the needs and moods of the market. Thus, co-operative will stabilize the prices over longer period. Thus, seasonal fluctuations are avoided for safeguarding the interests of the producing units and ultimately the consumers.

Better Selling Methods

Co-operative societies, apply better methods to push the rural products. Even they resort to advertising, branding, to claim superiority in the market. Such efforts are beyond the reach of the individuals.

Lower Cost of Production

These marketing co-operatives are rendering valueable service to the class of producers by providing the requisites of better farming. They buy and provide better seeds, fertilizers, and implements and economical rates, as they enjoy the benefits of large scale units, operating in the market. Such benefits are available to large scale units, operating in the market. Such benefits are not available to producers as individuals.

Essence of Integrated Programme of Credit

The programe of credit expansion, as a part of integrated approach on the part of Government of India, is going to be the greatest success, provided marketing co-operative are married to credit co-operatives. Collection or recovery of loans granted is done easily by marketing co-operatives. If other agencies are employed, the recovery remains a dream. Hence, marketing co-operatives should be given the role to play in the collection of loans and they should become part and parcel of the over all co-operative structure.

Control of Quality and Better Grading

To make greater success, better seeds are provided, producers are advised to produce or grow only certain breeds, which makes grading more easy and economical. Here, the producers are better rewarded as quality results into higher prices. Since individual production is limited, he cannot resort to grading, but co-operative will make him to have the cake and eat it too.

Elimination of Trade Abuses

The malpractices which are common in private trading centres are not resorted to, because co-operatives will be rendering the service, rendered by the merchant middlemen. As it is a common approach strengthens the bargaining capacity. The 'Scientific theft' is no more there. This is another reason to increase earning to our producers.

Realisation of Higher Prices

Maximization of income to the producing class is the objective of co-operative marketing. This can attained only when price that the producer gets is higher. By co-operative efforts, they will get better prices for their produce, the price for the produce is realized by the co-operatives on behalf of the members. It is mainly due to the united effort, where bargaining capacity improves and gets stronger. Individual effort, to sell will bring him down where he is pulled down. However, co-operative attempt is the fine answer to this sort of exploitation.

PROBLEMS OR LIMITATIONS OF CO-OPERATIVE MARKETING

The Government has made a lot of efforts for the successful, efficient and effective functioning of the cooperative marketing but the progress of the co-operative marketing societies has been far from satisfactory in most of the states in the country because the producers and members do not patronize these societies for the sale of their produce. Instead they use the services of commission agents. Here are some of the causes of slow growth of co-operative marketing societies:

(i) There is a lack of sufficient storage facilities with the societies. They, therefore, try to dispose of the produce soon after their arrival; a fact which results in lower prices for the producers;

(ii) In some cases rivalaries among farmer-members resulting in indecision, which hampers the progress of the societies;

(iii) Producers are indebted to local traders and enter into advance contracts with them for the sale of the crop;

(iv) There is lack of loyalty among members to co-operative marketing societies because of their poor education and absence of the co-operative feeling;

(v) Co-operative marketing societies are generally located in big markets/ towns and quick and cheap transport facilities are not available for the carriage of the produce from the villages to the societies;

(vi) Members lack confidence in co-operative organizations, for most of the co-operative sector enterprises run at a loss;

(vii) Co-operative marketing societies (CMS) are not capable of carrying on their business to competition with traders and commission agents, because of the absence of adequate business expertise among their employees;

(viii) Farmers are in immediate need of cash after the harvest to meet their personal obligations. They, therefore, sell their produce to traders; they cannot wait for the time required to move the produce to the mandi;

(ix) The managers of the societies are often linked with local traders and become impersonal to the needs of a majority of small and marginal producers.

(x) There is lack of sufficient funds with the societies to meet the credit needs of the producers against pledging of the produce brought for sale. Nor do they make an advance payment of the value of the produce purchased or sold through them.

(xi) Societies do not provide facilities of food and shelter to producers when they visit the market for the sale of the produce; and

(xii) The affection and attachment of producers is lacking where producers are having misunderstandings. Again they expect too much from co-operatives. They feel they are exploited indirectly.

(xiii) Managers of societies do not offer business advice to members;

(xiv) Since private sector is dominating the scence of business, co-operative child is nowhere, which is ill-treated. Private sector is deadly against, to be the cause of its collapse. Thus, everybody except government, hates co-operative societies. Traders compete away the business by offering temporarily favourable terms. Since they cannot afford to pay reasonable price for the efforts of other agencies like warehousing, transportation, banks, manufacturers etc., they hesitate to have trade relations.

(xv) The societies do not act as banks for the producers;

(xvi) The major factors of successful business are adequate finance and better management. In these societies, there is no sufficient fund for providing future contingencies and for programme of growth and expansion. Personal interference, favoritism will have upper hand where syndicate and indicate will make their headway.

(xvii) This is the greatest limitation, that impedes the growth of co-operative sector. The managing body does not consist of enlightened and experienced people. The office bearers be polite, trained, and experienced who must know the basic principles of co-operation. If good managerial staff is required for efficient management, the society is to pay better price for the services of these people with knowledge, experience and business knack.

SUGGESTIONS FOR STRENGTHENING OF COOPERATIVE MARKETING SOCIETIES

(i) There is a need for brining about a proper co-ordination between credit and marketing co-operative societies to facilitate the recovery of loans advanced by credit societies, and make available sufficient finance for marketing societies.

(ii) In the selection of the officials of co-operative marketing societies, weightage should be given to business experience and qualifications. After their selection, the officials should be given proper training so that they may deal deficiently with the business of the society. The efficiency should be rewarded, wherever possible.

(iii) The co-operative feeling among members should be inculated by proper education by organizing seminars and by the distribution of literature.

(iv) The societies should acquire the transport facility to bring the produce of the members from the villages to the mandi in time and at a lower cost.

(v) The societies should give adequate representation to the small and marginal producers in their organizational set-up.

(vi) The public procurement and public distribution programmes should be implemented through co-operative marketing societies to increase their business turnover.

(vii) Marketing societies, like the private traders, should provide accommodation and the drinking water facility for their members when the latter come to the mandi.

(viii) The area of the operations of the societies should be large enough so that they may have sufficient business and become viable. Most of the societies at present are not viable because of the small volume of their business.

(ix) Co-operative marketing societies should diversify their activities. They should sell the produce and inputs, and engage in the construction of storage facilities.

(x) Co-operative marketing societies should develop sufficient storage facilities in the mandi as well as in the villages.

Formation of Cooperative Marketing and Processing Societies

Another major improvement for rural producers is the formation of Cooperative Marketing and Processing Societies. The farmers with common interest from Cooperative Societies, so that some of the functions performed by the intermediaries are taken over by these societies. These societies shoulder the responsibility of processing and marketing the produce for the member farmers. To increase the incomes of the farmers it is important to involve them in processing. The processed agricultural produce becomes a 'value added' product and the benefits accrue to the farmers only. A number of cooperative societies are engaged in this activity. A good example of such an activity is the Sugar Cooperatives of Maharashtra which is very powerful both economically and politically. There are similar examples in other states also for other agricultural commodities.

A real beginning was made in the integration of Production, Processing and Marketing of milk–a highly perishable product–with the initiation of 'Operation Flood I' programme. This was followed by Operation Flood II and III programmes. Under this programme the dairy farmers in villages are organized into village level cooperatives societies called the Dairy Cooperative Societies (DCS). In turn the DCSs in a district form a Milk Producer's Cooperative Union at the district level. These Unions take the responsibility of collecting milk from the DCSs, processing it in their dairy and marketing it. In addition, the Unions also take the responsibility of supplying the necessary inputs required for milk production to the dairy farmers. The inputs could be feed, fodder slips, health care, artificial insemination facilities, purchase of milk at an assured price and other related services. The Unions at district level form a Milk Producers Cooperative Federation at the state level. The federation renders the necessary help to the Unions and in turn to the DCSs for production, processing and marketing of milk and milk products. These types of organizations are popularly known as 'Amul' pattern societies. Diagrammatically, this can be represented as follows :

Cooperative Marketing System in India

Though the above measures have improved the system of agricultural marketing to some extent, a major part of the benefits has been derived by large farmers, who have adequate marketable surplus. However, the small and marginal farmers continue to sell a major part of their produce to moneylenders to meet their credit needs and these moneylenders offer them very low prices. Therefore it is essential to form cooperatives of the small and marginal farmers to enable them to obtain fair prices for their produce. The advantages that co-operative marketing can confer on the farmer are multifarious, some of which are listed below.

Increases Bargaining Strength of the Fanners

Many of the defects of the present agricultural marketing system arise because often one ignorant and illiterate farmer (as an individual) has to face well-organised mass of clever intermediaries. If the farmers join hands and for a co-operative, naturally they will be less prone to exploitation and malpractices. Instead of marketing their produce separately, they will market it together through one agency.

Direct Dealing with Final Buyers

In cases, the co-operatives can altogether skip the intermediaries and enter into direct relations with the final buyers. This practice will eliminate exploiters and ensure fair prices to both the producers and the consumers.

Provision of Credit

The marketing co-operative societies provide credit to the farmers to save them from the necessity of selling their produce immediately after harvesting. This ensures better returns to the farmers.

Easier and Cheaper Transport

Bulk transport of agricultural produce by the societies is often easier and cheaper. Sometimes the societies have their own means of transport. This further reduces cost and botheration of transporting produce to the market.

Storage Facilities

The co-operative marketing societies generally have storage facilities. Thus the farmers can wait for better prices. Also there is no danger to their crop yield from rains, rodents and thefts.

Grading and Standardization

This task can be done more easily for a co-operative agency than for an individual farmer. For this purpose, they can seek assistance from the government or can even evolve their own grading arrangements.

Market Intelligence

The co-operatives can arrange to obtain data on market prices, demand and supply and other related information from the markets on a regular basis and can plan their activities accordingly.

Influencing Marketing Prices

While previously the market prices were determined by the intermediaries and merchants and the helpless farmers were mere spectators force to accept, whatever was offered to them, the co-operative societies have changed the entire complexion of the game. Wherever strong marketing co-operative are operative, they have bargained for and have achieved, better prices for their agricultural produce.

Provision of Inputs and Consumer Goods

The co-operative marketing societies can easily arrange for bulk purchase of agricultural inputs, like seeds, manures fertilizers etc. and consumer goods at relatively lower price and can then distribute them to the members.

Processing of Agricultural Produce

The co-operative societies can undertake processing activities like crushing seeds, ginning 'and pressing of cotton, etc.

In addition to all these advantages, the co-operative *marketing system* can arouse the spirit of self-confidence and collective action in the farmers without which the programme of agricultural development, howsoever well conceived and implemented, holds no promise to success.

The system is functioning satisfactorily, since all the inputs required for milk production are supplied with an assurance that irrespective of the quantity of milk supplied, the pre-announced, assured prices will not change. This type of arrangement is in vogue in most of the states in the country and it is estimated that about eight million litres of milk is collected every day through these societies. The fact to be reckoned here is that the dairy farmers are the shareholders of the organization. Hence, the value addition through processing of milk into butter, ghee, ice-cream, milk based sweets and other milk products stays within the organization itself. In addition to dividends, the dairy farmers also get a bonus at the end of the year in proportion to the quantity of milk supplied which depends on the profits made by the organization. The payment for the milk supplied could be on a daily, weekly or fortnightly basis.

Figure 1
'AMUL' Pattern Organization

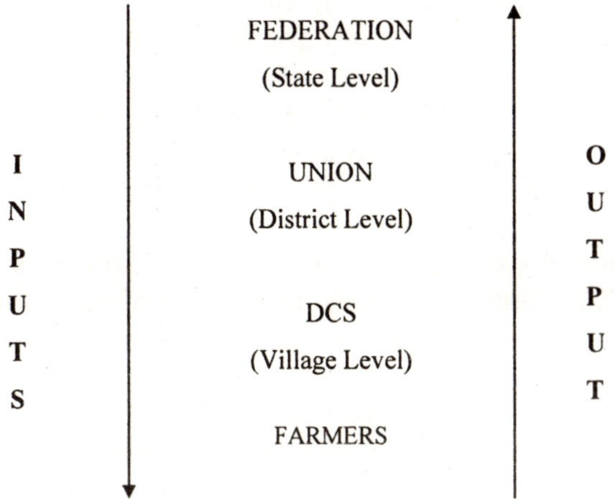

At the time of payment, the cost of inputs provided is deducted. Despite being successful and widely followed throughout the country, the proportion of milk handled by this system is hardly 20 per cent of the total production of about 50 million tones in the country. The initial aid for this scheme was provided by the European Economic Community in the form of skimmed milk powder and butter through National Dairy Development Board set up by Government of India. Operation Flood I concentrated on flooding all the metropolis with milk, while Operation Flood II and III concentrated on flooding the state capitals and district headquarters. By and large this scheme has proved a success. This system also provides for the conversion of milk during flush season into white butter and skimmed milk powder which has a shelf life. In the lean season when the quantum of milk collection goes down, the butter and skimmed milk power can be reconstituted into milk to meet the demand. These organizations have grown to the extent of selling milk products on brand names. For example the Gujarat State Milk Producers' Federation's immensely popular brand 'Amul'. Similar brand names of other states federations are; 'Nandini' in Kernataka, 'Aavin' in Tamil Nadu and 'Vijaya' in Andhra Pradesh for milk and milk products marketed by them.

The concept of organizing the farmers for production, processing and marketing of agricultural produce has been accepted because of its success in the case of milk. Similar efforts are on in the area of edible vegetables oils. Here again most of the states have already established Cooperative Oilseed Growers Federations with processing facilities and are marketing edible oil under their own brand name. Since the organization is viewed as a commercial venture, they follow modern management practices. In the case of vegetables oils also, brands like 'Safal' (Karnataka) and 'Dhara' are popular.

Similarly the Horticultural Producers Cooperative Marketing and Processing Society Ltd (HOPCOMS) at Bangalore, is engaged in the collection of vegetables and fruits from their members for sale in Bangalore city. This started in the year 1959 as Grape Growers' Cooperative Society and then diversified itself to all horticultural produce. This society is now operating in about four districts of Karnataka and will shortly cover the entire state. The society has opened purchase centres at important locations that purchase vegetables and fruits from the farmer-producers. The produce thus collected is immediately transported to Bangalore city on their own trucks. The society has opened about 150 retail outlets in Bangalore city for sale of these vegetables and fruits to the ultimate consumers. In addition to retailing, they also undertake bulk supply to institutions, industrial canteens, etc. Here again, the intermediaries are rendered redundant as their functions are taken over by the society, keeping service as the prime objectie and a very low margin to cover the costs. The members producing vegetables and fruits are only happy to sell their produce to the society. The society operates on the following lines:

(a) the price is fixed as per market conditions.

(b) up to Rs 2,000 the payment is made immediately in cash and if above Rs 2,000 by cheque

(c) there are no malpractices in weighment and no unnecessary deductions are made for quality since the produce is graded before sale.

A similar arrangement exists in Andhra Pradesh also, under the name 'Fresh Marketing Society', they even ensure the consumers that the vegetables sold to them are always fresh. From the consumer point of view also these societies are popular, as quality products can be bought at fixed prices and accurate weighment.

The present policy of the Government is to encourage establishment of Food Processing Industries, since these are considered foreign exchange earners. This has given impetus to many an entrepreneurs and multinationals to invest in food processing industries. Already companies like MARICO industries, ITC Ltd, Lipton, etc. are in the edible oil manufacturing and marketing field. There have been new entrants like PEPSI also. Entry of Pepsi has given a boost to tomato cultivation in four districts of Punjab. They need about 600 tonnes of tomatoes everyday for the manufacture of tomato puree and paste for export. They have signed contracts with the farmers for growing and supplying tomatoes which they process. The farmers are given high yielding tomato seedlings and other necessary inputs for cultivation, and are supervised by agronomists and extension staff of the company. The agreement with the farmers stipulates that they sell 60 per cent of their production to Pepsi at a fixed price and they are free to see the balance anywhere they like. The average yield of tomatoes, which was 19.5 tonnes per hectare, has now boosted to 47.5 tonnes per hectare and certain individual farmers have even obtained yields as high as 75 tonnes. During the year 1992, they procured about 43,000 tonnes of tomatoes and disbursed Rs 8 crore the tomato supplying farmers. This type of integration of production-processing- marketing is required in the case of agricultural produce marketing. One can well imagine the boost such operations will give to the rural economy and the consequent expansion of rural market.

Another example worth the mention is that of 'Mahagrapes' in Pune. Mahagrapes is an organization of a number of Grape Growers Co-operative Societies in the Pune-Nasik region. To meet the stringent quality requirements of export market, this organization imported an equipment for harvesting, packing and precooling of grapes of a cost of Rs 75 crore from USA. This has enabled the Managrapes to export seedless grapes to UK and West Asia. During 1991-92, they exported 2,000 tonnes of worth Rs 8 crore. Their future plans are to reach an export target of about 12,000 tonnes valued at about Rs. 30 crore. There are about 1,000 farmers involved in this activity. Again, this is a case of a farmers/producers' cooperatives directly handling exports. All the middlemen and intermediaries are avoided and the margins at each level of operation accrue to the society, thus increasing the incomes of the farmers producers.

There are many more such examples in our country. The returns to the farmers can increase substantially if the farmer-producers united and take more initiative in processing and marketing. While the support or procurement prices have to be increased to commensurate with the increase in input prices, this may not offer a long term solution for achieving higher incomes. The farmers should be in a position to participate in processing and marking, where the value addition to the raw produce taken place. This would certainly help the farmer-producers realize higher returns.

The recent liberation measures initiated by the Government should have a significant impact on farm incomes. The Dairy industry, hitherto reserved for the cooperative sector only, is now thrown open to private sector also. With the private sectors clout of marketing, this should be a boon to the dairy farmers. The decontrol of molasses is a step in the right direction. The price for sugarcane is normally fixed in relation to the recovery of sugar, which is the main product. The molasses was almost ignored since this was under the control of the government and released at a very nominal price. But molasses, when distilled into alchol, attains a high value. This alcohol forms the basis for Indian Made Foreign Liquor (IMFL) and acetates. From acetates one can derive the numerous chemicals for pharmaceutical industry. But this aspect is totally ignored while fixing the price of sugarcane and only the sugar output is taken into account. Since the sugar mills will be free to sell alcohol at the market price, the realizations will be more, and further passed on to the farmers, at least in the case of Cooperative Sugar Factories. Since sugar is a controlled commodity and the releases are dependent upon the government directives (65 per cent production is procured by government for distribution through the Public Distribution System and only 35 per cent is allowed to be sold in the open market), as of today many factories owe, money to sugarcane farmers. The immediate impact of molasses decontrol could help in clearing of dues to the farmers by the factories.

In addition, many by products which were of no values earlier are now being used economically with the necessary technology being available. For example, rice bran, which was normally fed to cattle, is now being used to extract rice bran oil and the deoiled cake is fed to the cattle. Paddy straw, husk, cotton stalks are now being used for manufacturing hardboards. Bagasse, (the fibre left behind after extracting the juice from sugarcane) till now used as fuel is now being used for the manufacture of paper, a high value product. Such technological innovations in the utilization of by-products are necessary to ensure better income to the farmers.

Traditionally our country has been importing raisins from overseas. 'Mahagrapes' mentioned earlier, is now perfecting the technology for manufacturing raisins from grapes. If the raisin making technology is perfected, the prices of grapes during the harvest season can improve, since shelf life can be given to this perishable product. This effort of Mahagrapes has given impetus to mango farmers in Maharashtra also to think in terms of conversation of mangoes into mango powder. This powder can be remixed with water to make mango paste and then mango juice. Such efforts will surely have a positive impact on the farmer incomes.

The impact of the development of modern marketing concepts, tools and techniques has been very minimal of Agricultural Produce Marketing. With liberalization policies of the government laying special emphasis on food processing industries and thrust on exports, the scope of improvement in the system of agricultural produce marketing is enormous. This should help ensure better and higher incomes to the rural populace and consequently result in the growth of rural market.

Rural market research is still at a beginning stage . While Indian market research is worth Rs.4000 crore, it forms barely 10-15 per cent of the total research pie. According to ORG-MARG the size of the rural market research spend will be around Rs.50 crore.

10

RESEARCH IN AGRICULTURAL MARKETING

As per the guidelines narrated above, research work can be done in agro-related and rural produce related marketing areas. The basic concept and methodology more or less remains similar, only the questionnaire pattern differs. The response of rural people will be more verbal and lesser in writing. Hence, there is heavy reliance on the fairness of the interview and his knowledge to grasp the response of the public.

Some of the areas of agriculture produce and rural produce where research work can be attended periodically are (a) sales analysis of dairy produce in cities, (b) consumer preference for packed curds, milk and butter milk. (c) test marketing for packed foodgrains, (d) creating consumer interest in ready 'Atta Packets' rather than foodgrains, (e) consumer behaviour for fruit juices w.r.t. fruits (f) sales forecast for Basmati Rice. (g) sales forecast for processed foods and (h) consumer attitudes towards new varieties of seedless fruits. This is to get the response of urban people on rural produce. The response can be obtained in writing and assessment can be fairly accurate. This can be taken care of by professionals and consultants as it is comparatively easier to get the response from the urban people.

The second part of rural marketing that is where to get response, makes it difficult to collect data from rural people for consumer goods, toiletries, high value goods and automobiles. This market research is a challenging assignment to any executive. This is where verbal response will have to be heard and recorded by the evaluator who can understand the rural vocabulary better. At present the marketer has the challenge to enter the rural market to sell FMCGs and toiletries and other modern amenities. The first thing is these commodities are not considered very essential by the rural population. Secondly by rural standard all these commodities are heavy investment and comprise of semi-luxury and luxury goods. However, research work has to be done to tap, develop and cater to this unexplored market.

Table 1
Differences in Urban-Rural Market Research

Aspect	*Urban*	*Rural*
Primary data sources	Large number of middlemen, experts, sales force, consumers, opinion leaders.	Less number of all categories
Secondary data source	Internal data, Syndicate research, Published media,. Many sources, and large data.	Very few sources and less data
Sampling	Respondents form relatively homogeneous group. Income can be a criterion.	Heterogeneous groups. Income and land holding to be carefully applied.
Data collection	Use of sophisticated instrument, style and administration. Respondents comfortable with numbers ratings and timelines.	Require simplified instruments. Respondent comfortable with colours, pictures and stories.
Accessibility	Easy to access, through many suffer from research fatigue	Tough to access, geographical distances and psychological approachesions are barriers.
Time	Willing to do good. Have time, pressures, spares little time for researchers	Hesitant But devotes time
Respondents	Literate, brand aware, individuals respond individually	Semiliterate or illiterate, brand unaware. Difficult to get individual responses. Generally group responses.

The bigger market for FMCGs and other amenities in the rural population which accounts to about 70% of the total Indian population. This is a massive 70 crore people out of 100 crore people. Even considering that majority of them live on basic sustenance needs and are not in a position to buy, luxuries or modern amenities, the market potentiality is still very high and appreciable. Table 28.1 shows how research is helpful for proper decision making.

RESEARCH PROBLEMS IN AGRICULTURAL MARKETING

More and more research studies are required in the rural sector for various activities of productivity, improved quality and increased quantity of production. There are various rural life and daily routine where studies could be done. Some of the promised areas of study could be written as under:

Table 2

Main Title	*Areas of Study*
Marketing and Farmer	Farmer's approach in marketing, constraints in them Farmer's involvement in co-perative marketing
Market demand and supply	Projections of demand for different variety of crops Demand supply gaps/surplus
Processing	Location, facilities and capacity of processing various products Utilisation of processing capacities, costs, wanting material handling Value addition by processing of various types of products.
Marketing costs	Work-out of marketing costs, transport, marginal cost for middlemen for different products. Comparison of whole-sale prices for various agro-products of different regions of states and with neighbouring areas.
Packaging	Desirability, types and costs of packaging Consumer feedback and improvements in packaging.

Contd..

Main Title	*Areas of Study*
Marketing of agro-inputs	Requirement of quality and quantity of fertillsers and seeds.
	Water resources management
	Mobilization of manure.
Pricing	Market trends of prices for various commodities
	Difference in farmer's price and retailers' prices and consumers price.
Storage	Types and appropriate mode of storage for different products.
	Safety in storage from damages and losses.
Transportations	Costs and facilities of transportation.
	Decision regarding mode of transport and economy.
	Pilferage and other losses in the Indian transportation.
Co-operative Marketing	Steps for improvement
	Strengthening of co-operative societies.

DATA SOURCES IN AGRICULTURAL MARKETING

Under the topic of Agriculture Marketing Research Institutes, we have talked about NIAM, ICAR, SAMB, DMF, AGRI-UNI., ISAM, ICRISAT, FAO, ADC etc. All these organisations . are the data sources for agricultural marketing. They will have a vast data bank of various products of various states and regions at the national level. Some organizations like ICRISAT, FAO will have data of many countries which will help to enable to enable comparison.

DATA COVERAGE

Various data collected are published in organization bulletins, journals and business magazines and summary in news magazines and newspapers. The details will be about harvest output level, wholesale prices and retail prices of various regions/ states. The probability period and quantity of seasonal fruits in important markets, production foodgrains in various states, the comparison to previous year's production, reasons for deviations and natural gross production are important.

DATA AGENCIES

Some of the agencies/organizations which have means and facilities to collect data are as follows:

Table 3

State Agricultural Marketing Boards	Buying and selling quality of various foodgrains. Market charges payable on agricultural commodities.
State Agricultural Marketing Departments	Prices of various commodities from selected market.
DMI	Collect statistics on regulated markets and transactions of different commodities of different markets.
Directorate of Economics and Statistics, GOI, New Delhi	Import-Export of agricultural commodities. Market transactions of various agre-products
FCI	Stock of various foodgrains.

JOURNALS AND PUBLICATIONS

Here again the journals and publications are not comparable to those meant for consumer goods, automobiles and electric goods. The publications on agricultural produce, rural products etc. are in the infancy stage with low readership. The statistics relevant to rural industries and agro-products are published periodically and they are in regional, national (Hindi) and English language. The commonly heard publications are as follows:

Agricultural Situation in India	Monthly
Agriculture Marketing	Quarterly
Indian Journal of Agricultural Economics	Quarterly
RBI Bulletin	Monthly
Bulletin on Prices	Weekly
Bulletin on Food Statistics	Twice a Year
Commission for Agriculture Costs and Prices	Annual Report
Indian Agriculture in Brief	Annual Report
Newspapers like Financial Express, Economic Times Business Line Business Standard (Coverage now and then, not always)	Daily
Various government departments handling the agro-marketing co-operative sector and rural development	Annual Report

SPREADING TV MARKET INFORMATION (DISSEMINATION)

Taking note of the low literacy of the rural population, it becomes necessary to spread agro-based information, data and statistics through audio-visual aids in addition to publications. In view of this, both state and central governments take the assistance of AIR and Doordarshan by which coverage can reach the masses. There are separate programmes for villagers in these media where the explanation and exhibition will be made very clear in respective regional languages. Even wholesale prices for different produce are broadcast so that even a smallest farmer knows the price trends.

The market and agro-business related news, information and data are made available to the rural masses with the noble intention of keeping them informed on the latest developments. It is possible that the information (data and statistics) may not be very accurate. However, for the purpose of decisions of the rural level, even if the information provided is nearly accurate, that should be adequate. The accuracy of data depends upon the accuracies of information collection like the junior staff of agricultural departments, co-operative society staff and the information given by the farming community.

The important data required to be spread is wholesale prices of each important commodity, foodgrains, the arrival pattern (quantity, quality) in bigger markets and the sales pattern. For example, if AIR. Bangalore is announcing these prices, it should cover the market of 500 kms around it and mainly the immediate marpets surrounding 100 Kms. Similarly, other Media Stations tend to follow so that the farmers get hold of the situations of their areas.

Doordarshan regional channels have been doing a good job of spreading agriculture production, variety, storage, use of fertilizers and pesticides for the growth and benefit to farmers. This type of audio-visual explanation gives a better impact on information and education to the rural people.

CASE STUDY

The Rediff Business Special/Shobha Warrier

There was a time not very long ago when the marketing circles talked about nothing but the Great *Indian* Middle Class. The focus has now shifted on to "a bigger *market*", *Rural* India aka Bharat. Manufacturers, marketers, makers of consumer durables...everyone, from multinational Coca-Cola to small-town garment unit, is making a beeline for Bharat. This has spawned a new demand for Bharat-friendly advertising agencies because for long, mass communications in India have suffered from a distinct bias for the *urban* consumer.

The Madras-based Anugrah Madison is one of the few agencies that specialise in advertising in *rural* areas. The agency has been in the news of late for winning awards for excellence in *rural* advertising.

A visit to AM, marked by interaction with its functionaries, offers rare insights into the *Rural Indian Market*. R V Rajan, managing director, is eminently qualified to speak on the subject. Rajan came to Madras in 1974 as a senior vice-president (south), Grand Canyon Echart. His job entailed frequent travels to *rural* markets. Sixty per cent of his clients like Shaw Wallace (fertilisers and agro-chemicals) and MRF (bullock cart and tractor tyres) had operations in *rural* areas; their customers were farmers.

In 1986, Rajan started his own agency Anugrah. His contacts became his patrons.

Consumer electronics major Philips was then seeking to sell both black & white and colour televisions and music systems in *rural* India. The time coincided with ad major Madison's search for an agency that specialised in *rural* advertising. Presto, Anugrah Madison was born. Thirteen years on, Rajan says he has not had enough of *Rural* India. "We will not canvas for work in the *urban market*. If it comes to us, we will do it," he says.

Back to Philips. For five decades, the brand catered to high-end segments of the *market*, though its audio products were ubiquitous in *rural* areas. The era of television had dawned and BPL was the *market* leader in 1985-95.

"It was a very interesting case study for us. We had to leverage the strength Philips had in the field of audio for pushing its television sales in *rural* India," recalls Rajan.

Sporting icon Sachin Tendulkar was the mascot of Philips then. Adverts featuring Tendulkar were very popular among the *urban* people. However, an AM survey revealed that matinee idol 'Superstar' Rajnikant was more popular among Tamil Nadu's *rural* masses than Tendulkar.

But AM did not scramble to sign on the movie star. Instead, it promoted Philips television as Enga Veettu Superstar (Tamil, for superstar of the family). There was no mention of Rajnikant, nor was his photo used anywhere in the advert. The very word 'superstar' was enough to remind people of Rajnikant.

Rajan ruled out ads on satellite television channels: dish antennae were yet to sprout on *rural* rooftops. "It is difficult to attract the *rural market*. Unlike the *urban market* where the aspiration levels and behaviour patterns of the people, especially the youth, are the same all over the country, *rural* India behaves differently. What appeals to the *rural* people in Tamil Nadu may not appeal to those in Andhra Pradesh. For example, the slogan Enga Veettu Superstar will not appeal to the Andhra people because their superstar was the late N T Rama Rao. The reigning actor is Chiranjeevi who is the 'Megastar'. So, we changed our slogan to megastar."

AM's executives would spend a great deal of time in *rural* areas, interacting with villagers, eating their food, drinking their drinks, talking their lingo and generally observing each and every aspect of life. They discovered that cinema is an inextricable part of life. Typically, life in a south *Indian* village moves at a leisurely pace. So fast-paced adverts won't work — that was a lesson.

Educating the *rural market* is more challenging, says Rajan. "It is easy to influence *urban* people because of their exposure to television and periodicals. But in *rural* areas, an ad agency has to develop direct contact with the people."

Anugrah Madison discovered that women and children were found to be the demand generators, but it was man who decided the brand. He did that after consultations with other male members in society. The rural market was two-tiered: the higher end comprised opinion-leaders. The Old Order was made up of successful farmers, village legislature members and elders. The New Order comprised youngsters who go to the nearest town to study in a college or work. These are the people who come back to the village with news about the latest consumer products, the most popular brands and "in-things".

Anugrah Madison would organise "Philips Super Shows" in towns like Salem, Tiruchi, Coimbatore, Madurai, Tirunelveli. Opinion leaders and Philips dealers would be heard out. The general public would be invited to have a dekko at the latest products. The people would get enthralled by their favourite film stars' shows on the television sets. Word of mouth publicity would later update the entire village.

Next strategy was to communicate directly with the masses through wall paintings, radio, regional press and rural cinema. A van equipped with audio-visual gadgetry would tour 4,000 villages. "The government had by then popularised vans which were used to propagate the family planning programme. We knew vans were the most effective interactive medium you could have in rural areas," remembers Rajan.

Advertisment colouring competitions for children and jingle singing opportunities for aspirants followed.

At the end of the six-months-long campaign, sales of Philips colour televisions went up by 27 per cent, those of B&W sets by 15 per cent and of audio products by 60 per cent. All this at a time when the consumer durables market was recording a negative growth. "But Philips registered a positive growth in places where we ran campaign," recalls Rajan.

REFERENCES

Anderson *et. al.* (2005), *Smart Communications Inc Case A*. ECCH Publication. *Rajesh K Aithal * and Arunabha Mukhopadhyay / Rural Telecom in India: Marketing Issues and Experiences from other countries.*

Anderson James and N. Biliou (2007), Serving the World's Poor; Innovation at the Base of the Economic Pyramid. *Journal of Business Strategy.*

Balakrishnan Mandira (1977), Rural Market: End of a Long Road for Consumer Marketers. *Decision*, July, 177-184.

Beshouri (2006), A Grassroots Approach to Emerging-market Consumer. *McKinsey Quarterly*, 2006, No. 4.

Bhalla, G. S. and Gurmail Singh (2001), *Indian Agriculture-Four Decades of Development*, New Delhi, Sage.

Bharat Nirman Initiative, 2005-09 (2005), Government of India. New Delhi.

Bhatnagar, S. (2000), Enhancing Telecom Options in Rural India: Some Options, *India Telecom Conference*. Stanford.

C.K. Prahalad and Stuart L. Hart (2002), The Fortune at the Bottom of the Pyramid. *Strategy and Business*, Issue 26.

CDOT (2007). *Rural Access and Broad Band Solutions*, New Delhi, CDOT.

CMIE (1996), Indian Agriculture Sector, Income Statistics, *Monthly Review of Indian economy & Indian Social Sectors*. Mumbai, CMIE.

ETIG (2003), *Rural Economy 2002–03*, New Delhi, *Economic Times.*

Ganguly, A. S. (1985), The Growing Rural Market in India. *Marketing in India*. New Delhi.

Grameen Foundation (2005), *Village Phone a Tool for Empowerment*, USA.

Gunasekaran V. and F. Harmantzis (2007), Emerging Wireless Technologies for Developing Countries.

Technology in Society, 29 (2007) 23–42.

Gupta Rahul (2006), Rural India Calling. *Voice and Data*, June.

ITU (2006), The Un-wired Continent: *Africa's Mobile Success Story*. ITU. Geneva.

Kashyap Pradeep & Raut (2005), *Rural Marketing*, Book New Delhi. Biztantra Publication.

McKinsey Report (2007), The 'Bird of Gold': *The Rise of Indian Consumer Market*. McKinsey Global Institute.

NCAER *Rural Infrastructure Report (2007)*, New Delhi, NCAER.

Pentland A, Fletcher R, Hasson A. Daknet (2006), *Rethinking Connectivity in Developing Nations*. Silver Spring, Prahalad C K. (2004), *Fortune at the Bottom of the Pyramid*, New Delhi, Pearson Publication.

Prahalad, C. K. & Allen Hammond (2002), Serving the World's Poor, Profitably. *Harvard Business Review*, September.

Vodafone (2006), *Vodafone policy Paper Series*. Number 2, March.

Vyas, V. S. (2002), Changing Contours of Indian Agriculture. in *Indian Agriculture in the Changing Environment*, Raj Kapila & Uma Kapila (Editors), Ghaziabad: Academic Foundation.

Wellenius, B.(2002), Closing the Gap in Access to Rural Communication: Chile 1995-2002, *Info* 4,3.

World Resource Institute (2001), *Digital Dividend Study*, June.

Bailay, R. (2003), Small Packets, Big Business. *Far Eastern Economic Review.s*

Balu, R (2001), Strategic Innovation: Hindustan Lever. *Fast Company*.

Bullis, D. (1997), *Selling to India's Consumer Market*, Westport, CT: Quorum.

Dawar, N. and Chattopadhyay, A. (2002), Rethinking Marketing Programs for Emerging Markets. *Long Range Planning*.

Kannan, S. (2001). Rural Market–A World of Opportunity, *The Hindu*.

Kripalani, M. (2002), *Rural India, have a Coke, Business Week*, 24.

Kripalani, M. (2003), *Finally, Coke Gets it Right, Business Week*, 47.

33-Luce, E. (2002), *Hard Sell to a Billion Consumers: Marketing India: The World's Second Most Populous Country is a Magnet for US Brands but its Market is not Easy to Penetrate,* says Edward Luce. Financial Times, 14.

Merchant, K. (2003), *A Salesforce for Indian Villages: Marketing: Women are Poised to Run an Online Direct Selling Portal that Promises to Reach the Smallest Communities.* Financial Times, 9.

Moorthi, Y.S.R (2002), *We're Like this Only.* Retrieved October 31, 2003, *from http://learning.indiatimes.com/bm/guruspeak/moorthi.htm.*

Prahalad, C.K. and Lieberthal, K. (2003), The End of Corporate Imperialism, 81, 109-117.

Srivastava, Prashant. Personal Communication. October 21 and October 31, *Journal of Student Research.*

Monish Bali (2000), "The Rural Market Likes it Strong", *The Economic Times,* [Interview by An Awasthi], August 23.

Neeraj Jha (2000), "Gung-ho on Rural Marketing", *The Financial Express,* June 19.

T. P. Gopal Swamy (1997), "Rural Marketing, Environment-Problems and Strategies, Wheeler Publishing.

www.hill.com

www.indiainfoline.com

The Marketing Mastermind Case Study HLL-Rural Marketing Initiatives ICFAI Press, pp. 62, Feb. 2003.

Poverty Estimates for 2004-05, Planning Commission, Government of India, March 2007, Accessed: August 25, 2007.

"Inclusive Growth and Service Delivery: Building on India's Success", (PDF). World Bank (2006). Retrieved on 2007-04-28.

"In Pictures–Middle Class, or Upper Class?". *India Together.* Civil Society Information Exchange. August 2003.

Planning commission of India. Poverty estimates for 2004-2005.

NSSO Report.

The World Bank (2004) and Census and Statistics Department (2002). Legislative Council Secretariat Hong Kong. Retrieved on 2007-08-01. "Note: The Gini coeffecient in the datasheet is calculated on a scale of 0 to 1 and not 0 to 100. Hence, on a scale of 100 India's Gini coeffecient (1999-2000) is 32.5 rather than 3.25".

Jeremy (February 22, 2007), "Indian children suffer more malnutrition than in Ethiopia". *The Times,* Retrieved on 2007-04-28.

http://news.bbc.co.uk/nolpda/ukfs_news/hi/newsid_6677000/6677645.stm

Datt, Ruddar & Sundharam, K.P.M. "22", *Indian Economy.*

Sarkaritel.com: Corporate News & Features: Highlights of Economic Survey 2004-2005.

India CIA World Fact Book. August 7, 2008. Retrieved August 20, 2008.

The Multidimensions of Urban Poverty in India,Centre de Sciences Humaines, New Delhi

Lifting The Poverty Veil J. Ramesh, *India Today.*

World BankICRIER.

Reuters, August 10, 2007. Accessed: August 15, 2007.

"Report on Conditions of Work and Promotion of Livelihoods in the Unorganised Sector" , National Commission for Enterprises in the Unorganised Sector, Government of India, August, 2007. Accessed: August 25, 2007.

India's Middle Class-Tracking the Growth of India's Middle Class-Economic Studies-Country Reports-*The McKinsey Quarterly.*

The Tribune, Chandigarh, India-*Business.*

Poverty in India, World Bank.

"Can India Eradicate Poverty? Will India's Economic Boom Help the Poor?"

"World Hunger-India".

George, Abraham, Wharton Business School Publications-Why the Fight Against Poverty is Failing: A Contrarian View.

Poverty and Riches in Booming India.

Poverty Estimates for 2004-05, Planning commission, Government of India, March 2007. Accessed: August 25, 2007.

www.http://news.bbc.co.uk/nolpda/ukfs_news/hi/newsid_6677000/6677645.stm

Datt, Ruddar & Sundharam, K.P.M.

Sarkaritel.com: Corporate News & Features : Highlights of Economic Survey 2004-2005.

India CIA World Fact Book. August 7, 2008. Retrieved August 20, 2008.

The Multidimensions of Urban Poverty in India,Centre de Sciences Humaines, New Delhi.

Lifting The Poverty Veil J. Ramesh, India Today.

"Report on Conditions of Work and Promotion of Livelihoods in the Unorganised Sector", National Commission for Enterprises in the Unorganised Sector, Government of India, August, 2007. Accessed: August 25, 2007.

India's Middle Class-Tracking the Growth of India's Middle Class-Economic Studies-Country Reports-*The McKinsey Quarterly.*

The Tribune, Chandigarh, India-*Business.*

Poverty Estimates for 2004-05, Planning Commission, Government of India, March 2007. Accessed: August 25, 2007.

www.http://news.bbc.co.uk/nolpda/ukfs_news/hi/newsid_6677000/6677645.stm

Sarkaritel.com: Corporate News & Features : Highlights of Economic Survey 2004-2005.

India CIA World Fact Book. August 7, 2008. Retrieved August 20, 2008.

The Multidimensions of Urban Poverty in India,Centre de Sciences Humaines, New Delhi.

Lifting The Poverty Veil J. Ramesh, *India Today.*

"Report on Conditions of Work and Promotion of Livelihoods in the Unorganised Sector" [6]], National Commission for Enterprises in the Unorganised Sector, Government of India, August, 2007. Accessed: August 25, 2007.

India's Middle Class-Tracking the Growth of India's Middle Class - Economic Studies-Country Reports-*The McKinsey Quarterly.*

The Tribune, Chandigarh, India-*Business.*

Poverty estimates for 2004-05, Planning commission, Government of India, March 2007. Accessed: August 25, 2007

www.http://news.bbc.co.uk/nolpda/ukfs_news/hi/newsid_6677000/6677645.stm

Sarkaritel.com: Corporate News & Features : Highlights of Economic Survey 2004-2005.

India CIA World Fact Book. August 7, 2008. Retrieved August 20, 2008.

The Multidimensions of Urban Poverty in India,Centre de Sciences Humaines, New Delhi.

Lifting The Poverty Veil J. Ramesh, India Today.

"Report on Conditions of Work and Promotion of Livelihoods in the Unorganised Sector" [6], National Commission for Enterprises in the Unorganised Sector, Government of India, August, 2007. Accessed: August 25, 2007.

India's Middle Class-Tracking the growth of India's Middle Class-Economic Studies-Country Reports-*The McKinsey Quarterly.*

The Tribune, Chandigarh, India-*Business.*

Poverty estimates for 2004-05, Planning commission, Government of India, March 2007. Accessed: August 25, 2007

www.http://news.bbc.co.uk/nolpda/ukfs_news/hi/newsid_6677000/6677645.stm.

Sarkaritel.com : Corporate News & Features : Highlights of Economic Survey 2004-2005

India CIA World Fact Book. August 7, 2008. Retrieved August 20, 2008.

The Multidimensions of Urban Poverty in India,Centre de Sciences Humaines, New Delhi.

Lifting The Poverty Veil J. Ramesh, *India Today*

"Report on Conditions of Work and Promotion of Livelihoods in the Unorganised Sector" [6]], National Commission for Enterprises in the Unorganised Sector, Government of India, August, 2007. Accessed: August 25, 2007.

India's Middle Class-Tracking the Growth of India's Middle Class-Economic Studies-Country Reports-*The McKinsey Quarterly.*

The Tribune, Chandigarh, India-*Business.*